Play
and
Learning

Play
and
Learning

EDITED BY

Brian Sutton-Smith, Ph.D.

University of Pennsylvania
for
Johnson & Johnson
Baby Products Company

In cooperation with: Richard A. Chase, M.D.; Roberta R. Collard, Ph.D.; Mihaly Csikszentmihayli, Ph.D.; Michael Ellis, Ph.D.; Greta Fein, Ph.D.; Howard Gardner, Ph.D.; Catherine Garvey, Ph.D.; Dale F. Hay, Ph.D.; Corinne Hutt, Ph.D.; Barbara Kirschenblatt-Gimblett, Ph.D.; Michael Lewis, Ph.D.; Robert B. McCall, Ph.D.; Hildy S. Ross, Ph.D.; Thomas R. Shultz, Ph.D.; Jerome Singer, Ph.D.; Dorothy Singer, Ph.D.; and Helen Schwartzman, Ph.D.

GARDNER PRESS, Inc., New York
Distributed by HALSTED PRESS
Division of John Wiley & Sons, Inc.
New York • Toronto • London • Sydney

Gardner Press, Inc.
19 Union Square West
New York 10003

Distributed solely by the Halsted Press Division
of John Wiley & Sons, Inc., New York

Library of Congress Cataloging in Publication Data

Main entry under title:

Play and learning.

    Edited report of the 3d Johnson & Johnson Baby
Products Company round table conferences.
    1. Play—Congresses.   2.   Child development—
Congresses.   I.   Sutton-Smith, Brian.   II.   Johnson
and Johnson ; inc. Baby Products Company.
HQ782.P515   155.4'18   78-14990
ISBN 0-470-26509-4

Designed by Raymond Solomon

Printed in the United States of America

Conference Participants

Richard A. Chase, M.D., The Johns Hopkins University School of Medicine, Baltimore, Maryland 21218

Roberta R. Collard, Ph.D.,School of Education, University of Massachusetts, Amherst, Massachusetts 01003

Mihaly Csikszentmihayli, Ph.D., Committee on Human Development, University of Chicago, Chicago, Illinois 60637

Michael Ellis, Ph.D., Department of Physical Education, University of Oregon, Eugene, Oregon 97403

Greta Fein, Ph.D., The Merrill Palmer Institute, 71 East Ferry Avenue, Detroit, Michigan 48202

Howard Gardner, Ph.D., 315 Longfellow Hall, Appian Way, Harvard University, Cambridge, Massachusetts 02138

Catherine Garvey, Ph.D., Department of Psychology, Johns Hopkins University, Baltimore, Maryland 21218

Dale F. Hay, Ph.D., Department of Psychology, S.U.N.Y., Stony Brook, Long Island, New York 11790

Corinne Hutt, Ph.D., Department of Psychology, University of Keele, Keele, Staffordshire, ST5 5BG, England

Barbara Kirschenblatt-Gimblett, Ph.D., Department of Folklore and Folklife, University of Pennsylvania, Philadelphia, Pennsylvania 19104

Michael Lewis, Ph.D., Institute for the Study of Exceptional Children, Educational Testing Service, Princeton, New Jersey 08541

Robert B. McCall, Ph.D., Boys Town Center for Study of Youth Development, Boys Town, Nebraska 68010

Hildy S. Ross, Ph.D., Department of Psychology, University of Waterloo, Waterloo, Ontario, N2L, 3G1, Canada

Helen Schwartzman, Ph.D., Institute for Juvenile Research, 1140 South Paulina Street, Chicago, Illinois 60612

Thomas R. Shultz, Ph.D., Department of Psychology, McGill University, Montreal, Quebec, H3A 1B1, Canada

Dorothy Singer, Ph.D., Department of Psychology, Yale University, New Haven, Connecticut 06520

Jerome Singer, Ph.D., Department of Psychology, Yale University, New Haven, Connecticut 06520

Brian Sutton-Smith, Ph.D., Graduate School of Education, University of Pennsylvania, Philadelphia, Pennsylvania 19104

Other Contributors

Barbara D. Goldman, Ph.D., University of Waterloo, Waterloo, Ontario

Jennifer M. Shotwell, Harvard University

Dennie Wolf, Harvard University

Contents

Preface

This report is the third of the Johnson & Johnson Baby Products Company Round Table Conferences. The first two were concerned with mother-infant relationships. The third focused on the character of play, how it changes with development, and what effects it seems to have. The idea that I should arrange such a conference was initially proposed to me by Dr. Richard Chase of Johns Hopkins University. Throughout both the preparation of the conference and the conference itself he was of invaluable assistance and support. During most of the meeting he was the active chairman, while I attempted to glean information for an appropriate final discussion. During planning I was also given tremendous assistance by Robert B. Rock, Jr., Director of Professional Relations at Johnson & Johnson. He and his staff carried on the needed correspondence and circulated documents amongst the participants. We had decided early on *not* to have prepared papers, but rather to have all members become familiarized with the recent writings of the other participants, so that a more informal presentation and more comprehensive discussion would be possible. To this end, representative papers of all participants were circulated.

The present work is an edited version of the statements that they made and of the questions and discussions that followed, all of which we recorded. The advantage of this approach is that greater simplicity and clarity of expression sometimes result; one can also gain a stronger sense of the person behind the questions and comments. The disadvantage is that issues are not always pursued in a cumulative way, and expression is sometimes barely grammatical. The tolerance of the participants, in fact, varied considerably with respect to permitting us to use the original tape; instead, some submitted a heavily edited or even a written form in its place. It was my own impression from the conference that the more interesting speakers sometimes turned out to be the least grammatical on the tapes. An exciting, gestural, parenthetical oral discourse seems to be entirely consistent with a low level of grammar; I trust that this does not place too great a burden on the empathy of the struggling reader. We have converted the tapes into what we think is a readable and useful book.

Following each discourse is an appropriate bibliography, so that the reader can further pursue topics of particular interest. Preceding each speaker is a brief introduction which serves to guide the reader to those interests he or she wishes to pursue, or to alert the reader to those alarums he or she would rather avoid.

Early in the arrangement of this conference each participant was asked to focus his or her remarks on the following questions: "What is

play?" "What is the role of play?" and "How can the quality of play experience in children be improved?" These structural, functional and prag-
matic questions pop into the discourse, and the reader needs to know that
they are in the background of the participants' thoughts.

Only the names of those who actually were present at the conference
are listed on the title page. In two cases, however, conference members
prepared their paper in cooperation with their associates whose names
are listed in the contents.

INTRODUCTION

There are many ways in which a conference can be organized, and even more ways in which the book that arises from that conference can be put together. The chapters of this book have followed the conference itself in pursuing a largely chronological plan of organization. The speakers have been ordered according to the ages of the subjects about whom they speak. While this has the advantage of providing the reader with a developmental overview of the kind of research which is current in this field, it has the disadvantage of doing disservice to many other potential forms of organization. It is the purpose of this introduction to consider some of these alternatives and to raise some of the many questions that the reader might ask of the participants in the conference.

(1) Rather than use an order based on chronology, it might have made sense to organize the conference according to the two major paradigms that have dominated play theory from its inception. The *primary paradigm* is the one we find in the philosophical and psychological literature from at least as early as Friedrich von Schiller in the late eighteenth century to Mihaly Csikszentmihayli, one of the conference participants. In this paradigm play is an activity taken up voluntarily, usually by a solitary player, and often with objects which are under his control. As a result of his activity or fantasy with those objects, the subject makes individual gains either in cognitive or creative organization. The *secondary paradigm,* which we find in anthropology, folklore, and sociolinguistics, says that play is a way of organizing collective behavior, that it is a form of human communication and that it reflects the enculturative processes of the larger society. By and large, in this conference the primary paradigm was dominant, psychologists being relatively overrepresented. The theoretical chore for the observer, however, resides in the problem of overriding this distinction with a theory that speaks to both individual and cultural functions.

In the present round table there seem to have been two kinds of primary paradigm researchers as well as one kind of secondary paradigm researcher. First there are those researchers whose studies are largely of *solitary play* and *play with objects,* and who show a strong preference for

1

"arousal" (Berlyne, 1960) kinds of theory. That is, they are very much interested in the intrinsic motor within the solitary player which determines why he plays with this object rather than that object, and much concerned also with what it is about the stimulus character of the objects that affects his play. While they differ somewhat in whether they characterize these internal motors in metabolic, neurological, physiological, or informational terms, this group is similar in placing their major focus on intrapsychic characteristics of the human organism or the stimulus characteristics of the objects with which it plays. These are dominantly psychologistic ways of thinking. We include here the discussions introduced by Shultz, McCall, Ellis and Hutt.

A second subgroup also concerned with individual functions is mainly involved with play as a *cognitive* process. The influence of Piaget is detectable but not pronounced here, and the emphasis is upon various kinds of concept formation or symbol formation. McCall (once again), Collard, Fein, Gardner and the Singers are included in this group. Csikszentmihayli's phenomenology is most fairly placed within this cognitive group, even though it is the cognition of entertained experience.

Secondary paradigm thinkers who participated in this conference were anthropologist Schwartzman, folklorist Kirschenblatt-Gimblett and sociolinguist Garvey, although the last of these straddled both approaches. But psychologists Lewis, Hay and Ross, with their emphasis on the primacy of social interaction, also made their contribution primarily to this tradition by suggesting the ways in which cultural influences might well be mediated through small-group behavior.

While few of the members of the conference set out to explicitly define play, one can borrow from their statements the following concepts. These are not so much their definitions of play as they are the concepts they frequently used when discussing it.

Play is defined as:

Schultz: arousal modulation

Lewis: having choices, manipulation of ends-means behavior, flexibility, internalizing the constant and variable mother

McCall: power to influence events, imaginary play as fantasy, exploration of social influence

Collard: active manipulation of objects which increases stimulation through the objects' reactions to those actions; functional conceptualizing

Fein: nonprototypic variability, variable transformations

Hay: quick and light movement, laughter

Garvey: exploration of opposites, rudimentary concepts, transformation of relationships within a system (such as language)

Ellis: creation and resolution of uncertainty, stimulus generation

Gardner: dramatization, patterning

Hutt: neural priming, information consolidation, metabolic recuperation, conceptual reorganization, heart rate variability

Singer: self-generative processing, attitude towards the possible

Kirschenblatt-Gimblett: the manipulation of alternative frames, foregrounding

Schwartzman: paradoxical statements, text and context commentary

Csikszentmihayli: flow

Sutton-Smith: adaptive potentiation, the envisagement of possible realms.

(2) In addition to a broad difference between psychological and anthropological paradigms, there are many more particularistic differences to be found in the discussion.

It is clear, for example, that there is a tendency for the kind of play which is studied by the investigator almost to become a value in itself. Thus one feels at times that one type of activity—either unstructured or structured play, dramatic play or fantasy, sociodrama, games and riddles, surgery, rock climbing—is perceived as more truly a form of play than any of the others. There is even a detectable tendency for some of the scholars as males or females to vary in their defense of either the more or less structured, more or less closed or open-ended forms of play, which are most favored by their own sex. Perhaps it is not surprising to find that the common experimenter effect in psychological research is paralleled by a theorist effect in psychological play theory. We all have our preferences, and these become more particularly apparent in open-ended discussions such as those that follow, than in more formal papers.

(3) Yet another way to organize one's thinking about the conference is in terms of some of the major research issues of play's antecedents, the transitions into play, the synchronic and diachronic structures of play, and the consequences to which play gives rise. This very way of stating research issues, of course, states the task as a linear metaphor, as if there is something that precedes play, then play itself, and then something that arises out of play. While this way of thinking may not be entirely false, it does more justice to the primary or psychological paradigm we have noted, than to the secondary or anthropological one. It is more sensitive to experimental manipulations than multiple cultural interactions. For example:

(a) *Antecedents*: Here we are concerned with the issue of how play arises: what leads to it? While psychologists usually seek to focus attention on particular contingent events prior to the play, folklorists and anthropologists seek to direct attention as well to the larger cultural contexts in which the play occurs (Kirschenblatt-Gimblett, Schwartzman). This is an important difference, because a psychologist is usually concerned with an antecedent that he can manipulate in some way and thus experimentally show its worth, whereas the anthropologist is more concerned with understanding the natural context which is antecedent, rather than interfering with it. Once he has interfered, it is no longer in the state of nature or culture he wishes to explore. In short, it is one thing to control context, and another to study it; this makes a great difference to the way one goes about the study of antecedents. Still, everyone agrees that there should be such antecedents, even though, oddly enough, some of the definitions of play that we have given emphasize play's transcendence of its antecedents. And in the discourse that will follow it is argued that sometimes it is just as legitimate to see the play as anteceding behavior as the other way around (Hay), which is analogous to the preparatory theory of Groos (1901).

What should be looked at as an antecedent also varies with the concern over object play, cognitive play or social play. In *object play* the antecedents have been variously named as a given state of arousal (Shultz), the preexistence of a period of exploratory behavior with the object (Collard, Hutt), a subjective uncertainty about the object (McCall), a setting which has been culturally defined as a play setting and objects which are culturally defined as play objects or toys (Fein), a setting which provides privacy and solitariness (Singer), appropriate temporal schedules (Hutt), and the functional complexity of objects (Ellis).

In *symbolic play*, prior stages in symbolic development (McCall), and individual differences in symbolic processing (Gardner) have been emphasized.

In *social play*, antecedents have been said to be mother-infant play contingencies (Lewis, Fein, Collard); peer power relationships and negotiations (Gimblett, Schwartzman, Garvey); cultural and SES attitudes towards the desirability of play (Schwartzman, Singer); and immunities and constraints provided by membership in play groups (Chase, Garvey, etc.).

(b) *Transitional Relationships*: Not always separable from antecedent influences upon play are the various transitional phenomena on the borderlines of the state of play. First there is *boundary behavior*, which includes initial, interstitial and terminal signals (Hay, Garvey). Then there are the decisions which must be made as to whether this is literal or nonliteral behavior: is it play or not (Hay, Garvey, Singer)? Once the play begins, children can be just as occupied with the communication management as they are with the play (Garvey), which leads to the view that there may be an *oscillatory* relationship between play, its antecedents and its boundary behaviors. The time and space frames are fluid (Hay), and players go in and out of play and negotiating roles (Garvey). They may be making formation, definition, disconnection, maintenance or counter-definition statements (Schwartzman). Play is as much a sociological grab-bag of childish politics as it is of play, so that there is a constant oscillation between life concerns. There also has to be a real question of whether play should be thought of only in terms of its relationship to exploration, which usually precedes play (Hay). Exploration can also lead to exploration. Negotiation can lead to negotiation. Play can lead to play. And in addition they may interact in complex manners. None of these variables may simply precede play or be transitional to it; perhaps they are really part of the substance of the sociology of play itself.

(c) *The Structures of Play*: The intrinsic nature of play can be described in many ways, as the previous definitions indicate. The most systematic interpretation, at least of "flow," was offered by Mihaly. Several times members of the conference deprecated locating play in certain behaviors alone, but at the same time others found behavioral evidence in exaggerated gesturing (galumphing) and play speech, quick, light movement, and furtive looking at the spectator. There seemed to be more agreement about its affective than its cognitive quantities: that is, about the laughter, enthusiasm and positive attitude that are associated with play. There was a discussion of play as idling (Hutt), and as perseveration and perceptual avoidance (McCall), but some concern also was shown about the cultural relativity of any of these attempts at definition (Kirschenblatt-Gimblett, Schwartzman). Despite an unwillingness to specify any play morphology, several speakers found it useful to characterize certain kinds of play in *structural* terms: as routines (Hay, Kirschenblatt-Gimblett, Garvey), formats (Schwartzman), stereotypies (Ellis), or games (Kirschenblatt-Gimblett). Others found it useful to characterize play structure separately from more institutionalized interactive phenomena such as games. Thus play was referred to in terms of a process orientation or ends-means manipulation (Lewis), or foregrounding (Kirschenblatt-Gimblett); as a special kind of rule formation (Schwartzman); and as kinds of transformation procedures within systems involving conceptual contrasts across realms of behavior (Garvey). Play was referred to as a kind of meta behavior, a communication system about behavior itself (Schwartzman). It was argued that there might be special rule systems for play itself, involving a series of increasing reversals (Kirschenblatt-Gimblett, Sutton-Smith).

(d) *Development*: The issue of play structure gives rise to the temporal question of how any such structures or structuring processes change over time. Two kinds of temporal phenomena are involved, the synchronic and the diachronic. *Synchronic phenomena* refer to changes over small time spans within particular play episodes. Within such episodes, is there a rise and fall of intensity (Shultz)? Are there biorhythms that govern such changes (Ellis)? Is there a tempo or style to play (Fein)? Finally, is there over such small time spans a change in the degrees of stereotypie and variability in play (Fein)? *Diachronic shifts* are of larger proportions, and in effect the arrangement by age levels of the chapters in this book implies that there are such large-scale changes over age in children's play. An important issue is whether there are broad stages across kinds of children's play routines, games, sports (McCall), and whether distinctive kinds of play (games) have stages within their nature (Kirschenblatt-Gimblett). Do these stages take on any distinctive character, for example from expressive imitation to competence to inversion (Kirschenblatt-Gimblett)? Finally there is the question of whether children's play and adults' play are really two different kinds of thing (Csikszentmihayli).

(e) *Outcomes*: Are there consequences for child socialization in children's play (Garvey)? Are there consequences for the child's subsequent cognitive capacity (Singer)? Does the child who plays become more flexible, more cognitively organized (Garvey), more linguistically complex (Hutt), less aggressive, happier (Singer), capable of more metaphoric usage and verbal art (Singer, Kirschenblatt-Gimblett), more successful (Singer)? Or is play mainly compensatory for inadequacies at the time of its occurrence? Remarkably, this last viewpoint, a well-known psychoanalytic one, had little sponsorship in this conference.

How do responses, mechanisms or cognitions in play reenter into relationships with the other strands of the player's life? That is, how is the transition from play accomplished in the other direction?

References

Berlyne, D.E. *Conflict, Arousal and Curiosity*, New York: McGraw-Hill, 1960.
Groos, K. *The Play of Man*. New York: Appleton, 1901 (Reissued New York, Arno Press, 1976)

Chapter 1

PLAY AS
AROUSAL MODULATION

Thomas R. Shultz

INTRODUCTION

Sutton-Smith: Dr. Shultz presents a picture of arousal as an internal mechanism acting something like a built-in thermostat which serves to modulate human behavior in certain ways. In his model it is the preceding state of arousal of the organism which helps to determine what it does next. If it is in a high state of arousal it engages in realistic survival activities; if it is in a low state of arousal it might seek to play.

Questions raised during this presentation and the discussion are as follows: how does one tell the difference between a state of arousal which is play and one which is not? Is it the state of arousal that leads to play, or is the state of arousal something that is itself caused by the play? That is, is it the independent or the dependent variable? Can one talk of arousal without taking into account cognitive factors such as uncertainty, novelty, and complexity? If one considers such cognitive factors, does one really need the concept of arousal at all? Cannot the same phenomena be described in these terms alone; that is, in terms of information theory? Or again, if cognitive factors have to be taken into account, then doesn't the context of parents, teacher and setting enter into whether arousal does or does not occur? And when play takes place, is it really to increase arousal, as Shultz argues, or is it to decrease arousal, as has often been maintained in play therapy? Is play arousing or defusing? Is it both? Or are there levels of prior arousal that permit play, and others that do not, as in a child's play before and after surgery? Again, if there is no well-established physiological base for the concept, why bother with it at all? Do we need a concept of arousal which is thought to be mediated by some internal neurophysiological process, as in this presentation, one that is different from a

concept of arousal that might be relevant to voluntary and intentional activities? Should we speak of a duality of arousal concepts?

Whatever the answers to these questions, it was clearly meaningful to
the participants of this conference to view the matter of arousal or excitement or uncertainty or tension or some equivalent, and the rise and fall
of these phenomena, as being in some way essential to the nature of play.
In the later papers of Drs. Ellis and Hutt, arousal concepts were again introduced, adding to the view of Dr. Shultz that such concepts were of
considerable value in play interpretation. Furthermore, the notion that
play may represent a form of *voluntary* arousal modulation, implicit at
least in this presentation, is a striking insight.

Shultz: The principal axiom in this theory is a very simple one. It
specifies that play serves a very basic and important function for the
child, *namely that play serves as the mechanism to modulate the child's
level of arousal.* The idea is this: when his arousal level is too low and certain other conditions are satisfied, the child plays, with the result that his
arousal level increases to some more preferred level. And conversely,
when his arousal level is too high the child stops playing, or perhaps
avoids playing, with the result that his arousal level drops to some more
preferred level. I realize that many of you will not find these ideas particularly earth-shattering or new. In fact, I know that some of you also have
used essentially the same formulation in your own work. These ideas can
be traced back to the so-called collative variables of Berlyne (1960), such
as complexity, novelty, and uncertainty, all of which presumably act to
increase the arousal of the organism. And probably these ideas can be
traced back even farther to the work of Harry Helson (1964) on levels of
adaptation and the work of Don Hebb (1955) on optimal levels of arousal.
Now of course in those days—and I'm thinking mainly of the fifties and
sixties—clear distinctions between exploration and play, such as those we
find in Hutt, were not really being made; the discussions were focused
mainly on exploration, and play was added as an afterthought. I'm sure
we'll have a good deal more to say about that. However, although these
ideas are old I don't feel too badly about resurrecting them, because I
really don't think they've gained much widespread acceptance among behavioral scientists. The arousal paradigm, for example, is largely ignored.
In an important recent book edited by Bruner, Jolly, and Sylva (1976), I
find, at least on my first reading, that it has been pretty much ignored. In
fact Bruner himself appears to argue against an arousal notion of play
when he claims, in an influential paper called "The Nature and Uses of
Immaturity" (1972), that play has the function of lessening environmental consequences and thus actually serves to lower the arousal state of the
organism. He argues that the organism can learn more efficiently at more
moderate levels of arousal (The Yerke-Dodson law). In trying to reconcile

Bruner's arguments with an arousal notion of play, I would like to suggest that during play, sources of arousal which are *outside* of the control of the child are indeed lessened or diminished, but that within the context of these lowered survival pressures play does have the effect of increasing arousal. In the play itself the child and his playmate are able to control how high the arousal will go, how long it will be maintained, and when it's going to be decreased or reduced. I'm bringing this up to note that an arousal theory of play is not universally and unequivocally accepted. Given the generally controversial nature of the theory, I would like to present briefly some sources of evidence for it.

Evidence from Smiling and Humor

Some of this evidence comes not so much from the field of play as from what I would consider a very closely related phenomenon, namely the phenomenon of smiling and laughing and the enjoyment of humor. There's a recent paper by Strauss and Waters in the *Psychological Review* which brings together evidence that the infant's smiles are produced by an increase and then a decrease in tensions. It seems to be true, according to EEG studies, that even the earliest so-called endogenous smiles are associated with low oscillating states of arousal. They're called endogenous because these smiles occur in the absence of any known external source of stimulation. Most often they occur when the baby is asleep. The smile occurs just as the arousal rises above and then falls below some threshold level. Our own research on the appreciation of humor by older children and adults suggests the operation of a very similar kind of sequence—a biphasic sequence involving first the induction and then the reduction of arousal. However, no one has yet succeeded in obtaining physiological indices for such arousal fluctuations in humans. But basically what we find in humor is that there are two structural features to a joke: first of all, an incongruity which more or less catches the listener by surprise and presumably serves to increase arousal; then there is a resolution. This is the effect of the joke, which makes sense out of the incongruity, explains it, says why it's appropriate, and presumably returns the arousal quite sharply to the baseline level. As I said, we don't have physiological indices of this, but if these two cognitive structural features of humor would indeed be shown to correspond to arousal fluctuations, then our evidence would suggest the following: first, that arousal increases are pleasurable—that is, discovering the incongruity alone contributes a certain initial amount to the enjoyment of the joke. Secondly, as the arousal decreases there is also pleasure, since the construction of the resolution seems to add another increment of enjoyment to the joke. Dan Berlyne (1960) referred to this kind of thing as an arousal boost/jag mechanism.

The idea is that a sharp increase in arousal produces a certain amount of pleasure—that's the arousal boost—and that this pleasure is further enhanced if the arousal is sharply reduced. That's the arousal jag.

Evidence from Nonhuman Primates

I think if you're talking about human play there are probably even better sources of evidence for an arousal theory of play in Michael Ellis's (1973) work, but I'm hoping he's going to tell us about that. I would, though, like to tell you about some evidence from nonhuman primates that I feel would tend to support an arousal theory of play. I think that the material is among the strongest sources of evidence for such a theory. First of all, it's become quite clear that primate play does not occur in just any situation. Play only seems to occur when the animal is essentially free of survival pressures—when it is not suffering from the heat, the cold, or the wet, when it is not being harassed by predators, and when it is free of various physiological pressures such as hunger, thirst, drowsiness or sex. I think it's reasonable to assume that any of these environmental or physiological pressures may increase the animal's level of arousal and thus preclude play according to the formulation I'm describing to you. Perhaps drowsiness doesn't fit into that, because there one can see that the arousal level is too low for play to occur. We'll see some evidence for that. Dealing with these kinds of pressures seems to have a definite priority over play, at least in the lives of nonhuman primates. I think a good demonstration of this kind of reciprocal relationship between serious behaviors on the one hand and playful behaviors on the other, comes from the work of Japanese primatologists. They work with a group of wild Japanese macaques. These monkeys are in an enclosed but otherwise natural habitat, and the investigators create a state of semidomestication by provisioning the animals with an abundant supply of food. It turns out that the effect of this available food supply is a dramatic increase in play and in other innovative activity, especially among the younger animals in the group. I'd also like to mention at this point some observations reported by Jane Van Lawick-Goodall (1971) on social play in wild African chimpanzees. She found that a very important part of social play among chimps involves tickling, which is interesting to me because that's what my research on humor was in part concerned with (1976). Chimps tickle each other pretty much the way we do, with a probing, flexing movement of the fingers, although they have other ways of doing it as well. They tickle each other in a variety of locations including the abdomen, under the chin, and the groin. The response to tickling in chimps is very often a kind of smiling one, or play face as it is called among the primatologists; sometimes it is even laughter.

Question: When chimps tickle each other, how do you know they don't laugh from fear?

Dr. Shultz: A chimp won't tickle just any other chimp. The most common tickling pairs will be mother-infant or sibling-parent pairs, but occasionally you find other strange things. There was even a case in Goodall's work of an infant chimp playing with an infant baboon. As you may know these two species are often at odds with each other as they get older, but when these two groups of animals would pass each other, these two playmates would seek each other out, and one of the things they would do was to tickle. If any other baboons came by, that was the end of the game; they ran away. So it apparently occurs only between the very trusted, not with just anyone. Related to that is the idea that what you see in these tickling games is a kind of approach-avoidance situation. Van Lawick-Goodall reports many instances in which one animal tried to get another animal to tickle it, enjoyed the tickling for a while, then withdrew as the tickling became too intense; then perhaps the animal would return again to keep the cycle going a little longer. I found it interesting that the tendency to withdraw from being tickled would be much stronger when a more dominant and larger animal was doing the tickling. In other words, an animal who was tickled, say, by a dominant male in the group wouldn't stick around very long. It's as if it would be too arousing, and the tickled animal would move quickly away. If that same animal were tickled by a smaller animal in the group, say an infant, the animal would be much more likely to stay in the game longer. All of this leads me to suggest again that it is perhaps arousal levels that are mediating the play going on in these tickling games. At low levels of arousal the animal may initiate the tickling games. The play serves to increase the level of arousal, which is immensely enjoyed, and then when the arousal gets too high he withdraws from the game, at least temporarily.

These naturalistic observations are interesting, but of course under more tightly controlled laboratory conditions one can create situations which provide even more direct evidence. I'm going to summarize very briefly for you the findings of a large number of experiments done with chimpanzees here in New Orleans by William Mason (1965; 1970). Mason found that there are a number of conditions which serve to inhibit play, that the reverse of these conditions facilitates play, and also that play has certain various consequences. The idea is that it all makes sense in terms of the concept of arousal.

Mason lists as inhibitors of play: intensity of play, extreme novelty, separation, and noise level. He gives the consequences of play as: distress vocalizations, skin conductance, social responsiveness, and noncomforting.

Let's consider first those factors which Mason has found to inhibit play. There are four of them. The first is the intensity of the play itself. Mason created a situation in which a human experimenter is engaged in play with a chimpanzee; the experimenter controls the content and course of play, and he plays with the animal in typical chimpanzee ways. Mason reports that as the experimenter's play increase in intensity from mild to vigorous, the number of play contacts made by the animal decreases. The animal seeks to play less as the play becomes more intense.

A second factor which seems to inhibit this social play is extreme novelty. Mason reports that large increases in the unfamiliarity of surroundings depress play. Moderate increases in unfamiliarity, however, act to increase play.

The third inhibiting factor is separation from cagemates. The young chimp is separated from his cagemates for a length of time, and when he is reunited with them, you see clinging behavior: they cling to each other. Mason argues that the clinging behavior acts to decrease arousal. What this means, of course, is that the animal is going to be playing less than he would if he had not been separated from his cagemates. So separation also inhibits play, although again it seems that a minimal separation serves to increase play more than does no separation at all; again, play is facilitated by moderate rather than low levels of arousal.

The fourth factor here is noise level. Mason has an experiment using a human experimenter who plays with the chimp and a human experimenter who clings to the chimp, and the chimp gradually establishes a preference for one experimenter. Virtually all chimps spend more time with the play experimenter, but as Mason introduces white noise into the situation he finds that with increases in the level of white noise there is less contact with the play experimenter and more contact with the clinging experimenter. When he puts all these characteristics together, it's quite striking that they all seem to lead to a decrease in play; they seem to inhibit it. Yet they don't appear to have anything in particular in common except for arousal. At least that's Mason's argument, and I guess I would agree with him. All of these data make sense in terms of the concept of arousal; they are all variables which increase arousal to such a level that play becomes very unlikely.

Question: What distinctions are you making between arousal and intervening activity? I mean, all these things often might lead to different activities.

Dr. Shultz: You mean incompatible activities. They do, in fact. They lead to activities which Mason has other evidence for—activities which decrease arousal. He sees play as an activity which acts to increase arousal, so that it's going to be less likely to occur in cases where arousal is already quite high. Instead the animal is going to engage in clinging or some other variable which will act to decrease arousal.

Play as a Source of Arousal

Unlike these variables which increase arousal and decrease play, play itself serves to increase arousal. Mason has essentially four pieces of evidence for it. (a) One piece of evidence is that neonate chimps' play behavior increases the rate of distress vocalizations. The experimenter with the neonate chimps will manipulate the limbs, tickle the chimp, restrict spontaneous movements, engage in all those activities that are involved in typical chimp play, and what happens is that the neonate chimp reacts with many more distress vocalizations than in a comparison condition where there is no stimulus, or where there is light pressure on the abdomen, or where the experimenter clings with the chimp. (b) The second source of evidence is that in neonate chimps, tickling increases skin conductance. These galvanic skin responses (GSR) are commonly used measures of emotional arousal: if the experimenter tickles a newborn chimp, GSR goes up considerably. There's an increase in skin conductance. (c) A third sort of consequence of play (this is in older, juvenile chimps) is that play seems to increase social responsiveness. What the experimenter does here is to play with the chimp and then suddenly assume a passive role. The chimp's reaction to this is to emit a whole range of social overtures towards the experimenter, relative to a condition in which the experimenter had simply been passive throughout that initial period, or to a condition in which the experimenter had been doing other kinds of social activity with the chimp, such as petting or grooming. So play seems to activate or energize a whole range of social responses. (d) The fourth piece of evidence is that play is noncomforting to the chimp. The basic evidence here is that when the chimp is put in a situation which is stressful, as when he is given electric shock to the foot, or is placed in an unfamiliar environment, or separated from his cagemates, and then the experimenter either clings or plays with the chimp, it's been found that although clinging does reduce any index of distress, play does not so comfort the chimp. For example, play does not reduce the stress vocalizations, but clinging does.

Dr. McCall: I quarrel with the generalization that play creates arousal. When youngsters are involved in play which is appropriate for them there's often a decrease in arousal. The theory of play therapy was that play created adjustment, not arousal.

Dr. Shultz: I think that's a very good point. These data in fact conflict rather sharply with the play therapy theory.

Dr. Collard: Prior to surgery, young children one, two, and three years old could play out their fears, but for about five or six days after surgery they couldn't stand the sight of surgical toys. Yet about ten days after surgery, when they were being prepared for stitches and tubes being re-

moved and so forth, they could play with them again. Therefore whether
or not play will be possible depends upon the intensity of arousal, and
how close and how real it is.

   Question: Were there nonsurgical-associated toys involved in the
study to show that this was indeed tied to the kind of toy?

   Dr. Sutton-Smith: Only in Gilmore's research (1971), I believe.

   Question: I think that's crucial—whether children in surgery will play
or not play, or what toys they play with. It might help settle whether we're
talking about general arousal or about specific toys and a certain emotional state. If the avoidance were, say, with the surgical toys as opposed to
the other toys, one might want to talk about it as fear, and say that it is
just a simple form of associational learning. I think it fits into the question
of competing responses. That is, if the children switch from one play
form to another, then although there's a decline in the play activity
you're sampling, there may be another kind of play, and so arousal might
be still appropriate.

   Dr. McCall: Has somebody done what strikes me as the necessary
study for the arousal notions (you can only do it with animals), and that is
to pharmacologically induce altered arousal states and observe the consequences on play? It seems to me that what's being talked about here is
that arousal is leading play. It's the independent variable. I'm happy with
it as a dependent variable, but this theory suggests that one plays because
of one's state of arousal.

   Dr. Ellis: I've done some research with the drug for hyperactive children that is marketed under the name of Ritalin. It's used to reduce the
distressing tendency for children to ignore social constraints and carry on
with whatever they want to do. In classrooms we found significant modulation of the activity. That is, the drug has a normalizing effect in the
classroom, but in the play setting you could never tell whether the hyperactive kid was on it or not. In a play setting it didn't produce any effect
and so was not contextually modified, which means it acts in a very complex way. That's the only drug stuff that I know of that asserts that it is
dealing with the arousal level of the child. So we argued on this basis that
these drugs were affecting the capacity of the children to modulate their
own activity—in other words, to go into deprivation temporarily because
the teacher wanted them to sit still. It made them sensitive to the requests
of others but did not alone depress arousal.

Evidence from Tickling and Peek-a-Boo

   Dr. Schultz: I'm going to enter at this point into my own research on
tickling games and peek-a-boo games in the human infant. My theoretical position is that the pleasure that infants derive from these games is

mediated by the arousal and reduction of uncertainty. In the case of tick-ling, the uncertainty is about whether one's being attacked, and in the case of peek-a-boo, it's about whether the disappearing loved one is going to reappear. This position, I think, is consistent with the idea of play as a phylogenetic vestige, which is the notion that although play perhaps is not concerned with immediate survival needs, it may at one time have been related to survival. As Carolyn Loizos (1967) has said, play patterns may be remnants of phylogenetically ancient behaviors that have become freed, through environmental changes, from their original functions.

Our research put this idea to the test by manipulating variables which were presumed to affect either the arousal or the reduction of this uncer-tainty. In the case of tickling, we varied both the intensity of the tickling (that is, from light to vigorous tickling) and the identity of the tickler, who could be the infant's own mother or a female stranger. In the case of peek-a-boo we varied just the identity of the player, who could again be the mother or a female stranger. The subjects in this case were twelve boys and twelve girls at each of two age levels. They were either six months or nine months of age, and the infant's responses to each play episode were scored independently by two experimenters using that scale. If the baby cried, he had a 1; 2 for mild distress; 3 for indifference; 4 for a smile; and 5 for a laugh.

Let's take a look at the tickling results first. The main effect resulted from the identity of the tickler. I don't think that's especially interesting; it just reflects the fact that the response was more positive when the mother was tickling than when the stranger was tickling. What I found more in-teresting was that the table shows the interaction between the intensity of the tickling and identity of the tickler. Vigorous tickling was enjoyed more if it came from the mother than if it came from a stranger, and there's a significant difference between the two. However, in the case of light tickling, it didn't make any difference who the tickler was: enjoyment of light tickling was intermediate between those other two scores. I found this to be true in a pilot study with both sexes. In the regular study we did we found this interaction for boys only. What you see here, therefore, re-fers to boys. The girls didn't show the effect, so I'm wondering how reli-able it is. Let me give my explanation of it and then make a comment.

TABLE 1–1
Mean Scores Reflecting
Enjoyment of Tickling

Tickler	Intensity of Tickle	
	Light	Vigorous
Mother	4.08	4.38
	=	>
Stranger	3.83	3.67

Presumably, vigorous tickling aroused greater uncertainty than light tickling did. After all, vigorous tickling resembles an attack more than light tickling does. I think that this uncertainty is more likely to be reduced if it's the mother who's doing the tickling than if it's a stranger because the infant is used to the mother, used to playing with the mother, and so in this instance can more easily interpret the tickling as a mock attack, or as play, than when the tickler is someone unfamiliar. I found it interesting that this pattern very much mirrors some results that Michael Lewis and Jean Brooks-Gunn obtained about infants' reactions to approaching people (1972)—that is, you would interpret standing at a distance as a kind of equivalent to light tickling, and direct approach as equivalent to vigorous tickling.

Dr. Lewis: Did you look at the behavior of the mother and the stranger while doing that? Just as the baby knows the mother better, the mother knows the baby better. And one wonders first of all if there's any difference in how vigorous the tickling is, based on past experience. I also wonder if there are any accompanying behaviors such as smiling and so on.

Dr. Shultz: Well, unlike more naturalistic studies like yours and Brooks', in our study we very rigorously programmed what was going to happen by training the mother to tickle just the way the experimenter was doing it. There was to be no smiling or talking, just the tickling, and mothers were elaborately trained to distinguish the vigorous tickling from the light tickling, how long it would go on, and that kind of thing. It was as standardized as we could make it. And the mothers were quite good about it, I thought.

We also asked each mother some questions regarding whether she ever played tickling or peek-a-boo games with her infant, at what age she began playing these games, the occasions on which they were played, how many hours she spent with her infant, whether there were siblings in the family, and the like. We thought such data might be relevant to the way these experimental games would be enjoyed, and in the case of tickling, at least, this turned out to be the case. These data show that the number of infants giving various reactions to light tickling from the mother are a function of whether or not they had previous experience with tickling. They also show that if the mother customarily played tickling games with the infant, the infant gave a more positive response to light tickling from the mother than if the mother had never played tickling games. I think the results point to the role of past experience and the anticipation in enhancing arousal. The argument goes as follows: light tickling from the mother, to which these data refer, is probably a fairly neutral stimulus by itself, not terribly upsetting, not terribly exciting; but those infants who were used to playing tickling games with the mother may have laughed more, these data show, in anticipation of their customary and presumably more vigorous game interactions. In other words, they expected something more vigorous.

The questions for an arousal theory have to do with the following: (a) social functions of play, (b) initiation and termination of play, (c) play content, and (d) developmental trends.

If one concedes that these early social games (tickling, peek-a-boo, etc.,) have the function of modulating arousal levels in the infant, then does it not also make sense to consider whether they serve any social functions for the people who play them? In other words, since all the primate species are essentially social animals, I think it makes sense to view these games as having a function not only for the individual animal but also for interactions between animals.

Would you, for example, agree with Mason, who argues that these so-called exploitive behaviors, including play, serve to disengage the child from his attachment to the mother? Or would you think that such games might instead act to strengthen attachment bonds? I think there is actually some evidence from nonhuman primates, particularly in Van Lawick-Goodall's work, that social play does indeed seem to strengthen attachment bonds, not only those between mother and infant but also between the infant and other members of the social group. I mentioned earlier some other cases in which play seemed to be very involved in the attachment process.

Now, if you concede that arousal theory has some validity for early social play, would you think it also has validity for other varieties of play? Not that it could explain everything about these types of play, but would it explain certain things such as when the play will be initiated, and when it will be terminated? I think that other theories haven't really been able to tackle that problem; I have a suspicion that the arousal theory might be able to.

The third question concerns the *content* of play. Could an arousal theory of play help to explain why play seems to function on certain themes to the near exclusion of others? Why, for example, is so much of primate social play agonistic or aggressive in nature? This fact, as Blurton Jones (1967), has indicated, is just as true of human kids as it is of other primates.

The fourth question has to do with developmental trends in the emergence of play, the fact that play at first increases in frequency with age and then starts to decrease in frequency as the organism reaches maturity. How can something like that be accounted for? How would it be accounted for in terms of an arousal theory, and how would that explanation fare in contrast to other theoretical approaches?

Dr. Lewis: I want to pick up on a point that's confusing me. You make some connection between arousal and uncertainty. Fenichel discusses a particular case which has always intrigued me: throwing a child up in the air. Why for some children is this tremendously exciting and fun, and for others fearful? For example, I remember as a child growing up in New York, going with my peers to Coney Island and riding the roller coaster. I can recall always being terrified of it, but there were some who seemed to enjoy it. Fenichel makes the point that the child who can enjoy that is the child for whom it is not an uncertain condition. That is, being thrown up, there is surety that the child will be caught by the parent. Then and only then can the game be fun. So it seems to me that we have uncertainty, which is a kind of cognitive construction, and arousal, which is something else. One may lead to the other, but I think that we might want to keep them apart. Could we talk about what you've been saying in terms of uncertainty without bringing in arousal at all? Some people have suggested that one primary function of the organism, of living, is to reduce the uncertainty. Could we take the construct of uncertainty without the concept of arousal and talk to the question?

Dr. Shultz: I guess the only objection I would have to that is that uncertainty is only one cognitive process or variable which is said to lead to increases in arousal. It is only one, for example, of Berlyne's list of collative variables, others being incongruity, complexity, etc.; and there are as well the various conditions that came up in Mason's experiment. I think if we want to view all these things as some sort of unified theory we need something a little more general than the concept of uncertainty, but uncertainty is clearly one that should be involved.

Dr. Chase: I find Michael's challenge interesting. That is, at what stage in the development of understanding of an area of behavior is it appropriate to be looking for an all-encompassing theory? Obviously you can do it at any time you like. I understand what you're saying about uncertainty better than I understand arousal, which is the higher level of abstraction. I realize there are other issues, such as novelty, which you want to include in a general arousal theory, but it seems to me that discussing the general arousal theory is a bit premature. It's possible to stretch it, but the farther I stretch the less clear I am about what it is. I don't think the physiological enquiries really settle it, because I don't know of any drug—either an arousing drug or a sedating one—that doesn't have multiple and complex effects. There's a whole class of sedative drugs which have very different effects on the nervous system, so I don't think we're going to settle this question through physiological investigation. It seems to me that we're looking at descriptive issues, and certainly in the work of tickling and peek-a-boo you represent very plausible ways of designing experiments that can be handled quantitatively; but then when you subsume the information under an arousal concept I find I get quite uncertain.

Dr. Ellis: I would like to introduce another idea which is at about the same level of abstraction and generalization as arousal, and that is the concept of *information*. I think that the collative properties of Berlyne (1960) can easily be put together in that one concept of information. The other observation that I would like to make is that while catching the baby being thrown may be a certainty, there are a host of other opportunities that being hurled in the air and being recaptured from the air will bring to the child, such as producing information that is pleasant to the child. We don't have to have arousal. I don't think the physiologists have gotten us anywhere yet. They may well do so in the future, but until they do, information, which is something we can deal with at a very simple level, can stand in its stead. It's just as useful. An argument that I would like to push here is that when you talk about information, you're talking in fact about the reduction of uncertainty in the environment; so my definition for play activities would be creating and resolving uncertainties. It is the passage of information into the organism which is pleasant.

Dr. Gardner: I agree with that. I was wondering about having a third control in the experiment, so that the baby would not know who the tickling person was, because I think information is part of the arousal system. If we heard a sudden loud noise that sounded like an explosion, we might all jump and leave this room; but if we knew that that explosion was about to take place because someone announced: "They're just going to excavate the room next door," we'd sit here and say, "Oh, that's the room being excavated." So I think a bit of information has to be part of an arousal system. That's why I think if the baby were lying there and the hands came and tickled, and the baby didn't have information about whether it was the mother or not the mother, there might have been no arousal or maybe just as much arousal, if only we could have measured it physically at the time.

Dr. Shultz: Paradoxically, the attempts to pin everything we've been talking about in one variable have convinced me, for five minutes or so, that you need both an uncertainty *and* an arousal aspect to your definition. There are all sorts of things I'm uncertain about, but I don't care, and that's very important. There are all kinds of things I can get aroused about, but only a subset of those are likely to involve me in things which we would call play. I think that any effort to make play explanation completely cognitive, as an information or uncertainty approach alone, would make me uneasy. Furthermore, when you said information you threw in the word "pleasure" in your very last phrase—information that's pleasant for the organism—in an effort to make it also affective, I think. So I see the need for both aspects, cognitive and affective.

Dr. Sutton-Smith: How happy are we with the notion of modulation, uncertainty, excitement, or arousal? Does the notion of modulation in this presentation strike a chord?

Dr. Fein: I'd like to throw out an example which perhaps speaks to that, but which is also why I have difficulty dealing with the ways in which those notions are being discussed here. My example comes from the other end of the spectrum. The kids are going to sleep at night, the lights are out, and you tape what they're doing. We have gotten some very nice records of this kind of presleep speech play in which you have whole reams of stories being told partially and in a limited and fragmented way. One of the nicer ones comes from a 22-month-old who's having a long conversation with his grandpa on the phone, only there's no phone in the crib. It's a conversation containing all sorts of mixed elements of what they've done sometime in the past, what they might do in the future; it brings in other objects and other parts of the child's experience. The child falls asleep as he's playing. It is as if he is reproducing information, and reproducing that information as part of a very pleasurable and yet dearousing, quieting episode or sequence.

Dr. Sutton-Smith: This may be a matter of "chats" or "lulls." Lullabies are supposed to be gentling and decrease arousal. The chat is supposed to be arousing. One of the points of a paper by Beth Lomax Hawes in *The Journal of American Folklore* (1978), is that the American mother, as compared to the Japanese mother, tends to chat the baby to sleep. That is, she arouses the baby and sings, etc., and either he falls asleep in the middle of this or she puts him aside and then he falls asleep. So this baby is reproducing a typically arousal-modulation American pattern. The Japanese pattern is that you keep lulling and quieting the baby and holding him long after he's gone to sleep. The American mother "arouses" the infant and the Japanese mother "quiets" him. Dr. Fein's children may indeed be "arousing" themselves; that is, providing their own modulation which terminates with decreased arousal.

Dr. Fein: There's no mother in the room in these tapes. You'd have to know whether there had been one there and whether that kind of thing had gone on at some former time.

Dr. Sutton-Smith: My abstraction from your point is that in the American system, arousal is treated as a bridge to going to sleep, a bridge to self-initiated decrease.

Dr. Singer: It's like going to sleep while watching "Kojak." There's actually a technique that I've used and recommended to people who are having trouble falling asleep. Usually the reason people have trouble falling asleep is that they have a set of unfinished business that is important to them. As they think about it, it rearouses them. But they can distract themselves by thinking about some less important aspect of their life: perhaps remembering a vacation they've had or, in the case of one woman I know, imagining watching an elaborate ballet dance. That holds people's interest momentarily; it distracts them from all the unfinished business.

Then, while they're replaying this ballet, the normal sleep-producing mechanisms take over and they just konk out. It's an attempt to reduce the level of uncertainty in one's experience, or, presumably, the arousal that may go with the uncertainty.

Dr. Garvey: I don't understand the arousal concept, but I don't want to throw it out all the way because I would like to reinterpret Greta's example. The other variables that have been mentioned here, such as information or uncertainty, all imply at least something out there that we are uncertain about or need information about; whereas what Dr. Shultz has proposed, if I understand it correctly, is more or less like some kind of an independently operated internal thermostat. He implies, at least, that the organism requires variation within a given range, and that this does not imply something on the outside, although it may indeed interact with things on the outside. One question, then, is, If you have this internal mechanism, why produce play rather than some other filling effort? We haven't answered that question at all. And another point, to reinterpret Dr. Fein's example, is that what this child may have been doing with this internal variation or flux is a filling operation. His cognitive space must be filled visually, perhaps by things he can see or feel or touch. And if these things are not there when the lights are out, then he may fill the cognitive space that would be there. This is a very strange and indeterminate model of arousal, where there is no thing in the outside environment to provide more information.

Dr. Shultz: I think it makes sense to view the organism as needing some sort of modulation and arousal, and I think there are obviously kinds of behaviors other than play which admirably fulfill this need. Consider, for example, the various survival or work pressures that organisms face. But the point is that play seems to occur when all these things are taken care of. The organism still presumably has this need to modulate arousal, and this could perhaps be a definition of play. All of those activities that the organism will engage in when it has these survival pressures, work pressures, etc., taken care of, those things we will call play.

References

Berlyne, D. E. *Conflict, arousal and curiosity.* New York: McGraw-Hill, 1960.
Berlyne, D. E. Humor and its kin. In J. H. Goldstein & P. E. McGhee (Eds.) *The psychology of humour.* New York: Academic Press, 1972.

Blurton Jones, N. An ethological study of some aspects of social behaviour of children in nursery schools. In D. Morris (Ed.) *Primate ethology*. Chicago: Aldine, 1967

Bruner, J. S. The nature and uses of immaturity. *American Psychologist*, 1972, 27, 1–22.

Bruner, J. S., Jolly, A., & Sylva, K. *Play, its role in development and evolution*. New York: Basic, 1976.

Emde, R. N., & Koenig, K. L. Neonatal smiling and rapid eye movement states. *American Academy of Child Psychiatry* 1969, 8, 57–67.

Fiske, D. W., & Maddi, S. R. (Eds.) *Functions of varied experience*. Homewood, Ill.: Dorsey, 1961.

Gilmore, J. B. Play: A Special Behavior. In J. Herron & B. Sutton-Smith (Eds.) *Child's Play*, New York: Wiley, 1971.

Hawes, B. Lomax. Folksongs and Function: Some Thoughts on the American Lullaby. *Journal of American Folklore* 1978, 87, 140–148.

Hebb, D. O. Drivers, & the C. N. S. (conceptual nervous system). *Pyschological Review*, 1955, 62, 243–254.

Helson, H. *Adaption-level theory*. New York: Harper & Row, 1964.

Itani, J. On the acquisition and propagation of a new food habit in the natural group of the Japanese monkey at Takasakiyama. *Primates*, 1958, (1), 84–98.

Kawai, M. Newly acquired pre-cultural behavior of the natural troop of Japanese monkeys on Koshima Islet. *Primates*, 1965, (6), 1-30.

Lewis, M., & Brooks-Gunn, J. Self, other, and fear: the reaction of infants to people. Paper presented at the Eastern Psychological Association, Boston, 1972.

Loizos, C. Play behaviour in higher primates: a review. In D. Morris (Ed.) *Primate ethology*. Chicago: Aldine, 1967.

Mason, W. A. Determinants of social behavior in young chimpanzees. In A.M. Schrier, H. F. Harlow, & F. Stollnitz (Eds.) *Behaviour of nonhuman primates* (Vol. 2). New York: Academic Press, 1965.

Mason, W. A. Motivational factors in psychosocial development. In W. J. Arnold & M. M. Page (Eds.) *Nebraska symposium on motivation* (Vol. 18). Lincoln: University of Nebraska Press, 1970.

Shultz, T. R. A cognitive-developmental analysis of humor. In A. J. Chapman and H. C. Foot (Eds.) *Humor and laughter: Theory and Research Applications*. Chichester: Wiley, 1976.

Sroufe, L. A., & Waters, E. The ontogenesis of smiling and laughter: a perspective on the organization of development in infancy. *Psychological Review*, 1976, 83, 173–189.

Van Lawick-Goodall, J. The behaviour of free-living chimpanzees in the Gombe Stream Reserve. *Animal Behaviour Monographs*, 1968, 1, 161–311.

Van Lawick-Goodall, J. *In the shadow of man*. Boston: Houghton Mifflin, 1971.

CHAPTER 2

THE SOCIAL DETERMINATION
OF PLAY

Michael Lewis

INTRODUCTION

Dr. Sutton-Smith: Considering that the bulk of play studies in the literature have focused on children's independent relationships with objects (Piaget, 1951), Dr. Lewis's thesis that all of these depend upon the earlier relationship with the mother is quite startling. It is also adopted by Catherine Garvey in her book *Play* (1977). Much of the present discussion focuses on the way in which the relationship to the mother may become transferred to the child as player. Attention turns from the mother's constancy and variability, and her intentionality, to the child's own competence, to his need for symbolizing because she is variable, and to his flexibility. In a way the social determinism of this point of view is being worked out through a variety of cognitive variables, such as ends-means relationships and the like. There are objections raised that infants explore the external world even without their mother's example, and that infants show individual differences, with some more socially oriented and some more object oriented in nature. Dr. Lewis responds that he sees the mother as the external source of the baby's arousal, regardless of whatever internal modulators may also exist.

Dr. Lewis: I am going to present the essential premise that play at the beginning of life is a social act, and that if one wanted to construct a theory of play one would have to argue that initially, at least, play is a social act. If you will allow me that statement, then indeed I might want to throw out as an arousing comment that caregivers play; children do not play, and the infant does not play. And I would offer as a hypothesis that play is a consequence of a social act between a caregiver and the child. What I'm struck by is that mothers ask very young infants an inordinately large number of questions. I mean, it's mind-boggling! If you watch what a parent is doing when asking a child a question, you'll see that it might fall into our category of play and it certainly falls into the category of arousal. The mother looks at her baby and says, "Does that feel good?" "Do you like it?" "Huh, huh?" accenting her facial gestures and her speech gestures. It is an act of arousal. We tried to study this in the context of interaction and conversation, and what happens is, of course, that the mother accepts any indication of arousal on the part of the infant as an answer to her question. So if the sweet little thing burps as a consequence of being fed, and the mother's asked the child, "Does that feel good?" the burp is interpreted by the mother as an answer. We know it's an answer because she does two things. She stops asking the question, and then proceeds to supply the verbal response. So something that looks like play also has an arousing component. Here, if I were to argue from an arousal position, I would say that the caregiver is the one that causes it; that is, even the arousal is somehow external to the child for a time. It couldn't be disputed that the child has clear arousal fluctuations, as a biological system, but this other kind of arousal is coming in from the environment, particularly from its caregiver, and it tends to set the child up as a social being.

I want to talk about two kinds of relationships. The first is relationship as play, and the second is relationship in order to play.

RELATIONSHIPS AS PLAY

Let's go to relationships as play. It seems to me that if we're going to get into that hairy field of adaptive functions, and so on—what you might call social biology—we would have to argue that the most adaptive function for the infant is its adaptation to its social environment. I don't want to go into great detail; I think Bowlby in his 1951 monograph demonstrated that if the child isn't cared for by someone or doesn't form a relationship, the child will die. There's a great deal of evidence being accumulated that the most important adaptive function of the infant is to its social environment. So that when I talk about relationship, the point that I would like to make is that there's a décalage between learning about the social world and learning about the object world. The social world is learned about earlier than the object world. Therefore very early play is part of social relationships. The precursors of the things that we call play have their origin in early social relationships.

Therefore the first point I want to make is that the child's adaptive functions are to its social environment. This comes under the general notion of relationships as play, which comes under the broader statement that play at the beginning is a social act, not a solitary act. Within interactions with social objects, interactions themselves and reciprocal behavior are learned, and it seems to me that these again are the precursors of play. Now let me develop this point a moment. I would be interested in developing a theory of social biology in which you would have early reflex systems which would modulate the child's social behavior, and then these early reflex systems would give way to learned behavior.

Some of you may have followed the literature on imitation in very young infants. People have demonstrated this as occurring at two or three weeks of age. But I think proving the existence of imitation with two- or three-week-old infants is a difficult problem. It's difficult for the theory of genetic epistemology because circular reactions, which that theory presupposes, aren't present yet, and you can't account for it in that way. And it's difficult for anyone interested in a cognitive basis for growth because there's not enough cognitive material to account for this imitation. So a reflex system seems to be the choice to explain early imitation. The interesting finding that emerges is that this early imitative behavior seems to become increasingly difficult to demonstrate as the baby gets older, so that by six weeks of age it has apparently disappeared, and a new kind of imitative behavior emerges, one that you have to work at (like a circular reaction) in order to get an imitation. What I'd like to argue, or ultimately describe, is a set of reflex systems which propel the child into sustained social interaction. Once these reflex systems disappear, as the Babinski would disappear, as the sucking or the rooting reflex eventually disappears, then imitation has a social function.

It would seem to me that the point at which these reflex systems start to disappear and learning takes over is the point at which we could start to talk about the child's notion of both relationship and things concerning play. There's something very interesting about social interactions which is not present in object interactions, and I think it's a problem for Piaget and for people interested in genetic epistemology. As you recall, Piaget argues for the development of means-end relationships through the child causing something to happen quite accidentally and observing an outcome to that action. Now, the problem with objects and object relationships for the child and for the development of means-end behavior is that objects do not have intention, but the social caregiver does in fact have intention. That is, the social caregiver can intend for its behavior to be contingent upon the behavior of the child. It is our belief that the caregiver, through this intentionality, helps to construct in the child both what I would call a socioemotional and a motivational construct, which I call competence. Means-end behavior will turn out to be a crucial activity because the child learns a means-end behavior and then attempts to alter the means-end. And it's in the altering, in trying something new, as well as learning that which it needed to learn to begin with, that something which I want to call "playful" occurs. There is no need for the child not to repeat the same act, but nevertheless the child doesn't only repeat the same act; it tries something different. I think the child tries something different (1) because of an ends-means competence mode, so that it is willing to try something different; and (2) because it's enjoyable to try something different.

Let me present that point very quickly. Years ago I did some work on binary choice experiments, and as you know those are pretty simple-minded. You give a kid two buttons and if he presses one a light comes on or an M&M comes out or something silly happens. What you notice is that after a while, the child catches on that one event of the two is receiving more reinforcement than the other, and that's how the binary choice situation is hooked up. What becomes optimal strategy then, since it's a stochastic model and since the child cannot possibly guess which is the right button of the two to press, is to constantly press the button giving the most reinforcement. Now indeed, rats will do that, but children don't do it. The question is, why don't children do it? I would suggest that children don't do it because they want play. That is, having caught on to the fact that it's random, they want to try something new, try to get the reward in some other way, by choosing the event which occurs least often. Now the likelihood that they will choose it correctly is fairly remote, but nonetheless they persist. If the left side is paying off 70 percent and the right side 30 percent, they will adjust their behavior approximately to 70 and 30. People tried to do a whole set of mathematical models with this; some have suggested that there is something to guessing the 30 percent side. I would like to call that play. Since we don't really know what play is, you won't be too offended if I do so, since for me this means-ends, this switch from what is known to what is not known, is in fact a precursor of this activity we call play. I think it's very adaptive, rather than lacking in adaptive functions.

Caretaker as Constant and Variable

One of the other important features of social interactions as opposed to nonsocial interactions is something which has often puzzled me. Social interactions are both predictable and variable; much more so, I think, than object interaction. People have argued that object relationships, as opposed to social relationships, are learned earlier because they're simple. In a certain sense that's true, but let me again explain my confusion. The mother is both a constant and a variable stimulus, and that must present an overwhelming task for the infant to master; that is, to be able to master both the constancy that this is someone that's the same and at the same time someone who is quite different.

Question: Are you for this moment pragmatically suggesting that play might be equivalent to a randomizing strategy in the double-choice situation when you don't know which way to go?

Dr. Lewis: No, not at all. Play is when you've learned a means-ends behavior. Once you've learned something, you then wish to try something different. We may be getting closer if we tie it into something called exploration. There's really the problem of the child having to learn both how to do one thing and at the same time how to constantly do different things. That is, play may be that process which allows us a tremendous amount of flexibility in our commerce. Instead of learning how to do one thing or another thing well, and just that thing only, what the child is doing is learning how to do many different things at the same time.

Dr. Garvey: In *The House at Pooh Corner*, Winnie the Pooh is standing on a bridge and there's a marvelous example of object permanence. He drops a pine cone in the water and then runs to the other side to see if that pine cone is going to reappear, and it does; but if he drops another one in he can't tell which of the two pine cones is his own winner. So he then has to choose a larger pine cone and a smaller pine cone. He throws them in the water, runs to the other side of the bridge, and sure enough, now he can tell which is the winner because they're different sizes. He then has to elaborate this marvelous game. He gets sticks, because he can mark them. So now this thing that starts out with object permanency becomes a symbolic game. It becomes a game of rules. I think he elaborates, and the game becomes more interesting for him, which may be what you're trying to say.

Dr. Kirschenblatt-Gimblett: I think the notion of "galumphing" that we encounter in Stephen Miller's (1973) work is useful here because it's very much about means-ends relationships. One argument he makes in reference to play is that play involves an elaboration of means. Whereas normally we try and get to the end in the most efficient, streamlined, direct fashion, in play one of the great joys is to complicate and overcomplicate that relationship, so that if the idea was to put the ball in the basket you can take a ladder and put it there.

Dr. Fein: There seems to be a period after the consolidation of the means-ends behavior when you have a surplus of behavior—that is, of these variable transformations—and then afterwards even they settle down into a conventional idea. This to me is a very critical, important issue. It doesn't happen all the time, and it seems to happen in some relation to what has become competent or not quite competent or almost competent, after which you get a variability period and then you give it up.

Dr. Lewis: I think we've made the point and I thank you both. If it wasn't clear before, it's certainly clear now.

I want to stick with this caregiver as both a constant and a variable object because I think that's terribly important. I don't quite know how it fits into play, but I know the child has this task of varying symbols, as opposed to signs, in order to facilitate play. The mother must be a symbol rather than a sign because she is variable, so the child has to develop a representation of her. She is not merely a fixed sign. There is some very interesting primate work, using macaques, on what happens if you keep the mother and infant together. If the mother and infant are separated from everyone else and kept together, when you bring the mother and infant into a room with lots of other adult females and children, the child can't recognize the mother. He can't go and find her. The child hasn't learned to represent her. So it seems to me that this variability of the caretaker leads to the development of symbols and representations, and this is also something which I would have to consider as being within a playful framework.

RELATIONSHIPS BEFORE PLAY

I don't want to develop these ideas any further at this point. What has been studied more is which relationships are important in order for play to take place. I would like to make two points. The first concerns the attachment-security notion, which says simply that if the child is able to form a secure and attached relationship it will facilitate the child's play, exploration, and manipulative behavior. I think that none of us would deny that that is probably the case. What's equally important, I think, and what comes from my belief that social relationships precede nonsocial relationships, is that the caregiver directs the infant through the relationship to objects. I think this is terribly important. I have in mind an example such as this: if the mother and child interact, the child pays careful attention to the mother, and while the child is attending to the mother, the mother then is capable of directing the child's attention to an object other than herself. I think this has important pedagogical implications; namely, that a child's relationship to the teacher enables the teacher to direct the child's involvement with nonteacher relationships. We had in a day care setting a little five-year-old child who had terrible language dysfunction. We were not sure of the cause. It turned out she was not an abused but a neglected child; she had been consistently left alone. One of the things you found in questioning her was that she would never look at you, so that if you asked the child questions such as, What is the color of the wallpaper? or What does the picture look like? and you pointed to a picture, the child was unable to answer because she had not learned how to focus her behavior so as to interact with the questioner, and be able to provide the answer. Many of you, if you've worked with disadvantaged children, have noticed that they tend not to look at you; they tend not to enter into a social relationship, and therefore the construction of nonsocial relationships—their interactions with objects—becomes harder.

Dr. Kirschenblatt-Gimblett: I'm concerned about your term "disadvantaged." I don't understand at all what you're saying. What do you mean by disadvantaged and what are you implying about what they do?

Dr. Lewis: Let me retract it. It will just lead us afield, and I don't think for the moment, it fits the discussion. Let me simply say that one can interact with children who will not look at you, will not enter into a social interaction with their teacher, and because of that are not able to profit from object relations that the teacher is trying to develop.

Dr. Kirschenblatt-Gimblett: Are you working with black kids or white kids?

Dr. Lewis: This was a black child.

Dr. Kirschenblatt-Gimblett: This is terribly important because there are cross-cultural differences in sociolinguistic norms. The avoidance of eye contact in Afro-American culture is directly associated with deference and respect, and I think it's most important that we keep that in mind.

Dr. Lewis: It just happens not to be the case with all black children. Indeed, with many poor black children you will get a tremendous amount of eye contact and interaction.

Dr. Kirschenblatt-Gimblett: I just ask that we introduce culturally-specific norms in interaction.

Dr. Lewis: Both points are well taken. The idea that I would like to pursue is that it's through the caregiver relationship that the child's and very young infant's behavior can be directed towards social objects.

Dr. Garvey: I'd like to bring a little evidence that supports the preceding notion of the focus of mother and child on one another as the beginning point. In Dan Stern's (1977) continuing work he sees a very, very clear pattern in the play sessions with infants up to six to eight months old, where the focus of the interaction is infant-mother directly, with nothing intervening. Aversion of eye contact either simply terminates the relationship, or it picks up again. After eight months both partners are able to focus on something other than each other; the mother and the baby can now jointly focus on a third object. This seems to be the very essence and basis for the possibility of any further learning.

Dr. Lewis: Let me develop and use the word empathy, if I don't arouse too much controversy. I would certainly argue that empathy, which has to do with intersocial relationship (which is obviously necessary in group play), again comes out of this early mother-child play.

Dr. Garvey: It seems to me you're describing the prototypical case for the natural history of social relationships; that it begins with a close sharing of the two people—in this case the mother and the infant—then expands and involves more space, more objects, more people, a broader range of experience; and that we see this natural history of social relationships at other stages of the life cycle. Is it agreeable to you to have this point of view on what you're saying?

Dr. Lewis: Yes. The question then would have to be, how would you make a distinction between play and, say, communicative states?

Dr. Garvey: Quite right. I think that's a job that you haven't yet tackled. It seems to me that you're describing the growth of relationships, not play.

Dr. Lewis: I'm suggesting that within that relationship this means-ends activity and this variation on themes takes place which is play. That would be how I would relate it, in particular, to play behavior.

Dr. Collard: But from nonhuman material I have two cases in point where the mother was not involved. Maybe you wouldn't call this play. I'm thinking about the Harlow monkeys who were raised on the artificial mothers. In this situation they would move off and apparently explore even though they had no mother. The other case was when I was observing the Japanese macaques. The mothers would keep them in between their legs, and when they tried to escape they would yank them back by the tail or whatever they could get hold of. These babies would try to go out and get a stick or a leaf or a rock, and before they could get it mama would yank them back; she didn't want them away from her. Now in both cases this looks as if there's an intrinsic wish to manipulate, explore, and handle, which isn't necessarily involved with infant-mother interaction.

Dr. Lewis: I'm a little reluctant, on such things as play, to go to cross-species examples. I think we have enough trouble with human beings without trying to infer a great deal about other groups. Still, I would not be unhappy to say that organisms, human organisms, have a built-in desire to explore or to play. That may take care of the whole problem for us. I mean, it's just a given, and depending on the context, it gets expressed. Let me just emphasize how much mother-infant play goes on. We know there is a considerable amount also in nonhuman primates, so what I've said would not necessarily *not* fit there either.

I would like to mention one final point concerning the notion of competence and play. My belief is that because there's intentionality, the outcomes can be more readily linked to action than they can be to nonsocial objects. That's one terribly important function of social objects: they have intention and, therefore, can link behavior, although I think of the exception in some of John Watson's work (1969) with the mobile, which was highly contingent. There's no question that if we knew all the dimensions we could make machines into people. It seems to me, however, that this quality, this intentionality of the caregiver, facilitates in the child, motives for acting in the world. These motives then have to be linked to these means-ends actions. Let me see how I can do that. I'm trying to link competence to the mother-child interaction and then to develop the theme that the child will try to cause things to happen through feeling that its behavior has an effect. Given that this is true, a competence motive or a trust motive would also lead the child to try to do things in a different way. That is, competence both leads the child to act one way and enables the child to be secure enough to act in new ways.

Dr. McCall: This is the second time I've heard you talk about the intentionality of the caregiver and how important that is with respect to the infant. I don't understand it very well. Can you tell me how the intentionality of the caretaker gets communicated to the child, and in what behavioral ways, leaving aside ESP? What specific attributes does intentionality have? What aids specific effects?

Dr. Lewis: Intentionality is something in the head of the mother, let us say. The behavior is quite simple in that what she does, she does in relationship to the child's behavior. That is, if the child smiles she will respond to that smile. What I'm talking about then is nothing more than what I would call contingency or reinforcement principles. If we wanted to reduce it to a behavioral level, we would simply say that the caregiver is more contingent in her or his behavior in relationship to the child's behavior than are nonsocial objects.

Dr. McCall: Appropriate contingent response.

Dr. Lewis: Exactly.

Dr. McCall: And that's all you mean by intentionality?

Dr. Lewis: That's all I mean.

Dr. McCall: May I suggest you give up the word "intentionality"?

Dr. Lewis: Some people are made unhappy by it. There is, as you know, an elaborate notion of helplessness and mastery amongst people working on the contingent literature. It's really toward that literature that I would direct you.

Dr. Hay: I wanted to follow up the question about intentionality, and I thought you could do more with it beyond talking about contingency without necessarily talking about ESP. It seemed to me the answer might arrive if you took a broader unit of play than just the response to a bout of play. A social partner might have a plan for that bout of play, and yet the responses within it might be coordinated, or they might be goal-directed. And that's somehow a different level of analysis from the response-response contingency. I wonder if you can do anything with that as an index of intentionality?

Dr. Lewis: The nature of the unit as play, as well as the nature of the intentionality within it, is immense, and I'm not terribly hopeful that we'll solve that question. I think you're right, however. I think the mother does have a plan. For example, contrast the mother when she's holding the child on her lap and is clearly going to be engaged in play with the same mother who wants to do the dishes and puts the child up in an infant seat close to her. Let's look at just the verbal exchange between them. We have some very interesting data on these, involving twelve-week-old infants and their mothers. What you find is that in both conditions the mother talks for an equal length of time. There's no difference. The difference lies in what I would call conversation and exchange. When she's doing the dishes, the mother is interested, not in interacting or playing (whatever term we want to use), but in maintaining contact, and she does this by talking. When she's holding the child in her lap, she's interested in some form of interaction, and in the exchange between the mother talking and the infant talking. These conditional probabilities of switching undergo significant kinds of change. Here, if you like, a larger play bout is being defined. Again we can refer to her intention: she intends to do the dishes, and she intends also that her child be with her as she does the dishes, and she seems to intend to keep up the conversation, whatever "intention" might mean. Whereas in the other situation she intends to play and interact.

Dr. Hay: All I'm suggesting is that there may be some external indexes of intentionality beyond response-response contingency—that you shouldn't throw it out.

Dr. Gardner: I'd like to make a general comment on your presentation. If it's to be interpreted just as a framework within which to think about play and development, I don't have any particular quarrel with what you said. But if it's to be interpreted as an empirical theory, and a potentially testable account of what's happening, I think that it's possible to have a different point of view. I take what you're saying to be roughly that the social aspects of development, particularly the mother-child relationships, take the lead in play and exploration of the world, and there's a kind of décalage when you first learn to relate to your mother, who serves as a means for you to learn about things having to do with objects. Now, I don't have much data to go on for my alternative account, but, to anticipate some of what I'm going to be saying later, it seems to me there are two different ways in which it could happen. One is that for certain children the relationship with the mother or the caretaker could become an end in itself, and the child's exploration would become focused exclusively on social events, while the world of physical objects would get underplayed. It wouldn't be explored at all. It may be the case for certain children that their development occurs via the route of interpersonal relationships and contact with the mother, etc. For other children it may occur much more by the route of object relations, with the mother not being so important, and certainly not necessary, in a logical sense, for the exploration of the world. Indeed I'd even say that which route is taken may depend in part on how arousing the mother and the objects happen to be in a particular environment. If, for example, for one reason or another the mother is too arousing, she may come to be neglected as a means of development, and the object world, which is more predictable, will become the route by which it proceeds.

Question: As in autism.

Dr. Lewis: I would certainly agree that we spend too much time arguing that there is one way, and only one way, to develop. It seems to me that it is not unreasonable to suggest that there may be parallel routes between objects and social relations. Some children may be essentially social and never become object-oriented, or may become less object-oriented, and some may go the other route. But I don't think it starts out with object relations. In that sense I would hold to the view that there is a sequence wherein play starts out as a social act and may end up not as a social act. I think we have to talk about outcomes, since in adults the range of activities we want to call play, from symbolic play to exploration to sports to the whole gamut, is so broad that I believe we would be naive to assume that there was a single developmental course for them all. They may have somewhat different developmental histories. I think that's terribly important, because otherwise we're going to be looking for a single developmental course, and I'm sure there isn't one.

References

Bowlby, J. *Maternal Care and Mental Health.* Geneva: World Health Organization, 1951.

Garvey, C. *Play.* Cambridge, Mass.: Harvard University Press, 1977.

Miller, S. Ends, means and galumphing: some leitmotifs of play. *American Anthropologist,* 1973, 75, 87–98.

Piaget, J.*Play, dreams and imitation in childhood.* London: Routledge, 1951.

Stern, D.*The First Relationship.* Cambridge, Mass.: Harvard University Press, 1977.

Watson, J. S., & Ramey, C. T. Reactions to response-contingentstimulation in early infancy. Paper presented at the Society for Research in Child Development, Santa Monica, Calif., April 1969.

CHAPTER 3

STAGES IN PLAY DEVELOPMENT BETWEEN ZERO AND TWO YEARS OF AGE

Robert B. McCall

INTRODUCTION

Dr. Sutton-Smith: Dr. McCall will take up where Dr. Shultz left off, with arousal modulation. He accepts the notion of some internal processing mechanism, but will rephrase it in psychological, rather than neurological, terms. He suggests that the human organism is an information-processing one that is moved by an internal state of "subjective uncertainty" to explore the world, and by a disposition to "influence events" to play with that world. He introduces the concept of perceptual avoidance to cover the data which shows that some stimuli can be so discrepant they are not responded to. Whether this is avoidance, or just a shutting out of stimuli, or a positive aversion, is discussed by the panel.

Making the assumption that playful attempts to influence the environment will be affected by the child's level of cognitive structure, Dr. McCall proceeds to outline a stage theory of development from zero to two years. It has similarities with Piagetian theory but is derived empirically from longitudinal psychometric data and gives a somewhat different view of those stages. McCall, like Piaget, considers these stages in internal structural terms only, whereas if Lewis is correct, each of the stages might well derive from, or at least be strongly affected by, some pattern of prior participation with the parents. Lewis argued strongly that it is the mother's intentionality with respect to objects that makes those object relationships meaningful to the child. McCall gives a most interesting example of the way in which this whole situation is reversed by the age of twenty-one months, when children show that they know they can influence the behavior of others. They, not the mothers, are now the source of the stimulation.

SUBJECTIVE UNCERTAINTY, EXPLORATION, PLAY

Dr. McCall: I would like to take a conceptual orientation to some of the topics we've been discussing, but I ask your indulgence. What I want to attempt to do is provide some perspective on a couple of issues that I see interlaced in the things we've been saying here. But a conceptual orientation implies a forest: to build such a forest, I must place a few trees out there, each of which will be grandly debatable. I ask your indulgence to let me place these trees out there, at least for a while.

The first thing one usually does when offering a conceptual orientation is to define the topic, but I won't do that. I'm not perturbed about not being able to define play. I find it relatively inconsequential and fruitless to spend hours trying to define what is and what is not play. I don't find it frustrating. The physicists don't seem to find the lack of a definition for gravity terribly frustrating, and psychologists don't mind the absence of a definition of intelligence. Secondly, I am not concerned about the fuzziness of the distinction between exploration and play. In trying to make such a distinction, I've attempted to take Dr. Hutt's point of view and integrate it with those of others, but it really doesn't matter much. In their natural stream of behavior, children, especially infants, show an admixture of what we have been calling exploration and play, and can vacillate between one and the other. It may not be quite as profitable as it seems to distinguish between these two. On the other hand, the distinction is convenient, and you will hear me use the words "exploration" and "play," by which I mean something similar to Dr. Hutt's view.

The perspective I would like to give the panel is on the relationship between cognition and exploration and play. I would also like to be developmental. This is a flag I'm waving these days, and it seems appropriate for this group. Most of us are developmental psychologists, but I dare say we haven't spent five minutes talking about development. Development implies change over age. We describe organisms of different ages, but we don't often describe change within an organism over age. I would like to deal with that.

Rather than worry about the definition of play, I have taken another attitude. I think there are two dispositions of organisms. (I use the word "disposition" advisedly. It is not a drive.) One disposition is to acquire information. In its simplest form, that is knowing the shape of something, its texture, its color, what it does, and so on. Another disposition is to influence the environment, be it animate or inanimate. Obviously these are related events. When you explore an object to acquire information about it, some of that information may involve the responsivity of the object to your manipulation, which, in turn, tells you about your influencing potential. Moreover, you can explore your influencing potential. I see these as functions or dispositions that are salient to the development of mental ability or intelligence, broadly defined, and to exploration, and eventually to play, because I would think of *imaginary play as fantasy exploration of social influence.*

A great deal of what children under two do is explore, which means acquiring information about an object. I have a pet theory that I have been pushing for twelve years. I do not want to present the empirical data here. That's contained in a paper by McCall and McGhee (1977). However, I would like to describe the proposition to you. It says that exploration or attention to an entity will follow an inverted U function, or what Berlyne (1966) calls subjective uncertainty—you could say information potential. This curve is described in Figure 3-1. Subjective uncertainty is often operationally defined as stimulus discrepancy. A totally familiar stimulus has no subjective uncertainty and receives some minimal ambient level of exploration. Things that are moderately different from it provide increasing amounts of information, and therefore subjective uncertainty, and will be increasingly explored up to a point, after which there is a decline. Too much uncertainty does not elicit as much exploration. Why the decline? Piaget said the child can no longer make the relationship between the new object and what the child remembers. But you will notice that my curve of exploration goes below this point. That is, relative perceptual "avoidance" is postulated for extreme levels of subjective uncertainty. A stimulus can be discrepant yet recognized as being quasi-familiar, and this leads to very relative perceptual avoidance. It's not a case in which a child simply cannot draw the relationship between what is familiar and a stimulus. Let me give you a commonplace adult example. I went to my tenth-year college reunion. As I was walking, I saw someone on the other side of the street. Who is that? (It's important that we were on different sides of the street. I was under no potential social embarrassment.) While I scanned my memory, I closed my eyes! I detected the person as familiar but not recognizable. Presumably, I closed my eyes to shut off the intake of additional perceptual information while I scanned my memory. We now have evidence to show that infants also behave this way. However, it is difficult to construct situations in which the subjective uncertainty is sufficiently great to produce relative avoidance, although we have done it.

Please make a distinction here. So far, we have talked about the exploration of entities that bear some relationship to what the child knows well. Those stimuli that are totally novel are not explored for their relationship to existing memories but for their physical stimulus characteris-

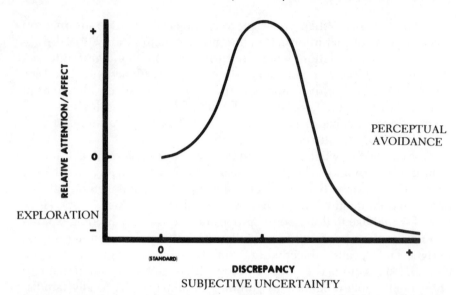

Figure 3-1. The theoretical distribution of relative attention (and affect) to stimuli that vary in magnitude of discrepancy (and therefore subjective uncertainty) from a well-familiarized standard stimulus. Reprinted with permission from McCall, R. B. and McGhee, P. E. The discrepancy hypothesis of attention and affect in infants. In I. C. Uzgiris and Frederic Weizman (eds.), *The structuring of experience.* New York: Plenum, 1977, p. 181.

tics; for instance, contour, density, etc. Methodologically, if one uses only two stimuli in exploration or play studies, are they novel or discrepant? If they are discrepant you may find the novel explored more, the same amount, or less than the familiar. If one stimulus is totally unrelated to existing memories, then it will be explored for its physical stimulus properties.

Dr. Hutt: In some respects, a novel object has *some* characteristics in common with previous experience. Is there such a thing as a totally novel stimulus?

Dr. McCall: For a very young infant, perhaps there is. But I would not be surprised if infants attempt to relate every new stimulus to some memory.

Dr. Gardner: It seems to me your example is a literal illustration of perceptual avoidance: you looked away from the person whom you suspected you knew. But I think that's a complete accident; you might just as well have looked at him more carefully.

Dr. McCall: I think not. Other people report babies deliberately looking away from certain stimuli, but since they don't usually scale the stimuli it's difficult to interpret these results.

Dr. Lewis: Adults move their eyes away when they're thinking about a solution.

Dr. McCall: The assumption is that the intake of more information in-terferes with the scanning of memory.

Dr. Gardner: So that exploring is not ceasing; it's going inside.

Dr. Lewis: It's internal?

Dr. McCall: Yes, if you regard scanning the memory as exploring.

Dr. Lewis: Do you really want to use the term "avoidance"? One could talk about competitive response. Do you really want to make it negative?

Dr. McCall: I have no investment in the word "avoidance." It was a convenient label to reflect the fact that infants looked less at these discre-pant stimuli than at very familiar ones, and that some evidence suggests that negative affect accompanies the response (McCall and McGhee, 1977).

Dr. Lewis: You have invested in it as if you want to talk about fear or a negative affect being associated. Lacey certainly wouldn't have talked about it as an avoidance, but would have said that you have to process in-formation internally, and therefore the energy is not invested in the ex-ternal event.

Dr. McCall: It is only negative if this behavior indeed functions to shut off the input channel and includes negative affect.

Dr. J. Singer: Again, if we take a Tompkins (1962) kind of theory of affect, then you propose that gross discrepancy or extreme novelty might lead to a startle response, in which case you do get a negative affective reaction which would imply some avoidant behavior.

Dr. Lewis: That's to do with the processing of the information: the re-sponse of avoidance. Not that it is perceptually discrepant. It's what you do once it is.

Dr. J. Singer: That's one way you could justify that there might be a situation in which you would literally avoid something. For example, in some of those Harlow cartoons, the baby monkey is holding onto the cloth mother, and then a little doodle bug comes in with all kinds of noisy claps. The monkey leaps desperately back to the cloth mother because of the tremendous novelty.

Dr. McCall: These situations are not totally clear, despite the fact that they are frequently cited as examples of fear in response to extreme in-congruity or discrepancy. In our situation it is clear that discrepancy or subjective uncertainty is the causal variable, because the same stimulus that produces this relative avoidance under some circumstances will pro-duce a maximum attentional response under others.

Dr. J. Singer: I've done a number of experiments with adults which show that if you're engaging in any kind of extended search of your own memory, or if you're producing fantasy while in a face-to-face situation (not in a very complex, visually stimulating situation), you either have to shut your eyes or frequently shift your eyes away from the stimulus, to the left or the right, depending on which side of the brain is more active in what you are doing. But there does have to be the shift, or some people literally put their eyes out of focus. We've tested for that, and males, at least, do so. Females seem to be able to blot out the stimulation centrally. Of course, these are adults. Anyway, there is the need to frequently use the same visual system to process material from long-term memory in order to make a better match. But I would add to it, the fact that you approach a situation with an intention to match initially, and I don't think you mentioned that. Even as you were walking down the street when your friend approached you had somewhere back there the thought that you might meet somebody you knew.

Dr. McCall: In the adult example, it's hard to argue about that. With babies, I can't imagine that they've had any experience or training to promote comparing a new stimulus with a remembered entity. I can't imagine an organism surviving without the disposition to relate what it sees to stored engrams of some sort. To take in information is a highly adaptive response; I can't imagine an organism without it. Similarly, to influence the environment in some way is fundamental.

DEVELOPMENTAL DATA

Let's be developmental. It seems trivial to suggest that exploration and play with an object are going to depend on the cognitive development of the infant, but few people have talked about this. I would like to offer a developmental perspective on the first two years that derives from a set of data that are in an SRCD monograph (McCall, Eichorn, & Hogarty, 1977). As you may know, the Berkeley Growth Study gave infant tests to babies every month from the ages of one to fifteen months, every three months until age thirty months, and every six months thereafter. We took those individual items, subjected them to a principal components analysis separately at each age, and then correlated the components scores across age. The theory that emerged from this strategy looks very much like Piaget's, despite the fact that the tests were created before Piaget did his major theoretical work, and the fact that we were not exactly looking for Piaget in miscellaneous data.

We found stages, if you will. The first principal component represents the best distillation of the test at a given age, given the item pool. It estimates the predominant character of the behavior the test was designed to study. My inference is that the first principal component estimates the predominant mental behavior at this given age, allowing for the fact that the conclusion arrived at is itself dependent' on the items on the test. Now, there may be periods of the life span during which the composition of that first principal component is relatively consistent. But there may be a break in the continuity in which the composition of the first principal component changes from one age to the next. This is a qualitative change, not a quantitative one. Another dimension over which development can proceed involves individual differences. We can correlate the component scores in the first principal components across age, and search for dips in the size of the cross-age corelational pattern. If intelligence were unitary and essentially consistent, you would expect the cross-age correlations to increase and level off, but that is not what we found. Dips in the size of the *rs* occur at certain places, and they happen to occur precisely at the same time that the predominant character of mental behavior shifts. These changes occur at approximately two, seven, thirteen and twenty-one months of age.

Dr. Singer: It sounds superficially similar to Werner's notion of spiral development. You reach a certain point, and then as you, in effect, tool up for a new stage there is this kind of a gap.

Dr. McCall: It also looks like Piaget's stages, especially their content and even the ages.

Stage I. The zero- to two-month period has been described as a period of time in which the child is attentionally responsive to entities in the environment that match the child's inborn sensory-perceptual dispositions. I hasten to add this does not mean the child is passive. Rather, attention is allocated to stimulus characteristics for which the child's sensory-perceptual system is maximally tuned; typically these are edges of stimuli, brightness contrasts, staccato movements of objects, and the like.

Stage 2. Between two and seven months of age the child becomes more motorically facile and therefore more capable of manipulatively exposing objects to himself for exploration. However, the infant does this with complete subjectivity. I can phrase the notion as "the world is what I do with it." Knowledge of objects is so tied to physical actions with those objects that objects do not exist out there; they do not have an independent, external existence of their own. But the infant is influenced by the information and responsivity of the object, so you see Piaget's primary and secondary circular responses, which may represent one of the first playful explorations of influence.

Stage 3. From seven to thirteen months is a transition stage. It's the beginning, but not the end, of means-end differentiation and coordination. The baby can now begin to separate the object from the action, but the object doesn't become totally independent until the end of that stage, at about thirteen months. It is now that you begin to see imitation of new behaviors. Prior to this stage, although there are reports of imitation in babies, they are essentially response facilitations by imitation, not the initiation of new behaviors. For example, the parent will imitate the baby and thereby facilitate the release of that particular response again from the baby, but this is not a new behavior which is currently absent from the repertoire. During this period the child progressively becomes able to imitate more and more behaviors that are more and more discrepant from behaviors that are currently in the child's repertoire. Near the end of the stage the child will enter into reciprocal imitation.

Stage 4: At thirteen months, means and ends become quite independent. The child understands that the object exists out there (as in Piaget's tertiary circular reactions), that objects may possess dynamic properties of their own. Now children can have true social relations. Now they can engage in reciprocal imitation. Note that imitation and influencing go hand in hand. We wanted to know if the baby who saw himself imitated would be likely to attempt to reinfluence that person. The context was that infants had two toys available. There was a priori selected target behavior for one toy. When the child displayed that behavior the examiner simply repeated the same action. For other infants, when the subject displayed the target behavior the examiner performed an alternate target behavior with another object which was not imitative but which was equally contingent on the infant's execution of the target behavior. Does the baby say, "Oh! I just influenced that person. I'll do something else and see what they do then"? So the dependent measure was whether the child, after performing some action following the examiner's, paused to observe whether that action again influenced the examiner. The prediction was that if the experience of being imitated is salient and represesents an ideal circumstance in which the infant can discern that he has an influence on another person, then more pause-looks should occur after being imitated than after the equally contingent nonimitative action. However, such an effect should occur at a specific age, after entity-entity relations are possible (thirteen months) but before symbolic relations (twenty-one months). Indeed, more pause-looks occurred after imitation than after nonimitation, especially at eighteen months of age. The supposition is that when infants see themselves imitated, it is clearer to them that it was their action that elicited that behavior out of the other person than if the other person had responded nonimitatively.

Dr. Garvey: There are two things going on. One is the actual action.

Dr. McCall: Which we ignored.

Dr. Garvey: Then there is the contingency. And I would expect some waiting for the contingency because there had been contingent action.

Dr. McCall: The contingency, if I understand your question, was the same in either condition. It was simply whether the examiner, who responded contingently to the baby's action, imitated the action or in fact performed another action that was nonimitative but equally contingent.

Dr. Lewis: How would you handle the data when the infant looks at the mother, the mother looks, and they engage in a looking sequence, turning and looking? The infant turns toward the mother, the mother then doesn't turn toward the infant, and the infant seems to produce a behavior such as a threat to get the mother to come back. But that is at three months rather than at thirteen months.

Dr. McCall: I'm not implying that there are no contingent relationships prior to this fifteen-to-eighteen-month period. Of course there are. But they don't involve the level of cognition I have been describing, in which there is the ability to extract the relationship and apply it to a new situation apart from the original actions. In those earlier cases it's a perseveration of the same response. In these cases, infants are trying new behaviors. For example, if the child did something with the object, and the examiner imitated and repeated that, the child did not necessarily repeat the same action the next time. Maybe the child even picked up the other object and did something else and then looked. The cognition of "I influenced you" is separable from the specific actions only after this fifteen-month age point. That's what I mean by talking of this period as one of entity-entity relationships. The child can associate two entities out there without having to act on them, and that association is now portable and not tied to those particular entities. That's when you get consensual vocabulary. Vocabulary is an auditory label applied to an object, and it exists largely apart from the infant except insofar as they may utter it. But they may learn the label from an adult when they are not acting on it, just perceptually receiving it. It's only when this is possible, when there's a complete separation of oneself and one's actions from the external world, that I suspect that vocabulary—true consensual vocabulary, not reinforced operants that happen to approximate words—is possible.

Dr. Fein: In the nonimitative condition, what if the examiner picked up any other thing and did any other thing with it?

Dr. McCall: In the experimental design there were two target behaviors, and it was a specific response that the experimenter knew to make with the other object.

Dr. Fein: Did you have any data about whether the infant was watching the examiner's behavior in the first place?

Dr. McCall: Yes, that was a precondition for the data analysis.

These results have implications for early social relations. When two three-monthers are put together, one child eventually performs an action with an object and the other child sees it, comes over, and there's physical contact over the object. This is the only way they know to deal with the world. They do not know how to influence at a distance, without touching. Later in development, a child will do something, and the other child will come over and, instead of having a fight over the toy, pick it up and do the same thing with it. Now they take turns, which is exactly what Dr. Dale Hay discusses in her paper. In the next stage the second child imitates the first one but tries the action with a new twist. It's a tertiary circular reaction, and each child watches what the other one does. The final stage is social influencing at a distance with "malice aforethought."

The child knows mentally that if he does something that is attractive to that other child, he is going to influence him, so he rolls a ball and then steps aside and waits. He *knows* that it is going to elicit a response from the other child, and he waits with the cognition, the anticipation, that he will influence the playmate. Such exploration of influencing can drive parents nuts. I submit that the "terrible twos" represent influencing techniques, and the child is relatively less concerned with the particular action or the nature of its consequences—just so there are consequences. They are willing to endure certain kinds of punishment for the privilege of exploring these influencing relationships.

Stage 5. When the child reaches approximately twenty-one months of age, real portable sympolic relations begin. In them the *relationship* between two entities is transferable and extractable from those particular entities to new contexts. Now you will see a playing child serve tea to a teddy bear. The tea is imaginary, the teddy bear is drinking it, and so forth.

I would like to argue that we need to start to be developmental. We need to look at changes over age, not only in this arena but in most of the ones that we consider to be part of developmental psychology. Development implies change, not only continuity, not only stability, although that may be the reality in some cases. We should not be shocked to find that we don't get correlations across age in infant tests, for example, or between other behaviors. We should rejoice when we fail to find a correlation. It means something has changed, and we, as developmentalists, now have something to study.

References

Berlyne, D. E. Curiosity and Exploration. *Science*, 1966, *153*, 25–33.

McCall, R. B., Eichorn, D. H., & Hogarty, P. S. Transitions in early mental development. *Monographs of the Society for Research in Child Development*, 1977, *42*, 1–108.

McCall, R. B., & McGhee, P. E. The discrepancy hypothesis of attention and affect in human infants. In I. C. Uzgiris and F. Weizmann (Eds.) *The structuring of experience*. New York: Plenum, 1977.

Tomkins, S. S. *Affect, Imagery, Consciousness* (Vol. 1). New York: Springer, 1962.

Weisler, A., & McCall, R. B. Exploration and play. *American Psycholgist*, 1976, *31*, 492–508.

CHAPTER 4

EXPLORATION AND PLAY

Roberta R. Collard

INTRODUCTION

Dr. Sutton-Smith: Members of this conference already were familiar with the distinction in the literature between exploration and play. In the prior paper, Dr. McCall sought to base this distinction on two dispositions in the human organism, one to acquire information and the other to influence the environment. In this paper, Dr. Collard will seek to base the distinction on two kinds of concept formation, which she terms *perceptual* and *functional,* and at another point calls *stimulus reduction* versus *stimulus creation.* This analysis will be supplemented by a second paper in which Dr. Collard will detail the behavioral consequences of looking at the baby's behavior in terms of the exploration-play distinction, as this can be found to vary under various conditions of home and institutional care. She has found great differences between institutional and home babies in their willingness to explore and play. The more stimulated home babies are more eager to do both. However, just adding the stimulation of toys and other children to institutional babies can lead to "stimulus overload," so that exploratory behavior becomes more stereotyped and defensive, and play behavior decreases. Dr. Collard will discuss the time phases from focused to flexible activity indicated by this data, and will question whether play definitions can be located in such behavioral descriptions any more than in internal monitors, or whether they must be located in characteristics of the setting.

In general the complexity of the presented data on infants serves to bring into the foreground the difficulties of interpretation, perhaps oversimplified in the prior discussions.

(a) THE ROLE OF EXPLORATION AND PLAY IN CONCEPT FORMATION IN INFANCY

Dr. Collard: It is generally agreed that early concept formation is based on perception and on action or function (Piaget, 1952; Kendler, 1961; Sigel, 1964; Gibson, 1969; Flavell, 1970). When babies explore and play, they are learning the elements of perception and action which are later combined into concepts (Bruner, 1972). Early concepts, which are based on generalization, can later be combined into more complex concepts or principles.

Learning is a cumulative process. Early exploration involves the perception of the stimulus properties of objects and their generalization to other objects, which leads to their classification into perceptual concepts. For example, in their exploration of similar objects, infants learn to generalize perceptual properties such as color, form or number, which are basic classifications on which higher order classifications and abstractions depend. Similarly, the response of objects to the infant's actions leads to the formation of action or function concepts. In their play with objects, infants learn to combine simple action schemas into more complex ones and to generalize the complex schemas to other objects. For example, simple action schemas such as grasping, waving, and releasing may be combined into the complex schema of throwing an object, and then the schema of "throwing" can be generalized to other appropriate objects.

It may be primarily through *exploration* that the perceptual properties of objects are learned and primarily through *play* that actions are generalized and the functions of many objects, learned.

Hull (1920) defined concept formation as a generalizing abstraction involving the discrimination of a particular element which is common to a variety of stimuli. Leeper (1951) described concept formation as the process of experiencing successive stimuli and the selective perception of certain aspects of those stimuli which are common to several of them.

Probably some of the ability of infants to respond to similar stimuli in similar ways is built in, but also some of it must be built up through learning. To generalize similar properties of objects involves the perception of likenesses and differences, and it is known that the ability to discriminate differences between some visual stimuli is learned through experience, as Riesen's experiments (1958) with visually deprived infant chimpanzees have shown.

Eleanor Gibson (1969) sees perceptual learning as the basic process which leads to the formation of generalized concepts. In perceptual learning there is a discrimination of the distinctive features of stimuli and a generalization of similar properties. The common features of a group of stimuli are abstracted to form a class concept.

According to Piaget (1952), during the sensorimotor period of infancy (from birth to about eighteen months), certain objects become organized into classes or groups through the generalization of their perceptual qualities or through the baby's actions upon them. For example, objects with certain properties may be grasped, mouthed, or thrown. A baby's actions on an object (such as banging it on a table) may also produce interesting results which provide intrinsic reinforcement for learning them, and then the baby can generalize these actions to other objects.

Berlyne (1970) has classified infant behavior into reflex and voluntary (or intentional) behavior, and then classified voluntary behavior as exploratory and instrumental. Instrumental or goal-directed behavior involves actions which produce an effect (Hulsebus, 1973). Contingency awareness, or the knowledge that one's behavior has an effect on the environment, plays an important role in motivation (Watson, 1966). Much instrumental behavior is learned in play in which the baby is intrinsically rewarded by the results of his actions and tends to repeat the actions which led to the effects. For example, striking a toy which makes a noise produces a sensory reward which then leads to a repetition of the action. The action of striking with the hand or with a stick can then be applied to other objects or can generalize to similar actions, such as striking a pan with a spoon. Other instrumental learning which is generalized to many situations is behavior in which the baby learns to go around a barrier or to climb up on something to reach a goal.

J. J. Gibson (1950) distinguishes preverbal stimulus generalization from conceptual thinking in verbal symbols which involves logic and classification. Tracy Kendler (1961, 1972) and Vurpillot (1977) believe that "true" concepts occur only at the level of verbal symbolization and that what I have called perceptual or action concepts should be called "preconcepts." However, Leeper (1951) and Lenneberg (1967) see concept formation at the level of perception and action as the most primary cognitive process and see language (or naming) as a secondary cognitive process. In other words, the *meaning* of an object or situation in perception or action usually precedes verbal labeling, and such meanings are often learned in exploration and play (Bloom, 1975). In my work with institutional infants, I observed that twelve- to fifteen-month-old babies learned to label objects most readily when I repeated the name of the object while they were playing with it or when the object was part of a meaningful action, such as when I named a particular food they were eating.

Olver and Hornsby (1966) distinguish between semantic concepts, which include concepts based on perception or on action or function, and syntactic concepts, which include logical classification in which the relationship between a class and subclass are understood. Bruner and

Olver (1963) have suggested that perceptual concepts develop first, function concepts second, and verbal or logical concepts last.

Psychological Processes Involved in Concept Formation in Infants

Research on psychological processes of infants related to concept formation has been done in the following areas: attention, memory, discrimination, generalization, classification, object concept, and learning sets. Most of these areas are included in the general studies on learning and perception in infancy (Gibson, 1969; Cohen & Salapatek, 1975; Lipsitt, 1967; Horowitz, 1968; Reese & Porges, 1976). In the following summary, I will refer the reader to reviews in these areas.

1. *Attention and habituation.* Most of the studies on attention in infants have concentrated on visual attention to patterns, objects, or human faces, although an increasing number have been concerned with attention to sound (Appleton, Clifton, & Goldberg, 1975; Horowitz, 1975). The orienting response to stimuli indicates alerting or curiosity and is increased by stimulus novelty or discrepancy (Sokolov, 1963). Attention in infants has been measured by cardiac deceleration to stimuli or stimulus change, by visual alerting, search or viewing time, or by habituation toward stimuli (Lewis, Goldberg, & Campbell, 1969; Kagan, 1971; Cohen, 1973; McCall, 1971, 1974; Karmel & Maisel, 1975; Mackworth, 1976; Clifton & Nelson, 1976). Habituation is measured as the decrease in response rate to a stimulus during one period of time or over several periods of time.

2. *Memory* has been inferred from the responses of infants to a novel or discrepant stimulus after habituation (or familiarization) to another stimulus (Sokolov, 1963; Fagan, 1970; Cohen & Gelber, 1975; Fantz, Fagan, & Miranda, 1975). Memory is implied by the ability to discriminate novel stimuli from familiar ones.

3. *Discrimination* has been inferred from infants' preferences for one stimulus over another, as measured by differential looking or manipulation or by a tendency to choose novel stimuli over familiar ones or to choose stimuli associated with positive reinforcement (Ling, 1941; Fantz, Fagan, & Miranda, 1975; Reese & Porges, 1976).

4. *Generalization of habituation* has been inferred from infants' preferences for a stimulus with properties which are discrepant from a class of objects with similar properties to which the infants have been habituated (Cohen, Gelber, & Lazar, 1971; Collard & Rydberg, 1972; Collard & Dempsey, 1976). Generalization also occurs in terms of an infant's actions (Piaget, 1952) or in terms of the function of stimuli (Nelson, 1973; Goldberg, Perlmutter, & Myers, 1974).

5. *Classification* has been measured by serial manipulation or by the simultaneous grasping of identical or similar objects from an array of ob-

jects or by grouping the objects into classes (Ricciuti, 1965; Nelson, 1973; Forman, Kuschner, & Dempsey, 1975).

6. *Object concept* or object permanence can be viewed as a construct if it involves one person or object, and as a concept to the extent that it is generalized to other objects or persons (Bower, 1975; Gratch, 1975; Vurpillot, 1976).

7. *Learning sets* are concepts in the sense that they involve principles of learning which can be generalized to other learning situations (Harlow, 1949; Fagen, 1977).

Studies on Classification and Generalization in Infants

Of the psychological processes involved in concept formation listed previously, only the studies on classification and generalization of habituation in infants will be reviewed here.

Classification. One of the first studies on classification in infants was made by Ricciuti (1965) who observed that twelve- to twenty-four-month-old babies, when presented with an array of four yellow cubes and four gray spheres arranged randomly, tended to manipulate the identical stimuli serially or to group them by shape. There was an increase in serial manipulation up to eighteen months of age and in grouping up to twenty-four months of age. Ricciuti explained these behaviors as possibly based on preference, because the younger babies tended to manipulate the spheres first, and infants tend to prefer spheres over cubes.

Forman, Kuschner, and Dempsey (1975) gave infants eight to twenty-four months old a series of six arrays of five objects each (cylinders and blocks), with two or three identical or similar shapes in each array. They found a developmental sequence of manipulation which progressed from banging two identical objects at the midline to stacking them vertically, lining them up horizontally, and finally grouping them spatially.

Nelson (1973) presented children from twelve to twenty-two months of age with objects having different functions and which also varied in color, form, and size (such as toy planes, cars, toy animals, and eating utensils) and observed that the children sorted the objects by function more than by color, form or size. However, two-year-olds *are* able to sort by form or color or size if they are asked specifically to hand the experimenter all of the objects in an array with particular properties (Denny, 1972). Goldberg, Perlmutter, and Myers (1974) found that two-year-olds could remember more hidden objects if the objects were in a particular category (such as toy animals, eating utensils or food) than if the objects were unrelated. This study illustrates that classifying or grouping objects can facilitate learning in very young children.

Generalization of Habituation. Habituation (or decrease in responsiveness to a stimulus with time of exposure) can generalize to similar stimuli. Generalization of habituation is the extent to which a response which has been habituated to one stimulus will be diminished to similar stimuli (Caron & Caron, 1969).

In the first published experiment on generalization of habituation, Saayman, Ames, and Moffett (1964) allowed three-month-old babies to look for three minutes at a red cross or a red circle and found that if the familiar stimulus was then paired with one changed in *both* color and form, the infants spent more time looking at the novel stimulus, but they did not do this if the stimulus was changed in *only* color or form. Cohen, Gelber, and Lazar (1971) repeated this experiment with four-and-a-half-month-old babies, using red or green circles or triangles, and also found that the infants fixated much more on the novel stimulus when the familiar stimulus was paired with one changed in both color and form than when only color or form was changed.

Welch (1974) did a similar experiment with four-month-old babies, using visual stimuli containing elements which differed in color, shape and arrangement. The babies were allowed to look at one stimulus for sixty seconds; the first stimulus was then successively paired with three novel stimuli for ten seconds each. The babies looked more at the novel stimulus when its elements were varied in two or three dimensions than when they were varied in only one dimension. Cornell (1975) observed four-month-olds to show more visual fixation when both orientation and pattern were changed in the elements of the novel stimulus than if only one were changed. These studies show that more looking (or exploration) occurs as the degree of novelty or discrepancy of a stimulus is increased relative to a more familiar stimulus.

In 1962, I observed that after babies twelve to fifteen months old had played with a red or a blue toy for six minutes and were then given a choice between a red and a blue toy of the same shape but of a shape different from the familiar toy, they tended to choose the toy of the novel color. When they played with a series of red or yellow or blue toys for a total of six minutes, they also tended to choose a toy of a novel color afterward (Collard, 1962). From these experiments, I concluded that the babies had generalized their habituation with the property of color to other objects of the same color which then led them to prefer an object of the novel color.

Collard and Rydberg (1972) allowed eight- to twelve-month-old infants to play for two or three minutes each with two or three objects having similar properties of color or form (red versus blue or square versus round), and found that the babies tended to choose a stimulus with novel properties afterward. The infants chose more objects with novel properties after exposure to the series of objects (a total of six minutes) than did infants exposed to one of the objects for two or three minutes. Because infants' response rate was observed to decrease over a six-minute period in their play with one of the objects and also over a six-minute period with a series of three objects having similar properties (played with for two minutes each), it was inferred that generalization of habituation had occurred to the property of color or form.

Collard and Dempsey (1976), using the same paradigm, also found that eight- to twelve-month-old babies could discriminate two versus three units as measured by their preference for the toy with the *novel* number of units and that they also could distinguish three versus four units, measured by their preference for the object with *more* units. For example, if the babies played for three minutes with a disc that had three small cylinders attached to it, and then for three more minutes with a disc with three small cylinders of different sizes and in a different pattern from the first toy, they were more likely to choose a toy with two units attached than one with three units. Conversely, if they played with two-unit toys, they were more likely to choose one with three units. In the study on discrimination of three versus four, most of the babies chose the toy with four units on it whether or not they had been previously familiarized with toys having three or four units. This result either means that their preference for *more* units was stronger than the *novelty* of the three-unit toys or that they had not habituated to four units during the familiarization period. In any event, preference for the toys with four units indicates that they could discriminate three versus more than three. In the number experiments, the total surface areas of the units presented for choice were equal, and the units in the choice toys were included in the familiarization toys.

Babies under a year old can also show generalized learning toward photographs of human faces. Cornell (1974) observed that after five- and six-month-old babies were exposed to a series of photographs of men or women (the same person in different poses or different persons in the same pose) they paid more attention to a photograph of a person of the opposite sex. Fagan (1976) exposed seven-month-old babies to three poses of the same face and then paired another pose of the familiar face with the photograph of a different person in the same pose; the infants looked longer at the picture of the new person. As the infants were able to discriminate different poses of the same face, Fagan concluded that they were able to abstract characteristics of the features of the same face in different poses.

Summary

To summarize, it can be said that the infant's early exploration and play lead to learning the elements of concepts which involve attention, discrimination and memory. The elements of concepts, which may be the perceptual properties of objects or the effects of the infant's actions on objects, can then be generalized to form concepts. These early concepts order the baby's responses and also form the elements on which later learning and concept formation are based. Concepts facilitate learning and thinking by organizing and simplifying information processing. The logic involved in later classification is based on prior learning of perceptual properties and functions. In learning language, abstract verbal symbols are applied to categories which already exist in perception and action. The infant learns the perceptual properties of objects primarily through exploration and the action or function properties of objects primarily through play.

Discussion

Dr. Kirschenblatt-Gimblett: It's not quite clear to me how this would relate to the play issue.

Dr. Collard: I'm talking about concept formation, and these are kids playing with blocks.

Dr. Kirschenblatt-Gimblett: Then it's using play material as a way of getting at concept formation.

Dr. Sutton-Smith: But in a way it's related to Greta [Fein's] notion of prototypes. These activities are presumably the sorts of activities by which the child differentiates similar characteristics across phenomena. Those patterns then become able to be detached from the realistic phenomena and are found much more nonprototypically in other play behavior.

Dr. Collard: Piaget says that insofar as actions become generalized they are the prototypes of concepts. He would see this on an action level or a sensorimotor level. He would say that schemas are concepts. He also said that in schemas themselves, insofar as perception and action are generalized to other objects or other stimuli, these are prototypes of concepts. All of these are prototypes.

Object permanence, to the extent that it is generalized to include all disappearing objects, would also be considered an action concept. Concepts such as, for instance, container behavior, in which an infant would have to know "inside" and "outside," and barrier behavior, where he would have to know "behind," would be spatial concepts, as would "near" and "far" in reaching. The properties of objects that babies can generalize or classify, either by sorting or by habituation, would be things like color, form, size, number or weight. Infants certainly adapt, when they reach for an object, in terms of size and what they think is the object's weight. If it unexpectedly turns out to be light, their hand will fly up in the air.

Dr. Gardner: I gather that the thrust of the message you're giving us is that the early people who made a sharp division between concepts and preconcepts were insensitive to what infants can do.

Dr. Collard: Right.

Dr. Gardner: And that strikes a responsive chord with my thinking. But now I'm worried about what it is that you're disqualifying. If the infant sucks at the nipple but doesn't suck everything else—that is, if you put certain things in front of its mouth, it won't suck; it will mouth or do something else—is that classifying in your definition?

Dr. Collard: I'm simply saying that in generalizing properties, I am listing those that have been found in research to be generalizable. If you look on generalization as a necessary part of concept formation, these would be the pieces out of which concept formation is made.

Dr. Gardner: Are you sticking to the distinctions that Piaget makes between exploration and play in terms of "more assimilation equals more play"?

Dr. Collard: Well, I don't really define it that way. I have been able to tease out exploratory responses and play responses with only two ambiguous responses. Transferring is an ambiguous response, although 85 percent of the time it's associated with what I'm calling an exploratory response. Mouthing is an ambiguous response. I imagine you could mouth-play with an object. On the other hand, over 90 percent of the time mouthing is associated with looking or with what I call an exploratory response. Also both of these do not decrease over time because you get some infants mouthing a lot at first, and then down she goes. You get other infants who delay mouthing, and up it goes, so it's sort of a straight line. Transferring is apt to be associated with things like handing an object to the experimenter, and dropping it on the floor. They drop it on the floor, you put it on the table, they'll pick it up with one hand, transfer it to the other, and drop it again. But only 15 percent of the time it's associated with play, and mouthing is interspersed between two play responses only 10 percent of the time. Also they don't go down. The things that do go down, that do habituate, are primarily looking and manipulation other than transferring.

Dr. McCall: Looking at this makes intuitive sense to me because play responses are different from exploratory ones, but I guess I'd like to push you on your more general thoughts as to why you call these behaviors play. In some senses you could say the first set of responses involved exploring and gaining information about some first-order characteristics of the objects, and you could say the second set concerned exploring and gaining information about second-order characteristics, so what cause does that give us to call it playful?

Dr. Collard: Perhaps my second paper will answer that question.

References

Berlyne, D. E. Children's reasoning and thinking. In P. H. Mussen (Ed.) *Carmichael's manual of child psychology* (Vol. 1). New York: Wiley, 1970, pp. 939–981.

Bloom, L. Language development. In F. D. Horowitz (Ed.) *Review of child development research* (Vol. 4). Chicago: University of Chicago Press, 1975, pp. 245–303.

Bruner, J. S. The nature and uses of immaturity. *American Psychologist,* 1972, *27,* 1–22.

Bruner, J. S., & Olver, R. R. Development of equivalence transformations in children. In J. C. Wright & J. Kagan (Eds.) Basic cognitive processes in children. *Monographs of the Society for Research in Child Development,* 1963, *28 (86).*

Bruner, J. S., Olver, R. R., & Greenfield, P. M. *Studies in cognitive growth.* New York: Wiley, 1966.

Caron, R. F., & Caron, A. J. Degree of stimulus complexity and habituation of visual fixation in infants. *Psychonomic Science,* 1969, *14,* 78–79.

Clifton, R. K., & Nelson, M. N. Developmental study of habituation in infants: the importance of paradigm, response system, and state. In T. J. Tighe & R. N. Leighton (Eds.) *Habituation: perspectives from child development, animal behavior, and neurophysiology.* Hillsdale, N. J. : Lawrence Erlbaum, 1976, pp. 159–205.

Collard, R. R. A study of curiosity in infants. Doctoral dissertation, University of Chicago, 1962.

Collard, R. R., & Rydberg, J. E. Generalization of habituation to properties of objects in human infants. *Proceedings, Eightieth Annual Convention of the American Psychological Association,* 1972, pp. 81–82.

Collard, R. R., & Dempsey, J. R. Number concept in eight- to twelve-month-old infants. Paper presented at the International Congress of Psychology, Paris, 1976.

Cohen, L. B. A two-process model of infant visual attention. *Merrill-Palmer Quarterly,* 1973, *19,* 157–180.

Cohen, L. B., & Gelber, E. R. Infant visual memory. In L. B. Cohen & P. Salapatek (Eds.) *Infant perception: from sensation to cognition.* Vol. 1: *Basic visual processes.* New York: Academic Press, 1975, pp. 347–403.

Cohen, L. B., Gelber, E. R., & Lazar, M. A. Infant habituation and generalization to repeated visual stimulation. *Journal of Experimental Child Psychology,* 1971, *11,* 379–389.

Cornell, E. H. Infants' discrimination of photographs of faces following redundant presentations. *Journal of Experimental Child Psychology,* 1974, *18,* 98–106.

Cornell, E. H. Infants' visual attention to pattern arrangement and orientation. *Child Development,* 1975, *46,* 229–232.

Denny, N. W. A developmental study of free classification in children. *Child Development,* 1972, *43,* 221–232.

Fagan, J. F. Memory in the infant. *Journal of Experimental Child Psychology,* 1970, *9,* 217–226.

Fagan, J. F. Infants' recognition memory for a series of visual stimuli. *Journal of Experimental Child Psychology,* 1971, *11,* 244–250.

Fagan, J. F. Infants' recognition of invariant features of faces. *Child Development,* 1976, *47,* 627–638.

Fagen, J. W. Interproblem learning in ten-month-old infants. *Child Development,* 1977, *48,* 786–796.

Fantz, R. L., Fagan, J. F., & Miranda, S. B. Early visual selectivity. In L. B. Cohen & P. Salapatek (Eds.) *Infant perception: from sensation to cognition.* Vol. 1: *Basic visual processes.* New York: Academic Press, 1975, pp. 249–345.

Flavell, J. H. Concept development. In P. H. Mussen (Ed.) *Carmichael's manual of child psychology* (Vol. 1). New York: Wiley, 1970, pp. 983–1060.

Forman, G. E., Kuschner, D., & Dempsey, J. *Transformations in the manipulations and productions performed with geometric objects. An early system of logic in young children.* Final Report to the National Institute of Education, University of Massachusetts, 1975.

Gibson, E. J. *Principles of perceptual learning and development.* New York: Appleton-Century-Crofts, 1969.

Gibson, J. J. *The perception of the visual world.* Boston: Houghton Mifflin, 1950.

Goldberg, S., Perlmutter, M., & Myers, N. Recall of related and unrelated lists by 2-year-olds. *Journal of Experimental Child Psychology,* 1974, *18,* 1–8.

Harlow, H. F. The formation of learning sets. *Psychological Review,* 1949, *56,* 51–65.

Horowitz, F. D. Infant learning and development: retrospect and prospect. *Merrill-Palmer Quarterly,* 1968, *14,* 101–120.

Horowitz, F. D. Visual attention, auditory stimulation, and language discrimination in young infants. *Monographs of the Society for Research in Child Development,* 1975, *39(158).*

Hull, C. L. Quantitative aspects of the evolution of concepts, an experimental study. *Psychological Monographs,* 1920, *28* (*123*).

Hulsebus, R. C. Operant conditioning in infant behavior: a review. In H. W. Reese (Ed.) *Advances in child development and behavior* (Vol. 8). New York: Academic Press, 1973, pp. 111–158.

Kagan, J. *Change and continuity in infancy.* New York: Wiley, 1971.

Karmel, B. Z., & Maisel, E. B. A neuronal activity model for infant visual attention. In L. B. Cohen & P. Salapatek (Eds.) *Infant perception: from sensation to cognition.* Vol. 1: *Basic visual processes.* New York: Academic Press, 1975; pp. 78–131.

Kendler, T. S. Concept formation. *Annual Review of Psychology,* 1961, 447–471.

Kendler, T. S. Personal communication, 1972.

Leeper, R. Cognitive processes. In S. S. Stevens (Ed.) *Handbook of experimental psychology.* New York: Wiley, 1951, pp. 730–757.

Lenneberg, E. *The biological foundations of language.* New York: Wiley, 1967.

Lewis, M., Goldberg, S., & Campbell, H. A developmental study of information processing within the first three years of life: response decrement to a redundant signal. *Monographs of the Society for Research in Child Development,* 1969, *34* (*133*).

Ling, B. C. Form discrimination as a learning cue in infants. *Comparative Psychology Monographs,* 1941, *17* (2).

Lipsitt, L. P. Learning in the human infant. In H. W. Stevenson, E. H. Hess, & H. L. Rheingold (Eds.) *Early behavior: comparative and developmental approaches.* New York: Wiley, 1967, pp. 225–247.

McCall, R. B. Attention in the infant: avenue to the study of cognitive development. In D. Walcher & D. Peters (Eds.) *Early childhood: the development
of the self-regulatory mechanisms.* New York: Academic press, 1971, pp.
109–136.

McCall, R. B. Exploratory manipulation and play in the human infant. *Monographs of the Society for Research in Child Development,* 1974, *39 (155).*

Nelson, K. Some evidence for the cognitive primacy of categorization and its
functional basis. *Merrill-Palmer Quarterly,* 1973, *19,* 21–39.

Olver, R. R., & Hornsby, J. R. On equivalence. In J. S. Bruner, R. R. Olver, &
P. M. Greenfield. *Studies in cognitive growth.* New York: Wiley, 1966, pp.
68–85.

Piaget, J. *Origins of intelligence in children.* New York: International Universities
Press, 1952.

Reese, H. W., & Porges, S. W. Development of learning processes. In V. Hamilton & M. D. Vernon (Eds.) *The development of cognitive processes.* New
York: Academic Press, 1976, pp. 413–447.

Ricciuti, H. Object grouping and selective ordering behavior in infants twelve to
twenty-four months old. *Merrill-Palmer Quarterly,* 1965, *11,* 129–148.

Riesen, A. H. Plasticity of behavior: psychological aspects. In H. F. Harlow &
C. N. Woolsey (Eds.) *Biological and biochemical bases of behavior.* Madi-
son: University of Wisconsin Press, 1958, pp. 425–450.

Saayman, G., Ames, E. W., & Moffett, A. R. Response to novelty as an indicator
of visual discrimination in the human infant. *Journal of Experimental
Child Psychology,* 1964, *1,* 189–198.

Sigel, I. E. The attainment of concepts. In M. L. Hoffman & L. W. Hoffman
(Eds.) *Review of child development research* (Vol. 1). New York: Russell
Sage Foundation, 1964, pp. 209–248.

Sokolov, E. N. *Perception and the conditioned reflex.* New York: Macmillan,
1963.

Vurpillot, E. Development of identification of objects. In V. Hamilton & M. D.
Vernon (Eds.) *The development of cognitive processes.* New York: Academic Press, 1976, pp. 191–236.

Vurpillot, E. Personal communication, 1977.

Watson, J. S. The development and generalization of contingency awareness in
early infancy: some hypotheses. *Merrill-Palmer Quarterly,* 1966, *12,*
123–135.

Welch, M. J. Infants' visual attention to varying degrees of novelty. *Child Development,* 1974, *45,* 344–350.

(b) EXPLORATORY AND PLAY RESPONSES OF EIGHT- TO TWELVE-MONTH-OLD INFANTS IN DIFFERENT ENVIRONMENTS

Dr. Collard: Corinne Hutt (1966) has suggested that the difference between exploration and play is that exploratory behavior occurs when novel stimuli raise one's arousal level and the organism seeks to reduce stimulation, whereas play occurs when the arousal level is low and the organism seeks to increase its level of stimulation.

Piaget (1952) observed that when his infants were given a novel object, during the first few minutes they made exploratory responses towards it (such as looking at and touching it), while afterward they tried out various schemas on it (such as shaking, waving, or striking it). I found that home-reared infants made significantly more exploratory responses during the first three minutes of play with a novel toy, and more play responses during the second three minutes (Collard, 1962). Hutt (1966) observed exploratory behavior to precede play in two year-old children.

I have defined exploratory responses made by infants toward objects as those responses in which the object is directly exposed to the senses, and the baby learns about its perceptual properties (Collard, 1962). Play with an object consists of those responses in which the baby actively manipulates the object and thus increases stimulation through the object's reactions to his actions.

I have classified the response made by eight- to twelve-month-old infants to a toy (which was graspable and unattached) into the following categories:

Exploratory Responses
   1. looking (responses in which the primary behavior is visual fixation or scanning the object)
   2. transferring the object from hand to hand while looking at it
   3. turning the object over or around while looking at it
   4. extending the object at various distances while looking at it
   5. fingering (rubbing the fingers over the objects)
   6. poking (touching the object with the forefinger)
   7. scratching (running the fingers across the object while alternately flexing and extending them)
   8. pulling at the toy as if trying to detach a part of it
   9. grasping and releasing the object with one hand while holding it with the other
   10. mouthing (responses in which the object is exposed to the tactile and taste receptors of the mouth)

Play Responses
1. banging the toy on the table
2. waving the toy
3. patting the toy
4. rubbing the toy on the table
5. pushing the toy across the table (without grasping it)
6. pulling the toy across the table
7. dropping the toy to the table or floor
8. casting the toy to the table or floor
9. other: for example, putting the toy on head; putting the toy under the table and making it reappear

Social Play with Toy
1. extending the toy to the mother or experimenter
2. handing the toy to the mother or experimenter
3. casting the toy to the experimenter
4. touching a person (usually on the hand or face) with the toy
5. banging a person with the toy
6. showing the toy to the mother (putting the toy near the mother's face and smiling, or pointing to the toy, often vocalizing)

The toy used in all of the experiments to be described was the same: a bracelet made up of four large wooden beads of different colors, strung on a keychain with a silver bell. Interobserver reliability in recording infants' responses to this toy over a six-minute period was between 85 and 90 percent on two consecutive trials and between 90 and 100 percent on varieties of response shown by the infants. Babies in the earlier studies (Collard, 1962, 1971) were matched in age and sex. A result was considered to be significant if its occurrence by chance was equal to or less than 05 on the Wilcoxon Test for Matched Samples.

The purpose of my original research was to see whether institutional infants living in a relatively unstimulating environment (except for stimulation by many people) explored less and developed fewer exploratory and play schemas than did infants reared in homes where they could move about freely, where there were more different objects to explore, and where adults had more time to play with them. I found that these institutional infants did show significantly less exploration and fewer schemas to the toy than did home-reared infants from lower-class families. Later I found that babies from middle-class homes who lived in an environment with even more varied objects to explore and whose mothers (who had fewer children) had more time to play with them showed significantly more schemas with the toy than did the babies from lower-class homes (Collard, 1971).

The infants who were in the institution at the time of my original study spent most of their time in their cribs and were exposed to a small number and variety of toys which consisted mostly of rattles, blocks, balls and soft plastic animals or dolls. A few years later, after the supervisor of the institution learned of the results of my study, the babies then in the institution were given a large number and variety of toys to play with and were placed on the floor in groups of ten or more for most of their waking time. In addition to the toys previously mentioned, they were provided with most of the Playskool and Fisher-Price ("educational") toys for infants, as well as a profusion of other toys. These babies were then interacting with about twenty different infants and more than a dozen different adults per day, and with at least three dozen toys, whereas the babies in the institution earlier would have been cared for by as many adults but would have had only two or three toys a day to play with in their cribs and visual but not physical contact with the other babies in a six- or eight-bed ward.

I discovered that these changes had been made when, in 1967, I revisited the institution to collect more data to add to that of my original study. For over a week I observed these babies, who were on the floor of a large sun porch (which was also an eight-bed ward), surrounded by babies from three different wards (usually ten to fifteen babies) and a wealth of toys. Instead of looking happier than the infants I had studied there earlier, they appeared to be stressed by overstimulation. Their exploration had a frantic quality to it; their attention span with toys was very short; they seldom smiled and often fussed or cried. Some of the babies withdrew completely by crawling under a crib and going to sleep on the floor. The institutional infants I had worked with earlier (for over a year) had smiled readily, had seldom cried, and had appeared to be slightly slowed down in their response rate to toys compared to home-reared infants.

Analysis of the responses to the experimental toy revealed that both groups of home-reared babies made more exploratory responses to the toy during the first three minutes and more play responses during the last three minutes (see Figures 4-1 and 4-2). They also made many more social play responses than the institutional subjects did.

When I analyzed the responses that the "overstimulated" institutional infants made to the toy, I discovered that not only did they make as many varieties of response as the home-reared infants had made, but they appeared to be extremely speeded up, making about half again as many responses as the original subjects. They particularly made many more exploratory responses, which consisted largely of stereotyped looking, transferring, and mouthing, and they made relatively fewer play responses, although their average number of play responses was only slightly lower than the level shown by the original institutional subjects whose

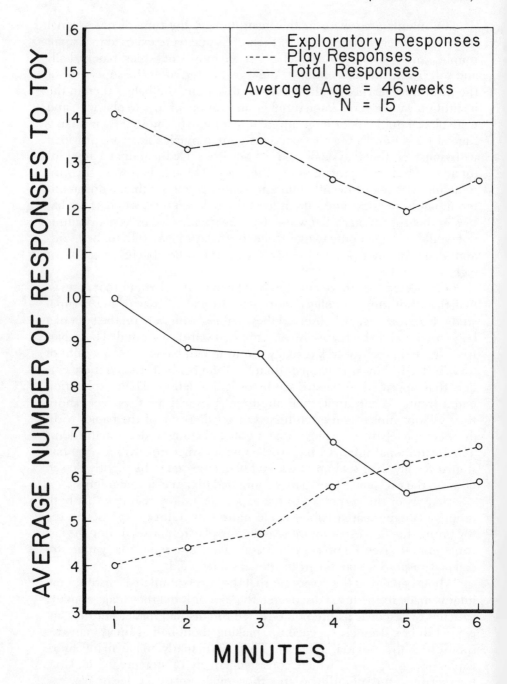

Figure 4-1. Exploratory and play responses of lower-class home infants.

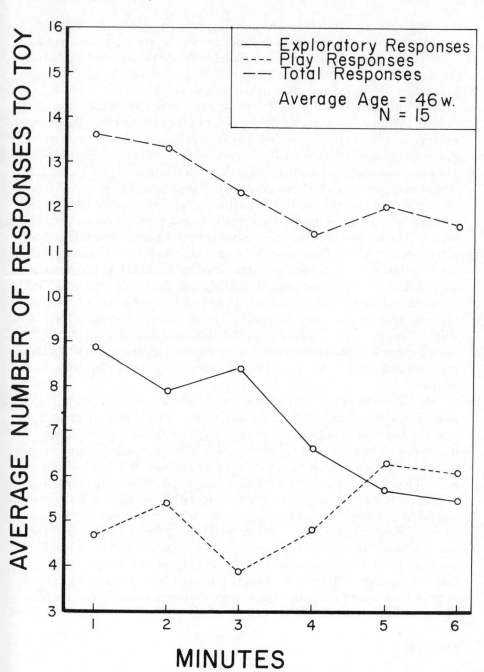

Figure 4-2. Exploratory and play responses of middle-class home infants.

response rate was much lower (see Figures 4-3 and 4-4). The over-stimulated institutional infants showed few social play responses, as had been true of the original understimulated institutional subjects, probably because both groups of babies were seldom played with by adults, who were mostly occupied with their physical care.

The understimulated institutional babies made fewer exploratory responses than the home-reared babies did, but they tended to make many stereotyped play responses such as waving and banging the toy, responses which would tend to increase their level of stimulation (see Figure 5-3). They also showed more body rocking than did the home-reared babies, a stereotyped behavior which would serve the same purpose.

These data support the theory that exploratory responses may be an attempt to reduce the level of stimulation, and play responses used to raise it. The institutional babies who had received a large amount of stimulation by a mass of objects showed a very high level of exploration with the experimental toy, while the institutional babies who had very few objects in their environment tended to play more than they explored. The home-reared subjects, who had been exposed to a moderate number of toys and many household objects, had more control over their level of stimulation through mobility than did the institutional subjects. Both groups of home-reared babies made more exploratory responses when the experimental toy was relatively novel to them, and more play responses afterward.

My observations of the overstimulated institutional infants make it appear that while stimulation with many varied objects may increase the number and variety of exploratory responses, the massive presentation of many stimuli can decrease attention span, either through distraction or through the high arousal level produced by stimulus overload. That the arousal level of these infants was high is suggested by their rapid response rate, their irritability, and their attempts to withdraw. High arousal level caused by stimulus overload can interfere with learning, because it leads to irritability or withdrawal (White & Held, 1967; Field, 1977). The amount of stimulation these babies were exposed to might have had less effect on them if they could have moved away from it or if its presentation had been paced to their assimilation rate, but because they were in a room with a closed door they could only explore rapidly, become irritable, or withdraw completely in sleep.

Discussion

Dr. Fein: This brings to mind something I began to think about with Bob McCall's review, and that is the connection between the kind of de-

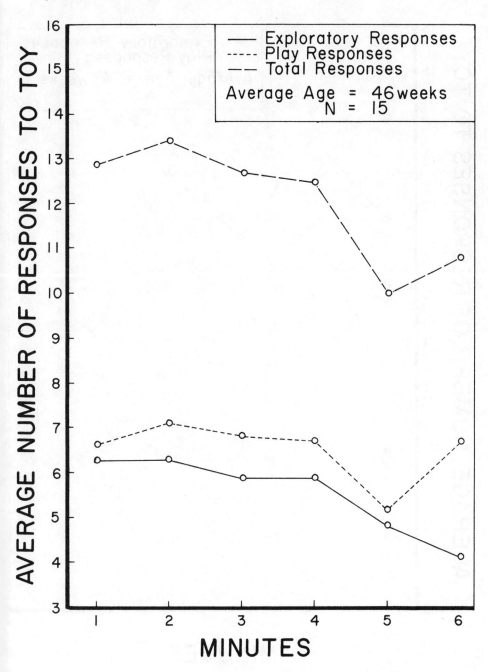

Figure 4-3. Exploratory and play responses of understimulated institutional infants.

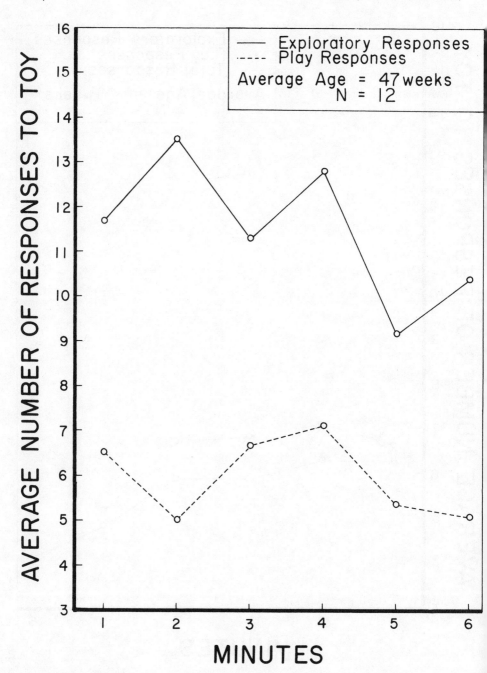

Figure 4-4. Exploratory and play responses of overstimulated institutional infants.

velopmental pattern that you're observing and that which others have observed. There is a temporal sequence of activity shifts within a particular time span, and it looks very much as if that is what happens developmentally also. The early phase is that of an object out there to be contacted as if it were an adhering part of that outside environment; the next stage involves detaching it from that outside fixedness and then doing these self-imposed activities with it; later come the more imaginative and symbolic kinds of behavior. And what strikes me increasingly, as I see these things unfolding over age, is the similarity between the developmental phenomena and the small span temporal phenomenon in terms of how you move into a situation and come to master it. It's as if these little babies are trying to master life in fairly rational, coherent ways, a process which is repeated each time we move into a new situation. Do you feel that's a permissible overlap between development and the ontogeny of temporal shifts in action towards objects?

Dr. Collard: Yes, but I also think you can look at this in terms of exploration as information processing and stimulus reduction, which would occur at first, and then at play as a stimulus creation that would occur as they begin to habituate to the other. I mean, first, with younger babies, you get your exploration starting very high and going down pretty rapidly, but exploration is much higher and there isn't as much play because they don't have as many play schemas as they do later.

Dr. J. Singer: Is it possible, however, that what we're making here is an artificial distinction between exploration and play, and that play may be a more subtle form of exploration? Once one has dealt with the more obvious physical properties of the object, then it has other potential properties that human beings can discover. So it may not be just the seeking for new stimulation that you're implying, but a continued exploration?

Dr. Collard: A cursory search for reaction.

Dr. J. Singer: That's another way one could look at it.

Dr. Collard: Right, that's good.

Dr. Fein: I guess, Jerry [Dr. Singer], what you've just done is precipitated a whole lot of frustration that has been accumulating in my soul over the past few years, and I might as well propose my irrational solution. We have this increasingly voluminous literature having to do with what play is, and it seems as if there have been two answers which have appeared already and now we've arrived at the second kind. The first is the intrapsychic answer, that play is what we think is going on inside the person who we say is playing.* The second way of responding to the question of what is play, is by looking empirically at the behaviors that are

*As in papers by Schultz and McCall—ED.

happening, and trying to establish definitive criteria for what behaviors are going to be called this and what behaviors are going to be called that.*
I think there's yet a third possibility which is metatheoretically peculiar but which reduces my anxiety, and that is to *define play in terms of the setting,* and say that play is what a setting permits to have happen in it, that a setting signals you to do what you're supposed to do. I really think that when we see kids playing, what we're doing is making setting inferences, and it's that setting inference that then puts us in business. I don't think we're always aware that we're making the setting inference. We're making some assumptions about the nature of the setting, how the person or the child in the setting reads it, and what we intended that settling to communicate to the person asked. It seems to me that the setting concept will help us then to work towards other questions such as: What is the state of the organism? What are those behaviors which then appear as we maneuver settings in different kinds of ways?

Dr. Hay: What I'd like to say is that there's a *behavioral setting* as well as an *environmental setting,* and that can go along very nicely with what you said. We are talking about the futility of trying to say, "This particular criterion behavior is exploration; that one is not." I think that's been true in attachment literature as well; it's very hard to identify a topographical behavior and say that it is exploration. I would be interested to know whether the play responses are accompanied by different sets of other responses, different affect responses.

Dr. Collard: Yes, you get much more *vocalization* with play, particularly with boys. They make a hell of a lot of noise, and then they yell their heads off and they laugh. The girls tend to look at the toy and vocalize to the mother about it. I remember the biggest surprise in my life was the first thirteen-month-old girl I was testing. We weren't supposed to talk during the test, and she kept turning around and pointing to her mother, saying, "What da, what da, mama, what da, what da, mama?" I didn't have any boys do it. But I did have a boy pitch the toy to me like a football exactly where I could catch it, and I found out later his daddy plays football with him. I said, "You mean he has a little toy football?" "Oh no, a full sized one." I got this beautiful interchange in which he would throw the ball to me, I would put it back at the standard position, he would throw it to me, I would catch it, put it back. Fortunately I was a pitcher. I knew how to do this. But you tend to get much more banging and vocalization and laughing work with the toy by the boys. With the girls you tend to get much more vocalization and smiling, etc., in terms of the mother. Remember, you haven't seen my situation. They're sitting on mama's lap and so to talk to mama requires quite a contortion. The mothers hold

*As in Collard—ED.

them so they won't fall off, and the girls have to turn all the way around to talk to them.

Dr. Sutton-Smith: It seemed, in your study, that the exploration and the play were dichotomous—that is, first the sober discovery and then afterwards the boost and that laughter, etc., when they began to play. I suppose in the more complex objects this exploration option would go backward and forward. It would oscillate. Do you have any thoughts on that? One suspects that with a more complex object the child will examine it rather carefully, then they may playfully bang it for a while and then notice something else and begin to examine it again.

Dr. Collard: Well, if you look at the graphs, exploration didn't cease; it kept on going. It actually tended to go down and then come up again. Four minutes is really a biological rhythm. Almost all kids will begin to tire, the graph line will zoom down, and then in the last minute it'll start up again. The zooming down means that they've started doing other things. After all, they are in a room. They do have mama there; they do have me there. They're apt to look up at the ceiling lights; they're apt to do something else. Then they'll get a recovery and begin to play or explore again, but you see it isn't all exploration at the beginning and all play at the end. But there's more exploration and less play at the beginning, and less exploration and more play at the end. That's what you can see very clearly on those two graphs.

Dr. Sutton-Smith: A biphasic phenomenon with different ratios.

Dr. Collard: Right.

References

Collard, R. R. Exploratory and play behaviors of infants reared in an institution and in lower- and middle-class homes. *Child Development*, 1971, 42, 1003–1015.

Collard, R. R. *A study of curiosity in infants.* Doctoral dissertation, University of Chicago, 1962.

Field, T. M. Effects of early separation, interactive deficits, and experimental manipulation on infant-mother face-to-face interaction. *Child Development*, 1977, 48, 763–771.

Hutt, C. Exploration and play in children. In P. A. Jewell & C. Loizos (Eds.) *Play, exploration, and territory in mammals.* New York: Academic Press, 1966, pp. 61–81.

Hutt, C. Towards a taxonomy and conceptual model of play. In S. J. Hutt, D. A. Rogers, & C. Hutt. *Developmental processes in early childhood.* London: Routledge (in press).

Piaget, J. *The origins of intelligence in children.* New York: International Universities Press, 1952.

White, B W., & Held, R. Experience in early human development. Part 2: Plasticity of sensorimotor development in the human infant. In J. Hellmuth (Ed.) *The exceptional infant.* Vol. 1: *The normal infant.* New York: Brunner/Mazel, 1967, pp. 291–313.

CHAPTER 5

PLAY WITH ACTIONS AND OBJECTS

Greta Fein

INTRODUCTION

Dr. Sutton-Smith: Dr. Collard discussed play as a kind of conceptualizing with objects. Dr. Fein will further detail this process in children between the ages of one and three years. She will discuss, in effect, a grammar of play involving relations and permutations of actions and objects, which is significantly related to the language behavior of the same children. The major discussion will center on (a) the status of objects and actions in describing play, (b) the change in the children's interest from the prototypical use of objects to a variable usage during the second year of life, then to a conventional usage by the third year. The suggestion will be presented that the latter conventional usage may ultimately provide a constant and underlying code permitting variation in another domain of behavior (role behavior for example). The importance of these distinctions lies in their suggesting that the dichotomy of exploration and play is insufficient. They are both points along some continuum of behavioral variability. In the present case, of course, we deal with the kind of continuum that has to do with the child's activities with objects. A third topic (c) is the relationship between the mother's toy-related responses and the child's subsequent adaptive competence. That is, does it make a difference if the mother plays with the child and its toys in a related or nonrelated way? (d) Finally, there will be a not totally successful effort to clarify to what extent we can define when either the young or the old are involved in pretend activity.

Dr. Fein: One of the things that is striking about play is that it is so obvious. When you see it you know it, and most people in a culture seem to know the same thing about it. To the ordinary observer it doesn't have any great mysteries, nor does it present a great definitional problem. And yet when as systematizers we come to study play, we have to contort a lot to figure out what exactly kids are doing when they do this obvious thing. I think that the struggle for us is to find the most useful unit of analysis for our purposes, which isn't the same as answering those grand questions of what play is in its totality.

ACTIONS ON OBJECTS

What I want to talk about is one way of analyzing play that I have found useful and stimulating, although I'm not sure how far it can be taken. It is a kind of analysis which looks at two domains, two kinds of units, and the relationship between them. It is a simple system which separates actions on the one side and objects on the other, and simply asks what the relationship is between a child's action and the object that he uses in the course of that action. When we spin out a system of multiple actions and open codes for a multiplicity of objects, intriguing possibilities emerge. The classical one involves the kinds of things a child can do with a cup. Children seem to understand that different actions can be imposed upon a cup: they can drink from it, they can put it on their heads, they can roll it: the cup lends itself to a diversity of action possibilities. At the same time the action lends itself to a diverse array of objects. A child can drink from a cup, or a shell. For each part of the action-object system there are substitutions possible, and a diversity of possibilities within each part. In our work we have tried to examine different pieces of that system of relationships. In one set of studies we tried to look at the substitutability rules. What rules govern the substitution of objects with respect to actions? Those studies led to the general questions: What is a cup to a child? What are the kinds of physical conditions that can satisfy cupness? and How do these conditions spread and become modified over time? In one study (Fein and Robertson, 1975), we tried to approach that question in a somewhat different way by posing at the outset that it might be useful to suppose that children operate on a prototypical object, a kind of classical cup or a kind of classical dog—the best possible kind of cup, or the best possible kind of dog in the sense of it being what would come to mind if you had to describe a cup or a dog to a Martian. When we use this frame of reference we are able to identify a range of objects which are more or less like the prototype. Having done that, we are able to contrast what children do under different kinds of prototype conditions. It is exceedingly difficult for young children to manage-pretend substitutions with less prototypical objects. In other words, in order to pretend to drink out of a cup, they need to have as cuplike a cup as possible. In another series of studies we looked within the prototype system to see how children's choices of object-action relationship change over time. What is the best possible thing to do when you're confronted with an array of cups, spoons, dolls and other kinds of objects? And it's there that we began to notice (and we were again surprised), on presenting a child with this simple array of materials, the diversity with which the possible action-object that you and I would call a cup might be used: as a potty seat, a hat, a ladle, to pour hair lotion, and in an array of action contexts. And it seems that this spread happens when the child hits twenty-four months—there's just a tremendous amount of playing around. Then by thirty months the system seems to become constricted; the child comes to decide that in the scheme of things a cup really is a cup and that's what it ought to be used for, and you begin to see a kind of stereotyping going on in terms of the objects and the choices that children make.

STYLISTIC AND STRUCTURAL VARIABLES

Another thing we've done with the action-object relationship system is to make a distinction between the stylistic attributes of play and the structural characteristics of play. You can look at (a) the number of different actions a child uses over a given amount of time or you can look at (b) the number of different objects that the child chooses to use over a given amount of time. Or (c) you can intersect those and look at what is sometimes called the *tempo* of play; that is, the action-object changes which occur over time. It's these kinds of variables that we've referred to as *style variables*.

We have tried to define structural variables in keeping with the Piagetian notions of developmental phases in the organization of play during the second and third years of life: whether children are involved in sensorimotor type exploration, whether they're beginning to do pretend-type activities, or whether they're using objects in terms of forming rows or stacks or piles or more abstract kinds of relationships. When we take that way of looking at the same situation we then add to it situational modifications which we would predict would influence the stylistic variables, rather than the structural variables, the idea being that if the child is structurally at a certain level of development, that's where he is. And when you alter the situation you put him in, basically what you will be modifying are stylistic, not structural, variables. In one study we put some children in a situation that was familiar to them, and other children in a situation that was relatively strange to them. There was a tremendous difference on the stylistic measures between those situations, and I'm sure you can predict what the differences were. In the strange situation, the range and diversity of play became considerably restricted and the tempo was reduced. Nothing happened to the structural variables. They seemed to hold their own. However, while across age we would expect age-related changes in structure but not in style, it turns out that there are age-related changes in both. With age the behavior of the kids becomes more diverse and they also function at a higher level. So the results were not quite as neat as we had hoped.

MOTHER'S STYLE OF PLAY

The other kind of study we've done builds on the idea that you can start with a set of actions and a set of objects and look at the different ways these can work out. We did an interesting mother-child play study. As we watched one-year-olds and mothers play together, we felt that there was a difference in what we would intuitively call the *elaborativeness* of the way in which mothers play with kids. But what did elaborativeness mean? We had some films that we kept looking at over and over again. It seemed as if the mothers who played more elaboratively were somehow introducing more variation when they stepped into the child's play. And as we looked and thought about it, it seemed as if the mothers who were the most elaborative were really doing a very simple sort of thing. They were taking into account the action-object relationship that the child was using at a given time, and when they stepped in they would make a modification. They would either modify the child's action or modify the child's object. So if the baby was banging with a spoon the mother would then bang with a stick, or bang with a ball, or the mother might pretend to eat with the spoon. In other words, there would be a change in one or another component of the child's activity, but usually not in both. When we looked at the mothers who were least elaborative, they seemed to change both parts of the child's activity. When you watched these mothers you felt they were not playing with their kids. They were playing, but they were playing quite independently, and if they connected with the kids at all, it was in a very demanding, intrusive way in which they tried to impose their activity upon the kid. Other mothers seemed to adopt a passive strategy. If they did anything at all they were doing exactly what the children were doing. They were neither modifying the play nor were they departing from it; rather, they were tracking their babies. We coded mothers' play moves according to whether or not it was an *elaborative* move, an *imitative* move, or an *unrelated* move. We expected to find that maternal play style would have an influence on how the children played, but it didn't. It seemed to have another kind of influence, which bothers me because I don't understand quite how it comes about. There's a very, very strong relation over time between the elaborativeness of the mother's play style and how the kids do on the Bayley test later on. The kids whose mothers use a lot of elaborative play do very well on the Bayley, and the kids whose mothers tend to be extremely disconnected don't do very well at all. I would have liked to have seen some sign that play itself was hooking into the relationship, but according to our data it wasn't.

Dr. Lewis: What ages?

Dr. Fein: The first observations were at twelve months, and the cross-lag correlations become very strong at twenty-four months.

Dr. Gardner: You said that you didn't find any differences in play depending upon the mother's style. Does this go for your impressions as well as for your data?

Dr. Fein: No; that's what's disturbing about it. It doesn't go with our impressions.

Dr. Gardner: You had the impression that children were reacting differently, but whatever it is that you're counting didn't yield that.

Dr. Fein: Perhaps it was our coding, or perhaps the situations we were seeing them in, but something was missing. My feeling is that what the elaborating mothers were communicating to the kids was a sense that in an adult-related negotiation there's a lot of fun and a lot of opportunity for you to do your thing and we're doing a lot of happy things together, and that's what they picked up in the play. We were watching the children playing alone, but I think we should have had a social play condition with either a peer or an unfamiliar adult if we were going to see that particular mother aspect come up in this play. I think there's a tremendous difference at that age between what kids do when they play alone, or when they're encouraged to play alone, and what they will do in a peer situation. In these data the strong prediction was from the mothers at time one to the kids at time two. That is, if you put them on two separate lines and looked over time at the relation between the mother's style to the kid's Bayley Score, for example—the mother's style at time 1 to the kid's scores at time 2—you would be doing a cross-lag analysis. There was not a terribly high correlation contemporaneously between the mother's style and the baby's Bayley scores.

Dr. McCall: What's the correlation between baby-baby and mother-mother over age?

Dr. Fein: What do you mean baby-baby?

Dr. McCall: In a cross-lag correlation panel you have two longitudinal correlations, of baby with baby and mother with mother.

Dr. Fein: The baby-to-baby Bayleys were fairly high from twelve to twenty-four months. I'm not sure exactly what they were, but they were relatively high. They were going over .5. The mother-to-mother was only around .2 to .25.

Dr. McCall: You have very serious problems interpreting a cross-lag correlation when those correlations aren't equal.

Dr. Fein: Not if you test the alternative, plausible hypothesis.

Dr. McCall: They're not different?

Dr. Fein: Excluding all the alternative possibilities, this was a reasonable interpretation, but again the causality is always in quotes when you use that system.

Dr. Collard: In this situation did the mother and baby each have their own toy or was there one toy between them, so that you were getting interaction between baby and mother with the toy?

Dr. Fein: There were a number of toys and some of them were duplicated, but some were not. It was a large array of toys and objects.

Dr. Collard: Because with the single toy situation, where the baby engages in social play with the toy with the mother, I found that the interest span lasted much longer because more interesting things happened than if the baby was doing everything by himself. You had a motivational factor there with the interchangeable mother-baby.

Dr. Fein: I suspect that those kinds of situational differences are enormously important. I think you get a very different kind of play when there is one containing object from when there's an array, depending on how rich the array of possibilities. That's something it would be nice to know more about. But I do think that probably the style of interaction is very different in those situations. I have a feeling that the large array really expands the option system, and to me that's closer to what I mean by play. You cannot really study the elaborativeness of the mother's play style, as we defined it, with only one toy. When you have a single object you're much closer to a tutorial situation, or you're encouraging a tutorial set, and even that depends upon the particular object that's being used.

Dr. Collard: In this work that I've done, the mother was asked not to initiate play but to respond to what the infant did. If she responded, the input would be more complex than if only baby alone responded.

Dr. Fein: That about summarizes the kind of work we have been doing. What we are moving towards now is trying to complicate what is already too complicated. We plan to look at how these systems function when peers are together, how they function in child situations both with and without adults present.

Dr. Sutton-Smith: Are you interpreting the parent or the socializer as having an effect on the diversity, while the structure's coming from some other source?

Dr. Fein: When we see Bayley scores we see as much social interaction as we see a cognitivelike performance. I believe that a lot of what's going on here is a form of socializing of adult-child relationships. What we originally were looking for was a closer kind of cognitive connection. I'm not sure we have that. If by *structure* you mean the progression from sensorimotor to symbolic play, then yes; I think that comes from another source. When children who play less imaginatively are put into relatively brief training situations, they recover too quickly for the initial deficit to have been a structural one.

Dr. Lewis: You talked about the prototypic quality of objects. Do you have the same notion for actions?

Dr. Fein: I wish I did. I don't know what to do with the actions. I think there is probably a way of making prototypes with the action system, but whenever I try to design a study that would try to get at the actions and their fluidity I fall apart on the simple awkwardness of objects. I can't get the interactions with objects to fit into a neatly symmetrical system, and so I have trouble balancing designs which will do that. When you have that kind of problem it sort of says, "There's something in the nature of the world that's resisting your theory, so back off." I think that the action side is something that's deeply internal, something like intentions, and I'm not sure our contingencies are adequate to deal with that.

Dr. Garvey: The actions and the action schemas that I tried to talk about are very simpleminded. One is the telephone schema, and another is the threat—escaping threat danger. I see these as action kinds of schema that enlarge, but not additively; they enlarge in a structural manner. The ends are usually learned first, filled in in the middle, and then elaborated. But it is true these components of action are matters that some people are worried about now, but that nobody has tried to do very much with, except maybe some philosophers and the attributionists. Heider had a rather good idea when he said that notions like *ought* and *can* and *may* and *willing* were components of social ideas, the components of actions. They were the primes, as a matter of fact, by which we cognize experience. We haven't gotten very far with that, and the people who are playing around now with computer simulation or an analysis of intentional behavior are trying to break down such things into components: to recognize "ought" components, "can" components, "willing" components as part of the way we judge social events. Now that kind of analysis needs to be applied to these kind of data but we don't yet have the apparatus, either theoretical or empirical, to deal with it in terms of human actions.

Dr. Sutton-Smith: These action schemas sound like pivot grammar organizations—object-action, action-object, etc. Does this play organization precede children's word permutations in language? Some children might establish these sorts of organizations in representational phenomena prior to their occurrence in language.

Dr. Fein: The only observations we have (and again this is still not finished) have to do with the difference between children who have been classified in their early language as expressive, versus those classified as referential. It's the expressive children who do a lot of pretend play, far more than the referential children, which again leaves me gasping because it is not what I would have expected.

Dr. Gardner: Why weren't you expecting it?

Dr. Fein: Well, if you think of the pretend system as closely linked to concepts of objects and words for objects and categories of objects, it would have seemed to me that the kids who had refined that categorical scheme would be the ones who would be able to do this substitutability kind of pretend activity. But it doesn't seem to work out that way.

Dr. Gardner: Maybe I could ask you about something I didn't quite understand. Were you saying that, roughly speaking, there's a U-shape in development, an inverted U, where in the beginning the child only wants to play with prototypical objects, then there's a period of freedom where a lot of things will be accepted as a cup, and then there's a kind of conservatism that re-emerges? What is the situation under which the child acts conservative at age three, and how flexible is the child if you change the rules, if you prod him into being more catholic, so he accepts anything as a substitute?

Dr. Fein: I do think that it's that U-shaped curve which makes sociodramatic play possible. There has to be some sort of stereotyping, some sort of agreement about what a thing is representing, in order for a group of children to do this sort of role-exchange representational storytelling that occurs in sociodramatic play. The children need to start with some sort of consensus about what their actions are and mean, and this is what I think becomes stereotyped; that is, the ways in which children represent caring for a baby, nurturing a baby, or feeding a baby become highly standardized. It's that standardization that makes it possible for kids to communicate with one another, that serves as a communication pivot for the complex sociodramatic play which adds new variations negotiated from that basis of shared agreement. So it's U-shaped, but only in respect to certain kinds of domains, and that stereotyping is in the service of further expansion and further elaboration. But then the elaboration is shared.

Dr. Gardner: I think this supports what you're saying. Do you know Claire Golomb's recent work, where she essentially invited the kid to accept more and more outlandish substitutions for the same thing and got them to go quite far? But as you say, there has to be a contract. And we're finding very much the same thing with our kids. We're studying a small group of kids very intensively. We have so many training effects they overwhelm everything else. But we find that when the kids are between three and four they are much more reluctant to engage in a lot of wild substitutions unless you play *their* game for a while. And so it really becomes very contractual. They want to do something. They have their own agenda, which they don't have when they're two. If you're willing to play with their agenda, which may be to take a walk or something, then they will humor you and do wild substitutions. So it's really a question there of competence-performance distinction. It isn't that the three- or four-year-old has lost the ability to make a nonprototypical substitution. It's just that under ordinary circumstances, why should he bother?

Dr. Fein: What makes it difficult, and why I sometimes throw up my hands, is that I have watched kids playing on the beach in Portugal, Long Island, and Lakeside, Michigan, and what's absolutely astounding is all the kinds of substitutions that can happen. What's so frustrating is to try to systematize the things that happen on the beach, in the sand, in the woods, in all these places where the materials that are available are the raw materials of nature and the child is fashioning the substitutional system driven mainly by the things he wants to imagine. We have a lot of trouble reproducing that in our laboratory.

Dr. Gardner: Those are what the ethologists call *indicators*. If there are objects around, you're going to use them. If there are no objects around you're more likely to create them.

Dr. Kirschenblatt-Gimblett: Is there any relationship between the shift from playing with highly prototypical objects to playing with low prototypical objects and the change from babbling to speech? Obviously babbling is exploring all kinds of sounds, and it seemed to me that objects with low prototypicality were interesting because they were like signs in their arbitrariness. It's totally arbitrary that *dog* should be that, or that *ship* should be this, and that arbitrariness is fundamental to language learning.

Dr. Gardner: There's another factor there which makes it somewhat less of an achievement, I think. Arbitrariness says, "Ah, what a cognitive achievement it is to think of this as a grandmother." But in the kids we call dramatists, who are very prone to this sort of thing, it's basically not caring what the thing looks like. If you want to argue where the cognitive rigor comes in, it lies in the child who recognizes in a strong way that this does not look like a grandmother, but who is willing to override that and call it a grandmother, as opposed to the child who is not willing to do this.

Basically, what I'm saying is that you have to throw this factor into the equation before honoring those children who are able to be arbitrary, and not because iconocism—the ability to represent an iconic relationship—is a cognitive skill.

Dr. Collard: When you say the two-year-olds could really stretch the kind of object that could serve a certain function, does this happen at the same time that they overgeneralize in language, where they'd use a word to mean many different things? I wonder if this is related.

Dr. Fein: Agewise that's about the time that we see it.

Dr. McCall: It strikes me that the age of approximately twenty-one to twenty-four months marks the onset of certain types of symbolic relationships in which the child can form a cognitive relationship between two entities and have that relationship exist for him as a relationship extracted from the two particular entities involved. Could that simply be an exercising of this new-found relational cognitive skill, such as we often see in children who suddenly get a new behavior in their repertoire? They do it ad nauseum for a while as if exercising it, and when it becomes well integrated, they feel comfortable with it and don't do it as often. Does that strike you as being plausible for your age function?

Dr. Fein: It does, Bob [Dr. McCall], but I'm not sure what it does for me. It's putting in different words what I think the age function is describing, but not explaining. Yes, they're doing what they want to do, they seem to enjoy doing it, and they're ingenious in how they do it. It's a moment of openness and then, at least within the part of the system we were seeing, the openness begins to be reduced. Yes, they are exercising a newly discovered function, *not* a behavior. They are tapping its boundaries, finding out how far it can go—"What can I do with this?"—mastering it, perhaps to go on to put it into higher order relationships which are much more complicated. I think at the next level you find the same sort of thing happening with role reversals, for example, when the ability to produce novelties opens up again and all sorts of silly things are shifting in and moving around, and then that too becomes somewhat constricted and stereotyped.

Dr. Gardner: Claire Golomb makes the point that it's very dangerous to do what she thinks Piaget did, which was to talk about the arbitrariness of early symbolic play. Even when there is a period of openness where there's a lot of experimentation, a lot of willingness to call this a grandmother, she argues that symbolic play is always rule-governed in the sense that you always find it's more likely to happen with certain kinds of objects than with others. And there's never a case where the child is chaotic and actively seeks to call anything anything else.

Dr. McCall: The constraints may come externally, from the shape or the forms of the objects, for example, as opposed to any internal governing rules. Could I ask a sort of general question? Does this discussion have to do with the developmental function or rule which would say that first a child has to learn something in order to be able to alter it, play with it, develop it, elaborate it, etc.? Are you talking about a sequence where first the process would take this kind of shape? If this other data we heard is true, we know it isn't curvilinear. Would it be fair then to characterize development as first discovering symbolic play is a thing that you have in common with others, and then it can become anything you want?

Dr. Schwartzmann: It seems like talking about object transformations or role transformations, as if we're talking about a glass and then it can become a grandmother. One of the things that Bateson emphasizes over and over again is that for something to become something else it has to be both *it is* and *it is not* that. It's glass, it's grandmother, and it's not a glass and not a grandmother. It has to happen simultaneously and be communicated in that fashion. I don't think it's helpful to separate those two things.

Dr. J. Singer: We're acting as if you learn something and then you have learned it—it's static. Take ourselves in this room. By this time we know everybody's name, but there's a hell of a lot more we can learn about each other as people besides that, and it's going to take several days and even then we will have plenty more we can learn about each other. I think the same thing applies to the task of the young child. The child may know clearly and distinctly that this is a glass and that it's used to drink out of. But there are lots of places that have glasses that are sitting on shelves, and there are glasses that are red, and there's a whole array of complexities that are still novel that have to be learned and assimilated into established schema. It's an ongoing task.

Dr. Garvey: A glass is not just *a* thing. But no one would be treating it like a grandmother, so that when a child does do that to it he's doing something beyond what its diversity has suggested.

Dr. Fein: In the course of this discussion I've been trying to revisualize what the kids are doing. It seems that as they move along they become clearer and clearer, in a very mental representational sense, about what a doll is, and about the whole network of linkages between the object doll and a baby, and about a host of nurturing functions which have been experienced and that become lucid and very clear. And in a sense it becomes a stable theme as the external shapings and modulatings and reformings of that stable core go on. It's that old thing that Karl Buhler said: when a child is playing with a stick as if that stick were a doll, would the child be surprised if the stick started to cry? I have a feeling the child would be absolutely knocked out—that the child has a sense both of what a doll is and of what a stick is, and the connection between them is for the sake of elaborativeness.

Dr. D. Singer: Taking a somewhat older age group, what we found in the study that was done under my supervision by Mary Ann Pulaski was that children prefer to play with unstructured toys—with Playskool blocks and all kinds of objects that have less definiteness. They play longer and more complex, elaborate games with them because these toys lend themselves to a variety of transformations. Initially they may be attracted to the structured toys, but as time goes on they are more attracted to the unstructured ones because these allow a greater multiplicity of settings and games.

Dr. Garvey: I think we're being very rigid about the notion of object and concept. It strikes me that there is a related group of concerns here that Roger Brown is now interested in, such as fuzzy concepts and the notion of vagueness. We might want to keep in mind as well that there are glasses and glasses; there is a point at which a glass is a glass and another point at which we would be hard put to say whether it was a glass or a vase. As the child is moving towards a more creative use of objects, he is probably at the same time expanding his notion of the central or core instances of concepts themselves and also becoming more at home with the vagueness of even objects and object concepts. You might see parallels there not only in language use but in cognitive development as it might be approached independently of language and play.

Dr. J. Singer: The research of Golomb shows that if you train kids to stretch through play intervention they actually perform better in conservation—handle conservation tasks at an earlier age. So in a way the stretch of imagination actually leads them to get a better sense of object constancy.

Dr. Gardner: I had a long talk with her [Golomb] about that study. It's a very brilliant study, the study that she was trying to replicate. But looking at what she did and at the way she interprets it, I don't think her interpretation is correct. What was entailed was a pretend game between experimenter and child in the course of which the experimenter all of a sudden stopped abiding by the play rules. So when the experimenter said he wanted to have a chair, and the child handed over the toy chair, the experimenter broke out of the pretend mold and replied, "No no, I want a real chair." The child was then trained, as it were, in saying, "Well it's not really a chair." I think it's not the pretend play but rather the going outside the frame of pretend play and getting the child to talk about what something is and what it appears to be. I think it's that part that trains the correct conservation response—which doesn't take away from the elegance of the demonstration. It's not necessarily the case that if you pretend play with kids a lot, they therefore conserve more quickly.

Dr. McCall: Is it at all possible that kids have learned during this kind of regimen that you respond to the opposite of what the appearance is, and that's why they're answering the conservation questions correctly—

because they conceive it as a nonconserver and are responding in the opposite?

Dr. Gardner: She claims—and I believe her—to have used the more qualitative assessments of testing the child's response, but it's a small N. It's about 15, and only four kids went all the way to conservation. It has to be replicated.

Dr. D. Singer: In nursery school play, if the child is engaged in, let's say, eating clay and making believe it's food, and then you carry it a step further and make the clay into a sandwich, he doesn't want to do that. He may even stop it. He's always aware of what is real and what is not real. In his own game he can label things accurately when he wants to, even without the training. I think this is part of symbolic play. He knows that.

Dr. Gardner: I think it's a little bit more complicated than that. I think the child is often able to do that but I think, at least at first, it's very much of a "herself" kind of thing, and it's not always clear that the child can react appropriately when you change the rules. A child can get very upset or may leave the play. I think that in many ways the child doesn't have any real distance from the activity except the way he happens to perceive it at that time. Someone once asked Piaget what the child would do if the hobby horse really began to hop. He said a child would never think to ask that question. I don't think it's prototypical of a little child, until later—at age five or six.

Dr. Kirschenblatt-Gimblett: It sounds as if deciding whether something is clear or not is up to the adult investigator or the adult player, and I wonder about that. It seems that the first frame or alternative frame of reference that children learn may in fact be the play frame—the mock. *This is not serious. This is different.* That may be the first alternative frame of reference that's dealt with at all. That play frame may be so incredibly primary that the mock pretend, "as if" play frame of reference has to be given greater thought as something that the kids have to deal with. Take animals, for instance: all that signaling that goes on. If the signaling isn't clearly done and received they misinterpret it for fighting, and you'll have a fight, not play. I wonder about this in connection with the present discussion.

Dr. Lewis: That may have something to do with the contract—the differences in different social objects. I'm sure that children would be much more likely to engage in certain kinds of activities than we would be, as adults. The child comes over to the parent and starts to pretend, even though he knows that the parent might respond in a very negative way. The parent, in attempting to teach the child something, is urging the child on to reality rather than to variations of nonreality.

Dr. Gardner: I'm not sure whether this is responsive to the question you raised, but I think that what I would say would be along the lines of what Jerome Singer was saying—that there isn't any one moment in time when the child becomes aware of what play is and what reality is, simply because play is a major way of approaching the world. Its origins go back to peek-a-boo, and hiding, and something not being where you think it's supposed to be. But the struggle to figure out what's real and what's not extends well into middle childhood, if it doesn't indeed extend to our conversation here around the table. I have a very bright eight-year-old who still is very uncertain about how things are to be taken. In a study we just completed, we wanted to see the extent to which children naturally go about characterizing characters from life and from fiction as to whether they have a realistic status or whether they're just pretend; even when you go up to sixth grade you find it's not a very spontaneous category for classifying things. While I agree with you that this is something that has its beginnings very early, I think figuring out what's pretend and what's not is really a long-term assignment.

Dr. Kirschenblatt-Gimblett: I wonder if much of what we're talking about is really play *antecedents,* not play proper, and this gets into the larger question that we're raising all along: what is play and what are the units of play, etc.? No doubt we'll extend this to ask ourselves some questions about games as well. But I wonder if a lot of what we're talking about is really play antecedents, and that for play proper you have to have an awareness that this is play, and that that awareness of play can and does occur very, very early.

References

Fein, G., & Robertson, A. Cognitive and social dimensions of pretending in two-year-olds. New Haven: Yale University ERIC # Ed. 119806, 1975.

Fein, G., Johnson, D., Losson, N., Stork, L., & Wasserman, L. Sex Stereotypes and Preferences in the Toy Choices of 20-month-old boys and girls. *Developmental Psychology,* 1975, 4, 527.

Fein, G. A transformational analysis of pretending. *Developmental Psychology,* 1975, 11, 291–296.

CHAPTER 6

SOCIAL GAMES IN INFANCY*

Dale F. Hay, Hildy S. Ross, and Barbara Davis Goldman

INTRODUCTION

Dr. Sutton-Smith: Dr. Hay's paper will identify the characteristics of the infant-mother, infant-stranger, and infant-peer social games with which she and Dr. Ross have been working. She lists their characteristics as those of mutual involvement, alternation of turns, repetition, and nonliterality. These characteristics will be described in detail in the following paper.

Because mutual involvement, alternation of turns, and repetition also characterize "serious" interactions, much of the discussion focuses on the means of distinguishing between the literal and the nonliteral. It should be added that repetition is often a signal of nonliterality and as such would tend to characterize "serious" interaction to a lesser extent. The difficulties of classifying a behavior that might mean one thing to one participant, but something else to another, particularly if an adult, are stressed. Although it seems that almost any behavior could be dealt with playfully, some argue that some behaviors are more likely than others to enter into play, and that some behaviors are in their nature playful (such as "galumphing," eyeing the spectators, behavior contrast, and "quick, light movement"). Others, however, prefer to identify the nonliterality of the event primarily by its context and by the attitude of the participants

*An earlier version of this paper by Hildy S. Ross, Dale F. Hay, and Barbara Davis Goldman was presented as an invited address to the Annual Meeting of the Canadian Psychological Association, Toronto, June 1976. The work reported was supported by a Canada Council Research Grant (S73-0700-SI) to Hildy S. Ross and a University of Waterloo Grant (037-7174) to Dale F. Hay.

rather than by the behaviors themselves: that is, by laughter, positive affect, or an enthusiastic response taking place in a recognized play setting. Yet others feel that one or more quite different characteristics of playfulness might operate on different occasions.

Another question centers on whether the games of infants are true emergents or have been modeled already in the infants' own games with parents. Or even, in the latter case, whether some play-prone children couldn't induce novel games of their own in ways that had not been modeled for them. Finally it is suggested that we may be looking at all this from too adult-centric a viewpoint; that the child's preferred mode of learning may be through the flexible means of play, and it may be this preference that forces the mother to use it, rather than the mother's modeling of it. Perhaps the mother must play with the infant to gain her more serious ends.

FEATURES AND FUNCTIONS OF INFANT GAMES

Kathy, an 18-month-old, was half sprawled across her mother's lap, sucking on a small block. A 24-month-old, Tasha, stood nearby watching them. Kathy's mother pulled a block from Kathy's mouth, saying "Get that out of your mouth. Dirty." Tasha hopped over to the other blocks on the floor a few feet away, got one, and placed it in her mouth as she approached Kathy's mother. She stopped near the mother, facing her, apparently waiting for her to pull the block from *her* mouth as she had done for Kathy. Kathy quickly approached, vocalized, and pulled the block from Tasha's mouth, then backed away slightly, holding the block. Tasha turned, got another block, placed it in her mouth and approached Kathy. Kathy approached and vocalized, pulled the block from Tash's mouth and placed it in her own mouth. Tasha got another block, placed it in her mouth, turned to look at Kathy, then stood, waiting. Kathy approached and pulled the block from Tasha's mouth for the third time. They stood looking at each other, about three feet apart, for four seconds. Then Kathy took a block from her own mouth and seemed to try to place it in Tasha's mouth. Tasha opened her mouth to accept the block, while Kathy's mother turned to Tasha's mother and said "Yukh." Kathy pulled the block back and walked away. She held out another block tentatively to Tasha but Tasha didn't notice as she turned, got a block from the floor, and placed it in her mouth. She approached Kathy, stood and waited, her head thrust forward with the block in her mouth. Kathy approached and tried to remove the block, but had to drop the blocks she was holding to do so. She removed the block and placed it in her own mouth, then backed away. Tasha got another block, the fifth, placed it in her mouth and approached Kathy. Kathy reached for the block, but Tasha backed away and held on to the block, saying "Mine," then hopped away.

This transcript describes an extended and patterned social interaction between two little girls. Both children were involved in the interaction, and each had a particular role to play. In this case the roles differed from and complemented one another: Tasha picked up a block and put it in her own mouth; Kathy removed the block from Tasha's mouth. They took turns—first one acted and then the other—and the interaction was repeated five times. In addition, the action was nonliteral; Tasha was not intent on keeping a block in her mouth, as evidenced by her willingness to give it up, and Kathy was not concerned that the block must be removed for health or safety reasons, as Tasha's mother might have been. This, and similar sequences of social interaction that we have observed in infants and toddlers, we have termed *games*.

The Three Studies

The games occurred during the course of three separate studies of social behavior of very young children; one involved the mother as a social partner, a second involved the infants and adult strangers, and the third was a study of peer interaction.

The mother-infant study examined the activities of young children and their mothers in a play setting. Mothers and children (who were 12, 18, and 24 months of age) were observed individually in a playroom. The mothers were asked to remain seated throughout the session, but to otherwise behave as they normally would. Two trials were made, each ten minutes long, with a different set of three toys present in each trial.

The major aim of the second study was to create a situation in which infants would approach, remain near, and play happily with a new person (Ross & Goldman, 1977b). Each of these strangers talked and gestured, and offered the infants a series of toys; they both initiated interaction and responded to the infant's overtures. Thirty-two 12-month-old infants participated in this study; four young women served as strangers. Altogether, in this study there were four, four-minute trials, with a different toy in each.

The third study, the peer interaction study (Goldman and Ross, in press), was originally conceived as a logical extension of our work on infants' reactions to new people, and the process they undergo in forming new social relations. Forty-eight children were involved; there were sixteen in each age group of 12, 18 and 24 months. Each 18-month-old came to two sessions a week apart, once with an older and once with a younger same-sexed peer. The 12- and 24-month-olds participated in one session each. For twenty-five minutes the two children were free to act as they wished in a laboratory playroom in which there were ten toys and their mothers.

None of these studies was designed to investigate infant games. Rather, these games were first noted when we looked at the videotapes of the peer study, where ball games were frequent. At the same time a relatively independent analysis of the infant-stranger videotapes using traditional measures (such as the degree of proximity or the duration of visual regard) failed to characterize the truly social nature of the play observed. An analysis of games was undertaken here as well. Finally, we had assumed that infants would play games with their mothers which were similar to those we had found with adult strangers and with peers; and we further assumed that such games might be an important part of their mutual attachment (Ross & Goldman, 1977a). An analysis of the mother-infant data verified the presence of such games.

We shall resist all tendencies to contrast the frequency or nature of games with mother, stranger or peer in our samples. Only the twelve-month age group was constant, and although all three studies were conducted in the same room, important differences existed in the toys available and the instructions given to mothers and strangers. We are more impressed with the similarities we found *despite* different situations, and shall focus on that.

In a total of 480 minutes, infants played 84 games with their mothers. Just under 500 minutes with the active stranger yielded 37 games, and in 800 minutes of peer interaction infants played 28 games. Games varied in length from four turns, two by each participant, to thirty-two turns, observed in one infant-stranger game. The average number of turns was ten. Some games were very brief and others lasted for many minutes. The number of games in all three samples averaged 1.6 in each dyad, but ranged to highs of 8, 5 and 13 in the mother-infant, stranger-infant and infant-infant pairs. In all, 18 of the 24 mother-infant pairs played games, 18 of 32 infants played games with the stranger and 11 of 32 infant peer dyads played games. Thus infants did not enter our experimental environment and occupy their entire time or even a large portion of their time playing social games, nor did all pairs play games. Games are notable not so much for their frequency or for the total time they occupied but for what they tell us about the infant's capacity for complex, structured involvement with a variety of social partners. As we analyzed the features of games, we came to a new appreciation of the skills that very young children bring to a social situation.

Common Features of the Games

Four features characterize these games: *mutual involvement, turn taking, repetition* of a two partner sequence, and *nonliterality*. An additional condition for describing an interaction as a game was the absence of any signs of negative affect. Each of these features will be discussed in turn, though it will rapidly become apparent that they are interrelated.

The most obvious feature of our games is that both partners must be clearly involved in the interaction, each performing some action in response to the other. If one child threw a ball, looked at the other, smiled, and waited, this might be classified as a game overture (in fact a quite common one) but it did not become a game if the other child just continued watching or didn't even notice. If the second child were to laugh, or bounce up and down, or chase the ball and throw it back each time it was thrown, then a game would be occurring. In a similar vein, one partner, the mother for instance, may have inserted a response to the ongoing behavior of her infant, with little awareness on the infant's part that this had occurred. For example, one mother counted the rings that her child removed from the peg but he seemed intent only on removing each ring. In another case, a child removed each ring, held it up, turned to look at her mother and waited, and the mother counted each ring in response to this overture; we labeled this interaction a game. In the first example, though the mother's response was clearly social and clearly dependent upon the child's, mutual involvement was lacking. In the second example, the infant looked to the mother and waited for her response, and thus both partners were involved in the interaction.

Following directly from mutual involvement is the game feature of alternating turns. Each partner has his own role to play in the games, and turn-taking regulates the interaction. Turn alternation is a rather impressive skill in that each partner, whether adult or infant, must leave room for the other to respond. Moreover the game participants often did much more than leave room for their partners' acts: they also signaled to them that they should now take their turn. Turn alternation signals ranged widely in our sample. Most common was simply waiting after the completion of one's own turn. Often alternation of gaze direction would be coordinated with pausing, as in peer ball games where the toddler would throw the ball, pause, look at the other child, look at the ball, then look back at the other child until he retrieved the ball. In the stranger-infant object exchange games, the stranger often paused for long periods with her hand extended, offering a block, waiting for the child to take it and complete his turn, or alternatively waiting for the infant to give her a block. In addition to waiting, infants and adults often withdrew physically from the action by stepping back, sitting back, or placing their hand in laps or by their sides. An example of this occurred in a game between an infant and adult stranger. The adult pushed the toy turtle toward the infant, withdrew her hand to her knee and watched the infant; the infant watched the turtle, put her hand rather tentatively on the turtle, and pushed it back a little. The infant pulled her hand back to her foot and watched the turtle; the adult pulled the turtle back and pushed it forward until it hit the infant's foot; then she put her hand on her knee. In all the adult took nine turns, and the infant took eight; at the completion of each turn the adult's and the infant's hands returned to their knees, legs or the floor by their sides.

Turn alternation signals were frequently even more explicit; for example, one infant stood shaking the tub and waiting for the adult to drop a block inside, or the adult pointed to the block in the infant's hand and then into the tub, with the same end in mind. Another infant waved his hands impatiently at his mother, in an apparent attempt to encourage her to return the ball. Adults often repeated the same phrase at the end of a turn, and infants also occasionally used verbal statements, such as "I'll get it, I'll get it" to mark one's own turn, or "Go Baby, go" to encourage the other child to throw the ball.

The third feature of our games was repetition, sometimes with variation, of the complete sequence of interaction, as exemplified by the transcript at the beginning of this paper. Tasha got the block and placed it in her mouth five times; Kathy approached Tasha and removed the block four times. Repetition could make an extended sequence of interaction easier for the infants, as each act need not be completely novel. This may have enabled the infants to pay attention to the maintenance of synchrony with their partners, when required, rather than forcing them to focus on the content of the turns. It is of interest that Piaget (1962) also mentioned the repetition of an activity for "mere assimilation" as an indication of a sensorimotor game.

A fourth feature of these games was nonliterality. Indications were given that the activities incorporated in a game were not meant literally, as ends in themselves, but playfully, to serve as means for a game. Repetition itself could signal that an interaction was not to be taken literally, as exemplified by the games involving exchanges of objects. To illustrate, if a child requested a ball from another child, and received it, it appeared to us as observers and to the child who originally had the ball that the first child intended a real object exchange. If, however, after receiving the ball, the child then offered, or rolled, or threw it back, then waited, arms outstretched, requesting it again, it became apparent that the action was meant nonliterally. Often the children's laughter or happy vocalizations indicated that their actions were to be interpreted as nonliteral; in other cases a literal interpretation was just highly unlikely. For example, a frequent infant-stranger game consisted of the stranger offering the infant a block, the infant accepting the gift, and then dropping it into a container. The exchange was not literal, as the infant did not retain possession of the blocks, nor was it a conscientious effort by the two partners to clean up the room before the next pair of subjects arrived. Rather the interaction was nonliteral; a game was in progress.

The four features of games—mutual involvement, turn alternation, repetition, and nonliterality—all play important roles as games are initiated, develop, and end.

The precise moment when games began was often difficult to determine. Mutual involvement may have been sought by a clear game overture, such as throwing the ball toward the other child and waiting, arms outstretched, for its return, or, as the strangers often did, demonstrating the action of throwing a block into the container, which was to be the infant's role. In other cases games began only when the second partner responded and indicated his desire for mutual involvement. Thus it was the imitation of a vocalization, rather than the vocalization itself, that started a game, or the infant's laughter when the adult accidentally dropped a block that induced the adult to drop the block again.

As the games progressed, the partners remained mutually involved and continued to alternate their turns; in addition, the interaction retained its nonliteral quality and freedom from negative affect. However, the partners did not appear to feel constrained to repeat all components of their roles in every turn. Each role in a game might contain several elements (for instance, smiling, vocalizing or performing some action). Some games became channeled over time, with extraneous elements dropping out of each person's role. For example, one game began with the infant, mother and a toy walrus held by the mother; the latter two pretended to drink from a cup offered by the child; later only the walrus was offered a drink by the child. Alternatively, new elements were sometimes added so that a role was elaborated as the game continued. Other games may best be viewed as composed of subroutines where the content of one person's turn changed and then his partner followed his lead. For example, both the stranger and the infant changed their roles in one game with the blocks and tub. At first, the stranger gave the infant a block and the infant took it from her and dropped it in the tub. After a few turns the stranger held the block over the tub and the infant swiped at the block so that it fell out of the stranger's hand and into the tub. Thus an entire game may have contained several successive subroutines which differed slightly from one another. The continuous nature of the game was maintained when the subroutines followed one another fairly rapidly, and also when they involved different activities with the same set of objects.

Games frequently ended when one partner waited too long or failed altogether to take his turn, thus ending mutual involvement. Though a game might be re-established by the other partner repeating his turn, following his partner's failure to act, at times he apparently felt constrained not to take two turns in a row, and the game would end. A frequent cause of the turn-taking failures was a seeming distraction of attention, often to some other toy or toy function. The adults, as well as the infants, sometimes were responsible for such game interruptions. A particularly striking example is the stranger who interrupted a highly organized, elaborate and infant-initiated game in order to build a tower with the blocks that were in front of her. Sometimes games were inadvertently ended by mothers as they readjusted the children's clothing, or repositioned them, causing one child to fail to take his turn. Occasionally a mother verbally directed an interaction to stop, or drew the child's attention to another toy. Object exchange games terminated through all the above turn-taking rule deviations, but also through redefinition of the interaction as literal. In these cases extended, nonliteral exchanges of blocks or the ball would be suddenly terminated by one child keeping the object, rather than relinquishing it; this was often accompanied by "no, mine," or turning away, or going to the mother with the toy.

The study of the features that characterize infant games yields much information concerning the skills that infants bring to social interaction. These skills are considerable, and include the infants' ability to repeat their own behavior, with or without variation; their ability to comprehend and to imitate their partners' behavior, often quite exactly and following only one example; their ability to get their partners' attention; and their ability to create interaction through those of their own acts that are interesting to their partners. All these are assumed to be part of the repertoire of children in the second year of life, though initiating interesting activities can be a challenge even to the experienced mothers in our sample. More complicated skills are also involved, including those necessary for turn alternation, such as the infants' monitoring their partners' activities, pausing in their own activity for their partners' turns, and using and understanding turn alternation signals. Furthermore the infants seem able to transform their own, generally literal, actions or those of their partners, into nonliteral vehicles for games. Thus infants engage in complex, extended, well-formed, and patterned interactions.

Diversity among Games

The term *game* has a very broad application, and its use in yet another context should be examined. How do our infant games relate to chess, hockey, hopscotch, or the Olympic Games? What is the commonality with tennis, Monopoly, or a simple game of catch? We have used the term game because the interaction was structured, involved turn-taking, and was repeated and nonliteral. The infant games we described are social: more than one person was involved in the interaction. This contrasts with the games described by Piaget (1962) for the first two years of life. On the other hand, the social nature of our infant games is consistent with most traditional games, including all those listed above. Rules appeared to regulate the interaction, though the rules may be fewer, simpler, more flexible, and differ in origin from those of more traditional games. Turn alternation and basic repetition of roles are two of the rules that the infant games have in common with other games. Constraints also existed within any given game, and would determine the nature of a turn. On the other hand, competition, generally considered a hallmark of games, is noticeably lacking. The apparent aim of the infants as they played was to engage their partners in a harmonious, integrated series of actions for a relatively extended period of time. Yet the aim of structured involvement with others does not seem altogether alien to the broad range of child and adult games. With young infants this aim may provide challenge enough, whereas older groups may both require and be capable of using rule-guided competition to further this aim.

One might still object to the diversity of interaction patterns included as games, but the philosopher Wittgenstein's (1953) analysis speaks well to any remaining doubts. He denied that there is any feature common to all games:

Consider for example the proceedings that we call "games" . . . What is common to them all?—Don't say: "There *must* be something common, or they would not be called 'games'"—but *look and see* whether there is anything common to all.—For if you look at them you will not see something that is common to *all*, but similarities, relationships, and a whole series of them at that. . . . Are they all "amusing"? Compare chess with noughts and crosses. Or is there always winning and losing, or competition between players? Think of patience. In ball games there is winning and losing; but when a child throws his ball at the wall and catches it again, this feature has disappeared. Look at the parts played by skill and luck; and at the difference between skill in chess and skill in tennis. Think now of games like ring-a-ring-a-roses; here is the element of amusement, but how many other characteristic features have disappeared! And we can go through the many, many other groups of games in the same way; can see how similarities crop up and disappear.

And the result of this examination is: we see a complicated network of similarities overlapping and criss-crossing: sometimes overall similarities, sometimes similarities of detail (*Philosophical Investigations* [Vol. 1], 1953, p. 66).

Wittgenstein draws an analogy between the concept of game and a thread, spun by twisting fibre upon fibre. "And the strength of the thread does not reside in the fact that some one fibre runs through its whole length, but in the overlapping of many fibres" (p. 67).

In our study of the features of infant games we cannot expect them to correspond in every detail to what others have seen as common features of traditional child or adult games, nor should we expect all infant games to contain the identical set of features. Yet these features should overlap and they do, substantially. Among the infant games, additional features are shared by subsets of the games that parallel those of child and adult games and reveal a capacity for complex structuring of mutual interaction even greater than that found in our analysis of the more common features of our games. Further, these additional features contribute to the considerable diversity among the infant games themselves.

The greatest diversity was in the acts that made up the roles of the games, a diversity which seemed in large measure to be created by the different physical objects available. Balls were thrown and retrieved; blocks were exchanged and deposited in a tub, or tapped together; dishes were transported from place to place and piled on one another. This feature seems to bear continuity with most traditional games which use objects and which are guided by the nature of the objects. Thus a tennis ball and racket, a football, and a baseball and bat all mediate different ball games.

A second source of diversity noted was in the extent to which each turn was an exact replication of itself. In no case, we might judge, were the two actions identical, yet there seemed to be a range of permissible variation which differed among games. In other words, the level of abstraction of the rules which guided the roles or turns of each player differed among the games. We were not always able to specify the abstract rules which guided the action; however, we could at times approximate them. To illustrate, in one game an infant played with a stranger, each partner had to make a sound with the blocks, usually by tapping them against each other or banging them on the top of the tub. Although turns were sometimes simultaneous, more often they alternated, and in two highly similar games there was a total of forty-one turns. The stranger tried two variations of making a sound with the blocks: she tapped the side of the tub, and she hit the top of a tower of blocks. The second variation was accepted by the infant, who in turn hit the block pile, but the first variation was never imitated or subsequently repeated by the stranger, and so we assumed either that the timing of the variation was incorrect, or that it did not meet the infant's definition of a permissible turn. In any case, this example illustrates that rules more general than "repeat, as exactly as you can, your previous behavior" are possible. The infant in this case was twelve months old and seemed to understand this abstract rule of making a sound with the blocks, as witnessed by her adherence to it. Rules in traditional child and adult games are also general and abstract, and allow variation among turns rather than requiring faithful repetitions of a previous turn.

Another feature noted in one game between a twenty-four-month-old infant and her mother was the presence of a hierarchical structure. This was noted for the infant's role, which on one level consisted of carrying a stock of plates and bowls to one corner of the room and then to her mother. Once near her mother, she handed her the objects one at a time, and the mother accepted them. The child then retrieved the plates and bowls one at a time, transported them to the opposite corner of the room, and then returned to the mother and exchanged the objects once more. The exchange of the dishes was thus embedded within the transportation of the dishes, and the infant's role assumed a hierarchical structure. We have yet to notice a similarly complex structure in the other games, though some approximate it. It would be premature to judge this infant as unique, for others may be capable of this level of organization, but have not demonstrated it in the laboratory. This child could be precociously displaying an ability which would be more general among slightly older children. It is, once again, a feature of some child and adult games— baseball, tennis, and bridge may serve as examples.

The final feature of the games to be examined is the reversal of roles, each partner assuming the role previously occupied by the other. Two examples from the peer study illustrate this process. In ball games each player had the role of throwing, and the complementary role of retrieving the ball. The roles reversed after each child retrieved the ball and prepared to throw it. An imitation game provided another instance of role reversal in which the role of initiating a particular vocalization and the role of imitating it were transferred between the two children. However, the clearest case came from the infant-stranger study. The game began with the stranger offering a block to the infant, the infant then accepting the block and depositing it in the tub. Then, after ten turns, and seemingly at the infant's initiative, the roles reversed and the infant offered the blocks; the stranger accepted them and placed each in the tub. Later in the trial the roles reversed again. Role reversals imply a sophisticated understanding of the nature of one's own role, one's partner's role, and the relationship between the two. Such understanding may belie the egocentrism often attributed to such a young child. And once again, role reversal is an essential feature of many traditional games; tag would not be the same game if one person were constantly "It."

Thus we have substantial additions to our list of game-playing skills which, though not demonstrated by all of our sample, are possessed by at least some. First, infants were able to create interesting mutual activities that take into account the nature of the objects present; second, they incorporated diversity in their own turns and accepted it in others, or were able to create abstract rules which governed the nature of the turns; third, at least one infant was capable of devising a role involving a complex, hierarchical structure. Finally, infants had the abilities to reflect upon the nature of their own role, their partners' roles, and the relationships between the two that seem necessary prerequisites to the ability to reverse roles.

Functions of the Games

Finally, we turn to the question of the function of infant games. Why might infants play games? This is a question we can scarcely hope to answer with any degree of confidence; yet by attempting to do so we may be able to explain why we feel infant games are worthy of study, and to provide a context for future work.

The overriding aim of the infant games is mutual involvement in social interaction. The regulated, repetitive structure of the games may facilitate the continuation of interaction.

At a different level, we think a game can also provide a rich learning situation for the infant and for his social partner. From the infant's point of view, it can be a time for learning about the properties of the physical environment. A block can be tapped or rolled or placed in a container; the dishes will balance only if stacked roughly in order of size; the rings can be fit on the peg, and each can be named by a different color; the ball can roll, is easily picked up, and squeaks when you squeeze it. Some of these properties could be discovered in independent play or exploration; others, however, might be demonstrated by the adult or peer in his turn, and subsequently imitated. Pausing while the other person takes his turn helps the infant attend to the content of the other person's role, and thus to learn from him what objects can do. Especially in the mother-infant study, we saw fairly explicit examples of teaching within games, as the mother named and counted objects. Some danger exists in expecting that the infant learns the properties of his physical environment entirely on his own; other people are often his guides.

Infant games also provide valuable training in the process of interaction. That is, infants may learn *how* to interact; their skills at taking and yielding turns, understanding nonliteral actions, creating abstract rules, and performing complex, hierarchical roles or reversing roles may develop in the course of games. Such skills may have an important place in future games; we see continuities with other forms of social interaction as well. Conversational interaction or dialogue also depends upon turn alternation skills and the giving and understanding of turn-yielding and turn-taking signals (e.g., De Long, 1974; Duncan, 1972; Sacks, Schegloff & Jefferson, 1975). Our analysis of these essentially preverbal games bears a good deal of resemblance to Garvey's (1974) work on verbal interaction at a somewhat later age. Thus infant games provide an opportunity for practicing social interaction skills which extend well beyond adult games in their application.

Other researchers have established that mother and infant can enter into a synchronous interaction which involves turn alternation. Such demonstrations have focused on the burst-pause pattern in sucking (Kaye, 1977) and in vocalizing (Schaffer, Collis, & Parsons, 1977; Stern, Jaffee, Beebe, & Bennett, 1975). Our findings extend theirs by going beyond the mother-infant dyad, and thereby demonstrating that synchrony is not an exclusive feature of the attachment relationship. Further, the data also indicate the rapidity with which infants and toddlers can organize and coordinate their social interaction: games with new adults and peers appeared within four minutes of their meeting. But equally impressive is the fact that our data show a wide variety of response patterns taking us beyond sucking and vocalizing, and demonstrating the infant's ability to create harmonious interaction with different content. The fact that our subjects are older than those observed by others leads us to at least speculate that the ability to employ diverse elements in achieving synchronous interaction is a developmental phenomenon. It is one thing for the infant to establish a synchronous interaction with his mother over the first months of life, based on certain well-established response patterns; it is quite another for him to meet a new individual and coordinate his responses with those of his partner.

Finally we should like to explore the role of infant games within the infant's already established and new social relations (Ross & Goldman, 1977a). Infants play games with their mothers and with adults and peers they meet for the first time. Mother-infant games, we propose, form a part of the relationship between them. The repeated interactions provide a basis for mutual involvement, and the content may be valued because it can be invoked when involvement is sought. When the infant attempts to establish a new social relation with an adult or peer, he may create a similar mutual repertoire of activities they can enjoy together. As with adults, shyness may be more easily overcome if there are things you can do with one another. Games may be directly transferred from among those played with parents or other friends, or new games may be derived that blend the repertoires of both players. Games could well become a part of the new social relationship and strengthen it. We are currently studying this process among peers. Until we can provide firm evidence of the transfer of games, let us illustrate with an example from personal experience. Jordan Ross, from the age of seven months, played a simple game in which he shook his head at his mother, and she in turn shook her head and said, "No, no, no." Positive affect was evident on both sides. Jordan's father and brother, his grandparents, aunt and uncles also played this game with him after watching this example. Then one day his mother picked Jordan up at a babysitter's house, and found the sitter's seven-year-old daughter, Jennifer, playing "No, no, no" with Jordan, much to his delight. We do not know if he had developed the game with his mother or with Jennifer, but whatever the case, Jordan had to be credited with full responsibility for teaching the game to at least one partner. Parenthetically, we might warn against the use of "no" in a game, or your child, like Jordan, may initiate forbidden actions in order to elicit "no" and begin a game. For many months he refused to acknowledge a literal *no*, and insisted on his own nonliteral interpretation.

We conclude that infants play games with a variety of social partners. Games provide an opportunity for mutual involvement and for learning about the physical properties of the environment, the actions of other people, and most important and most general, the process of social interaction. Games are often complex, well-formed, rule-governed, and extended. They may form part of the relations infants establish with others. Finally, an analysis of infant game-playing skills reveals a sophisticated social repertoire possessed by children who are between their first and second birthdays.

DISCUSSION

Dr. Hay: In view of the concerns of the conference, I now would like to discuss our observations in terms of the general construct of play. On what grounds might early games qualify as a form of play? Do we refer to them as such because infants and toys are involved? Or because to us, as adults, these interactions seem like fun? I would suggest that the games seem playful essentially because they do not seem *literal.* Thus it is the feature of *nonliterality* that brings infants' games into the domain of play. Given that nonliterality in fact may be a characteristic feature of play, it may be helpful to discuss some of the problems arising from its use.

The other features of the games—mutual involvement, repetition, and alternation of turns—can be specified in objective terms and recorded through direct observation. In contrast, the assessment of nonliterality requires inference. We first must assume the existence of a literal and a nonliteral version of an act (or set of acts), and then attempt to infer from the available information which version we presently observe. There are at least two ways in which such an inference can be made.

First we can search for supplementary information in the antecedent, accompanying and consequent actions of the actor. For example, if a child pushes another child and giggles, we can take that as evidence that it's not literal forcible contact, not a literal push or shove, but rather that it's being used as a means for a game. That inference, of course, is based on the assumption that the literal version of the act is within the child's repertoire—that there exists some awareness on the part of the child and some choice not to employ the literal form of the action.

There is, however, a second basis on which we as observers infer nonliterality without requiring awareness on the part of the child or the person serving as partner in the child's play. As observers, we tend to place our own adult-generated constructions on whatever it is the child is doing. For example, when a twelve-month-old infant and an unfamiliar adult take turns placing all the blocks in the room into a container, we' might say that the literal version of the interaction is clearing up a room. But that literal version is a construction we are placing on the activity. The child certainly is not aware of that literal version. In fact, although the adult might acknowledge the similarity between this game and house-cleaning, she probably was not consciously aware of the literal version while participating in the interaction. Indeed, adults engaged in interactions with infants probably often tend to assume they are playing—that is, behaving nonliterally—simply because they are dealing with children so young.

Thus we as observers can examine infants' games and determine a literal equivalent in adult life to a given interaction of which neither infant nor adult partner may be aware. Should we require awareness on the part of the players of these games? Should we take nonliterality to imply deliberate choice of the nonliteral over the literal alternative? If so, a problem immediately arises. In terms of the developmental progression of various classes of behavior, the nonliteral form of a given action may emerge long before the literal one. Dr. Ross has observed an example of this: her son, Jordon, who is almost two, uses the shooting gesture. She would hope that this is not a translation from the literal alternative but indeed that the nonliteral version has occurred earlier in development.

It is clear that our consideration of nonliterality has led us immediately to the venerable problem of awareness. This problem also arises in our attempts to specify the structure, as well as the nonliteral quality, of early games. In particular, are we justified in saying that these games have rules?

As observers we can categorize an infant's role within a game in terms of a central rule, such as "Tap your foot" or "Put the blocks in the container and laugh." As verbal adults, we can articulate such a rule. However, the infant engaged in the interaction may not be aware of the rule, or may not have the verbal proficiency to articulate it, or indeed may not have a concept of rules in general. Is "Tap your foot" then any less of a rule? Given that an interaction is structured, must the actors be able to analyze and articulate its structure for it to qualify as a game?

Clearly, then, the nonliteral quality of early games and their apparently rule-governed structure are inferred by adult observers and may not be apparent to the actual players. Nonetheless, attempts to learn more about these two characteristics of games should not be abandoned; troublesome though they be, nonliterality and rule-governed structure permit some distinctions to be made between social behavior in general and interaction, and between literal activity and social play.

A behavior might be termed social to the extent that it is directed to another animate organism (most commonly, a member of one's own species). Given then that there exists a general domain of social behavior, interaction would consist of that subset characterized by mutual involvement and coordination of responses among partners. These distinctions should be kept in mind in the realm of play as well. For example, if one considers remaining near a person to be a form of social behavior, then parallel play (Parten, 1932) could be considered social. However, it is not interactive.

Thus three of the four features of early games—mutual involvement, turn alternation, and repetition—specify their interactive nature. However, do they differentiate play from what is not play? Mutual involvement alone obviously does not distinguish play from literal interaction. Repetition and alternation of turns may characterize interactions that we would be loath to call play, including conflicts over toys (Ross & Hay, 1977). Although it is a troublesome, inferential concept, nonliterality seems to be the feature that best distinguishes these playful games from other sorts of interactions.

In making this distinction, it is also important to note that children in the second year of life drift in and out of states we might call play. For instance, children at this age frequently show and give objects to their parents and other people (Rheingold, May, & West, 1976). There are occasions when a sharing response such as giving seems to transform itself into a game of give-and-take, with objects being exchanged at a rapid rate, and then drifts out of that again into a state that we would not as readily term play. The time frame in which these one-year-olds operate is somewhat more fluid than our adult time frame, so that infants may move in and out of play; there may be abrupt shifts from nonliteral to literal interaction.

Thus, in sum, if we wish to discuss these early games as a form of play, we must use the very troublesome criterion of nonliterality, which may be an adult-generated distinction and not a child-generated one. This is a problem. It is the same problem we have been facing throughout these meetings, in terms of our attempts to define play. We must try to specify what cues we use when we label an action playful, and determine the extent to which those cues are in the eyes of the beholders as opposed to the minds of the players.

Dr. Sutton-Smith: I'm personally interested in this question of whether you should call them games or not. Despite Dr. Kirschenblatt-Gimblett's definition of games as competitive, involving rules, sides and winners, which comes from the work that J. M. Roberts (1959) et al. did, I find no real problem with this. It's like whether you should call intelligence, intelligence, because it's sensorimotor. The "games" of little children—at least the ones they play with mothers—are asymmetrical in the

sense that they are managed by adults. But they have the precursor characteristics of games because you have an opposition with some slightly
different outcome for each party. In that sense, insofar as there is a contrast between the roles of the partners and an issue that is differential for
the partners, these are precursors of games. However, if there is just turn-
taking with no outcome, as in your example, and as in Dr. Garvey's example, I believe it is better to call them an exchange routine or ritual.
If Kathy and Tasha then turned this into a tug of war over the block
in the mouth, I would call it a game. With examples like this, it
could clearly go either way, being interactive one moment and contestive
another.

Dr. Hay: As Wittgenstein noted in the passage we cited, the term *game*
has been applied to a variety of playful interactions. Two dimensions of
such interactions that seem particularly important are the rule-governed
structure of games and the existence of a win/loss outcome. Clearly most
of the interactions we have been considering do not have such an outcome. Further interactions that house win/loss outcomes, such as strug-
gles over objects (Ross & Hay, 1977), most often seem quite literal. Thus
most of the interactions of infants would not meet the criteria of competitive adult games. Whether these early examples are precursors is an empirical question. Do these interactions become increasingly competitive
or do conflicts become increasingly nonliteral? In any case, our use of the
term game does not seem completely inappropriate, given the turn-taking
structure and nonliteral quality of these interactions, and the range of
meanings of the term in common usage. For example, is there such a
thing as a game of "catch"?

Dr. Gardner: What I'm wondering is what do you think about the extent to which it's the case that child one does something and then child
two does something else, and the game is kind of emergent rather than
being clear in the mind of the first player.

Dr. Hay: What I do when I describe these games is to articulate a rule
that to me summarizes the interaction. I don't know if the infants are
aware of that rule. However, there are some limits on the content of turns
in a game. If the content of turns is too varied, then one of the partners
may not recognize the interaction as being a game. It doesn't fulfill the
criterion of repetition. In terms of its being emergent, I think that's probably perfectly right. There are some games in which it seems that the ini-
tiator has something in mind, if you want to say that loosely. Take the
twelve-month-old who kept kicking his foot against all odds; it finally was
communicated to the other child with him that the appropriate response
was to kick one's own foot. The second child did touch his toe and wiggle
his feet around for a while before he got down the response. On other occasions the game is defined by the second person. One child does some-

thing like dump the blocks out of a tub, and the other child laughs, and then the first child will repeat action and the other child will laugh, so that game emerges from the second child's response to an interaction that may not have been peer-directed at all.

Dr. Gardner: One thing that struck me was the extent to which the different cues may be important in playing the game. I was thinking about blind or deaf infants and the extent to which their play would be impoverished, because in each case there would be a feedback that they didn't get. My guess is that it's polysensory, and the game is likely to continue based on the extent to which the child is getting a lot of stimulation from the interaction.

Dr. Hay: I think it's also important that there is accompanying *affect*, which again we haven't categorized as neatly as we could; but while infants play games they are talking, they are laughing, and they are showing "quick and light movement." There are cues there which I'm using to call it playful activity. Whether or not we could systematize these cues into a set of defining criteria is the problem we have to deal with.

Dr. J. Singer: I think with respect to your question of intentionality or awareness, there's been a lot more theorizing around the issue of human beings structuring their behavior gradually around plans or some kind of organized sequences, some of which may eventually take the form of actual visual or auditory images; but the term plan can be broader than that. It can be viewed in the same way as a kind of computer subroutine or program that becomes structured. And one gets the impression in watching some of these that that's what's happening with the kids. Out of the emerging interaction, they form a structure and then react further to that structure.

Dr. Hay: I think that's true. There's order in these interactions, and the question is whether or not the children are aware of the order. I think that they're not unaware of the order. The fact that they do use these overt turn-taking or turn-yielding signals when the partner is not living up to the bargain or not performing adequately is an indication of some awareness on their part. They are not verbal and they do not speak on the level we do and so they're not going to be able to say, "This is the 'tickle, tickle' game," or "This is the 'foot kicking' game," as I can. I don't know if that makes it less of a game. I tend to think it doesn't.

Dr. Collard: Would some of these things be based on expectations of games that they played with their mothers? When there is an interaction going and the mother all of a sudden blanks out, you can see the baby try and try to get her attention and then just extinguish. He tries and tries to get it going again. It's as if there is an expectancy there that the mother's going to do something and she doesn't, and he keeps trying to make it work.

Dr. Hay: There's no question that there are interactions of very young infants that bear resemblances to these data in terms of the repetition, the turn alternation, the playful quality, the nonliterality. At this point, however, I don't have the data to suggest that these games that we see with strangers and peers emerge out of the mother-infant relationship.

Dr. Collard: If a toddler *never* had his belly tickled by somebody, do you think he would raise his shirt and walk up to somebody as we saw in your film?

Dr. Hay: One thinks not, but on the other hand, we can examine game initiations on the part of twelve-month-olds. In one study the partner was the mother; in another study it was another child; and in the third study, a stranger. Games that were played with the peer and the adult stranger suggest that even a short-term relationship is being established within the confines of twenty minutes in our setting, and interactional sequences emerge out of that relationship. You don't need to go and ask whether those particular games have been played at home.

Dr. Ellis: What if the adult had made the cleaning up the room into an interactive game?

Dr. Hay: Adults do that.

Dr. Ellis: But it points out an important issue, which is that I think it is possible for it to be both a game and play and work or product- and process oriented at the same time.

Dr. Hay: I think that's a common ploy of adults. I think it leads to frustration on occasions when the child decides to be nonliteral, you have to get out of the room in three minutes and you want the room cleaned up, and they're taking it as a game. We often do characterize what we do with them as play, even if we do have a literal objective.

Dr. Ellis: My next question is the reverse of the other. What if the child with the stranger is working at establishing the limits of a social interaction with the stranger, whereas it is not necessary to do that with a familiar person. In other words, this time the child is the one who is product oriented. He asks what are the social limits: is this stranger a threatening person, or does this stranger follow the paradigms that I've built from other human interactions that I've had? Now we have play that is in fact work on the part of the child. I'm babymorphizing.

Dr. Hay: I think that's a really good point, that interaction is serious business, that becoming acquainted with other people and learning what they're like, is indeed a literal objective. To the extent that one uses games as means to that end, you're right; we're again in an interplay of what is play and what is social *work*. Still, although this may be a literal motive, it is not the literal motive that would be read off the behaviors involved in the interaction.

Dr. J. Singer: There are whole groups of feeding games or cleaning or bathing games that parents will get into. The child sitting in a chair will turn away from a spoonful of cereal, but if the mother says something like "Let's put the birdie in the nest," the child will open the mouth wide, the spoon goes in, and the child chomps the cereal. This begins a happy game, and the resistance to eating disappears.

Dr. Lewis: I want to pick up on the use of happy. We've done this before and we've talked about playful versus play; I think it's an important distinction that we have to keep in mind. An interaction, a serious interaction, can be playful. Therefore, what do we do with that? Is that play now? Is that literal in your terms? And again, I think you can feed your child seriously. You want to get the food down because you have to go somewhere, and you can feed your child playfully. Both ways serve the function of feeding your child and they're quite different kinds of activities. I think we ought to stress that the socioemotion or emotional attribute and tone of the activity is going to in large part define for us whether we're going to consider it play or work.

Dr. Hay: I think those are the cues that we can use as observers. One of my central feelings—one of the things I was trying to say yesterday in response to Dr. Collard's work—is that the same, topographically identical act can hold different functions. What we know of its function is an inference that we're making based on certain cues such as affect, the distribution of responses in time, any metacommunicative signals that are present. We use whatever cues we can to infer the function of the behavior.

Dr. Lewis: We can classify games, perhaps, but we're not going to classify play. And if anything emerges as the central theme, it is that play can be anything.

Dr. Hay: Or any behavior can be playing.

Dr. Lewis: Any behavior or any routine.

Dr. Ellis: We're almost ready to give up right now on saying that a behavior, any sort of behavior, can be classified unambiguously as play.

Dr. Lewis: But I want to hold to the quality of play. There is something about its quality—we keep coming back to playful.

Dr. Hay: Isn't it that we're making an inference and we have to figure out what is consistently the evidence we use to make this inference?

Dr. Lewis: Well, we can measure facial expression and affect. I'm not saying that's the route to go. But if we want to start classifying, as we do with behavior, I think we have to move to a multidimensional classification which has on one side, if you like, something called these behaviors that we've been looking at. On the other side is something which may be called emotional expression. I would be reluctant to throw away these behaviors entirely because there's something heuristic about them. There are certain things that we are less likely to call play than others.

Dr. Hay: But I think it's important to realize that there are some things that we may have been quite unwilling to call play that can indeed be used playfully. For instance, a number of the responses that we've called responses to separation or attachment behaviors can be used playfully. We just have to extend our boundaries about the responses which we're willing to say can be used playfully, as well as in other modes. One thing that comes to mind is infants' *following* of other persons; it can be demonstrated that following can be used to fulfill an exploratory function as well as an attachment function (Hay, 1977). It strikes me here that it can serve a playful function as well, to the extent that children and young animals play "chase" all the time.

Dr. J. Singer: Maybe we should recognize that human beings need to function or are capable of functioning on several dimensions. The literal and nonliteral can exist side by side, and the art of enjoyable living (as I'm sure we'll hear from Mihaly [Csikszentmihayli] a little bit later) is to learn to turn work into play to some extent. We can accomplish a great deal with a child by suddenly changing the situation from one in which he is literally being bathed or fed or separated from, into some make-believe or pretend element of it, which then seems to have a component of fun, for some reason.

Dr. Fein: But I think you have to back up one step more, Jerry [Dr. Singer], because as I hear what Mike [Dr. Lewis] says, it's like prematurely laying something onto the baby. It seems to me the first decision is to say: are we going to accept an organism that is play-prone to begin with, or are we going to talk about an organism who has to be taught to play, who discovers play in the course of something that is done to it by the external work. I'd personally like to argue for a play-prone organism.

Dr. Hay: The play-prone organism may be taught *how* to play but not necessarily taught to play. I think that's important.

Dr. Fein: I think that's one of the strands, and I guess again the sort of anecdotal thing that would be terribly hard to bring into a laboratory would be when, say, there's a pet in the house, and it goes to the very young infant, and there are the movements of the baby with respect to the pet. There is the child's system of interaction with a very, very active and responsive other, and this produces lots of laughter, lots of repetitiousness, lots of eager interchange. If the child is given half a chance to create this kind of setting, he will do so.

Dr. Lewis: Do we really want to get into the issue of whether this is a biological disposition which needs learning and experience to mature and develop? Wouldn't we take this for granted? I'm hearing a nature-nurture creep in here and I was hoping that we might have a conference where it might be avoided.

Dr. Fein: Not when you talk about children's play emerging from social interaction, which is what I'm hearing you say. I think the child imposes on social interaction the possibility of playing with it, or doing other things with it. I think that's part of the child's contribution to the situation, to the creation of a situation.

Dr. Lewis: It seems to me, again going back to a means-end kind of analysis, that organisms discover that there are alternatives to behavior which they can use to arrive at an end, and this is an early discovery. This sets the stage for something that we might call play, or might be willing to, since you have a choice. And as soon as one has a choice, it seems to me one is disposed to something that I would think of as play.

Dr. Garvey: This is a very important point that Mike [Dr. Lewis] brings up. I certainly didn't use the word literal and nonliteral first, but I've used it over and over again, and I came at it from a linguistic point of view—linguistic in the sense that if we're talking about meaning, meaning only exists in the presence of contrast. You can't have meaning without contrast. If somebody smiles all the time, you have no reason to believe that he's happy if you have never seen him have any other expression but a smiling one. So it's only when a contrast exists that you can talk about a literal or a nonliteral orientation. And the contrast—here's the tricky thing—I think the contrast may not be in the physical behavior. We've tended to look at it that way. If you can literally drink then you can play drink. That's a behavior. But if we're going to go back to what we think we know about language and concept formation, perhaps it's the concept that must be there, not the behavior. Then the concept itself can be literally or nonliterally followed, which frees us of the behavior specifically. This could account for why Hildy's [Ross's] child can play shoot before he can actually shoot a gun or he can actually hold a gun, because he has the concept of shooting. Now he can treat it in two different ways, but he couldn't before.

Dr. J. Singer: He may not know that this gesture, along with the statement bang-bang, means that there's such a thing as a gun, which is a lethal weapon.

Dr. Hay: In some ways we are interested in the period before the child has a unified concept and has recognized that he can enact it either literally or nonliterally—before he is aware of the relation and contrast between particular literal and nonliteral activities. We feel that in the initial stages of the acquisition of some concepts (Jordan shooting a gun is one example), the nonliteral could proceed the literal, or even advance in the absence of any knowledge that related literal activities exist. These may eventually be unified or related to a literal concept, and perhaps the literal-nonliteral distinction should await this understanding. Yet the nonliteral half of the concept will retain its continuity even as the literal half is elaborated; it may contribute to this elaboration, and it will be used throughout in play. Its meaning in a playful context will remain relatively intact.

Dr. Garvey: But the concept will be elaborated later.

Dr. Gardner: I'd like to make a comment on this question of literality and nonliterality. I sympathize very much with the fact that you brought it up, Dale [Dr. Hay], and the way you talked about it, and the major reason I sympathize with it so much is because I'm wrestling with the same issue in an area we're looking at, where it's even more important to resolve this, and that's the question of early metaphor in children. If you read transcripts of what children say, or you engage them in games, they produce a high number of metaphors, at least some of which are clearly acceptable in adult standards. However, if it's an overextension or a generalization or a misnaming or any of those other things, then you don't want to give the child credit for a metaphor. It becomes a trivialization of the term. What we've fallen back on is looking for a series of indices which, when they co-occur, are good evidence that the child is really using metaphor. I think that's probably the strategy that you want to use for assessing nonliterality in children's play. I just wanted to mention a few of the things that you said which I think are good ways to go, and I'd like to add one you didn't say, which we find very helpful in discussing metaphor. One is the presence of laughter. Another is to have the adult do the wrong thing to see how the child reacts. A third is to look at how the child has previously used the word in the case of a metaphor, and trace the history of that usage. That's the use of contrast to infer a different usage, metaphorical, not realistic. In your case, if the child has always been the only one to drink from his cup and now for the first time is giving it to the walrus, that's some evidence of metaphoric use. A fourth thing that we find very helpful, and I think you could begin to see it in your kids, is whether when the child is engaging in what may be a play activity, does he out of the corner of his eye look at a third person, particularly if the child is playing with a peer? Does he look at his mother to get her reaction? We have found this a personally satisfying way to evaluate when the child thinks he has made a clever word play: namely, is he looking around to see how the audience is reacting? We get audience interest not in the case of metaphor, but in the case of our early symbolizations.

Dr. Hay: We see it in conflicts between infants. On an occasion one child tried to hit another child and then turned to his mother saying, "He's crying." The other child wasn't crying at all.

Dr. Gardner: And the point is no one of these indices is ever reliable. Only the convergences are helpful.

Dr. Collard: Somebody made an absolute statement saying any behavior can be classified as play. I think you have to qualify that both in terms of the context and in terms of the result. For example, if a child who can't swim falls in a swimming pool and makes flailing motions, that's different from what happens when he's playing in the bathtub. If a kid falls on his head on the sidewalk, that's different than if he's playing jumping and falling on the bed. I mean, I don't think you can say any behavior can be play without taking the context into account.

Dr. Chase: You're saying one can't use morphological characteristics alone to define play. It isn't a kind of behavior in terms of descriptive parameters.

Dr. Kirschenblatt-Gimblett: One of the things we don't really know about in all this is the nature of adult-infant or mother-infant interaction in naturalistic settings. Perhaps this is because we as adults operate so much from what we consider to be a normal, literal, instrumental mode that for us play is lamination or overlay on top of that. Therefore when Dale [Hay] talked about the kid pretending to play "bang-bang" when he obviously hadn't learned about the gun first, we made the assumption that it's an exception to what we assume to be the normal mode. Perhaps naturalistic settings, observations of mother or adult-infant interaction, might reveal that playfulness, the elaboration of means to the accomplishment of goals, is in fact the most common mode. This might account for why it is so difficult to sustain an interaction with an infant unless you play with the infant. In a sense what happens is that adults use play in a very instrumental way, and that way may be a very common feature of mother-infant interaction—bathing and feeding and sleeping and distracting and occupying and preoccupying—so that in a sense play has a very, very primary place in the interaction.

References

De Long, A. J. Kinesic signals at utterance boundaries in preschool children. *Semiotica*, 1974, 11, 43–73.

Duncan, S. Some signals and rules for taking speaking turns in conversations. *Journal of Personality and Social Psychology*, 1972, 23, 283–292.

Garvey, C. Some properties of social play. *Merrill-Palmer Quarterly*, 1974, 20, 163–180.

Hay, D. F. Following their companions as a form of exploration for human infants. *Child Development*, 1977, 48, 1624–1632.

Kaye, K. Toward the origin of dialogue. In H. R. Schaffer (Ed.) *Studies on mother-infant interactions*. New York: Academic Press, 1977.

Parten, M. Social participation among preschool children. *Journal of Abnormal and Social Psychology*, 1932, 27, 243–269.

Piaget, J. *Play, dreams and imitation in childhood*. New York: Norton, 1962.

Rheingold, H. L., Hay, D. F., & West, M. J. Sharing in the second year of life. *Child Development*, 1976, 47, 1148–1158.

Roberts, J. M., Artis, M. J., & Bush, R. R. Games in culture. *American Anthropologist*, 1959, 61, 597–605.

Ross, H. S. & Goldman, B. D. Establishing new social relations in infancy. In T. Alloway, L. Krames, & P. Pliner (Eds.) *Advances in the study of communication and affect*. Vol. 3: *Attachment behavior*. New York: Plenum, 1977a.

Ross, H. S. & Goldman, B. D. Infant sociability toward strangers. *Child Development* 1977b, 48, 638–642.

Ross, H. S., & Hay, D. F. Conflict and conflict resolution between 21-month-old peers. Paper presented at the Biennial Meeting of the Society for Research in Child Development, New Orleans, March 1977.

Sacks, H., Schegloff, E. A. & Jefferson, G. A simplest systematics for the organization of turn-taking for conversation. *Language*, 1975, 50, 696–735.

Schaffer, H. R., Collis, G. M. & Parsons, G. Vocal interchange and visual regard in verbal and pre-verbal children. In H. R. Schaffer (Ed.) *Studies in mother-infant interaction*, London: Academic Press, 1977.

Stern, D. N., Jaffe, J., Beebe, B. & Bennett, S. L. Vocalizing in unison and in alternation: two modes of communication within the mother-infant dyad. *Annals of the New York Academy of Sciences*, 1975, 263, 89–100.

Wittgenstein, L. *Philosophical investigations*. Oxford: Blackwell, 1953.

CHAPTER 7

COMMUNICATIONAL CONTROLS IN SOCIAL PLAY

Catherine Garvey

INTRODUCTION

Dr. Sutton-Smith: Dr. Garvey's paper carries forth the interest of Drs. Hay and Ross in interactional games. But now the children are a year or so older and the issue is the complexity of the way in which their social play is put together. Garvey emphasizes that children seem to demonstrate more complex behaviors in their play performances than we can readily find elsewhere in their behavior. They both play at their dramas and manage the interactions at the same time. This is the first time in the conference that attention is called explicitly to the *framing* of the play by the participants, although our earlier discussion of the differences between what is literal and what is not (in Hay and Fein) certainly related to this issue. Evidence is advanced suggesting that these discoursal aspects of speech play are highly advanced over the logical aspects.

Discussion centered on whether the plays generated by the children are largely imitative, constructive, or transforming of the life around them, and how it is children can possibly process so much information as quickly as they do to manage the games of which they are capable at age three. There was a discussion also of ritual plays and their echoic nature, in which content seems to be largely disregarded, not unlike discussions of the weather in adult discourse.

Dr. Garvey: Let me say something about the conceptual framework that I used to try to make sense of play, for myself, at least. I see play not as a particular type or types of behavior but as a mode of acting or orienting to experience. I look at it as if a child can play with the resources at his command, and these resources can be classed as: motion and sensation (tickling perhaps), object and object attributes, language, social constructs, and rules or limits. As the child's capabilities of dealing with and integrating these resources grow and expand, his play may be expected to reflect the developments in these different systems or aspects of experience. By no means do they stay simple. These various classes of resources immediately become combined in more and more elaborate ways. For those aspects of experience that we know enough about to treat as systems, such as language or social relationships, we can sometimes say that the play mode is characterized as involving transformations of relationships within that system. There are changes or discrepancies from the patterns of corresponding nonplay systems of the resource space.

PEER PLAY DYADS

The observations that I want to talk about today are based on a primary corpus of forty-eight same- and mixed-sex dyads of children, with ages ranging from two years, ten months up to five years, seven months, and another forty dyads of children of the same sex, ages three years, two months to three years, nine months. We looked only at pairs of children playing together with no adults in the room, and so we're talking about peer play now. We grouped the children into age-peer groupings within this whole corpus. We looked at a lot of aspects of the things that children did while they were in a laboratory playroom being videotaped. We looked at the way they talked and the way they played and a number of aspects of the interaction sessions. I've not addressed any questions concerning individual differences. I will have nothing to say about that. What I've been doing is trying to look for structures and processes underlying social play and social speech.

I'd like to distinguish at least two approaches to the study of play. The first is primarily descriptive, although the methodology need not be restricted to observation. The descriptive approach seeks to understand how play is possible, how it's conducted and organized and communicated. I'm most interested in *communication* as a part of the interpersonal control system. There is no question that the child must interact with a partner when he's playing, if he's playing socially, and he must control the partner as well as himself, or we can say he must control the amount of input and the rate of input that his partner contributes to the relationship, as well as exercising some kind of a monitoring system by which he controls his own amount of interest and perhaps stimulation. I'm not quite sure where the arousal notion fits in here, but if it does, and if we talk about social play, then we have to talk about how one handles the partner as a source of stimulation which must be controlled and monitored as some suitable level. A second approach to the study of play is one that treats play as an *indicator* or measure of some other nonplay capability. Here we're relying on the fact that although play seems to be rather fragile and ephemeral at times, it's a very serious phenomenon, and we rely on it all the time. I think now of the work of a number of people who are studying language who use make-believe situations to get the child to perform certain kinds of behavior, and with amazing success. So, thirdly, we really are counting on play or the ability to adopt an "as if" mode. It's a very sturdy thing. At least we are treating it as if it is. But in any case, we all assume that play can serve as an indicator of certain developing abilities and cognitive achievements that are not perhaps readily amenable to study by means of other techniques. Some things we think we can get at better by looking at them through play, rather than in other ways.

Rituals that I will talk about today—ritual play—can tell us something about turn taking and about the temporal controls of social speech, which is a very important aspect of social speech not well investigated up until now. But certainly a child must be able to handle cues to speaker exchange and inter-speaker pause relations. We could expect ritualized play, which employs strict turn alternation and controlled interspeaker pauses, to tell us something about these abilities.

What I'd like to do now is to go to an example of play, give you a handout, and play you a little bit of a recorded make-believe play session. I will then talk about it in some depth. Perhaps this will illustrate the point that I wish to make, that communication is a central part of play and the communication, of course, is very, very complex. The tape that I'll play now is an audio recording from our videotaped records. Let me say a few words about it first. This scene that you will hear between a girl of thirty-eight months and a boy of thirty-five months embodies most of the fascinating qualities of social play. We're concerned now with *how* you play, how it is done, what skills and expertise its operation reflects. Whether it's serious business or not, you can see that it's work in the sense that play is *achieved*. It's something that is actually worked out and jointly created. In this recorded example the children are very young. The boy, as you will note, is still seriously constrained by his linguistic encoding ability. He still shows traces of telegraphic speech in some utterances (utterances #2 and #10). In utterance #23, you see evidence of incomplete morphological development. On the other hand, the child shows some sophistication in producing cohesive speech; that is, he relates his speech to the utterances going before, and he does this in a number of different ways. In utterance #12 he uses sentance or clause conjunction. In utterances #14 and #25 he uses perfectly normal adult ellipsis to link his contribution to his partner's speech. We see skill in producing what we'd call elliptical discourse in adult speech in utterance #20. I suppose there that a clause corresponding to the proposition "if you will not put your head down, then I will spank you" is understood both by the child's partner and by the speaker himself. In utterance #23, "No, your teddy bear go away," a clause corresponding to "You can't have your teddy bear" plus some indeterminate conjunction such as "because he is going away" also appears to be understood and meant. Here I want to stress the fact that although the surface aspects of his speech, in terms of its morphology and its telegraphic characteristics, may be still rather immature, the discoursal aspects of the speech are in effect quite sophisticated for this age and show a good grasp of complex propositional structure that we might have some difficulty eliciting from the child by any techniques other than by listening to him play. His participation is most definitely shaped by the more linguistically and socially sophisticated girl, who is simultaneously playing the roles of director of the scenario, the prompter for the verbal script, and an actor in the scene. She is being her own (nonpretend) self in certain parts of the scene. She is undoubtedly a dramatist in Howard Gardner's best sense. Under her prompting the boy produces additional appropriate reasons for punishment. At the beginning of the episode, the girl is to be punished. Why is she to be punished? He says "Not good, you bad." "Why?" she asks, in the role of naughty baby. "Because you spill your milk." Now that is an appropriate reason for punishing a baby. The baby's bad and is being sent to sleep because it has spilled its milk. She rejects that and says, "No, because I bit somebody." And he accepts that as being an even better, or at least a perfectly acceptable, reason for sending the baby to sleep. Note, however, that even though she's more sophisticated in supplying these rationales, in utterance #11 he says, "Not good, you bad." When she says, "Why?" he is able to understand that to mean not *why am I bad?* but *why do you say I am bad?* or *what have I done that leads you to claim that I am bad?* I'm pointing out these details to reveal the extreme complexity of the interpersonal language use that you see in this little episode. This pretend episode is framed, so that there's not much question here that the individuals engaged in it are doing two highly redundantly marked kinds of things. One basis of this claim is the *way* they talk; there is their normal speech and there is make-believe, role-playing speech. So we sometimes have very clear breaks framing make-believe episodes, and if we didn't use language, I believe we'd be throwing away half the information we have that helps us to interpret what's going on.

In Table 7–1, I have checked those utterances in which the girl is talking or directing the boy in what to say next. She has some kind of scheme, it seems, as to what goes on, although I would say they collaborate in creating this. It's worth noting that at least four of her utterances are very clearly what we might call *metacommunications* about the play itself. The point that I want to make about this is that the girl's directing-acting switches are striking evidence of the early acquisition of role enactment ability. We have to keep in mind in considering this episode that there is a

TABLE 7–1*

	Girl (38 months)	Boy (35 months)
(G+B orient toward doll:		
G+B ♦ Caretaker)	√1. *Say, "Go to sleep now."*	
		2. Go sleep now/
(G ♦ Baby;	3. Why? (whining)	
Baby and Caretaker		4. Baby . . .
converse)	5. Why?	
		6. Because
	√7. *No, say "Because."*	
	(emphatically)	
		8. Because.
		(emphatically)
	9. Why? Because why?	
		10. Not good. You bad.
	11. Why?	
		12. 'Cause you spill
		your milk.
	√13. *No, 'cause I bit*	
	somebody.	
		14. Yes, you did.
	√15. *And say, "Go to sleep.*	
	Put your head down."	
	(sternly)	
		16. Put your head down.
		(sternly)
	17. No.	
		18. Yes.
	19. No.	
		20. Yes. Yes, do . . . Okay,
		I will spank you. Bad
		boy. (spanks her)
	21. My head's up.	
	(giggles)	(spanks her again)
	22. I want my teddy bear.	
	(petulant voice)	
		23. No, your teddy bear
		go away. (sternly)
	24. Why?	
		25. 'Cause he does.
		(walks off with teddy
		bear)
(G drops baby role):	26. *Are you going to pack*	
	your teddy bear?	

*Text of pretend role-play episode from a Group 1 dyad. (√ indicates meta-communication; ♦ indicates role transformation; material in parentheses indicates paralinguistic features and actions; the italicized utterances are those in which the girl speaks out of pretend play role, presumably in her real identity. Total time to end of utterance 25–90 seconds, giving an average rate of one utterance every 3.6 seconds for this pretend episode.

rapid alternation in one person's behavior which implies states of being in two different identities, that of self in directing the episode and in interacting with a willing but less capable partner, and the other identity, the adopted one of being a child and a baby. The pretend role is enacted, I think, with some verisimilitude here—for example, with whining and pestering the parent. The partner's two identities, then—pretend parent and actual playmate—are interacted with differently. The parent receives pestering demands and disobedience, and the playmate receives helpful directions as to what to say and how to say it. To emphasize this point: not only is she being two different people at the same or nearly same time, but she is treating the partner in two different ways which are appropriate to the partner's corresponding two complementary identities. I believe we will find *role-enactment* skills to be closely related to the more widely researched but still not clearly understood complex of skills often called *role-taking* abilities. Mead's theory would lead us to reason that acting the role of the other would be a contributory step to conceptualizing the other as distinct from oneself; that is, in learning others' similarities and differences to self and in learning to relate self to others. Our example indicates that role enactment is not merely a matter of reproducing vocal characteristics such as whining and saying goo-goo; it is all physical actions, such as spanking the bad baby or using other appropriate moves like taking away the child's teddy bear. Although we have all these things—vocal characteristics, physical actions, and adoption of moves and props appropriate to the other person as well as to yourself—role enactment also consists of bringing to bear on the transformed situation other-appropriate motives; that is, motives appropriate to the other person, emotional states appropriate to the other person, concerns, reactions, and certain threads of practical social reasoning. This is one of our more amusing episodes, but it is certainly not a rare episode among our forty-eight dyads. We have this type of enactment all the time. This episode is interesting, I think, because the girl exhibits a good deal of skill, and it's interesting further in that there is such a disparity between the linguistic development of the two children. And we might even say in relation to utterance #20 that the boy is having a little trouble with the proper (linguistic) sex assignment. He spanks the girl and says, "Bad boy." I don't think it's worth speculating that he is imitating what his parents have said to him. In fact, I don't think it really matters at this point except to say that she's clearly leading the situation and is clearly in advance. But what he does and what he is able to do, partly in response perhaps to her "scaffolding," is still a fairly complicated and complex achievement. So it seems to me that event is comprised of complexes of situated motives and acts and outcomes. By motives I mean things like "You're bad; you must go to bed." "I don't want to go to bed." "I'm going to tease you by repeatedly asking 'Why, why, why,' and whining, and then disobeying." These kinds of motives, acts and outcomes have perhaps been experienced and observed in and through the child's own identity. Perhaps our children have indeed been spanked. Perhaps they have bitten someone. Maybe not. I'm not at all sure. Nor would I want to go and find out. But in the pretend enactment these bits of knowledge and the way they're put together are reworked from another person's perspective; that is, from the role that each is enacting. I did mention that the episode was framed, and you noted the very sharp contrast between the child's utterances #24 and #26, one with the whining, babyish "why" and the other, the request for information, in the child's normal speaking style. Note also that the tempo of the interaction was fairly brisk. At the point of silence that you heard after utterance #21, the boy was acting; he spanked her again after she said her head was up, although he said nothing. The turn-taking mechanisms in this episode were working fairly efficiently. There are two instances of simultaneous speech, one in utterance #3 and the other in #2. But as in adult speech, simultaneous speech is resolved rather quickly and the alternating-turn pattern takes over again quite quickly.

The point I wanted to make was that successful pretend play rests on effective communication, and very heavily so. It takes cooperative efforts, and role enactment requires role taking of a fairly high order. The boy "knows" that a reason for parental punishment can be provided. That is, parents do provide some reason for punishing a child. He also knows that taking away the toy constitutes punishment to the child. Both children seem to give evidence of knowing that the play state is distinct from a nonplay orientation. The resource that we see being played with here is knowledge of parent-child relations and interaction appropriate to the relationship.

Dr. Gardner: Was this teddy bear a possession of the boy?

Dr. Garvey: It may have been before. The toys were in the room, and if the boy had been playing with the toy before, that would justify that.

Dr. Gardner: You said that the word "your" by the girl is interesting.

Dr. Garvey: That's right, but she's out of the baby role now.

Dr. Gardner: So she's now stipulating that it's his.

Dr. Lewis: I thought perhaps she got worried that he was taking her teddy bear away and wanted to terminate this pretend, since she's using the teddy bear as a security. In the context of #22—when you get spanked and you go to bed, you get your teddy bear.

Dr. Garvey: Yes, she knows that.

Dr. Lewis: Now all of a sudden he's taking that thing away, and it sounded almost as if she was getting disturbed.

Dr. Garvey: From study of the tape and the videotape, I'd say this was a quite unconcerned request for information. He's walking off and maybe terminating the play episode. I don't think she's personally concerned about losing the teddy bear.

Dr. McCall: Isn't it the case that the teddy bear is part of the props of the room and he who possesses it has nine-tenths of it, or something like that? It's hers when she wants it in the play context, but when he's moving off with it he's possessing it. It's therefore his. By the way, for whatever it's worth, I did not hear the bit about "bite" in #13. I heard her say, "because I spanked somebody." The dialogue makes more sense if that is in fact what she said.

Dr. Chase: Is parent-child play stylized?

Dr. Garvey: In the whole episode?

Dr. Chase: Yes.

Dr. Garvey: In the dyad's thirteen-minute session they did a good deal of parent-child playing. She wanted very much to play mother, and he didn't really want to, but in this episode she has captured him. She may not have her preferred role but he has joined her in a parent-child enactment.

Dr. Lewis: To what extent does this theme of the punishment recur and under what conditions? Is that recurrent in the episode?

Dr. Garvey: No. We have another dyad that did spank the toy bear. The toy bear was a child and he had hit his father, and the mother and the father spanked him. But we have very little of that actually.

Dr. Lewis: If in fact what happens to the child when it transgresses is that it gets spanked and put to bed and it gets its teddy bear, then this is the acting, the playing that is made up. Do we want to distinguish between that and the child who makes up a consequence which in fact does not normally happen? That is, in some sense it's not happening so it is symbolic and a display. Yet when it does happen that's the way it happens. It strikes me as being different from the case where in fact what happens is not normally what happens.

Dr. Garvey: I think if we engineered our play sessions by limiting the props, etc., we could get more comparable observations. The children did tend to play the same kinds of things, but they played a lot of different things as well, so I don't have enough observations of this.

Dr. Lewis: If this child made up being spanked and put to bed with a teddy bear, and that didn't happen to this girl when she transgressed, would that kind of play be different from what happens when all she does is to set up a situation and then repeat everything that normally happens?

Dr. Garvey: That's also hard to answer. You need an awful lot of data from the same children, I think. That's just not the focus we had, but you're right; it would be an interesting question. It might speak to creativity in play, but I can't answer that from our data. A virtually complete account of a child's daily life would be necessary to answer that question satisfactorily.

Dr. Fein: When you watch children over time, in a child care program, for example, you can see a lot of that kind of thing happening. I'm thinking of one incident that we observed where two children were playing babies and a third child was a mother who was very nurturing, warm, and comforting. She got bored, left, and a new mother came in, and this one was a very harsh, spanking, punitive, restrictive mother. Now the two babies were the same. What was marvelous was that they reorganized themselves together to account for each mother. It would be lovely if we could find a way of balancing all those possibilities, but it's very impressive how, given the willingness and the spirit of the play situation, these refocusings can happen fairly easily.

Dr. Schwartzman: If you study a group of kids over a long period of time, so that you have some idea of their history of relationships with one another in and out of play, I think you see a different dimension. Even where it's still true that kids are using the mother-child interaction, they're using it to comment on their own relationship with each other, with their peers. You can't get this if you study kids that have never interacted with one another.

Dr. Garvey: That's right; or even on a short-term basis like this where we see them together for just fifteen minutes.

Dr. Lewis: I really would like an answer as to whether they replicate or transform behavior in play.

Dr. Gardner: I have two answers which are contradictory. The first one is that by and large children and everybody else repeat in their play or their imagination what they already do. They don't really invent. Even novelists don't really invent. I think it's just a quantitative thing; over time one can extend the prototypical so that it's somewhat less prototypical. What we see here is a very prototypical kind of exchange. If the kids played a lot there'd be some loosening of the edges, but basically I don't think anyone invents. If they do it's James Joyce, certainly not a three- or four-year-old. On the other hand, there is something very funny that I think goes on, and I don't really understand it but I've seen it enough to be intrigued by it. That is, the child will play the role of the teacher. That's a very common thing. It's done by three- and four-year-olds all the time, and it makes no difference that the child may be in the nicest day care center or nursery school where the teachers are, from our point of view, warm and supportive. Still, the way the teacher is played is like a classical schoolmarm that we've had or that we've seen in movies—always strict: You do this, you do that. If you were a Jungian, you'd say it was an archetype. I don't think it's an archetype. What I'm not sure, though, is whether in a certain sense the child isn't also very surprised that the teacher acted in that schoolmarmish way. The only way the child has of illustrating behavior which is different from its own is to take the opposite kind, just because a person in a position of authority is somewhat more directive. There's no modulation. There's an exaggeration which is contrary to the child's experience.

Dr. Lewis: It seems to me there are two dimensions there, and that one might have more to do with coming to understand the experience they had and the other more to do with creating new experiences—I mean, it may serve a different function for what is a symbolic kind of activity. Either all you do is to keep as close as possible to the original score or you do something quite different when you vary that score.

Dr. Kirschenblatt-Gimblett: A difference is suggested between imitation and reconstruction. I think Michael's [Dr. Lewis] point then asks us to make yet another distinction that involves a permutation transformation, which would take us one step further. In that case we would have three kinds of play: (a) imitative, in the sense of some very mechanical reproduction—a very mechanical and unimaginative model of what's going on; and (b) reconstruction, which is what Kate [Dr. Garvey] has been suggesting is happening; and then, if you like, (c) transformation or permutation, which is perhaps what Howard's [Dr. Gardner] example of the schoolmarm involves.

Dr. Ellis: This is totally alien to me and I'm fascinated by it. I would like, as a stranger to it, to ask whether even you, with your sophistication, are working at a level of too great a simplicity relative to what's really going on, because it seems to me that there are multiple roles here. Just see if this works for you: each of the protagonists here is him- or herself; each is also a baby or a caretaker; and in addition, the prototypical parents or caretakers. There are a very large number of roles that are woven together in all this. Let's ignore the details. There's three of each, and each one recognizes the other person as three; but also the other person has to have something of the three for the person, so there are twelve of them, let's say. In addition to that, the average length of an interaction (verbal exchange) is 3.6 seconds, which discounts the fact that some of the work, some of the play, has also to be encoded and uttered, which takes a lot of time. So what we're seeing here is an absolutely bewilderingly complicated and high-speed interaction. I've never seen it quite so graphically presented. If that is so, we must stop all the rest of the conference and work on this interaction. What I'd really like to ask is a sort of metaquestion: are all those observations apparent to you guys as well as to me, or have I just sort of disappeared into a path of complexity?

Dr. Garvey: You mean the number of roles that are going on here?

Dr. Ellis: Yes, and the speed.

Dr. Gardner: I'd like to respond a bit to the question Mike Ellis raised. I think you're right, but I think one should pose some possible caveats. The first is that while all these awarenesses are present in a certain sense, they're not present at the same time. I would think that the child is a package of schemes, and while these schemes can be aroused by the environment, which in this case would be the other child, I'm not at all sure how coherent they are. I think one has to be aware of our own wittedness in making sense of this. The second thing is that maybe you can program a computer to do this quite easily. If you simply put in a couple of programs you account for most of the boy's utterances—when he says "why," you say "'cause," and if there's another "why," say "'cause" and add a sentence. I don't think that this mechanistic thing is going on, but I put that on the table lest you attribute the same degree of sophistication about this utterance to the child that you are worried about.

Dr. Ellis: So you can establish two limits. One would be a simple algorithm for producing this and the other is mine, which is just bewildering to me. It's enormously complex, too complex. And it may be that the participants in this have some of these things arranged in hierarchies. I don't know whether that's the appropriate use of the word, but they chuck out whole parts of this as a result of prior experience. So it's somewhere between.

Dr. Garvey: I think Dr. Gardner's point is a very good one. We can become simply swamped by the complexity of all this, but a great deal of it could be computerized. Matilda Holtzman (1971) has worked out a computer program for producing normal elliptical speech under certain restrictive conditions. So could some of the types of exchanges be produced—reproduced, possibly—with a program?

Dr. Lewis: I think the difference is repeating, for example, something that you know; that is, there's a subroutine, which is that you get spanked and you go to bed with your teddy bear. And again it speaks to just the representing rather than the elaboration. But this could occur even with adult behavior. The fact is that whatever we do is done in an incredibly fast time, and that's a problem to any information kinds of theories. The rate at which we talk and understand and comprehend and then respond is bewildering when we think of the exchange time as just getting the information to your head and back out through your mouth. So the question is that there seems to be a shared meaning which you don't have to come to understand; you have to come to locate it, which is much faster. You say something which you share and the other person knows what you mean; you don't have to reconstruct it.

Dr. Ellis: It's like both laughing at joke 88.

Dr. Lewis: That's right. And that would then allow something less mechanistic, and yet you would still have a subroutine to call upon which gives you very fast access to knowing.

Dr. J. Singer: I can give you a personal anecdote of playing a game like this, although I was much older. I was ten years old, and I had a cousin, a girl, who was fourteen. She got me involved in a game that was very similar to this, except it was more romantic. It was essentially two lovers, though there were also some other girls around. It was a group game— sociodramatic play—and it became fairly complicated because eventually it involved a girl having a baby, after having gone through the tunnel of love, and the idea was for this all to be written down. Since I was the best writer of the group, although younger, I was going to write this for *True Story Magazine*. It all went along very well, except that I created great embarrassment for myself when I went in in front of the entire family assembled at dinner and said, "I can't figure how to write this story exactly because she's supposed to have a baby and we're not even married yet." So that at a key level there was a fundamental part of the whole story that I didn't understand, even though I was going through all the motions of the enactment and actually writing it down. So you can have a whole set of schema which are worked out and fairly differentiated and whole other areas that are gaps. We can't tell how much is a gap or a void in this case. He's playing along remarkably well, it seems, and yet we don't know how much he's missing that she's comprehending, that she's already practicing.

Dr. Lewis: Well, you get an idea when he offers a reason: spilling the milk. She doesn't like that one. That apparently doesn't fit into the story.

Dr. Garvey: But his reason is credible.

Dr. Lewis: That's right. You wonder why she rejects it.

Dr. Garvey: It's not wicked enough.

Dr. Lewis: I would bet that she bites. And many a night she's been sent to bed with her teddy bear for biting. There's that subroutine.

Dr. Garvey: I'll never find out.

Dr. Lewis: Oh, come on!

Dr. McCall: I think we're also missing here the raw physical stimuli. The sight of the teddy bear may well have keyed off the statement, and not indeed a memory of what happens at home. As she puts her head up, that's a stimulus for another schema. I think that while you are correct in seeing many different roles, and while I too am amazed at how they can shift, actually, in terms of the step by step interaction they are not contemplating twelve roles simultaneously. They only go from one to another, back and forth, and those are actually in their sequence, if you link stimulus and response. Considered in sequence, the total package is not nearly so complex as it appears.

Dr. Kirschenblatt-Gimblett: There is some evidence to suggest that some of the paralinguistic and social-interactional skills can be more developed than the cognitive skills. For example, in riddling, kids can often figure out that you have to ask a question that someone else can't answer, but they can't actually formulate it properly as a riddle, so they'll ask you this bizarre question, give you a bizarre answer, and while it would not be a riddle in the true sense of the term they'll have the information right. I mean preriddles. John McDowell's work, for example, demonstrates this beautifully. He shows that if you analyze the intonational pattern, they've got the right riddle intonation in terms of stress and pitch of voice, which means that you don't give it away by emphasizing anything. They've got that down pat. They've got the interaction together and they've got the bizarreness of the answer, but they've got no connection between answer and question. So those kinds of internal and cognitive features may take a while in coming, whereas some of the interactional and paralinguistic features may be very well under control.

VERBAL RITUALS

Dr. Garvey: There's a different kind of play which I call *verbal rituals.* Actually you can ritualize anything, but these happen to be ritualized verbal exchanges. These, however, are of different levels of complexity. The first thing that's ritualized seems to be "Hi, bubba; hi mommy," ritualizing a greeting kind of exchange. And the second one, "You are too; no I'm not," is ritualizing an assertion-counter assertion. These exchanges make sense in terms of taking the resources you've got and then playing with them, but the ritual is a particular kind of play that shows an amazing amount of both self- and perhaps other-control in terms of timing and interactive behavior. The reason we've analyzed this type of ritualized verbal play is that it shows an extreme degree of interpersonal- and self-control on a parameter of speech which is a natural and necessary one; that is, the timing of speech and silence. The other reason I'm measuring it is that in another study we found that interspeaker pause duration in the conversations of the children seems, so far as we can see, to be somewhat longer than the interspeaker pause duration that adults use, as reported by Jaffe and Feldstein (1970). Over an entire adult conversation, interspeaker pause for adults averaged .66 seconds in their study. You see that the average values are considerably longer for children. That might lead you to conclude that children take longer to answer and to raise the question of why that would be. Perhaps we might predict that among the classes of those determinants would be complexity and predictability of encoding and decoding. I think there are some very interesting phenomena here which we are just beginning to study. This type of performance, I think, has considerable relevance to the question of interpersonal control. If what you have to say is not complex, and is very predictable, you can attend to the rhythmicity of the turn taking. Not only is the duration of utterance and interspeaker pause mirrored back and forth, but it seems that both pitch and intensity are also mirrored. Those dimensions are harder to analyze and measure. It certainly isn't a simple matter of the number of syllables determining how long it takes to say a phrase; of that we're fairly sure. Let me stop there. This was just a point to be made about the degree of interpersonal control that children can exercise in playing with a very simple resource—language— much simpler than the cognitively and conceptually more interesting matter of pretend enactment. But the rituals show a great precision of control in terms of timing.

Dr. J. Singer: The children almost echo each other, don't they?

Dr. Garvey: I think they do. A sound spectograph analysis shows this. It's rather difficult to do a lot of them, but we have made a few. Yes; pitch configurations and intensity are echoed.

Dr. Schwartzman: Do you have any information on what sorts of things precede this kind of ritual?

Dr. Garvey: No single thing, certainly. Rituals can fall out of almost anything. I can't see any determinants of when you fall into a ritual and when you don't. These long, repetitive rituals are more characteristic of our younger children, and as the children get older the rituals tend to become more complicated and shorter, perhaps because they're more complicated. Action patterns can be ritualized too, but these examples are primarily verbal. In the two rituals of Table 7-2 there's not even direct gaze, which I think is amazing. You'd think they would use gaze to help cue onto the timing, but apparently that is not necessary.

Dr. Ellis: I reckon that it makes it even more complicated than that because now we have the whole thing operating at two levels.

Dr. McCall: I don't think that you have to postulate that the child understands that complete cognition; only that he is exploring the response-contingent attributes to this situation. One could argue that it makes it simpler if this child does something—any damn thing—in response. I find a lot of what irritates parents about a two- and a two-and-a-half-year-old are instances in which the child really doesn't care that you get mad, just so you do something. You know—"I want corn flakes this morning." "Good." So you pour out the corn flakes, pour in the milk. "I don't want corn flakes this morning." The child doesn't care if it's corn flakes or potato salad. He wants to get a response out of you. It's the same thing in simple language. A child will sit at a table and say, "Cup, mommy, cup." Now if mommy's at the stove with her back turned, it turns out that an auditory response from mother doesn't seem to be effective, as she stands there busy with the cooking. She says, "Yes, that's a cup." "Cup, mommy, cup," and the child keeps on saying it until the adult turns around and says, "Yes, that's a

TABLE 7–2
Ritual Verbal Play Episodes

	Utterance Duration	Pause Duration	Utterance Duration	
I. B (43 months)				G (43 months)
			1.6	1. I say "Hi, Susie."
		1.7		
2. Hi, Bubba,	1.1			
		1.5		
			1.0	3. Hi, Mommy.
		.6		
4. Hi, Bubba.	1.1			
		.7		
			1.0	5. Hi, Mommy.
		.2		
6. Hi, Bubba.	1.1			
		.5		
			.9	7. Hi, Mommy.
		.3		
8. Hi, Bubba.	.9			
		.6		
			.8	9. Hi, Mommy.
		.7		
10. Hi, Bubba.	.9			
		.8		
			2.2	11. I'm not saying that anymore.
II. G (42 months)				B (43 months)
			1.2	1. I'm not.
		.6		
2. You are too.	.9			
		.6		
			.9	3. No, I'm not.
		.6		
4. You are too.	.5			
		.6		
			.5	5. No, I'm not.
		.7		
6. You are too.	.5			
		.6		
			.5	7. No, I'm not.
		.5		
8. You are too.	.5			
		.5		
			.5	9. No, I'm not.
		.5		
10. Yes, you are too.	.5			
		.6		
			.6	11. No, I'm not.
		.6		
12. Yes, you are too.	.7			
		.7		
			.7	13. No, I'm not.

cup." The cup is irrelevant. The child already knows the label. It's the social-influencing technique. I see the motivation for much of speech, for early peer-peer interactions and parent-child interaction, revolving less around the content of the enterprise and more around the contingent-response games and exploration. I see imaginary play as possibly being a fantasized exploration of social contingencies— *What will this other person do? What happens when they do this?*—without risk.

Question: The series of "why" questions that you get at three and early four would probably be related to that: "Why this, why that," where sometimes the kid really does not know the answer, but a lot of times it's just exploring the possibilities of the "why" question. It's a new concept—"why."

Dr. Lewis: Therefore the content does make a difference, whether you're repeating known subroutines or in fact changing them. That would be a way to separate those out from what you're saying, which I would agree with, whether indeed you're trying to do something different from just engaging in a social behavior.

Dr. McCall: Often the content is not the most important thing.

Dr. Garvey: I don't think you can say it's either/or. I think it's both.

Dr. McCall: Certainly it becomes admixed. But I think that a lot of what the child is requesting, such as in the corn flakes example, is irrelevant to the purpose of the interaction. I recall one episode with my own son, where "you don't touch the TV" was the rule. The child knew the rule perfectly well—went up to touch the TV. But he didn't go up because he was interested in the TV. He went up reaching for the TV with his hand, but looking back at me. He knew what was going to happen. He was just going to see what Dad's going to do here and what's going to happen. Very often you get children who are spanked as a form of punishment who, in the face of an imminent spanking, will say "spank me." I speculate that the reason they do that is because the punishing attribute of spanking is the loss of control of the other person; and saying "spank me," or the child directing any other punishment, is a regaining by the child of the control of the situation.

Dr. Kirschenblatt-Gimblett: I just have to comment that much of what we've been looking at by way of these routines and rituals suggests that a good deal of the interaction isn't an end in itself, and that that's not peculiar to children. I think we overestimate the instrumentality of adult behavior, and that in fact much of what adults do when they interact is for the sake of interaction, and that it's perhaps more prevalent and more obvious among children, but by no means unique to them.

Dr. Garvey: Erving Goffman has been telling us this for years and years.

Dr. Kirschenblatt-Gimblett: Right.

Dr. J. Singer: There's a whole set of ritualized expressions. You get into an elevator with someone and you say, "Hot enough for you?" or something like that. You really don't care if it is hot enough for them or not. There's just a level of light conversation that tides over an uncomfortable moment or a pause or a confrontation with strangers.

References

Bates, E. *Language and context: The acquisition of pragmatics.* New York: Academic Press, 1977.

Garvey, C. Some properties of social play. *Merrill-Palmer Quarterly,* 1974, *20,* 163–180 (a reference for published work on the ritualized verbal play).

Grimm, H. Analysis of short-term dialogues in five- to seven-year-olds: Encoding of intentions and modifications of speech acts as a function of negative feedback loops. Paper presented to the Third International Child Language Symposium, London, September 1975.

Gleitman, L., Gleitman, H., and Shipley, E. The emergence of the child as grammarian. *Cognition,* 1972, *1,* 137–164.

Holtzman, M. Ellipsis in discourse: Implications for linguistic analysis by computer, the child's acquisition of language, and semantic theory. *Language and Speech,* 1971, *14,* 86–98.

Jaffe, J. and Feldstein, S. *Rhythms of dialogue.* New York: Academic Press, 1970.

CHAPTER 8

EXPLORING EARLY SYMBOLIZATION: STYLES OF ACHIEVEMENT*

Jennifer M. Shotwell, Dennie Wolf, and Howard Gardner

INTRODUCTION

Dr. Sutton-Smith: Dr. Gardner will discuss the topic of individual differences, an issue little touched upon in this conference, where most of the approaches have been from a developmental point of view with the expectancy of successive stages, and so on. He asks whether play symbolization is the same for all children or whether there may be different pathways for different children. He will also raise the question of whether each symbolic medium (play, graphics, etc.) may have its own particular pathways. Like Garvey, he has found play the most suitable medium to study children's behavior in these early years. Between one and two years it was difficult to study symbolic behavior except through play. He presents a typology of children as either dramatists, patterners, or mixed types. The behavior of the dramatists was not unlike that of the players labelled by others as imaginative (Singer, Hutt). There may be some parallel also between dramatists and nonprototypic responding (Fein), stimulus generating (Ellis), or functional conceptualizing (Collard), although

*This paper was prepared for presentation at the Symposium on "Fundamentals of Symbolism," Burg Wartenstein, Austria, July 16–24, 1977. The research described herein has been supported by the Spencer Foundation. We thank Shelley Rubin, Ann Smith, and Pat McKernon for their help with all phases of the study, and Jen Silverman for her illustrations. The author and coauthors are located at Harvard Project Zero and the Boston Veterans Administration Hospital.

these latter concepts were developmental rather than typological ones. Gardner also maintained that what Lewis had to say about the mother-infant determination of play behavior would have more relevance to his dramatist type than to all children. Patterners, on the contrary, are more likely to show a solitary concern with objects. This argument is strengthened by the finding of parallels between parental and child symbolic behaviors.

In the discussion there is also argument over whether the experimenters themselves may tend to favor one rather than another symbolic style, and may in consequence be getting more information from children who are geared to interpersonal rather than solitary or object-related behaviors. In short, the experimenters might be modelling some of the behavior they were seeking to elicit. The enthusiasm of the discussion suggests that the limited size of the N was a trigger to speculation.

In this chapter we are departing from the usual mode insofar as Dr. Gardner has chosen to replace his own oral presentation at the conference with the paper on which it was based, a paper coauthored with his colleagues, Jennifer M. Shotwell and Dennie Wolf. We first present the paper and then proceed with the conference discussion.

Dr. Gardner: Scholars from various disciplines consider the use of symbols as a hallmark—perhaps *the* hallmark—of human cognition. Moreover, those researchers concerned with the foundations of symbolization generally locate its origins in the first years of life: the acquisition of proficiency in symbolization is often seen as the central challenge of the first half-decade of life. By the time children are five, six or seven, they are already quite skilled with several symbol systems (language, visual arts, movement/gesture) and usually have at least an initial facility at handling such realms as number, music and film.

While the above characterization is not controversial, very little is known definitively about the early course of this critical human ability. And while few scholars have assumed that the development of symbolic capacities is a simple process, much investigation has tended to either lump all symbolic systems together, or to carefully study one, while ignoring its relation (or lack of relation) to other symbolic systems. As a result, at least four crucial questions about early symbolization remain to be confronted:

1) Is early symbolization "of a piece," such that skill with one symbol system implies, or correlates highly with, other symbolic skills?

2) To what extent are the facts of early symbolization determined by genetic (biological) considerations, cultural factors, models provided by parents or peers, or some combination of these forces?

3) Does mastery within each symbol system follow an ordinal scale—

that is, do all children pass through the same set of stages in the same order (as apparently occurs in those cognitive domains studied by Piaget)?

4) Is the course of symbolization similar across children, or are there instructive individual routes to symbolic mastery?

To secure answers to this set of questions, a group of researchers at Harvard Project Zero has, for the last several years, been examining the early course of symbolization. A chief source of information has been a longitudinal study of a small group of first-born middle-class children. These youngsters have been observed on a weekly basis since age one as they have developed toward symbolic competence in seven different areas: language (particularly story-telling), symbolic play, two-dimensional depiction, three-dimensional construction, movement, music, and understanding of number. The study is still very much in progress (we are in the third year of what we hope will be a long-term study); the sample is small (to the original sample of five children we have recently added four subjects); and data analysis has been largely informal (we are just now preparing our first computer run).

Nonetheless, although answers to the questions raised above must be made tentatively, a progress report on certain findings may help to crystallize the issues under discussion. As a result of such an interim summary, individuals with a different slant toward early symbolization can evaluate our efforts, indicating which impressions may be parochial and which more far-reaching, and may themselves help to secure crucial cross-cultural data which will place our findings in proper perspective.

It is admittedly difficult to assess findings without some familiarity with the methods used to procure them. However, for the purposes of this conference it seems preferable to take the liberty of foregoing the specifics of methodology and to devote our efforts instead towards rendering a detailed description of certain findings.

In what follows we shall describe the early course of symbolization in two of the symbolic media under study: symbolic play and three-dimensional construction. It should be noted first, however, that young children's play is, initially at least, hardly differentiated by "media" concerns. As researchers, we have had, in a sense, to define boundaries somewhat artificial to children's everyday play. For our purposes, symbolic play has been formulated as the ability to represent actual or imagined experience through the combined use of small objects, motions, and language; the medium of three-dimensional construction has been conceived as entailing the meaningful articulation of spatial relationships, especially as exemplified in the subjects' activities in block play and clay modeling. Thus both media are grounded in a child's everyday experience of object handling, but between them they encompass a wide range of how this experience is explored—a considerable range of symbolic systems.

A large part of the story of early symbolization involves tracing the growth of increased competence with symbolic systems. Accordingly we will, with regard to symbolic play and three-dimensional construction, present three levels of competence which can be readily discerned in our population. Yet one of our chief discoveries has been that not all children realize symbolic milestones in the same way. Indeed, to the extent that one can generalize about so small a population, there appear to be at least two discrete paths to (or styles of) early symbol mastery. One group of children (hereafter called *patterners*) shows a strong interest and skill in configurational uses of materials—an interest apparently rooted in a persistent curiosity about the object world around them, how it works, how it can be named, varied or explored. Such children are typically more interested in design and mechanical possibilities of materials than in their uses for communication or for the recreation of personal experience. For instance, given a set of variously shaped blocks, patterners tend to be interested foremost in exploring problems of symmetry, pattern, balance, or the dynamics of physical relationships between the blocks, and might well create a design by matching a number of small blocks to a larger one.

In contrast, the other group of children (hereafter called *dramatists*) exhibits an interest in sequences of interpersonal events, ones having dramatic or narrational structures. Beginning from a strong interest in the world of persons and feelings, such children consistently seek to embed objects within interpersonal exchanges or to exploit their semantic properties in the service of the sharing of experience and effective communication with others. For instance, given the same set of various shaped blocks, a dramatist is likely to call a large one "the mommy," a small one "the baby," and have them re-enact a shopping trip.

As we have come to know these styles better, we have become convinced that they go beyond "media preferences," "verbal vs. visual inclinations," or "person- vs. object-centeredness"—though each of these entrenched characterizations bears some truth. Rather, they seem to represent fundamentally different, but equally valid, routes toward general symbolic competence—routes originating both in children's overall personalities and in their underlying mental structures. The depth and complexity of the style issue, however, is best conveyed through rich example. Consequently we turn now to the central tasks of our paper: first, as a background to our own findings, a brief sketch at three early ages of general cognitive and media milestones; next, a summary of the principal steps entailed in the development of skills in the two relevant media; and then, a fuller discussion of how the acquisition of such media-specific accomplishments (shared across children) may be effected quite differently by patterners and dramatists.

EARLY COGNITIVE DEVELOPMENT ACROSS MEDIA:
SHARED ACHIEVEMENTS

Any investigation of styles of early symbolization should take into account two bodies of data. There is, first of all, the general trajectory of cognitive development, which has been set forth over the past few decades by Piaget and his followers. Second, and of equal importance, are those capacities and constraints which color the ways in which children will utilize any medium or symbol system. In Table 8-1, drawing both on

Table 8–1:
General Early Achievements

Approximate Age in Mos.	Cognitive Milestones	Achievements Across Media
12–14	Stage 5 of Sensorimotor Intelligence: —action schemes no longer tied to immediate objects and persons; become independent of "here and now"; —advent of walking and single-word utterances.	Formulation of Units of Action: —basic vocabularies of schemes associated with different media (e.g., in drawing: marking arcs, dots, continuous scrawls); —media separated from other fields of action (e.g., originally marking activity was a blend of motor, visual, and, often, sound effects) and define fields of interaction between self and others.
24	Stage 6 of Sensorimotor Intelligence: —capacity for internal representations of past experience; —ability to make organized searches for hidden objects, perform deferred imitations; —two-word utterances.	Ability to Combine Units of Action into Meaningful Sequences: representational possibilities exploited in language and symbolic play (e.g., two-word utterances allow formulation of simple semantic relations). Organization of Units Increasingly Finely Articulated: sensitivity to dimensions of judgment, classification, range of similarity relations. Renaming and Romancing: flexibility of signifier-signified relationship explored as children frequently give another appropriate name to a familiar object (e.g., a shoe held by its laces is an "airplane") or donate elaborate meanings to unarticulated products.
30–36	Preoperational Stage: —semiotic function acquired; remains primarily egocentric, limited in terms of inventive flexibility; —simple sentences.	Hierarchical Organization of Information Sequences: coherence within a more integrated structure of units previously chained together by relatively simple relations (e.g., now can build arches, supply tuneful renditions of familiar songs). Representational Possibilities Realized in Two- and Three-Dimensional Media: interest in and ability to use common social dimensions, categories (e.g., number, shape, size and color). Extended Recall and Elaborated Media Vocabularies: acquisition of a variety of less conservative forms within which to explore notions of self and other. Effort to Make Explicit the Processes of Representation: for example, directing adults on how to draw a face or to be a frog.

the accumulated wisdom of developmental psychology, and on our own sources of data, we have summarized these background factors at each of the three ages to be treated here: 12–14 months, 24 months, and 30–36 months of age. Taken together, these various indices of development suggest certain broad understandings which children have developed across various media.

Even as certain broad patterns characterize the cognitive development of every normal child, so, too, a set of basic medium skills has been found in each of the children that we are studying. These common skills provide a preliminary answer to one of the questions guiding our inquiry: it appears that progress in the media under consideration does indeed follow an ordinal scale, with any child who gains competence in symbolic play, or in three-dimensional play, passing through the same set of milestones in the same order (though, we should add, at widely varying speeds). In Tables 8-2 and 8-3 we have summarized the fundamental achievements negotiated by each of the children in the study, arrayed once again in accordance with the three age levels. In the case of three-dimensional construction (Table 8-2) we have examined milestones in both clay and block materials; in the arena of symbolic play (Table 8-3) we have described the child's achievements in replaying (the capacity to re-enact pieces of experience) and in object substitution (the capacity to treat one object as if it were another).

PATTERNERS AND DRAMATISTS: STYLES OF ACHIEVING MILESTONES

Although the milestones outlined in the above tables were negotiated by all the subjects in our longitudinal study, we observed considerable variation in how each child came to understand these matters. To the extent that children do achieve symbolic competence in a medium via somewhat diverse routes and varying time schemes, the identification of major steps in medium development (as only briefly sketched in the preceding tables) has been instrumental in separating out critical individual differences among children—differences which may coalesce in stable constellations of traits persisting over time and across wide variations in format and materials. By conceiving of these sets of frequently associated characteristics as *styles* of symbol use, we suggest that they entail coherent manners of working, of selecting information, capturing it in forms, and organizing it into a coherent message. As such, differences in style between children may signal markedly different routes toward achieving the same fundamental steps in ordinal scale development.

Table 8–2:
Three-Dimensional Achievements

Approximate Age in Mos.	Block Material	Clay Material
12–14	Stacking: —extension of interest in specific locales ("here-there," "on-off," "in-out"); —a refinement of a "dropping" motor scheme into directed placements; —this stacking scheme transferred across a variety of appropriate materials (e.g., blocks, cans, etc.). Semiotic Function: —not provided by spatial location; —occasional use of ritualistic play schemes suggestive of attempts to donate meaning to forms (e.g., pushing two blocks along the floor with "vroom" sound effects as if a car).	Product Awareness: —more attentive handling through a wider set of manipulatory techniques (e.g., squeezing, patting to flatten, attempting to roll coils, poking deep holes, tearing of huge wads); —crude attempts made to repair broken clay models (e.g., pressing a broken circular coil back together again).
24	Constructions now combine vertical, horizontal axes. Significance attached to visual aspects of certain forms, arrays: —e.g., repeated building of ritualistic "house" forms; interest in symmetry within one plane. Semiotic Function: —meanings rendered primarily through ritualistic forms, or through linguistic techniques rather than through use of three-dimensional grammer; —initial emergence of spatial location as significant for meaning (e.g., poking holes in upper half of wad as "eyes").	Initial Specificity of Depictive Placement/Shape in Displays modeled by others: —e.g., naming a line of small upright cones as "seals." Shaping Techniques Explored with More Control: —some assembly of premade forms; —usually inappropriate adding on to a model (e.g., adding a wad as "nose" onto the nose of a clay face).
30–36	Construction along vertical, horizontal, sagittal planes. Ability to build arches: —e.g., —little production of solid structures with blocks. Semiotic Function: —meaning modulated by three-dimensional grammar (e.g., meaning contributed primarily by spatial location, not language); —growing differentiation and specificity of spatial relations provides basis for assignment of significance to certain spatial relations (be it in terms of order, design, or depiction); —symbolic play crucial in fleshing out referential potential: it donates meaning and provides a vehicle for replicating large-space experience on smaller scale (e.g., child builds an arch and drives a car through it; or child carefully forms a clay circle, says "donut" and pretends to eat it).	Elementary Shaping: —simple modulation of meaning through shaping, but primarily at level of meaningful assembly of premade forms.

Table 8–3:
Symbolic Play Achievements

Approximate Age in Mos.	
12–14	Replaying: —exploration of relation between self and other through imitation and replaying rudimentary abrreviations of familiar events (e.g., feeding games; hello/good-bye). Object substitution: —substitution of one generally similar object for another (e.g., a spoon for a phone receiver; a concave round block for a cup). Replicas: —initial understanding that small toys can be used as, or made to act like corresponding objects in the real world (e.g., can pretend to feed a doll).
24	Replaying: acquisition of simple signifier-signified relationship; —combination of fragments of events into a sequence of familiar daily events which can be replayed; —simple stereotypic roles (e.g., kitten, caretaker) can be played as role-switching becomes increasingly available. Object substitution: —ability to freely transform numerous objects into items needed for play; —use of renaming to capture perceived significant similarities between objects (e.g., the top of a salt cellar is called "phone" because of its shape and pattern of small holes).
30–36	Emergence of Inventive Fantasy Play Replaying: scenes cohere through a dynamic of *event* rather than pure sequential or additive recall; —mood, character, less stereotyped emotions portrayed in more dramatically detailed role play. Object substitution: adept at animating numerous toy figures, regarding them as person-like; ability to imagine and act upon make-believe objects (e.g., pretends to see a fly, swat it, carry it to trash, wash hands).

The different styles of approach—those of the dramatist and the patterner—can be discerned quite early (even before the vocabularies of specific medium use have been defined) in the type of relational play with objects favored by certain children. Dramatists' play with small objects often includes other people (e.g., dropping objects into an adult's hand), while patterners are, from the start, fascinated with relations between two objects (e.g., repeatedly putting a ball in and out of a cup). As children reach twelve to fourteen months of age, differences in stylistic preference emerge more clearly, particularly as the areas of three-dimensional construction and symbolic play begin to take shape as media "fields" for action and re-enactment. In the following discussion, using examples drawn primarily from two young girls, Julie and Anita, we will examine how mastery of these two media is modulated by the patterner/dramatist distinction.

12–14 Months: Emergence of Styles in Three-Dimensional Construction and Symbolic Play

Some of the earliest three-dimensional materials to be used by children are blocks and clay. Children learn to make conventional stacks of blocks at approximately the same age and yet have not acquired enough control and flexibility of the three-dimensional medium to introduce much variation into the stacking activity itself; as a consequence, one clue concerning early individual differences is in those activities which prove sufficiently interesting to *divert* the child away from independent conventional uses of the materials (i.e., stacking). We found that dramatists tend to exploit the occasion of block stacking as a turn-taking game (e.g., after the adult adds a block, Julie adds a block, then the adult, then Julie, etc.), or to donate meanings to blocks through symbolic play, without troubling to effect appropriate spatial locations or combinations. For example, Julie, in response to a request to build a train, pushes a block around like a train instead. Patterners, on the other hand, when diverted from such conventional uses of three-dimensional materials as stacking, tend to get caught up in examining or organizing attributes of the small objects. For example, rather than build a tower as requested, Anita carefully selects all the coin-shaped blocks from the assortment and shows them to her mother. Or, at another point, she picks up each block, one at a time, examining each with great deliberateness, and then mouths and drops each; she makes no effort to combine them.

Differences among children regarding the assiduous attention paid to the physical aspects of the materials also seem to have some early implications regarding sophistication of clay modeling. Those children whom we have classified as patterners display persistent interest in exploring a range of effective techniques with clay (e.g., pressing, pulling small pieces off, squeezing, poking, crude rolling attempts, attempting to rejoin pieces). Dramatists, on the other hand, tend to become engaged with clay at a more superficial level (e.g., primarily employing techniques immediately modeled, or simpler techniques such as pulling apart, eating, throwing, or placing in and out of a container).

Emergent individual differences prove even more salient in the realm of symbolic play. This is in part due to the tremendous flexibility as to *means* which can be employed (children can utilize movement, language, or spatial orientation, in varying combinations); it is also encouraged by the child's open choice as to which aspects of personal experience may be emphasized or replayed.

Thus, profoundly concerned with establishing structures suited to the mutual sharing of experience, dramatists' earliest communications center on imitations and simple role-exchange games like peek-a-boo and teasing. Via imitation, the children also refer to routine events through mimicking the actions of others or through abbreviating personal action into gestural signifiers. The early substitutions of such dramatists arise largely in the context of replaying familiar experiences, depend on gestural abbreviation, and focus on discovering a wide range of persons and objects that can fulfill the same role in an event. For example, Julie uses a small spoon and cup from an array of a tea set and dolls to pretend to feed herself, to feed her mother, to give her mother a drink, and to feed one of the dolls.

By comparison, patterners seek effective means to capture and explore the salient aspects of the object world. Interested in the possible uses and transformations of objects from the first year, a patterner's earliest communications are often "sharing" and "showing" games which center on exchange or manipulation of small objects. At the stage where flexible manipulation and association give way to simple symbols, such children appear to pursue representation as a way of distinguishing between objects. Frequently exploiting the configurational aspects of present objects rather than the replaying of past experience, patterners' early symbolic play exhibits less interest in the playing out of personal event-structures across a range of agents, than in exploring object-attribute relations. For example, when Anita is presented with a toy tea set and dolls, she briefly groups the cup, spoon, and doll together, but then becomes deeply involved with collecting and stacking all the four small plates, all four of the large ones, and then nesting the stack of small plates inside the stack of larger ones. As she places three spoons on top of this display, she makes smacking noises with her lips and starts to hold a spoon toward the adults, but then turns back as she once again becomes entranced with the problem of unstacking and rearranging the plates.

These examples illustrate that (as when, in three-dimensional construction, children are able to build towers) both children have now attained a common stage of understanding how objects may be used as replicas and how personal experience may be replayed. The fullness with which the children go on to develop these understandings, however, and the directions in which they exploit them may vary considerably.

24 Months: Consolidation of Styles

The power of individual differences becomes dramatically evident as the two media become increasingly available to children for the symbolic recreation of significant aspects of their experiential worlds. Children's growing control over these media by the age of twenty-four months facilitates consolidation of some of the personal style concerns which were just revealing themselves at children's first birthdays. This strengthening of interests and approaches has, in turn, its own implications with regard to the development of symbolic interests.

At this age, because of the more inflexible form of the grammar of three-dimensional construction and its inherent dependence on attention to attributes of physical objects, dramatists, who tend to overlook such aspects of experience, display a somewhat restricted articulation of their spatial environment. Although both patterners and dramatists combine blocks in constructions involving both horizontal and vertical axes, dramatists seem less interested in experimenting with novel forms of construction and more engaged in transferring a simple form donated by interpersonal interests across a range of materials; in contrast, patterners undertake block building involving complex experiments with problems of balance and symmetry. Thus Julie, over a period of play sessions, builds houses consistently comprised of at least two vertical elements, as pictured below:

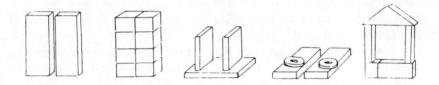

Anita combines blocks in constructions such as pictured below:

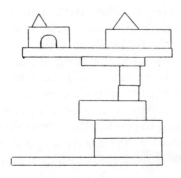

Similarly, concerned with the dynamics of interpersonal events, dramatists often pass quickly over, if they do not ignore, other relationships between objects. Differences between the two styles of handling objects are illustrated in the following examples, where both children have been given a set of twelve blocks, evenly varied over color (red, yellow, and blue), size (large and small), and shape (round and square):

Observation 1: Anita selects all the small round blocks and puts them in one hand, then selects all the large round blocks and holds them in the other. After she sets these groups down, she gathers all the small square blocks in one hand, stacks the large square ones, then stacks all the small square ones on top. Later the experimenter makes a long line of square blocks, with all the large blocks grouped together followed by all the small ones. Without prompting, Anita makes a corresponding array with the round blocks.

Observation 2: Julie builds a tower of the large circles, placing a small red round one on top. Then she makes pairs by placing blocks on top of one another: a large yellow square on a large yellow circle, a large red square on a large blue circle, and a large blue square on a small red circle. As she does this she repeats "applesauce, applesauce" softly. Then she hands one of the pairs to her mother and one to the experimenter, who both pretend to eat them as Julie pretends to eat hers. The experimenter asks for some milk and Julie hands her another block, and one to her mother also. When she becomes distressed at not having a block as "milk" for herself, she is satisfied by her mother's offer to share the block Julie has just given her.

Thus, although both children can build towers, the finer grades of relationships between objects based on size, color, and shape, are passed over by the dramatist, who exploits the materials as props for symbolic play.

In the same vein, children's differing styles inform their methods of modeling clay. Although both groups of children are equipped with a similar range of manipulatory clay techniques, dramatists tend to rush by problems of careful shaping, and would rather rename the clay, thereby transforming it into objects of current experiential interest. At this age, for example, Julie holds up a wad she has only superficially squeezed and calls it "hamburgers and french fries." Patterners, on the other hand, tend to get caught up in problems of shaping or of making pleasing configurations with the materials. Thus Anita, at the same age, forms a number of rings from the large and small coils the experimenter has rolled, and holds each finished form up for display. Spending quite a while experimenting with the contours of one ring, she finally arrives at a satisfactorily (and inventively) curved circle and lays it aside as "finished."

While the behavior of dramatists appears somewhat suppressed within the grammar of three-dimensional activity, it is the patterners who seem handicapped in bringing to fruition the possibilities of symbolic play. As described in Observation 2, the dramatist has donated a simple event-structure to a previously ambiguous situation, and has engaged in clear symbolic behavior. In contrast, the patterner's play seems to differ from her play a year ago only by her ability to recreate order across a more divergent set of objects. It is important to probe, then, just how far patterners have progressed in grasping some form of the signifier-signified relationship.

During the latter part of the second year, such children begin to be able to make symbolic use of their sensitivity to object attributes: what arises might be called a capacity for similarity relations, as patterners become avid practitioners of seeing one object as if it were another. The groundwork for these similarity relations has been laid by early manipulative exploratory play in which objects have been grouped by size, arranged in rows of the same number, or matched by shape or color. What changes toward the end of the second year, yielding patterners their own characteristic forms of object substitution, is that children go from simply noticing attributes to operating on them for representational purposes. The effects, in the realm of symbolic play, of patterners' operations on attribute-mapping structures are illustrated by the following example:

Observation 3: Anita is given the set of blocks and invited to tell a story with them. Anita comments, "Make house." Anita (with some help from the experimenter) builds an arch and then places a small conical block on top of it. She changes her mind and places the conical block in the center space under the arch. She again changes her mind and builds a tower of blocks, using the cone, beside the arch. She knocks it over all at once with a laugh, but then quickly rebuilds the arch. When she again places the conical block atop it, she comments, "Hat."

30–36 Months: Complementarity of Styles

At the age of two, the child's characteristic style of approaching media is clearly evident and serves as a point of departure for the majority of her activities. But by the age of two and a half or so, the child's increasing elaboration of each style launches a period of complementarity, whereby children favoring one stylistic approach master the rudiments of the other style: dramatists often elaborate narratives to a point where they can make use of attribute-mapping skills, while patterners' classifications and constructions become articulate enough to imply events. Thus we see the patterner, Anita, sorting out a range of small items (i.e., three different colors of large and small blocks, people, cars, and animals). In response to the experimenter's request to "put all the ones that are alike together," she lifts the items one by one from the heap and places each in a locale on the floor, grouped according to type. During the process she names the little girl doll "this be Anita," and the grandmother doll, "that gonna be mommy," with no other comments. It is Anita's interest in the classificatory scheme, and her careful attention to each object, which provides the setting for the interpersonal relationship which she is able to map onto two of the objects. On the other hand, when Julie is posed the same task, she gets one of the dolls on top of a small block, and comments that he is "sleeping . . . cover him?" She then wants to make "other things for him . . . need a . . . need a . . . make a house for him" and goes on to construct a simple house. In the process of making a bed for another small figure, she lines up all the large blocks flat on the floor, then places two small blocks upright at each end of the line. The two small blocks match the respective colors of the end blocks. It is her interest in providing for the needs of a doll-replica that leads Julie to a structure carefully ordered by shape, symmetry, and color.

At the same time, increased exposure and sensitivity to the symbolic productions of a wider circle of symbolizers (including peers) may facilitate the acquisition of complementary styles. Not only do children become acquainted with different symbol-user models, but new demands may be placed on the child. As it must behoove dramatists to become comfortably adept at handling culturally-valued categories of number, size, shape and color, so it must be advantageous for patterners to develop better tools to handle increasingly wider and more complex forms of interpersonal dynamics. At this same time children become highly sensitive to the typical uses of materials (e.g., even the most convinced dramatist makes structures with blocks because that is what blocks "are for").

While children may be led to the development of a complementary set of skills through the articulation and elaboration of their originally favored modes, much of their play retains the flavor of this first-flowering style. Consider what happens when both types of children are encouraged to enter into a "pretend" game, as the experimenter "makes believe" that one of their friends has come to visit for a tea party. Both the patterner and dramatist are initially confused and only gradually enter into the symbolic play to the extent of being able to address the imagined person. It is illuminating, though, to note how each child takes grasp of an unfamiliar play demand and also how each brings such play to a conclusion. The patterner needs prompting at first to attend to the imagined guest's needs, but then connects by providing herself and the guest with *real* objects (i.e., forks and plates). She ends the play by stepping out of the imaginary realm, drawing the activity instead to concrete objects by requesting the experimenter to name a number of the props used in the play event. The dramatist, on the other hand, enters into the play by spontaneously answering the guest's needs with an *imaginary* object (i.e., offering the guest her "coat"). Likewise she ends the play within the structure of the imagined event by telling the invisible guest "bye bye" and providing the imaginary props necessary for her departure.

However, as the following examples illustrate, it is clear that patterners' and dramatists' play has, by now, come to share a pool of attribute-structure and interpersonal event-structure skills.

Observation 4: With a set of ambiguously shaped blocks (some of which suggest people, some of which are more conventionally blocklike) and cars, the experimenter starts a story of a "lady"-block in a car, hunting for a parking space along a row of cars. There is one car pulled out of the row so there is an empty space. The experimenter then leaves the story to Anita to resolve. Anita slides the lady's car into the empty space, "Go in here." The experimenter asks what else the lady will do.

Anita: "No room." (This is an imitation of an expression used by the experimenter in the part of the story already started.)

Experimenter: "Now that she has a parking space she can go somewhere. Where shall she go?"

Anita: "Up the hill." (She makes a walking gesture with the person block up a ramp of blocks previously designated as "hill.") She becomes more engaged with the ramp, laughing as she slides the lady-block down it. She walks the lady over to a yellow man figure and says "Hi, man." Then she builds an arrangement of blocks and figures. (See below) She slides the lady-block down the ramp toward the man, then places the lady-block at the foot of the ramp and experiments with sliding a variety of blocks down the ramp.

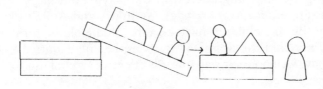

FIG. 8–3

Observation 5: Given a set of ambiguously shaped blocks, Julie first sets up two rectangular blocks on end, announcing "this one's a woods . . . here's the woods"; then she adds a block arching across the first two, saying "that for a hole." She pushes another one through underneath, saying "beep beep." She continues to build onto the structure, ending up with a construction as pictured below. She then replaces the triangle and square block with two more barrel blocks, saying "that's the dinner . . . that's Froggie's dinner . . . it's a table for him." Then she says "He wants to eat with a spoon," and she feeds Froggie (a large stuffed frog), repeating twice "Here's some for you." She gives him the blocks shaped and patterned like bricks, saying "Dis a for him." Then she puts one brick block in each of the four barrels which are on top of the structure, saying "Here we go now. Ah put this in here too." She takes up a clothespin which has a face drawn on its head, and the experimenter names it as "Fred" and greets it, "Hi, Fred." Julie also greets the clothespin, "Hi Fred"; then names the clothespin "George," and calls the experimenter "George."

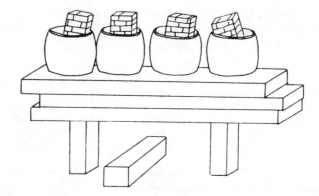

By the age of two and a half, patterners are able to create interpersonal events (Anita speaks for the lady, continues the action a bit further, makes the lady speak to another figure) at the same time as they exhibit their interest in object interrelations (block building, sliding various figures down the ramp). Just as well, dramatists can exploit the attributes of objects (naming upright blocks as "woods," making an orderly symmetrical block construction, exploring the notion of correspondences between objects by placing each brick-patterned block in a barrel) while maintaining a compelling interest in the playing out of personal events (Froggie's dinner, feeding Froggie). As Julie's and Anita's play demonstrates, by this age children have become creditable performers in both the patterning and the dramatizing styles; having acquired both sets of skills they are well on their way towards effective symbol use.

CONCLUDING REMARKS

We regard the findings sketched above as both partial and preliminary—partial because they represent only one part of a broader investigation of the processes of symbol use, and preliminary because we are still gathering and analyzing data.

We have also regarded our findings as parochial to some degree, although we have yet to trace out a full articulation of their limitations. Since there has been little previous research done in the area, possibilities for validating findings on early symbolization are just opening up. Other researchers now inquiring along these lines provide opportunities to confirm our findings with respect to individual differences and the acquisition of skills in diverse symbolic media. From the valuable long-term intimacy we have acquired with our small population, we hope eventually to posit ordinal scales for each individual style, for each medium, as well as for the general course of symbolic development. The resulting descriptive model, together with the tools and techniques used to construct it, can then be made available to other researchers. We look forward to the examination of our findings in the contexts of different social classes or special populations, different experimenters or types of experimental situations, and in diverse cultures, including ones in which symbolic play is not encouraged.

Although we must currently regard our findings as tentative, it nevertheless seems fruitful to engage in some speculation: what would be the significance of the proposed scales and styles, should they be validated? In our view these findings suggest that, even as there exists a range of expressive media, there may also be a variety of routes which individuals can follow in mastering one, or several, of those media. It seems probable that most people could (and eventually do) become relatively adept within the various stylistic approaches, but what does it mean when an individual seems to have recourse to only one mode of symbolic expression? Stylistic rigidity may signal the limited world of the emotionally disturbed, learning disabled, or even the psychotic individual. Our findings also raise the question of whether the missing skills can be taught; or a single style sufficiently exploited to "make up for" the missing skills—and what might be the role of education in this process? And the possibility also arises that certain persons, such as great artists or scientists, may be similarly wedded to a single style, finding in that commitment the tools for forging a powerfully personal vision.

Finally, we have speculated about what the possible sources of the styles of symbolization might be—are they carried genetically; are they modelled after parents, siblings, or other members of the society; do they result from a subtle interaction between predispositions on the part of the child and adjustments on the part of the parents? Although our present data do not directly address such questions, we have considered these issues particularly with reference to possible neural substrates which might lead to a patterning or dramatizing style. While we will leave further exploration of this possibility to the conference, it is intriguing to reflect that, in the case of a capacity as fundamental as symbolization, the human may have evolved at least two alternative routes to the attainment of competence.

DISCUSSION

Dr. Lewis: These distinctions make such good sense; I think we all feel that. What other things do we know? How about impulse control, activity level? You may not have the data, but what's your feeling? Are we looking at introspective behavior? I'm trying to see what other words we might call this dimension.

Dr. Gardner: Our feeling about impulse control is that the two kids who are patterners are both very tight kids. They are very reluctant to make their feelings known. In fact, whenever you try to engage them in a storytelling or dramatizing kind of mode they very quickly shift you into a pure naming mode or something like that. As they get older this loosens up a bit. But the sort of thing that is characteristic of many kids, and particularly of dramatistic kids, is that no matter what you give them they tell you what's going on in their home and they act out spankings. It's just the sort of thing you don't get in the patterner. As far as tempo is concerned, I think the answer is complicated, but I think you get sustained activity from the patterner. That is, a patterner may arrange forms for a long period of time. You won't see that happening with a dramatist. On the other hand, the patterner very quickly cuts off a game in which you're acting out some event, whereas the dramatist may carry it on for a while. But I suppose if you pushed me against a wall I would say the dramatist tends to be faster paced.

Dr. Schultz: I have a question that focuses not so much on the individual differences idea but back to the basic developmental processes idea. To me, one of the great mysteries in developmental psychology has always been what could account for something like the development of symbolic function. You're following kids right across that age range where presumably it starts. The reason this has always been so mysterious, it seems to me, is that there's essentially a great discontinuity between what Piaget describes as a stage 4 and stage 5 child and suddenly being able to use symbolic function in stage 6. Do you have any ideas about what happens that could create this situation?

Dr. Gardner: This is a question that I've been preoccupied with ever since I went into psychology. That to me is the BIG question. The way I'm going to evade it is to say that I think it becomes less of a mystery the better we can describe exactly what happens on a week-to-week basis. The most heartwarming part of the study is that with the second set of kids we're finding very few surprises. That is, we really can predict pretty well what's going to be happening in the following weeks. And I think when you look at it at a descriptive level you see that things which are present very early, like peek-a-boo games, exchange games, getting objects, banging them together, putting objects together, lead into the time when you can give a name to the particular object, take a couple of objects and make them stand for something which you've seen before, or take some words and some objects together and replay an event that happened before. There's no question that all the sorts of things which Piaget and other people talked about are very important. You need an object concept. You need to have a certain memory in particular modalities. You can't recreate visual experience unless you can remember what things look like, and you can't recreate experiences auditorialy unless you remember what they sound lke. So we in no sense want to underline the fact that these tend to co-occur around the time of symbolization. I guess what I'm trying to say is it seems less like a quantum leap and more like a regular, though species-specific, unfolding as you trace the microstructure, and I think that's encouraging.

Dr. Fein: I have difficulty with a part of it and that is, can you tell us more concretely what it is that your patterners would be doing at twelve or eighteen months that would put them into that category?

Dr. Gardner: One of the things we're finding with the new children which we didn't notice before is a surprisingly mature classificatory ability around kids when they're thirteen or fourteen months old. I think this is the sort of thing which Riccuiti wrote about, and Katherine Nelson to some extent. A child whom we would call a patterner, when given a set of objects in a box, would pull out instances of the same object; that is, identical things, one at a time, and possibly also members of the same category. Obviously they have to be pretty prototypical. And this suggests an early and keen attention to the size, shape and dimensions of those objects. This is something that one wouldn't expect to happen with the dramatist.

Dr. Fein: What would the dramatist do?

Dr. Gardner: The dramatist would reach, without even looking at what the object was, and hand it over to the mother and hope that she would do something interesting with it or give it a name or something like that. He wouldn't pay much attention to the size and shape. Every kid around that age spends a lot of time taking things in and out of containers. Our speculation is that the patterner does that more and is exploring the placement possibilities more than the dramatist.

Dr. Fein: Suppose a child takes one of the boxes, pretends to drink out of it, and then picks up another one and pretends to drink and then hands it to the mother?

Dr. Gardner: Well I think that would be a case where the child is showing instances of both kinds of behaviors. And I suppose the issue, if my distinction makes any sense at all, is whether it's a distinction which only applies to extremes, or a distinction which is useful for a majority of kids. I think the empirical answer would be that you'd have to do that with a lot of kids to see whether in fact the sort of thing you described is what commonly happens. Do the kids have aspects of both, or is it the kind of story that I'm trying to tell where the kids are more likely to do mostly one or mostly the other?

Dr. Lewis: Siegel, in his classificatory system, talks about just these two different kinds of behavior as an ontogenetic kind of change. The child would start off matching objects on features such as size and volume and color. Later he matches them more as the dramatist would: those things which go together as from a story; namely, the pipe, the matches, a cigarette. They would go together because they related to a high-level category. Does that fit, do you think?

Dr. Gardner: Well, the biggest issue for anyone who makes a claim for individual differences is that the distinction isn't just a crypto developmental difference. Most of the proposed individual differences have turned out to be really developmental differences, you know; field dependence, stuff like that. The case I'm making would be that we don't agree with Siegel; we think these are two fundamentally different modes and the children may favor one first. As you [Dr. Lewis] were talking today, it seemed you were giving a perfect description of what I would think would be important for a dramatist (the influence of the mothers' games), but really would not be terribly relevant for a patterner.

Dr. Lewis: Well, Siegel (1964) would be opposed to both of us because he would say that first the child explores the object world.

Dr. J. Singer: It seems to me there is a whole host of stylistic differences that come together. I think you were a little too hasty in dismissing field dependence/independence. I think the controversy is not resolved as to whether it's simply a developmental level or a style. At least a good deal of recent evidence on interpersonal behavior suggests that field-dependent people, by acquiring more information from the external environment, function more effectively in a whole set of social situations than the field-independent persons, so it depends in part on the task demands, the nature of the particular situation. An argument could be made for that being the genuine style rather than a difference in some kind of developmental arrangement. There are other differences too. There's the reflectivity-impulsivity of Kagan that seems related to this. There's a whole series of styles. We ourselves, in our research, have what we call children who engage a lot in imaginative play versus kids who don't show very much imaginative play. It seemed very similar to what you were talking about.

Dr. McCall: What about Jensen's level 1 and 2? We have in a sense an associative-type child here who's putting edge to edge. He doesn't look at the gestalt, whereas the other one is more symbolic and tries to integrate at some higher level than purely sensory associativeness.

Dr. Lewis: That's Siegel's point.

Dr. McCall: But it does not necessarily have to be ontogenetic. In Dr. Gardner's case that may not be the explanation, but both of them may be describing real phenomena.

Dr. D. Singer: I don't know how large the sex differences are, but I was just thinking of the work with left and right hemispheres, and I guess you'd have to have a larger N than what you had to determine whether this is a right hemisphere function.

Dr. Gardner: It's too early, and we do not think it is related in any straightforward way to alleged distinctions between the two hemispheres.

Dr. D. Singer: But you are working with older children too. And I think it's not too early to tell in the older ones.

Dr. Gardner: Of course we're very interested in that issue, and one of the things we have good measures on is handedness. The kids are about the age now where one could do that, but given the kinds of relationships we have with the parents, that may be a bit too tasky for them.

Dr. McCall: There are some people who think there are no adequate measures of handedness.

Dr. Gardner: I think the best measure of handedness is to see which hand they use.

Dr. McCall: No, it isn't, because people learn to use different hands for different functions. Which hand does your child use to do this and that task? There is very little correspondence. You learn to use one hand or another for a variety of social functions. It's not so clear that it's all determined by your handedness.

Dr. D. Singer: Another approach is to give nameless forms to people. They shut their eyes and feel one with the left hand and then with the right hand, and you find that girls show less differentiation than boys. Up until around age eight, boys are already more specialized in terms of left and right brain, which may in part account for some of the language difficulties they have.

Dr. Lewis: Does the handedness data you have show any relationship?

Dr. Gardner: Not so far. My hunch, for what it's worth (and it's worth very little), is that the distinction we're talking about will not map in a very interesting way in two hemispheres. But in part my answer comes from the fact that I am becoming increasingly disenamored of attempts to call one hemisphere X and the other one Y. I think it's more complicated than that. But irrespective of that prejudice on my part, I don't think that this particular difference makes much sense in terms of any of the characterizations of the hemispheres that I've seen proposed.

Dr. Chase: I don't understand why you say that. It seems to me to lie right in the center of the asymmetries and functions in the brain that have been best established. Not that it's clear by any means, but certainly, for most of us, the left hemisphere is far more important to our language performance than the right.

Dr. Gardner: But what's interesting about the dramatist is not so much the fact that he uses a lot of language—because I'll bet if you did syntactic measures the patterners would be as good—but rather the interpersonal, story-narrative use of language which so far as I know doesn't map in any particularly interesting way to attempts to characterize the hemispheres. I think it would be true to say that right parietal functions are thought to be important for visual, spatial kinds of things, but to my mind that's not enough to say that the patterners are basically right-hemisphere kids and the dramatists are basically left-hemisphere kids.

Dr. Chase: Why dismiss it when it could turn out to be a very interesting story? In other words, I don't see that you have a reason to dismiss it.

Dr. Gardner: It's only unrequited love on my part. I wanted it to work out that way, but it has not.

Dr. Schwartzman: What are your hunches?

Dr. Gardner: Well, there's a big difference of opinion among the researchers. I tend toward the genetic hypothesis. Dennie Wolf tends toward the environmental hypothesis, which I guess means that it's the interactional hypothesis that's right. Not to be flip about it, I think that there's no doubt that parents can be categorized in style, and Dennie always says when she talks about this that there's no case in which a child is counter to the styles of the parents. I, on the other hand, think it's more complicated. Let's say you try a very patterning approach and the child isn't interested. You're going to try something else. So I think the kids bring some predisposition to it, but it would be very hard to disentangle the factors because you've got at least a year of interaction in the household before there are any signs of the distinctions we're talking about. I think it's quite clear that the sample I'm using is terribly parochial in every sense. I'm very interested in presenting this kind of material to anthropologists, from the point of view of knowing whether even the categories of symbolization that we talk about make sense in other cultures. Symbolic play is something that we take for granted as developmental psychologists in the United States, but it may be an irrelevancy as far as other cultures are concerned. I would like to get some cross-cultural perspective on whether patternizing and dramatizing make sense in other cultures, or whether it's again a Cambridge, Mass. kind of blinder.

Dr. Lewis: Are dramatists messy and patterners neat?

Dr. Gardner: I think that's part of the tightness that I talked about. Neither they nor their mothers like to fingerpaint. One has a feeling that one's dealing with something that's part of the child's being. If our distinctions go beyond those of other people, I would like to think not that they contradict them but rather that we hope to be able to give more nuance to our statements about how children will be able to work with a variety of media. So it's not just that a child is a verbalizer or nonverbalizer, but rather that children will use language in different ways, depending on what their approach is. For example, even though dramatists would be thought to be linguistically more precocious and maybe more aesthetic as well, in fact the first metaphors in metaphor games come from patterners. We take shapes, either just blocks or familiar shapes, and have the child rename them; and the names which are appropriate in a metaphoric sense—that is, have a perceptual kind of similarity—are more likely to come from the patterners than from the dramatists. The dramatists would like *you* to give a name to things, which isn't really the way to play a metaphor game. And let me say something about the number. We're noticing how children are acquiring number concepts, and again something interesting seems to have happened. The patterners are quite good at doing one-to-one correspondences when you get them into a number set, but their numbering in an oral sense is often quite chaotic. The dramatists are much less likely to honor one-to-one correspondences, but they're very good at coming out with the number sequence correctly.

Dr. Sutton-Smith: I wonder if I can ask you again about the symbolic series. Most of the time when we're dealing with Greta's [Dr. Fein's] work, or with Piaget's work, we've really got what you're calling a dramatist: first there is the decontextualization of the self from the original setting, then the playing with those actions separately, then the use of the toy to play one's own actions, then the use of the self to play another's actions, then the use of the object for the toy, and then the use of the self for the mother rather than the action. That is a symbolic series which some people are working with (Nicolich, 1977) and is clearly, in your terms, a dramatistic series. There's an impersonation of people and peoples' actions. There are identities and actions. I'm having a hard job fitting your system to that well-established sequence which goes from twelve to thirty months.

Dr. Gardner: Not at twelve months. We find at eighteen months that the child will begin to take objects and set them up in familiar and meaningful patterns. Given table-setting kinds of toys, the patterner by the age of eighteen or twenty months will set the things up so it looks like a table with a setting; so you will get a referential mapping, a symbolic mapping, but it will be one which is isomorphic to the way the situation would look in the real world rather than something that is enacted with families at the table. Each one's strength is the other one's weakness. The dramatist will give you a good dinner-table conversation but won't set the thing up in the proper way because she doesn't care. One thing we talk about is the possibility (and we don't have any way of measuring this) that patterners and dramatists may both pass through the same stages at about the same rate, but that there's an additional element which characterizes each child in his area of specialization. For example, the patterner may show you in one sense or another that he understands things about role substitutions and role play, etc., but he doesn't really explore this very much, doesn't do it very much, and so doesn't have the rich nimbus of associations that we found in Kate Garvey's transcript. It may be more of a style difference than a structure difference.

Dr. Sutton-Smith: Perhaps it has to do with the prototypical and the nonprototypical. If this is a valid dichotomy, then the dramatist would be less concerned with prototypical isomorphism.

Dr. Gardner: That's clearly true. There's no question about that. The patterner gets upset when you try to make something stand for something that doesn't look like that thing, but is on the other hand very good once there is a visual similarity. The typical patterner would walk through the woods and identify letters of the alphabet in trees—in branch and tree constellations. It's almost eerie. The dramatist will be much more accepting of naming, but will for that very reason not be as good at coming up with neat kinds of visual metaphors.

Dr. Lewis: I was a little disturbed by what you said about metaphors. Can you make up story metaphors such as "This story is to this story as this story is to something else"? The dramatist might be better at that. You sort of loaded it against him because you asked him for the dimension that you already know.

Dr. Gardner: I think that you're probably right. We've begun to do storytelling tasks with the kids, and that data is being analyzed. What we do is to tell stories building up certain expectations of characters. We may use puppets or we may not, and we see the extent to which the children pick up on these sorts of implicit aspects of the stories. My hunch would be that it is the dramatist who has a better sense of story genres and will recognize what's expected in stories and carry it through, but I don't know what the data is going to show. The kids are now three to three and a half, so that story tasks in which there's an active engagement on the part of the child are becoming possible for the first time. They weren't possible before.

Dr. Lewis: Therefore you can have different kinds of metaphors, so we can't even talk about metaphor in any single sense.

Dr. Gardner: That's why I said *visual* metaphor. There are expressive metaphors. I don't think we have any evidence yet that the dramatists would be better in expressive metaphor, one where there's a quality in common between two experiences rather than a physical kind of mapping.

Dr. Fein: I'm trying to see the kids we've seen in your framework. What might be happening in the early period frame is a distinction between the dramatists and all the others, because during those early stages when you have the first beginning forms of the pretend acts you really don't have very much of the patterning behavior. Then, as they became developmentally able, perhaps some of them would fall into a patterning style. But I guess I have a lot of trouble moving it back to the age level where there's no evidence for this kind of consistent patterning because the kids are so much into the sensorimotor use of objects.

Dr. Gardner: I'm wondering whether part of our different impression may come from the fact that we see these kids a lot and do a lot of different things with them. I think styles may be more likely to emerge under those conditions. Do you do longitudinal work where you can trace whether the kids are playing in a similar way?

Dr. Fein: We've seen most of our kids longitudinally. Very early there are kids who do a lot of pretending, and some who don't do very much. It is only later that the ordering and lining up and the selection according to characteristics of roundness or size appears.

Dr. Gardner: What age?

Dr. Fein: It doesn't happen till twenty months—twenty-two months, twenty-four months—that you begin to get any kind of consistency or high frequency in this kind of lining up, ordering, piling up of blocks in the formation of structures.

Dr. Csikszentmihayli: That doesn't correspond to my observations.

Dr. Fein: You see the block lining up early?

Dr. Csikszentmihayli: At twelve months.

Dr. Gardner: For example, if you give a kid a bunch of blocks and he picks two to knock together, which every child will do around that time, how likely is he to pick the two same ones? I would think that would be a nice measure of how much a child is paying attention to attributes.

Dr. Collard: I can give you that in marbles. George Forman has been working five or six years on that and he has percentages now by age with particular arrays, six different arrays . . .

Dr. Gardner: Does he speak to the issue of whether there are individual differences—whether the kids will just knock together anything as opposed to . . . similar marbles?

Dr. Collard: No, I'm sorry, but he has the percentages of how many kids at what age knock identical marbles together, and then differences also in their structuring—whether they're making graphic collections or symmetrical collections. And he has a graded series of ordering, from knocking two together to putting one on top of the other to making horizontal arrays that touch each other to making horizontal arrays which are spaced from each other to making groupings which are quite far apart.

Dr. Gardner: This is very much what we would expect to find in the ordinal scale part of our study where we take blocks and map out the patterns, and so far our findings are very developmental. It's not the case that the child builds in three dimensions at an early age. He just lays out a horizontal array. The point that I tried to make—to use words other than *patterning* and *dramatist*—is that there are certain children who pay attention to what we call the *event structure implications* of a bunch of objects, and other kids who pay attention to what we call the *object attribute aspects*—the size, shape, form, etc. And what I'm saying makes sense if you can take kids at a certain developmental level and divide at least some of them according to a consistent practice of one or the other. It's in no way an attempt to deny developmental sequences, which I think supercede these individual differences.

Dr. Collard: Well, Forman said a dramatist would roll the cylinders rather than classify. A lot of kids wouldn't classify. They found if they rolled them they'd go zooming across the room.

Dr. Gardner: But rolling is a kind of classifying too.

Dr. Lewis: Do you have any idea, given this distinction, whether the dramatists actually engage in more play? You see, in some sense you've said to these kids, "Go do something with these objects," and the dramatist—rich in symbolic play—goes in and constructs something. The "shnooky" patterner says, "What am I going to do for these guys? This guy wants me to do something. I'll put them together, I'll get all the like ones." So it would seem to me that they are both engaged in the same activity. A different assessment would be how often the patterner versus the dramatist spontaneously plays with the material.

Dr. Gardner: But you're using the word *play* in exactly the sense I don't want to use it.

Dr. Lewis: Well then, which type will spontaneously go into the box and pull the objects out the most?

Dr. Gardner: That's an interesting question, which I can't answer. But I'll tell you something which is a relevant observation. A new set of kids has been seen from November through February, so it's been four to six months, and we already know exactly what's going to happen. The bag is there; they go right for it. Some of them show memory things—if something isn't there they go to the location where it was before. There is no question that there are strong expectations built, but I think there's enough variety in the materials we bring that the child has a chance to show his strong suit. I think the child who decides to array things in terms of their object attributes, and who doesn't become involved in turn-taking games where he's paying attention to the mother's reactions, is engaged in play, too; but it's play that has a different kind of rhythm and different kinds of cognitive payoffs. My feeling is that it's not the case that one kid sits around and does nothing and the other kid is very busy, but rather that the kinds of things from which they gain sustenance differ, and to some extent it's those things from which they gain sustenance which they get involved in a lot. So as I said before, it's the patterner who will spend a long time arranging and rearranging things.

Dr. Ellis: I think you should recognize that the presence of your observer biases the outcomes, because presumably dramatists are more interested in playing games with you, the observer, than they are in the toys. And it would be a good idea somehow to do the kinds of things that Kate [Dr. Garvey] has done, to "snoop" on the interactions so that you, the experimenter, are not an intrusive event. When you've done that, from my experience, the patterners would play for much longer with their stuff, and the dramatists would be more disconcerted by the absence of someone to interact with and would find the isolated situation much more difficult.

Dr. Garvey: I want to make another suggestion in relation to this which might show you something. You said at about age three they begin to show more involvement in both modalities. At two and a half it would be very interesting to put one of each together and see who has the greater influence and whether there is any change in the behavior of one or the other in that direction.

Dr. Gardner: We've done some peer pairing but we let the parents choose the companion, so there may be a confounding. But it would be interesting to go back and look at those observations to see whether there is indeed some interaction.

Just a comment on Mike Ellis's point. I think that certainly what you say would be worth doing. I feel that we have spent so much time with these families that we really are part of the family. In that sense there are lots of pros and cons, but I think it would be erroneous for you to conclude that the child is performing for us anymore. Clearly there are relationships which have been set up, and the child is very upset when the examiner he or she knows doesn't come, etc. But the child hasn't been acting every week for three years. We have a pretty good idea of what the child is like. In fact Dennie says, without any desire to be self-serving, that we know the kids much better than the parents do in the sense of being able to predict what they're going to do in all kinds of situations.

Dr. Garvey: That wasn't Mike's [Dr. Ellis's] point, and his point is still a very good one: that you are getting more behavior out of the child who is interested in the interaction just because you are there.

Dr. Schwartzman: And the fact that he's very sensitive to the cues.

Dr. Garvey: He's getting more cues, too.

Dr. Gardner: I understand what you're saying but I have to give my intuitive feeling about it, which is that you might be more accurate in one case than in the other. There are two kids whom we're thinking of as being real patterners. In one case I think the child is completely at ease and goes about his business, which may not always be interacting with the experimenter. In the other case there was a time about which I think that you may be right: the child perceived us as being part of a situation which wasn't her kind of situation. I think that's what you're saying. In a way we're playing more to the dramatists than the patterners.

Dr. Csikszentmihayli: What you're describing makes me think back on some of the data which we collected recently when we asked a group of college students to keep a diary for about a week of all the things they did during the course of a normal day that were not necessary, that they did without any kind of purpose or any kind of social requirement. And we produced several thousands of these things in which people put down every three hours what they did during the day. One of the two largest groupings of things that people noted involved social interactions—talking, joking, doing things with people—which accounted for about 25 percent of all the things they did; and the other, which was also 25 percent, was a kinesthetic category—moving, doing things with their hands, structuring their free time essentially through the body. And these two categories were inversely related; that is, people who did one didn't do the other. There were other categories such as imagination, fantasizing, talking to oneself, etc., but the two largest ones were the kinesthetic and the social. This had all kinds of correlates in terms of personality variables and performance. I'm wondering whether what you're describing is the precursor of the kind of behavior that we found. Is there anything about body use that you are seeing among the patterners, structuring the environment through movement, etc.? Because the social and the dramatizing seem to be pretty much related.

Dr. Gardner: I can't really give you a good answer to that. Movement, in terms of gesture and body expression, is one of the seven media that we're monitoring. But we're monitoring it with dance as the ultimate vision of what movement can be like. What we find there is more the kind of task effect that some people were implying before; namely, that the dramatists are more willing to wiggle like a worm and that sort of thing, which isn't really what you're getting at. One nice thing is that we do have the videotapes from year one, so that someone with that question in mind, and some movement notation, could go back and see whether there are differences. But I don't have a good intuition for it.

Dr. McCall: Mihayli's [Dr. Csikszentmihayli's] comment jogs my memory. We have completed an analysis of the Berkeley study of the raw protocols from the Bailey test, which was given every month for fifteen months, and every three months thereafter ad nauseum. In the course of this analysis the individual items were factored at each age, and then correlations among factor scores across age were calculated in order to find patterns of continuity and discontinuity. The second factors, since this was a principal components analysis, were bipolar; and I am pretty sure there is a string of continuity of individual differences in the second and third years that represents a contrast between a perceptual orientation—a form orientation—on one hand, and the verbal symbolic on the other. This is an SRCD monograph. We did get similar results also in the analysis of the Fels data which was published in November 1972 in *The American Psychologist.* There is also a social dimension that continues during this period of time, but I don't think that's necessarily in opposition to something like *form* versus *verbal symbolic.* That's pertinent to what some of these other people are saying. The nature of your context is extracting out introvert- versus extrovert-oriented children, which characteristics do have a little heritability and do get mutually reinforced in families, as you described.

Dr. Gardner: This suggests something that I think is important for us to do. We are contracted to do a control study next year. The basic purpose of the control study is to take some kids we *haven't* seen every week of their lives and give them the same tasks, to see how they perform. We're doing it mostly for normative purposes, since our kids may be way off the map because they've been systematically drilled in all these things. What these comments suggest is that we ought to see some kids under a nonsocial condition, which will double our N, unfortunately. But I think that's a good point.

Dr. Garvey: The investigators cannot be blind to the kind of child that they're giving the test to. Right?

Dr. Gardner: Well certainly not now, no.

Dr. Garvey: And you've been working with them for several years.

Dr. Gardner: I think the complementarity there is a nice thing, because certainly if I were sitting here and saying that the world is composed of two kinds of people, I could be accused of saying we have *made* the world into two kinds of people. What's interesting is that despite our expectations, kids began to violate them when they became three years of age. And also the fact that when we see these kids when they're much older, in the grade schools, in our cross-section longitudinal study, we see what appear to be echoes of that early distinction, although it's not as entrenched.

References

Gardner, H. *The arts and human development*. New York: Wiley, 1973.

Gardner, H. *Developmental psychology: An introduction*. Boston: Little Brown, 1978.

Gardner, H. From Melvin to Melville: On the relevance to aesthetics of recent research on story comprehension. In S. Madeja (Ed.) *The arts, cognition, and basic skills*. In press.

Gardner, H. *The quest for mind: Jean Piaget, Claude Lévi-Strauss, and the structuralist movement*. New York: Knopf, 1973.

Gardner, H. *The shattered mind*. New York: Knopf, 1975.

Gardner, H. Sifting the special from the shared: Notes toward an agenda for research in arts education. In S. Madeja (Ed.) *Arts and aesthetics: An agenda for the future*. St. Louis: Cemrel, Inc. 1977, pp. 267–278. Also in *Journal of Aesthetic Education*, 1977, *11*, 31–44.

Gardner, H., & Gardner, J. *Classics in psychology*. New York: Arno Press, 1973.

Gardner, H., Winner, E., Bechhofer, R., & Wolf, D. The development of figurative language. In K. Nelson (Ed.) *Children's Language*. New York: Gardner Press, 1978.

Gardner, J., & Gardner, H. *Classics in child psychology*. New York: Arno Press, 1975.

Grossack, M., & Gardner, H. *Man and men: social psychology as social science*. Scranton, Pa.: International Textbook, 1970.

Mercer, B., Wapner, W., Gardner, H., & Benson, D. F. A study in confabulation. *Archives of Neurology*, 1977, 34, 429–433.

Nicolich, L. M. Beyond sensorimotor intelligence: assessment of symbolic maturity through analysis of pretend play. *Merrill-Palmer Quarterly*, 1977, *23*, 89–99.

Rosenstiel, A. K., Morison, P., Silverman, J., & Gardner, H. Discriminating among dimensions of critical judgment: A developmental study. *Journal of Aesthetic Education*, in press.

Siegel, I. The attainment of concept. In M. L. Hoffman and L. W. Hoffman (Eds.) *Review of Child Development Research*. New York: Russell Sage Fdtn., 1964.

Wolf, D., & Gardner, H. Style and sequence in early symbolic play. In M. Franklin & N. Smith (Eds.) *Early symbolization*. Hillsdale, N.J.: Lawrence Erlbaum, 1978.

CHAPTER 9

THE COMPLEXITY OF OBJECTS AND PEERS

Michael Ellis

INTRODUCTION

Dr. Sutton-Smith: This paper by Dr. Ellis recalls the first one, by Dr. Shultz; we will once again be discussing play activity in terms of levels of output, levels of arousal. But now the theoretical emphasis is more upon the information provided in the playroom than upon internal monitoring. Ellis's interest as a physical educator is on kinds of play objects and their effects on children's activity, which is a continuation of the ecological approaches of the early thirties but with a new level of sophistication (Herron & Sutton-Smith, 1971, p. 83). He finds that the children's level of activity is a very direct function of the object's complexity, but that other children universally provide more complexity than any objects can. In a different way this parallels both Hutt's later finding that children's language usage is more complex with peers than with teachers, and the discovery by both Garvey and Gardner that it appears to be only in play that a diagnosis of high-level functioning becomes possible. Ellis also finds evidence of certain biorhythms of activity and quiescence in the groups he studies which seem to transcend the object situation itself. Hyperactive children are shown not to be distinguishable from others in the play setting, although they are in the classroom setting, and this leads to the issue of which kinds of people are more dependent on external stimulation for response and which are more self-generating. There is a vigorous discussion over whether the concept of arousal is specific enough to be of much use in current play research. The effect of varying constraints and contexts are shown to have such an impact on the level of activity that questions are raised about notions of internal monitoring which

157

do not also take into account the mediational influence of cognitive variables.

Dr. Ellis: I come to you from a very different orientation. I really used to study the acquisition of motor skills. We wanted to understand activity because that seemed to be the boundary between the motor behavior that we were charged with being interested in and other kinds of behavior. And it's just that rather molar view of studying whole groups of kids interacting at the same time and analyzing the interactions as they took place, rather than manipulating the interactions in an experimental sense, that gave us an awful lot of our data. So we're different. The work that I'm telling you about is different in the sense that quite often we would study the interaction of eight to ten children at a time.

FUNCTIONAL COMPLEXITY

The first major theme that I want to talk about deals with the relationships between children and objects and between children and children. We did a group of studies which were designed to establish the parameters of preference for objects. We started manipulating color and form and complexity and so forth. The studies in themselves were relatively simple. Only when you take them collectively—when you look at, say, twelve studies of preference for various parameters of play objects—does a pattern begin to emerge. We were simulating playgrounds. In other words, children could run around the play object; they could actually climb into it and onto it. The characteristics of the toy or the object that attracted or maintained their behavior were what I'll call the *functional complexity* of the object, and that really is a kind of collative property. It's a variation on one of the collative properties of Berlyne (1960) in that it talks to or describes the potential for responsiveness on the part of the organism to the object. Does the object do something? If the object has a function that interacts with the response of the child, that is the parameter of the object that will maintain the attention. And we found that such things as color and form and complexity of the painting on the object were all microscopically influential compared to its potential for interaction, for sustaining an interaction. That is of course typical of science. You could have asked any parent about that and they would have given you exactly the same answer.

In addition, we would always run our kids in groups; in that sense it was just like a normal nursery school. Then after a while we would manipulate groups to start to look at the ways in which children played together, the number of social interactions they maintained as well as the number of object interactions, and we found that we could alter the level of social interaction, but only for a very short period of time (Ellis & Scholtz, 1977). We could put out an extremely complex object and capture the attention and the interactions of the children, but very soon the interactions with peers reasserted themselves as the preferred mode—and that makes sense too, from a functional complexity viewpoint. Peers are functionally far more complex than the most complex object that you can design. We might spend a month designing an object, only to find that the children could consume that object in thirty or forty seconds—then they would want to use it with a peer. That's why it staggered me that Roberta [Dr. Collard] found some data that you could sustain attention for four minutes. I know our children were older—between three and five or six years old. They would use up an object and get beyond exploration—What is this, what does it do?—and onto, How can we use this together? in very short order of time—thirty seconds, a minute. And we could see the ebb and flow of interaction with peers and objects. We could control that by altering the functional complexity of the objects, but in the end, no matter how hard we tried, the interaction with peers eventually asserted itself as the preferred mode.

Dr. Collard: The babies who had more varieties of response maintained their interest longer, and so did the babies who used social play with the toy. So the habituation depended to a large extent on what they did to the toy. The institutional babies started with less response and their interest went right down.

Dr. Ellis: The functional complexity would increase with the number of degrees of freedom offered the child by the object. Just to exemplify that: one of the items in a complex piece of apparatus was a rope. It was braided so that it was easy to grip (Gramza, Corush, & Ellis, 1972). If we tied it at the bottom, so that it had very limited opportunities for manipulation, they habituated to that object very quickly. All you had to do was untie the rope and change the functional complexity (Gramza, 1970); [the number of responses that became possible.] I think functional complexity applies to peers also. One of the neat things about peers, of course, is that as you interact with them their functional complexity increases because they are changed by your interactions; so you can spiral upwards. We did not until right at the very end begin to analyze the social content of the interaction. We were just happy to look and see whether it took place or not.

Dr. Schwartzman: The groups of kids that you had—were they always the same groups or did you change them?

Dr. Ellis: They were intact groups. Later on you'll find that we did start messing around with some groups, changing their composition, but we had a very naturalistic setting. The kids would come to our laboratory every day. It was part of their thing, and they were used to us changing it around because we would muck around with the lab to keep it interesting even if there was no experiment going on. It was the physical education part of their nursery school experience.

Dr. Hutt: Did you ever predict that certain objects had functional high value and then the children didn't do much with them?

Dr. Ellis: I can't think of an example where they didn't, but that's no big trick because the level of sophistication at which this was taking place was very simple. We were just artificially complexifying and building (Gramza & Witt, 1969; Gramza & Scholtz, 1974). We would cut holes in something that would enable them to climb under it. That would give them access to a different dimension of that object; always as we increased the degrees of freedom so we increased the number of responses, and that's not a particularly sophisticated or difficult thing to do. And it stopped rather early because we got bored with this in the sense that we felt we had established this notion of functional complexity, at least for ourselves.

Dr. Lewis: What were the ages of these children?

Dr. Ellis: Mid-threes to kids who were just about to go to kindergarten. It's a normal preschool kind of setting for the data that I just talked about.

Dr. Sutton-Smith: Besides cutting holes, what else did you do?

Dr. Ellis: We had trestles; we had a cargo net which was more complex than something that wouldn't move; we had blocks. These were huge four-foot cubes. Sometimes we would cut holes in them so you could get onto the top, and sometimes we would cut enormous holes so that you could get inside. We reckoned that it would be more functionally complex if there was just one big hole. Sometimes we made them out of plexiglas so you could see through them; sometimes they were opaque; sometimes they were translucent. We had carpet rolls that we built into things so that little kids could wriggle through them. The short rolls gave you fewer possibilities when they were fixed, but a short one when it was free gave you more possibilities (Gramza & Witt, 1969; Gramza & Sholtz, 1974). Our intuition as humans as to what is complex and what is interesting to little kids was remarkably reliable. We could tell which toys had more value, using the degrees of freedom model. We simply added: What possibilities has this?

BIORHYTHMS

We were also interested in trying to figure out whether there were norms for activity; that is, a concern with the expression of responses in a gross sense rather than with their content. The Department of Mental Health was extremely interested in hyperactive children. We were interested in the notion that the human is driven or impelled to interact with the environment. We decided that in children who were free ranging and were in environments where there were potential opportunities for high levels of energy expenditure—playgrounds and that kind of thing—we ought to see two systems working against one another (Wade, Ellis, & Bohrer, 1973). There would be the need to process information—in other words, to explore and play with the environment—and that costs energy. The second system that we thought would beat against that would be the activity-nulling effects of homeostasis; that is, the processes of restoring the oxygen consumption—getting tired.

We thought getting tired would interact with getting bored, and that since getting tired has a lag in it (it takes some time to build up tiredness or fatigue), we should see these things producing oscillations. We predicted that there would be periodicities in the activity of children, and we set out to find that. We predicted the presence of biorhythms. We didn't know how to find out when you've got a biorhythm, so we recruited a NASA space statistician who had studied vibrations in the tailpipes of Saturn rockets and told him we were looking for vibrations in the behavior of children. We used spectral analysis, which is a procedure for decomposing periodic events into sine waves. We did produce statistically satisfying evidence that there were biorhythms in the activity of free-ranging children where the task demands were for energy expenditure. We had a very long cycle of about 45 minutes, and on top of that was a small cycle of about 15 minutes. We said, "Let us propose that these two systems are operating independently, that the 7.5 minutes up and 7.5 minutes down (15 minutes) is a work-rest biorhythm that expresses itself in this situation, and that the long one (45 minutes) is an incitement-habituation curve." We also assumed that normal children were biorhythmic in their activity. We then said, "Well, what happens if we study children who are called hyperactive? What happens to them? After all, it may be that hyperactivity is caused by a mismatch between permissible biorhythms in the institution and the biorhythms of the kid." And in profoundly retarded, hyperactive children we found absolutely random behavior (Wade, 1973). There was no variance that could be accounted for by a sine wave. They were classified as hyperactive because their behavior was very intrusive in the institution, because there was a low-level random expenditure of energy, a low-level, asystematic, nonmodulated expenditure. It didn't matter what you did; they just carried on doing the same thing. They were extremely intrusive in the institutional setting, but they weren't biorhythmic like the "normal" children that we studied. We used heart rate as a measure of energy expenditure rather than as a measure of attention. Later we started to use heart rate or changes in the heart rate—that is, heart rate variance—as a measure of attention.

The point is that there were periods in which the child would be habituating to the environment, would become bored as a result, and would be impelled to action again. When there was another child in there, the biorhythmicity was much stronger. It seemed as though they could get in phase with one another and then they had opportunities to generate interactions and get on with the business of expending energy.

HYPERACTIVITY

The notion is that the hyperactive child is emitting more activity than normal. First of all, there's some evidence to suggest that hyperactive children do not, in fact, emit more energy-consuming activity than normal, but that it is in some way distributed differently, or it occurs in obtrusive settings. The concern that hyperactivity is necessarily caused by some damage to an energy state in the brain was questioned by us simply because we found that in a free-play setting we couldn't tell the difference between the normal and hyperactive children, who were nevertheless extremely intrusive in the formal setting of the classroom (Karlsson, 1971).

Dr. J. Singer: Could you define again *hyperactive?* You referred to hyperactive retarded, and I'm not sure whether you're also referring to hyperactive "normal" kids who are identified as disruptive in the classroom.

Dr. Ellis: In the end we decided we would like to separate this word out and we used *hyperkinetic*—too much movement. In the one group were the profoundly retarded who had this random, flat spectrum activity, and in the second group the hyperactive, inappropriately active children who were making it in the real world but were just a damn nuisance. But they were only a nuisance in constrained or on-task settings. We were calming these kids down in Illinois by providing them with methylphenadate (Ellis, Witt, Reynolds, & Sprague, 1974).

Dr. J. Singer: In the example you just cited where double blind observers could not discriminate which were the inappropriately active kids, what criteria were they using?

Dr. Ellis: We had a whole bunch of dependent variables which described the quantity and the nature of the activity emitted by a group of children. When we did the statistical analysis to sort them out and test for those labelled *inappropriately active* and *not inappropriately active,* we couldn't tell the difference in the playroom, but the difference was like six standard deviations on a normal scale for when they were behaving in a classroom. We couldn't tell the difference in the free-range setting as to whether they were on placebo or very large doses of methylphenadate. In other words, methylphenadate modulated the inappropriate activity in the constrained setting but not in the free-range setting. And our conclusion was that inappropriate hyperactivity is setting modulated. It deals with either the "unwillingness" or the inability of the inappropriately hyperactive child to respond to the task demands of constraint. The question is, what do we do about it? That has very important implications for the management of the stimulus density or the information density of the classroom. It may be that an inappropriately active child is one who cannot tolerate relatively low levels of information or stimuli from the environment. I'd not want to use the word *stimuli,* because stimuli need not necessarily carry information; they may only carry stimulus energy. We also found again that the peer influence was important. When we made a mistake and simply allowed a group to exist, rather than counterbalancing membership, a play episode would last for more than one setting. There was not independence between play settings. Big deal! Everybody would say, "Well, how did it take you so long to figure that out?" Hindsight is so much richer than foresight. We had structured our experiment another way, allowing the groups to remain intact. Those groups ran on themes, quite independently of the drug conditions the kids were on. Of course, they were playing monsters today and monsters were neat, so that when they came in the next time, or while they were waiting for their cab to take them back to the school, they would play monsters because they had played monsters the day before. And that masked out any effect. So my argument here is that insofar as we're looking at activity—the expression of energy-consuming responses—as biorhythmic, it seems to be modulated strongly by the number of peers. It's also modulated by the task demands, the activity demands of the setting. It's *not* modulated by methylphenadate, which seems to be extremely ineffective.

Dr. Collard: Weren't there possibly some children who might become overstimulated by having too much in the room and therefore become disorganized? I'm thinking again about the distractability of some minimally brain-damaged infants, where too much stimulation will throw them off, whereas with a lot of your hyperactive kids the pacing is terribly important. If you fit the pacing of what you're doing or what you offer them to their pacing and give them the freedom, they're okay; but with some children, too much stimulation will have the opposite effect.

Dr. Ellis: The important discrimination that Jerry [Dr. Singer] reminded me of is hyperkinetic versus hyperactive kids. You play white noise for hyperkinetic kids and it increases their response level. If you increase the tummy rumbling by making them hungry, their randomly asystematic behavior increases just before lunch time and decreases just after lunch time. That looks like appetitive behavior.

The theme that I want to get through here is that there seems to be a modulation of the behavior that is a function of the interaction between the child's need for information, if we accept the need, and the potential of the setting for generating information.

Dr. Sutton-Smith: I don't have any concrete images. Were these kids running around metered?

Dr. Ellis: Yes, we were monitoring multichannel telemetry.

Dr. Sutton-Smith: Did you have a rise and fall over forty-five minutes in the degree of output?

Dr. Ellis: Yes. Over, say, a minute, the heart rate seemed to be responding to the energy expenditure of the child. It's as if the sum of the antecedent energy expenditures is reflected in the energy transport necessary to remove their side effects. You're using the heart rate as a means of measuring how much fuel this guy has just consumed, and the consumption goes up and down. The heart rate variance, on the other hand, is how the heart's behavior is influenced by central processes. I think there are two separate mechanisms.

We also studied boredom, because the Department of Mental Health was interested in stereotyped behavior: head banging, picking, the surplus responses that are so damaging and so intrusive. We found that we could introduce what ethologists would call stereotyped behavior in about four minutes in quite normal children. In other words, stereotyped behaviors are normal; they are in fact a response to information in private settings (Ellis & Sholtz, 1977). They would emit repetitious off-task behaviors when the task was so simple that it had no information in it. We refer to looking at the light, body manipulations, repetitious grooming responses, playing with the clothes. We could induce a whole bunch of those kinds of stereotyped responses by merely getting the kid bored. You could say we carefully controlled the amount of information-bearing stimuli in the setting. We could retard it or accelerate it by manipulating the complexity and novelty of displays in the room. This thread of controlling the behavior of the child by manipulating the potential for generating information was something that paralleled the earlier work on functional complexity.

Dr. McCall: With respect to nervous or hyperkinetic behavior, were you suggesting that it's not nervous necessarily in the anxiety sense but that it's a gap-filling activity while little else is going on?

Dr. Collard: A displacement activity?

Dr. Ellis: You could call it that. Somebody else referred to the surplus behavior of fiddling with your leg. You look at people under the table and some people have their leg flipping around. We are emitting all kinds of time-filling behaviors that don't seem to be product oriented. You can't figure out what results from that—why they are doing that.

Dr. McCall: Do you see anything pathological in these behaviors? Do you speculate that they have developed these for different reasons, or have just come to learn this as a response that they habitually do in certain circumstances?

Dr. Ellis: I'm familiar with two explanations for the quasi-pathological, very large rocking behaviors, such as head banging. One explanation is from Berlyne (1960), who argues that there's a paradoxical effect. You chronically reduce the level of information available, and that induces anxiety—it's aversive—and over months this builds up. (You see it in animals as well, incidentally.) Then the organism becomes extremely anxious about this chronic deprivation and reduces that anxiety by emitting highly redundant responses as a way of diminishing anxiety. For example, polar bears and wooly monkeys and seals emit the same type of stereotyped responses. The Ellis explanation for that—and remember, I'm a physical educator so I'm interested in motor behavior—is that to maintain a motor response constant you have to track out all the disturbing elements that would alter that response. If you want to rock at sixty-five rocks per minute, there are all kinds of influences on you that tend to drift that off. You get tired. The chair is different. Then you have to null errors. And errors when being nulled contain information. I don't know how you would prove it except by starting to manipulate the influences that tend to induce error. My argument is that when a person is emitting highly timed, constant, stereotyped responses or spatially constant responses, he can in fact be answering questions. Can I track out to sixty-five rocks per minute? Can I produce the same response even though my arm is slightly different today from what it was yesterday? I'm not sure which one makes sense.

Dr. Lewis: Then it's an information task that the organism is involved in.

Dr. Ellis: The information is contained in the internal feedback, which says, "Is there now an error in the last response? How do I null it?"

Dr. Lewis: You could argue that it's an exclusion. The organism's strategy is just to exclude those error-producing events so that it can continue.

Dr. Ellis: That, in a sense, requires some information. You have to respond to the changing circumstances in order to keep something constant. They may both be very casuistic kinds of explanations, but one came from Berlyne and says they're so anxious that they produce redundant responses to reduce the level of anxiety. The other one says that a person is generating information by emitting highly stable redundant responses.

Dr. J. Singer: One possibility is that the person could introduce privately generated stimulation—that is, images, fantasies, memories, and that sort of information—into the situation that's understimulated, rather than having to engage in motor activities; or you could do both. I wonder if that doesn't tie in with some of your inappropriately active kids. Maybe their problem is that when they're in a constrained environment they still seek externally derived information. They lack some capacity or interest in producing privately generated stimuli—interior monologues, fantasies, little make-believe games that they could in effect play at their desks.

Dr. Fein: I think what Roberta [Dr. Collard] was saying was that it is not unusual to see kids who go crazy in free-ranging situations but hold together very well in constraining situations. So it seems to me your paradigm is suggesting that you have these two kinds of organizations, each of which may have very different implications for managing children as well as for therapy and situational organization. Have you experimented with the other part of it?

Dr. Ellis: I spent a lot of time worrying about the various explanations for play, and what you've just described is usually given as an example that play behavior is, to some extent, the burning of surplus energy. If we constrain someone, then he explodes into the unconstrained setting with nonproductive kinds of gross energy-expenditure behaviors—rushing around playgrounds or blacktops, cannoning all over the place. It's like little molecules let out of a constrained setting.

Dr. Fein: Yet there are some kids like this who are really dramatically different when one sits down with them. There then is a more defined, well-structured, guided convergent requirement, and everything gets put together, and there's just a new child.

Dr. Ellis: A research associate, Bob Korb, came out with a proposal for a way of thinking about that which would account for both sides of the coin. He talks about tractability, the propensity of the child to respond to the task-demand characteristics. A hyperactive child is a person who is intractable—who will go on emitting his externally related or externally generated stimuli whether that's appropriate or not; and the other side of the coin is the child who is differently and sensitively responsive to the demand characteristics of the setting. When it's constrained, they're constrained. When it's unconstrained, they're wild. His argument is that the drug, methylphenadate, increases the tractability of the inappropriately hyperactive child. In some way they respond better to the task-demand characteristics.

Dr. Hutt: It seems to me that the only construct that ties the phenomena together is that of arousal, because you can not only obtain independent evidences of arousal other than your behavioral measures, but you can make specific predictions, like the action of methylphenadate, from what you know about the arousal systems.

Dr. Ellis: I've been using the word *information* up until now because most people are a little happier with that. Now going beyond that is attractive to me. It is valuable from a biological viewpoint to postulate that arousal mechanisms that we don't know much about do, in fact, mediate play behavior. It's very attractive to me because I can see how that would have become stabilized in mammals over their evolution because they can see a selective advantage accruing to those organisms that are differentially susceptible to change in their environment, and who are impelled in a sense, when the environment remains constant, to introduce changes into the environment (Ellis, 1973). Those kinds of advantages seem to be reasonably obvious and could explain from a biological viewpoint how such a mechanism became selected. Now if you'll allow the concept of an arousal box—a mechanism that compares and rewards and which just lies somewhere in there—if you're a neuroanatomist you can even go probing around to see if you can find it. By inference it looks as though there ought to be such a mechanism. And if there is, and if the organism is differentially rewarded for information generating, then in an extraordinarily rich setting you can see how very rapidly the behavior of the organism responds to it.

Action within the environment would account for lots and lots of things that we've been talking about. In other words, when you say, "Why would a child do that?" sometimes I'll say, "Because by doing that he generates uncertainty in the setting and establishes a process for resolving the uncertainty."

Dr. Fein: I think the uncomfortableness I feel with these rather general information-processing arousal arguments is that they *are* so very general, and they do not in any kind of organized or structured way help to work out the kinds of components of an environment that a child has to break apart. Our discussion about inappropriately active children was suggesting that in fact there may be particular kinds of information which certain kinds of children have difficulty in dealing with because of the information subtleties. One of those really has to do with the question of what are the rules. What is the logic of the situation in terms of where you stop and where you start? That's one kind of environmental information which is essential to the whole cultural process of the child in terms of understanding the society, understanding the culture, understanding the situations, understanding the difference between home and school, the difference between a classroom and a playroom.

Dr. Ellis: It *is* very general, and I don't mind that. Now you're asking much more specific questions. We in my laboratory were remarkably unsuccessful in demonstrating the predicted physiological correlates of this concept (Ellis, Barnett, & Korb, 1973). We just weren't skilled enough or we just didn't know enough to be able to say, "Here is an 'arousing' situation. Can we see the concomitant changes in the biology or the physiology of the organism?" We tried very hard to do that, and failed. Now I saw in Corinne's [Dr. Hutt's] paper the first signs of some grip on this problem, and I'm excited by that, because as soon as we have another way of getting at it then I think we're off to the races, and it will become rapidly and markedly less general. But it does one other thing that I think is terribly important. Information must be defined in terms of the antecedent experiences of the individual. This forces you to pay attention to the enormous diversity in the interactions that we have seen. It seems to me that everybody is trying to force patterns on the content. I don't think there are patterns on the content that go across individuals, but that in a metatheoretical sense the patterns are in the interaction between the individual's past experiences and the content of the response right now.

Dr. Garvey: You mentioned the possible phylogenetic reasons. You made an ethological-like statement saying that perhaps this information, or moderating, *modulating* box, the arousal box, was very important in relating the organism to its environment; it becomes a stable operating system, or method of systems. That's a theme we haven't brought up very much in this conference but it's probably an important one. You just made an allusion to another theme that ties in with it, and that was the question of an engineer's notion of *tractability*. And someone else brought up the notion of *compliance*. In looking at Dorothy's [Dr. Singer's] TV, has it struck you as it strikes me how amazingly tractable and agreeable children are? When you say, "Let's play this" or "Let's do this," the so-called normal child, the one who does not present himself as a problem, is immensely compliant. This too has long-range effects in how children come to be children and adapt themselves to living as children. I'm not sure that it might not somewhere along the line be connected to information arousal, that is, that one of the forces that operates on the information has to do with the ability to read, and to comply with directives from adults.

Dr. Ellis: The hyperactive child is called so because he is quite often unwilling to comply. What were the compliance requirements of the setting and how did they influence the way hyperactives and normals responded?

Dr. McCall: I think I'd like to be devil's advocate. First of all, I agree with the response to Greta [Dr. Fein] that as a discipline, at least, psychology isn't going to get very far with play and exploration unless we look, as we have been trained to, at specific responses. I don't think play and exploration are matters of specific responses. There is a unity among each of them that is of a different genre; so I am not uncomfortable with these approaches at least, but I feel we're still in our initial stages of studying them. On the other hand, there's a danger with general orientations, and the danger is one that I see in the notion of the arousal level. I'm not enthused about the arousal notions in play because I don't think they contribute any information to me about play that differentiates it from any other behavior. If you take any behavior and you have to have some energy to get the behavior going, you can say that in a sample of subjects there's an average level of arousal at which this behavior typically occurs. But there will be variability. Now in the normal course of events some kids are going to be expending so much energy at rates that are incompatible with this average that you don't expect them to do that behavior when they are at high arousal. But when they are too low, then you expect them to be more likely to show the behavior that will put them at that average level. In the extreme it's obvious: if a kid is shaking and agitated he's not going to play, and if he's asleep he's not going to play. That's ridiculous, but I'm not sure it's so far away from the arousal notion. Now to call that average level "optimal" is an inference that I am unwilling to make unless I have extra information that says there is something utterly unique about this level such that the behavior cannot occur at any other level of arousal; otherwise, to say there's an average level of arousal at which this behavior tends to occur is to say very little. Next, a pure arousal notion does not tell me why the organism does some things and not other things. So I am caught in my own thinking that you have to have some energy concept to get behavior going, but how much more have we learned, or can we expect to learn, from an arousal notion? The one thing I can think of as useful is the idling concept. That is, that the organism has a certain *idling level*. From that derives the notion of the gap-filling behavior—dreaming, imagining, or hyperactivity. That tells me something. For the rest, I'm just not persuaded it's any different from any other class of behaviors. Take problem solving: you can't be too anxious or too little anxious. There's an optimum or average level of tenseness.

Dr. Ellis: That changes, of course, with task difficulty. But I think there *is* something that arousal concepts tell you. You can in fact predict the kinds of behaviors that result—the systems people have figured out. They have looked at the strategies used by people to diminish the quantity of information coming on board. They queue the information up, they chunk it up, they multiplex it, they leave some of it out, they say to hell with it and escape. There are all of those kinds of things happening when there are high loads of information. Now there seems to be something different happening when you put a person into a situation where the load is small. And you can do that systematically, as in the boredom studies. These special kids that we study in a research institute are a population apart; they're really used to these kinds of things. They come into little experimental rooms, and if there's nothing there, like "Go in that room and get bored, kid," they cannot cope with that. So we had a series of dummy tasks that you could accomplish in three seconds. In one of them all you had to do when a tone came up was to turn the tone off by pressing a button. The tone would go on about every 50 seconds. So what does the kid do for the 49.9 seconds that he's not cancelling the tone? There is nothing happening. There's a temporal certainty it's not going to be happening for a long time. During that time you begin to see all kinds of elaborations which I think in general, collectively and intuitively, we've called playful. They start to generate information-bearing responses. I think halfway between uncritically espousing the arousal-seeking model and completely rejecting it there is a point where we can at least say there are directions involved in the behavior, and I think it's that that's useful, and that will be a thread.

Dr. D. Singer: I think sometimes it's also a question of labeling. Because I've noticed that in one nursery school the tolerance for what we're now calling appropriate behavior may be greater, so that you can watch a child walk or run around a room for a long period of time, in a very aimless, hyperactive fashion, while in another school we see very quiet, controlled behavior. The climate is really different where the teacher in a sense has a contract (it's a hidden contract) that she doesn't tolerate this kind of behavior. Or I've seen even another kind of situation where the amount of energy put out by one child who, if the teacher hadn't changed the game, was such that he would probably have been called a hyperkinetic child in a hyperactive game. He was taking a block and stepping on it and trying to shoot off another block into the air as a missile, so that it would hurt another child. He did that for quite a bit of time until the teacher came over and redirected the energy and had him take the two blocks and make a balance beam. Now he was still very excited, very hyperactive, but something happened by using the same two materials in a different way. Suddenly all of the children who were his enemies and were frightened of him now got on line behind him to try the balance beam. He was still very active, still full of affect, and the center of attention, but the teacher had rechanneled all that. So you see all different kinds of behaviors in natural situations labeled one thing or another, and I'm sure if I could have measured that child his arousal system would have been as high in both games, but now one was suddenly socially appropriate and one was inappropriate, due to the teacher's redirection.

Dr. Garvey: In response to Bob's [Dr. McCall's] suggestion: if we can get off the average or the norm for intensity, don't you have some kind of data that you could use to compare other kinds of activities in terms of your periodicity, so that you're concerned not with the height of arousal but with the phase? Wouldn't that phasing change and perhaps be a way of distinguishing between kinds of activity? Say the child is waiting in between button pushes—does he show the same kind of sine wave?

Dr. Ellis: We were unsuccessful in doing that, but I have the feeling that Corinne [Dr. Hutt] *has* been successful here, and all we need to do now is to apply the procedures for saying, "Is that a reliable phasing?" "Is that reliably periodic?" We had developed the methods and failed to generate the behavior. I think Corinne [Dr. Hutt] has got the behavior, and a very simple short step is now to say, "Yes, these are the sine waves that describe this behavior." And I'm really excited about that because at last I see something that I think would be useful.

Dr. Garvey: The temporal distributions that I'm trying to hunt down in interspeaker pauses and speech have this kind of characteristic, and I think it's in those temporal parameters that we might find some very interesting processes distinguished, and different classes of experiencing.

Dr. Ellis: I had an experiment that I wanted to do which for technical reasons didn't work out. In it, the procedure would be either experimenter paced through high-to-low information content, or subject paced through high-to-low information content. The experimenter pace would be periodic, and the biological events accompanying the information process should follow that out. In the situation where the subjects could pace themselves they should be able to null the errors and maintain the parameters in a much narrower wave band. Those kinds of things are just around the corner, I think. They are quite specific predictions that come from the arousal mode, and I think it's wrong to say that the arousal mode doesn't enable you to make specific predictions. I think it does. The reason I stopped doing this three years ago and tried to figure out what we had done for the last seven years is that I felt that I no longer had the skills to get to the next step; I needed to acquire sophistication in cognitive processes. After all, processing information involves individual cognitive processing on the part of the subject-child or person, and I had no expertise in that—I'm great on heart rate and oxygen consumption! The other thing is that I felt I wanted to demonstrate the psychophysiological correlates of play behavior, and I didn't know anything about that either. Personally, as a researcher I'm now ready to move to a different plane of operating with the phenomena because I think that I've mined the kind of gross stuff that we did as far as it can go.

Dr. Singer: First of all, I want to stress again Greta's [Dr. Fein's] point about the situational aspects. I think your study makes that very striking in the constrained and nonconstrained situation, and probably what we need in this area is to do more studies of the taxonomy of social structures, and then tie those back to information seeking and information processing, or even arousal tendencies, in relation to different kinds of settings. I think we've done surprisingly little of that in this field.

Another aspect that's not exactly related has to do with the distinction between processing information from the external environment and self-generative processing. And here we have a lot of data (really more from adults, although there's some data from children also) that suggest that you get at least some striking individual difference variables that come up again and again. To give a couple of quick examples: you mentioned the vigilance or self-monitoring task, signal-detection kinds of experiments. We've done quite a large number of those in which individuals are monitoring a light that flashes off and on. It's a long, boring task and they're doing it correctly because they're being paid, and they're getting about 90 percent accuracy. But some individuals pretty quickly introduce a great deal of what we call task-irrelevant ideation, or stimulus-independent mentation. There's some form of daydreaming, which we tap, entering into the situation, though I won't go into methodology. This becomes important after a while, to the point where they're willing to give up their accuracy and give up the money in order to continue processing their private material, because at a certain point it does begin to interfere. At first it doesn't interfere, and they say, in effect, "The hell with it; I'd rather pay attention to my own thoughts," whereas others will stick with the external stimuli. There's also a whole literature now on sensation seeking, which grew out of attempts to measure behaviors within sensory-deprivation situations. Marvin Zuckerman at the University of Delaware has developed a series of scales and has done quite a lot of research on that; and in a recent study that I was involved in, we tested over 1,000 college students, looking at drug and alcohol use. We found the single best predictor, and one with a tremendously high discriminability, was the scale of external sensation seeking. In other words, the people who were constantly on the lookout in the external environment for sensation, for experimentation, and were not as interested in or didn't have the experience or the capacity for self-generating material, were the ones who went for the drugs or the alcohol use in college.

Dr. Ellis: In my field, we count alcohol usage as another legitimate recreational activity. It is frowned upon by our society and has noxious side effects, but then many recreational activities have noxious side effects.

I only have one other point, and I'm not going to elaborate it, but I bring it to you because we've almost avoided it in this conference and I'm afraid we'll never get to it. I have a feeling that one of our difficulties in studying play behavior is the inherent difficulty that this material presents for the scientific method. To capsulate that very briefly: the normal scientific paradigm involves demonstrating control of the subject's behavior in this demonstrating control of the subject's behavior in this field, and yet a common theme in play theory is that *play behavior is inner-directed behavior*—in some way, the contingencies and processes are internal. And so to study them in the conventional scientific paradigm requires us to acquire control over internal events and thereby subvert them. Some day I'd love to talk that all out with some people, because it's been frustrating for me to take the conventional paradigms and apply them to this intensely personal kind of behavior.

References

Berlyne, D. E. *Conflict, Arousal and Curiosity*. New York: McGraw-Hill, 1960.
Ellis, M. J. *Why People Play*. Englewood Cliffs, N.J.: Prentice-Hall, 1973.
Ellis, M. J., Barnett, L. A., & Korb, R. J. "Psycho-physiological Correlates of Play." Abstract describing an uncompleted project. Annual Report of the MPPRL, Children's Research Center, University of Illinois, 1973.
Ellis, M. J., Witt, P. A., Reynolds, R., & Sprague, R. C., "Methylphenadate and the Activity of Hyperactives in the Informal Setting." *Child Development*, 1974, *45*, 217–220.
Ellis, M. J., & Scholtz, G. J. L. *Activity and Play of Children*. Englewood Cliffs, N.J.: Prentice-Hall, 1977.
Gramza, A. F. "Preferences of Preschool Children for Enterable Play Boxes." *Perceptual and Motor Skills*, 1970, *31*, 177–178.
Gramza, A. F., Corush, J., & Ellis, M. J. "Children's Play on Trestles Differing in Complexity: A Study of Play Equipment Design." *Journal of Leisure Research*, 1972, *4*, 303–311.
Gramza, A. F., & Scholtz, G. J. L. "Children's Responses to Visual Complexity in a Play Setting." *Psychological Reports*, 1974, *35*, 895–899.
Gramza, A. F., & Witt, P. A. "Choices of Colored Blocks in the Play of Preschool Children." *Perceptual and Motor Skills*, 1969, *29*, 783–787.
Herron, R. E., & Sutton-Smith, B. *Child's Play*. New York: John Wiley & Sons, 1971.
Karlsson, K. A. "Hyperactivity and Environmental Compliance." Ph.D. dissertation, University of Illinois, 1971.
Wade, M. G. "Biorhythms and Activity Level of Institutionalized Mentally Retarded Persons Diagnosed Hyperactive." *American Journal of Mental Deficiency*, 1973, *78*, 262–267.

Wade, M. G., & Ellis, M. J. "Measurement of Free Range Activity in Children as Modified by Social and Environmental Complexity." *The American Journal of Clinical Nutrition,* 1971, *24,* 1457–1460.

Wade, M. G., Ellis, M. J., & Bohrer, R. E. "Biorhythms in the Activity of Children during Free Play." *Journal of the Experimental Analysis of Behavior,* 1973, *20,* 155–162.

Witt, P. A., & Gramza, A. F. "Position Effects in Play Equipment Preferences on Nursery School Children." *Perceptual and Motor Skills,* 1970, *31,* 431–434.

Chapter 10

EXPLORATION AND PLAY (#2)

Corinne Hutt

INTRODUCTION

Dr. Sutton-Smith: Dr. Hutt brings to focus much of the earlier discussion on arousal, activity levels, and information processing in the papers of Drs. Shultz, McCall and Ellis as well as the distinction between exploration and play in the paper by Collard. Treating her discussion in terms of various conceptual levels, she first approaches the adaptive value of play as a form of metabolic recuperation and neural priming; proceeds to discuss play in terms of its physiological correlate; namely, heart rate variability (with interesting if puzzling implications for the biorhythms of which Ellis speaks; and perhaps even for the biphasic quality of arousal discussed by Shultz, and the shift from prototypic to nonprototypic variability introduced by Fein); and proceeds to discuss play in terms of its linguistic complexity and conceptual reorganization. She introduces the startling (to this group) notion that children's learning may be done in the exploratory period, not in the playful period. This leads in turn to discussion of the kinds of mastery involved in play. Is it a consolidation, a reorganization, or a transformation (as earlier discussed by Garvey)? Are these not kinds of learning? Hutt goes on to show that as compared with exploration, play is a relatively less resilient behavior and is more dependent upon contextual (space-time) and mood variables. Exploration is a more direct function of player competence and object complexity.

There is a further discussion of the absoluteness of the exploration-play distinction and of the nature of the special operations which characterize play—whether here more than elsewhere production matches competence, as seems implied from some of the statements of play's complexity (Ellis, Garvey, Gardner, etc.)

Questions are also raised about our dependence on the children's language itself to infer the nature of the child's internal life during play.

Dr. Hutt: Perhaps some words of introduction are necessary regarding my personal orientation, in order to make more sense of the kind of line I've tried to take and the perspective I've adopted. My approach is principally a biological one; I was a student of Tinbergen, and my first essay in this area was an ethological one. Therefore I've tried to see human and animal phenomena in a biological perspective in which I don't see discontinuities in the nature of play but simply changes in the manner of manifestation. I've tried, therefore, to relate mammalian and primate play to children's play, but less to adult leisure activities. I also happen to believe that what goes on inside the nervous system, whether it's the central nervous system or the autonomic nervous system, has some relation to the behavior being manifested, and if we can get some insight from measures of psychophysiology or neurophysiology that would help us elucidate the behavioral phenomena, then we can only be the wiser by using them. But I don't see these indices as an end in themselves. Thus, I tend to shift from a biological to a physiological level to a cognitive level to a sociological level, trying, at any time, to make explicit the particular level at which I am operating. So in a sense I plead guilty to a certain amount of intellectual or conceptual promiscuity. I regard this as permissible where fertility is the outcome, and I promise to mend my ways if the result is sterility!

EXPLORATION AND PLAY

I have attempted to devise a taxonomy of play; that is, a classification of all those activities of children which adults customarily term *play* (see Figure 10-1), in order to distinguish two main categories from each other. These are *epistemic* behaviors (concerning the acquisition of information and knowledge) and *ludic* behaviors (those playful activities which bear upon and utilize past experience). As portrayed here, the taxonomy is particularly appropriate to the play of three- to five-year-olds, but with increasing age each of these modes may become more differentiated.

I devised this taxonomy because I was faced with a practical problem: having studied exploration and play, and succeeded in elucidating some distinctive features enabling us to recognize and separate these two categories of behavior, I was faced with a practical educational situation, insofar as the Education White Paper in Britain (D.E.S. 1972) provided for a tremendous expanse in nursery education. Thus all of a sudden the study of play became extremely important, and educational practitioners were looking to psychologists—developmental psychologists—to give them some guidelines. One of the most significant findings of our earlier

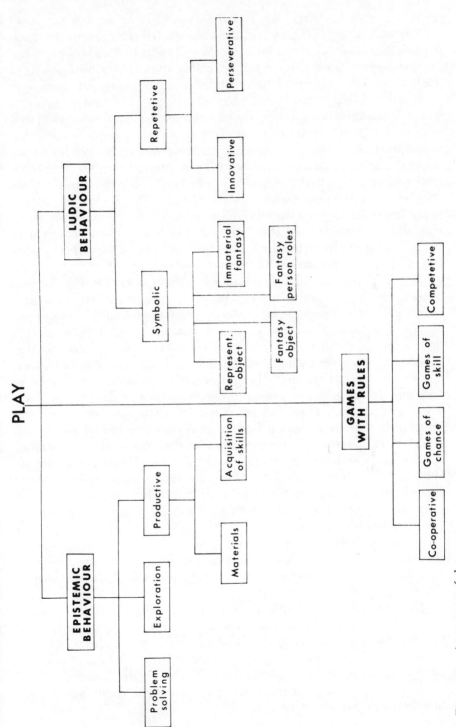

Figure 10-1. A taxonomy of play

series of studies was that children only got launched on an imaginative sequence with a toy that they had already explored (Hutt 1970a, b). Incidentally, much of what I'm going to say will apply to the child exploring
and playing on its own, since I have really confined myself to looking at
the transitions between exploration and play in the solitary situation.

We found that, once launched in a sequence of imaginative play, it
was very unlikely the child would find out about any *new* features of that
object other than by pure accident. To give you an example of a toy that
belled and buzzed on certain movements: suppose the children found out
about the bell and then used the bell in some game; thereafter, the probability was very high that they would not find out about the buzzer unless
they hit upon that movement quite accidentally. This finding has educational implications because this kind of play sequence, which ones sees
very often in a preschool setting, can preclude learning of a certain kind;
i.e., the acquisition of further information about a particular target object. I felt it was necessary to try to communicate this distinction to teachers especially, because the preschool ideology in Britain is that children
learn through play, and therefore children are permitted an abundance
of free play. It is thought to be only a question of providing the appropriate equipment—that children are then bound to "learn" in the sense that
they acquire information, are able to categorize, classify, and develop
fundamental cognitive skills through simply playing. I felt it was important to demonstrate that not all forms of play necessarily have this sort of
outcome. But one was in a semantic quagmire in that the term *play* was
being used for such a heterogeneous assortment of behaviors, and it was
imperative that these be categorized and distinguished in some way.
Hence the distinctions I have tried to draw, the main distinction parallel-
ing Berlyne's (1960) original one of specific and diversive exploration.
When I talk of play, therefore, I am referring to *ludic* behaviors. But
since ludic refers as much to the manner in which an activity is performed as to the nature of the activity, epistemic behaviors may also be
performed in a *ludic mode*.

Question: Solitary play is a model for your thinking here. Usually
there are other children in a play situation. From others they may learn
what they may not have discovered for themselves. Might that make a
difference educationally?

Dr. Hutt: Indeed. *Exploration* is not a category which is neatly
defined in temporal terms. There is alternation between serious exploration and more playful manipulation of the object or toy. This occurs both
in the social and the individual situation, whether the information comes
from a peer or from the individual himself. There is no clear-cut and dramatic transition from exploration to play; the child alternates for some
time between the two activities.

Temporal Differences

There are also certain temporal characteristics which are distinctive of exploration and play, and these too have implications for behavior theory.

In our studies we used three temporal schedules, the toy being available every other day, or daily, or twice a day. Morphological markers were used to delineate epochs of exploration. We could find no difference in the rate of habituation in exploration under the three temporal schedules; i.e., response decrement in exploration was not affected by the temporal schedule. Play, on the other hand, was very markedly affected by the temporal schedule (see Figures 10-2 and 10-3): massed trials elicited least play, while spacing the trials or exposures produced most play. Stimulus satiation, therefore, was reflected in play rather than in exploration, and one can see the adaptive significance of this. I shall return to the adaptive dialectic over and over again, because my primary question concerns the function of play, whether for the animal or the human organism.

If there is a certain amount of information to be obtained by the child from a source of novelty, incongruity, discrepancy, etc., the rate at which this information is acquired is dependent on two main factors: his *cognitive competence* and the *complexity of the object*. Factors like temporal schedules do not have much effect on the amount of exploration. A child will process the information about the stimulus object at a rate compatible with his cognitive competence. On the other hand, what he goes on

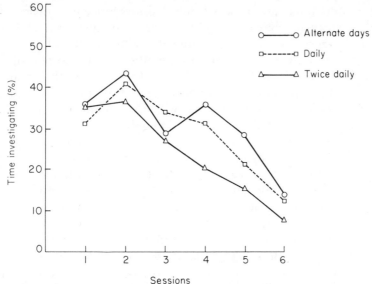

Figure 10-2. Decrements in investigatory responses under three temporal schedules: ●——● alternate days (n = 6); □——□ daily (n = 4); ■——■ twice daily (n = 4)

Sessions

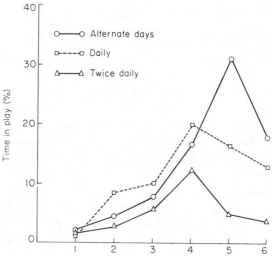

Figure 10-3. Amounts of 'play' involving the object displayed under three temporal schedules, with sound and vision: •———• alternate days (n = 6); □———□ daily (n = 4, except for sixth session when data for only two subjects); ■———■ twice daily (n = 4)

to do with the information thereafter is affected by a number of factors; e.g., mood changes, temporal schedules, past experience, and so on.

Physiological Differences

Entering the adaptive dialectic again, one may ask: what is the biological function of play and how is it selected for? Since playful activity can be inhibited relatively easily, and by a variety of environmental and organismic factors, its place in the motivational hierarchy is fairly low. Exploration, or epistemic behavior, on the other hand, is superordinate in the motivational hierarchy: no matter what the state of the organism or what conditions prevail, exploration is difficult to inhibit. For instance, rats and monkeys who are hungry will first explore the containers in which they are presented food before eating the food.

If, therefore, play has the adaptive and important functions generally attributed to it, why does it not occupy a high position in the motivational hierarchy? Should it be so easily inhibited by adverse conditions, negative affect states, fear, illness, etc? I am going to argue that the principal function of play is a very general one: that it acts as a neural primer. In other words, I wish to put play within a broader category of *arousal-modulating behaviors;* it is for this reason I consider *arousal* a crucial construct, though I agree with Bob McCall that there is a lot it does not explain satisfactorily. At the moment, however, it is the best I have to work with, and I can make better predictions using that construct than without it.

Now what are these arousal-modulating behaviors? There are a variety of behaviors classed as *displacement activities* occurring in mammalian species in situations of conflict. In humans, homologous behaviors are manifest as stereotypes or mannerisms of various kinds; Mike Ellis described some that occurred in stimulus-deprivation experiments. Stereotypies also occur in circumstances of overstimulation (e.g., children jump when excited) or where arousal is endogenously high, as in autistic children and schizophrenics. In this latter case the stereotyped behaviors are being used to block further novel sensory or perceptual input (Hutt & Hutt, 1968).

In attempting to reinterpret arousal in terms of information processing, Delius (1970) has argued that mechanisms for the reduction of processing rate have evolved and been actively selected for. Although the principal function of the nervous system is to process information, it also has to regulate and distribute metabolic energy as and when required. To a certain extent there is some incompatibility in these two functions. If the nervous system is engaged in the distribution and recuperation of metabolic resources, then its channel capacity, in terms of information processing, is reduced, and at such times behaviors which have the function of reducing information influx come into operation. Whatever behaviors are employed, they have in common the transient uncoupling of cortical regulatory centers from subcortical and autonomic processes (Hutt & Hutt, 1977). This uncoupling is reflected in a relative increase of *heart rate variability;* i.e., in the beat-to-beat fluctuation in heart rate (see Figures 10-4 and 10-5).

We can see now the advantage of moving from one conceptual level to another: the use of such a psychophysiological marker or index gives us a further insight into the state of the organism. Heart rate variability (HRV), for example, is associated with behaviors which are used by autistic children to minimize information input (Hutt, Forrest, & Richer, 1975). Thus HRV may be used as a marker of *uncoupling*, or of times when the nervous system is endeavoring to reduce the information-processing rate, either because channel capacity is already exceeded or because of competing demands.

Rapid eye movement (REM) sleep is such a period of uncoupling in all individuals, when certain recuperative functions are known to take place (Oswald, 1969). Deprivation of REM has detrimental effects. I am suggesting that ludic-behaviors play serves a physiological function in the awake organism analogous to that of REM sleep. During play there is temporary suspension of the cortical information-processing functions—the nervous system may be described as "idling," in the sense of an electromechanical engine, while at the same time allowing metabolic restitutive functions to take place.

The psychophysiological evidence from heart rate does in fact show that during ludic behaviors the organism is functioning in a very different

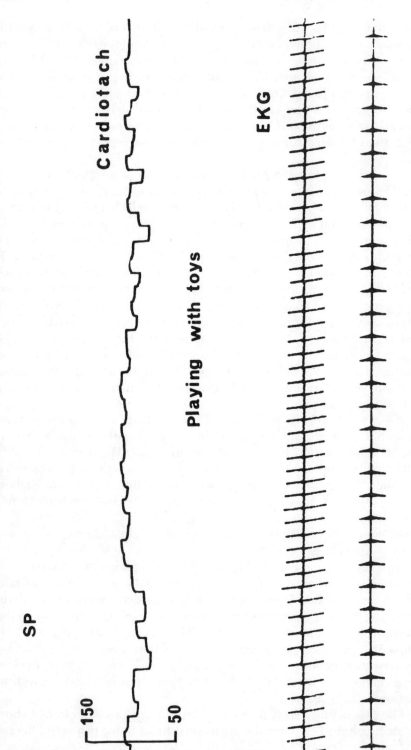

Figure 10-4. Heart rate and rate-of-exchange of HR (as shown in the cardiotachograph) during the play of a 2-year-old boy.

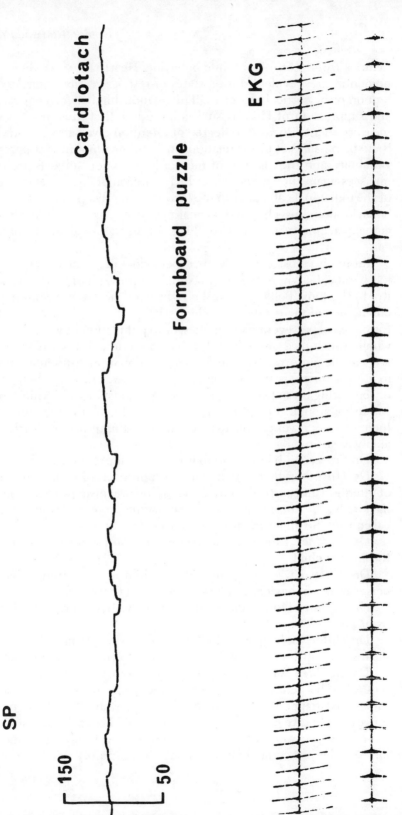

Figure 10-5. The more suppressed or stabilised HR record of the same boy during the solution of a formboard puzzle.

manner from that in epistemic behavior. Heart rate variability is a phenomenon most evident during states of rest; it is easily suppressed by attention or by cortical processes. The relationship between concentration
and suppression of HRV is such a close one that in adults it is used to
measure mental load—the degree of attention given to vigilance tasks—
there being a direct linear relationship between amount of suppression of
variability and the amount of mental load. When subjects are relaxed,
one sees again the emergence of heart rate variability. The arrangement
of the individual categories in the taxonomy has been determined by both
behavioral and psychophysiological measures. We can argue about their
actual placement later on if you like, but first let me paint the broad can-
vas.

From the most cortically-cued behaviors of problem solving on the
left hand side, where there is maximal suppression of heart rate variability, to the ludic behaviors on the right hand side, there is an increasing
emergence of heart rate variability. HRV is thus highest during the performance of perseverative activities; or to put it another way, the system is
wholly uncoupled and idling. We have mentioned that the same behaviors can be performed seriously in a functional, instrumental manner or
in a ludic manner. We are able now to use heart rate variability as a way
of separating these two modes: of twenty-six instances in which the child
was using an object in either an instrumental/exploratory manner or in a
ludic manner, twenty-one instances were distinguished by heart rate variability measures.

Dr. Singer: With lower variability during play sequence?

Dr. Hutt: No, higher variability. Suppression of variability is a result
of attention and cortical control. When the organism is relaxed, idling behaviorally, the autonomic system too is idling, removed from direct cortical control. So *high variability is more evident in play.*

Dr. Gardner: I did not understand the point you were making about
the autistic child.

Dr. Hutt: I was using the autistic child as an extreme example of
perseverative behavior, at the extreme end of that continuum.

Dr. Gardner: Do you have anything to say about ludic behaviors in autism?

Dr. Hutt: No, because I don't think they show ludic behaviors, if one
means to imply thereby that these are characterized by positive affect.

Dr. Gardner: When you were talking about what you saw as the purpose of ludic behavior, as I understood you, you said that one of the
things that happens is that the organism idles and this allows metabolic
processing to take place. So the test one would like to do, although I don't
know how you would do it, would be somehow to prevent ludic behaviors. Maybe you could do it in animals; you certainly wouldn't want to do

it in humans. If the autistic child is in fact characterized by an absence of ludic behaviors, one could look at the metabolic aspects of the child. I wouldn't know what to look for, but that would be a way of testing your notion that there's a kind of balance between ludicness and metabolic processing.

Dr. Hutt: The difficulty there is a practical one in that one doesn't know quite what sort of metabolic functions are going to be the most useful to test; but in principle it can be done.

Dr. Gardner: It's implied that when we interrupt REM sleep there are bad consequences. If one could somehow take an animal and disrupt him whenever he was playing, one could look for the same kinds of consequences.

Dr. Fein: In the classical Barker-Dembo-Levine experiment, when the play was interrupted the children became frustrated, and regressed; but the heart rate wasn't being measured in that experiment.

Dr. Hutt: I should also have said that from animal evidence we have a fair idea now of the neural distribution of the control centers of these arousal-modulating behaviors. Sleep is perhaps the commonest arousal-modulating behavior; both animals and children go to sleep when faced with great conflict. Delius's work shows that very closely adjacent centers in the limbic system are associated with both sleep mechanisms and displacement activities. That is an additional source of evidence linking these arousal-modulating behaviors.

Dr. Lewis: The level—that is, the rate—should differ between play and processing and/or exploration, and that might well affect the variability measure.

Dr. Hutt: We have looked at the dependence of variability on mean heart rate, and there is none. We did look at mean heart rate too but failed to find the close association with behavioral differences that there is with the heart rate variability.

Viewing ludic behaviors in this way, at a neurophysiological level, they may be seen to have this dual function of both priming nervous system when informational input is reduced and enabling the recuperation of metabolic activities. This view also takes into account the phylogenetic and ontogenetic changes seen in play: there is more play in domesticated than in feral animals, upon whom the pressures of survival are greater, and more play in the higher primates than in other mammals. In all species that engage in it, there is a diminution in play with age (as there is also with REM sleep): as the demands of the environment increase, the need for a primer grows less.

At a more cognitive level, play may be seen as a "time-out" phase for consolidation of information acquired during epistemic activity. Ludic behaviors, and symbolic play in particular, are primarily *expressive*. They reflect conceptual reorganization, attempts at social control, and cognitive competence.

CONTEXT OF DISCOURSE

I would now like to show you some results from a study of language usage in day-care children during ordinary discourse and during fantasy play. Day-care centers in Britain are not comparable to those in North America—they cater almost entirely to disadvantaged children. What is most striking about the language of these children is that it is very infantile. The most common production is a two-word utterance. On the other hand, when they were engaged in imaginative play they produced language of far greater complexity. The same measures of linguistic complexity were taken during normal discourse and during play; e.g., mean length of utterance, number of adverbs, mean number of adjectives, of qualifiers, etc. On almost every measure the complexity is far greater during imaginative play than in normal discourse (see Figure 10-3).

Dr. Lewis: It seems that not only do you have the normal discourse versus fantasy, but one might want to dimensionalize as well the amount of affect. That is, in normal discourse the child is possibly talking about things that don't interest him very much, that are boring, that are not very affective; whereas in fantasy there is a rich affective life. I am wondering if the dimension is between normal discourse versus fantasy or between low-affect versus high-affect states.

Dr. Hutt: That may be so, but for the moment I would like to stay with the play versus nonplay distinction. Both staff and children are predominantly working-class in these day care centers. Bernstein, for instance, would say that the emphasis of the staff is therefore on the acquisition of skills rather than upon the dimension of person perception and that accordingly they have an implicit theory of learning which is primarily didactic. Children are instructed; they are told to do things, not shown how to, and this mode of verbal interaction does not allow the child to express his competence. It is only the imaginative situation—one where the child is in control—which releases a performance congruent with that competence.

Dr. Fein: Are you measuring peer conversation or teacher-peer conversation?

Dr. Hutt: Peer conversation as well as adult conversation.

Dr. Fein: Then in the teacher-child language exchange, probably an important index of the child's competence is in what he understands about what he is told and in the contingencies of his response, rather than in the form of his production; if there is an asymmetry, then it is crucial to put comprehension potential into the pot, so that you can take account of the setting differences between the sociodramatic situations and the reality situations.

Dr. Hutt: I take your point; but the comparison is still valid, is it not?

Dr. Sutton-Smith: Maybe it says something quite different. Maybe it says—as I understood Mike Lewis to say—that we really need a high-affect situation where these children are talking normally, in order to see if the play situation is a superior form, a higher and more complex form, than they would use in an ordinary adaptive situation where they really have to communicate something quickly because of, say, danger. Would they be able to do as well there as they do here? That's the point. On the other hand, it's very interesting that the play situation is the more fluent and more complex one in relation to many others.

Dr. Lewis: You could argue that if the teacher in a discourse excited or aroused the child in an affectual sense, that might be comparable to a fantasy. I don't know if that's true. I think that these two dimensions are covariant. I recall trying to learn French, and that I did best when the teacher got me involved in speaking about things that I enjoyed speaking about and was interested in, rather than going through simple silly sentences.

Dr. J. Singer: We got very similar results in one of our studies when we classified the subjects initially, through interview, as more or less imaginative in their normal play behavior. We found that when we actually rated their language in a play behavior, not only did they get higher ratings for imaginativeness but they got more positive affect and some of the same scores—more modifiers and longer mean length of utterance, etc.

Dr. Lewis: I don't think that would alter the fact that it still could be covariant.

Dr. Hutt: I have no quantitative data on this question of affect, but thinking of episodes where there has been high affect, where the children are in fact relating to adults, not to peers, I find these episodes were not notable for greater linguistic complexity; language remained constrained and restricted.

Dr. Garvey: I'd like to make one more comment about the affect. You could extricate these dimensions, I think, because after all you're talking about motivation, not necessarily positive affect. So why not frame the arguments and disputes as being about motivation and affect as compared with fantasy play? Another aspect of fantasy play is that modifiers and specifiers have to be put in if communication is going to go on at all. So I suspect that there are a number of factors mediating these results that are perfectly amenable to study if one looks at the actual speech.

Dr. Lewis: Would these observations about affect, the arousal component, be compatible with what you said earlier about the function of play? If the children are more aroused, or more affectual, they may be producing more and better language.

Dr. Hutt: Not necessarily more aroused, but nearer the optimum for the individual—yes, in that state obviously their production is going to be better, both linguistically and behaviorally.

Dr. Sutton-Smith: Dr. Kenafick, in a 1977 dissertation at Teachers College, similarly had children working with each other on four play tasks in rotation; that was one set of conditions. The other set of conditions was the children working with the teacher on the same tasks. There was a recording of all the language, and the results were similar to yours. On almost all indices the children had a wider range of vocabulary and longer lengths of utterances when working with other children; however, they also had more primitive, more regressive references. And there was one feature in which the teacher did reach a high level, where more abstractions were brought forth by the children in the presence of the teacher. So it was not an either-or situation, although apparently there's some differentiation. We weren't at all sure why this was so, but there seem to be two different communication systems—one for teachers, one for children.

Dr. Kirschenblatt-Gimblett: Those are sociolinguistic norms, because obviously there are all kinds of conventions and expectations about how teachers talk to children and how adults talk to children, and these vary by social class and by setting and by all kinds of conditions. Just to introduce that kind of relativity variable is terribly important. I wanted to ask, in that connection, whether the normal range was established by speech in the school setting or whether the home setting was examined as well.

Dr. Hutt: Not in this particular study. We are looking at the home situation in another study, but we haven't any data yet.

Dr. Kirschenblatt-Gimblett: I was thinking of the kinds of situations where children are to be seen and not heard, to speak when spoken to, baby talk—just all those things that reflect a cultural orientation to language, and especially language for children. While that doesn't change the findings, I think it does frame them in a particular way.

Dr. Hutt: Yes, and one has also to take the semantic context into consideration. When these children are talking about a football match, as opposed to some domestic situation, their production becomes very much more elaborate.

Dr. Kirschenblatt-Gimblett: One of my students, an education major, did a study of four or five boys—young adolescents who had been marked as problem kids and slow learners—and became particularly interested in their play activity. They played street hockey on a block where their activity was disrupted every two or three minutes by a passing car, which meant that everything—all the equipment and everything—had to be cleared. They would run to the side, wait for the car to pass, then set everything up, put the puck back in place, and resume as if nothing had happened. They did this for hours. The level of organization, plus all the metalanguage going on, where one of them would call the plays, narrating, describing, accounting, registering—the language, the skill, the concentration—all of that stunned him, it was so at variance with any of those skills being demonstrated in a formal learning setting. It's not fantasy play; it's another kind of play, but it demonstrated skills far beyond anything that was normally expected from these boys.

Dr. J. Singer: It is fantasy play grafted on to a game with rules, because the extra dimension is that they were behaving as if this were being watched on television or being viewed with announcers. Sometimes they even stopped for commercials, if you like.

Dr. Kirschenblatt-Gimblett: Except for them this was part of the formal mode by which they played. I should add that they also got themselves organized to collect money to buy all the equipment and they kept it at one person's house. So the game had a centrality in their day, and in their lives together, which seeped out of the specific play itself into a set of social relationships involving money and purchase and storage of equipment and all kinds of things.

Dr. Ellis: The complexity of the organization doesn't surprise me in the least. You see that in any old random bunch of Canadian kids who are forced together into an environment: they would arrive at that level of organization within a week. It reminds me of what I referred to yesterday in the hyperactivity study, where there was a group life that transcended arbitrary breaks. And it seems to me that school for these children *is* an arbitrary break. Their group life is carried into the classroom, if they're in the same class, and of course they have the capacity to control the life in that classroom. It's a small task to manipulate a boring math lesson to produce interesting outcomes if you have a history of organizing. So it's interesting that you observed that they were marked as troublesome kids. In fact, they had an inappropriately better organization than anything the teacher and the other members of the class were ready for.

DIAGNOSIS

Dr. Hutt: I would like to say just a couple of things to elicit your reactions about imaginative play. First, I see it as a very good diagnostic indicator for play therapists and educators, in the sense that when a child plays he is signaling competence, knowledge, ease, familiarity; he is signaling mood state: "I feel happy enough, I am not anxious; I feel relaxed enough to play, to do as I wish; any constraints that apply, I entirely disown." As soon as there are external constraints, the activity ceases to be ludic. Secondly, if a child is in a situation of high arousal, as when he is hospitalized or when he is ill, it is difficult, well-nigh impossible, to engage the child in ludic activities, but it is quite possible to engage him in epistemic behaviors. One is confronted with this difficulty very dramatically with new children starting at preschool: when they come at age three, a number of them are apprehensive, shy, withdrawn, and unable to play. Any teacher who tries to engage that child in imaginative play is likely to meet with failure. On the other hand, it is quite possible to distract or alter cognitive set by involving him in some problem-solving situation—a jigsaw, a form-board puzzle, or some exploratory activity. This is an indication that the ludic behaviors are crucially dependent on mood state; and this fact may be a useful diagnostic tool for people dealing with young children in a practical situation.

Dr. D. Singer: Is the opposite true, that there are certain states in which you can engage the child ludicly but not epistemically?

Dr. Hutt: I haven't encountered them.

Dr. D. Singer: I'd like to comment on an experiment we did in the Connecticut Valley Hospital with disturbed children. One group that we didn't really want to work with was the autistic ward, but the director felt we should involve this ward simply because she felt the hospital administration wanted everybody to have the treatment effect. I believe, as you do, that the autistic children are suffering from too much arousal. We found that the woman who did simple rhythm work did better with these children. When they tried the clown theater—the other condition, the kind of ludic symbolism—these kids couldn't handle it at all. But with the simple exploring of materials and playing in a very structured way, we found they were responding tremendously, which I think supports what you were saying. And these were autistic kids in a high arousal state who were not able to handle any kind of symbolic material at all, but could do the simple rhythm kinds of things, which I guess fits in with their perseveration at any rate. There was another thing I wanted to mention as you were talking about the increase in language for the imaginative children. We looked at some of the language protocols of the children who were low in imagination and high in aggression, and what I found was a lot of repetition and name calling, but not the kind of rich language that we found in the high imaginative children. Now, in these aggressive kids the affect is high in many instances—they were running around and hitting each other—and the language and the mean length of utterance in some cases would have been the same when you counted the morphemes, because a lot of outpouring was going on. But when you actually looked at the content of the language in terms of adjectives and adverbs, they weren't using the kind of language the imaginative kids were. It was much more repetitious—"stinky, stinky, stinky," "hate you," "hit you," that kind of thing—without the elaboration we found in the high imaginative, less aggressive children.

Dr. Hutt: I would make a distinction there between high affect and positive affect.

Dr. D. Singer: Yes. We were scoring the positive affect. But what we saw was a kind of moving around, which we weren't counting. We were scoring only for positive affect. Hitting and jumping around the room earned a different score from our positive-affect score, which we looked at in a favorable way—the smiling and feeling good with the game.

Question: In the instance where the new child could not be engaged in play or ludic behavior by the teacher, but could be in problem solving, what about the child being engaged in ludic behavior by another child?

Dr. Hutt: If the new child is in a state of apprehension, that is still unlikely.

Question: You mean in the context of the new child being fearful?

Dr. Hutt: Yes.

Dr. Sutton-Smith: The paradox I see is in what you said earlier— that children tend, in play, not to examine objects any more for their epistemic characteristics. They've done that, and they've absorbed the objects into a fantasy schema. Then put that together with the high level of production competence shown in the social play you mentioned. Is play, then, concerned with production rather than competence? On one level there's a notion that play doesn't do much more than exploration; on the other is the notion that play does something different. I'm finding it difficult to put those two notions together.

Dr. J. Singer: I have to say that I can't accept your limitation of epistemic behavior. It sounds as if you're talking of studying the concrete properties of an object. But I think what happens is that once a child has more or less mastered the given properties of the object—its size and shape and other features—then he is disposed to explore the symbolic potential of the object by creating a novel environment. The environment may not be visible to others. We may clue in on that creative environment only by the child's change of voice or by references to settings that are not immediately given in the environment. So I'm inclined to feel that a new level of exploration is going on. It's a controlled exploration, and therefore not as arousing as the exploration of novel, externally derived stimuli, and that's one of the reasons for the positive affective property of make-believe play—that there is a sense of controlled exploration going on.

Dr. Hutt: I think the difference is a semantic rather than a substantive one, because I call these latter activities *conceptual reorganization and consolidation,* since the child is doing this in relation to schema that he has already formed. For exploration to be effective, it needs feedback. I am talking here not of the social, but of the solitary situation. If he is exploring socially, then what is the feedback that gives me information about his exploratory activities? For any reordering or rearrangement of information, I prefer the term *consolidation* or some other form of conceptual reorganization.

Dr. J. Singer: If you accept that consolidation is still a major part of the learning process—the mental reshifting—recombination . . .

Dr. Sutton-Smith: The word *reorganization* I find is more critical there, because that suggests novel gestalts. It doesn't just suggest a consolidation of responses which have already been laid out. It does suggest that too, but it suggests they are put together in novel ways. There is a difference.

Dr. Hutt: In the context of the schema, exactly.

Dr. Sutton-Smith: But that is genuine novelty when you have a new pattern for old elements, is it not?

Dr. J. Singer: I think that is what is happening on a day-to-day basis for all of us. We see some novel event in the street and then it comes back to us later on and we carry it a few steps further. We replay it mentally, and see some new elements in it.

Dr. Hutt: This is what reminiscence, reverie and daydreaming are about. That leads in rather nicely, together with Dr. Singer's point, to *individual differences,* which is one of the main questions I am concerned with. First let us take the children who show imaginative play and those who do not. If imaginative play has all these other cognitive functions that you have just mentioned, what is the implication or the significance of that for children who don't engage in much imaginative play? Are we failing to get at the crucial measures which might give us some clue as to what is going on in the nonimaginative children?

Let me contrast two children. Child A is engaged in a very sustained sequence of pushing trains forward and back, moving the wheels, twisting the carriage, a number of intricate manipulations, but no verbalization, only some vocalization. Child B, on the other hand, is much more verbally explicit; there is much linguistic production which enables us to categorize and say what is going on. What about the first child? Do we say that he is not engaging in imaginative play, or rather that we are not getting at the covert processes that are going on? Where the imaginative play is overt, where there is language to use as markers, we are reasonably happy about making a decision. What about the children who don't have such markers and whose play one cannot identify? If consolidation, reorganization, etc., are inherent parts of symbolic play, then are these nonverbal children going to be deficient in some cognitive respect? Another type of individual difference which I mentioned yesterday is that between the linguistically proficient children and those who show greater ability and skill in the spatial and numerical areas. We are beginning to find some correlation between these two types of children and their involvement in imaginative play. The linguistically proficient children show far more imaginative play. Now, is that an epiphenomenon, an artifact, due to the fact that we are using language in order to identify imaginative play? That is a question I would like to discuss at greater length. I wish also to look at the highly aroused and low aroused children—the introverted and the extroverted children. As you know, on the Eysenk dimension extroverts have relatively high levels of arousal. One can therefore predict in terms of sensation-seeking, stimulus-seeking, etc., the kinds of behavior that children are going to manifest. Since this kind of relationship is easiest to describe by using an extreme example, I will use autists. Autists are extremely highly aroused. When they are put in a situation where there is some novelty, they show classic behavioral and perceptual avoidance of complex or novel stimuli. In other words, they go and sit with their back towards the source of novelty (Hutt & Hutt, 1968). They are well aware of the location of the source of novelty, but it is unambiguously avoided. This lasts for a while, and then the child will eventually turn around and explore. But his level of arousal never gets to that optimum which permits him to engage in symbolic play; he moves straight over to perseverative behavior. Thus, superimposed upon that taxonomy one may place another dimension, that of *arousal*, with high arousal at the extreme right and left and optimum arousal in the area of symbolic behavior and the areas of skill acquisition—those skills in which children become very quickly playfully engaged; e.g., skipping, jumping, cycling. Thus, using both the behavioral and psychophysiological attributes of our taxonomy, we are able to predict the type of behavioral mechanism, the kind of play, children are most likely to show in phasic or in tonic arousal; i.e., what a new child might do at school or what a shy and introverted child might choose.

Dr. Collard: I'm going to Freud now. If you look at *identification with the aggressor,* which characterizes a lot of play (around Halloween kids playing ghost, kids playing doctor or dentist, kids even sometimes playing whoever happens to be in control of them), that to me would be a kind of role reversal where they are taking the active part. Now that I have permission to speak as a psychoanalyst, I want to throw out an idea and see whether it's original or not. The last time I was teaching about play and dreams, I happened to notice that the two functions of dreams, according to Freud, were wish fulfillment and mastery; and in play you can get the same two. Mastery, of course, would be playing out conflicts, identifying with the person who is in power (which of course is Whiting's theory, that that is the basis of identification). But the interesting thing to me was what Corinne [Dr. Hutt] said today about sleep—REM sleep—being restitutive and play being restitutive. And looking at the coincidence of the two functionings—in dreams wish fulfillment and mastery, and in play the same two—I thought there was an interesting and useful parallel.

References

Berlyne, D.E. *Conflict, Arousal and Curiosity*. New York: McGraw-Hill, 1960.

Bernstein, B. & Henderson, D. Social class differences in the relevance of language to socialisation. In J. A. Fishman (Ed.) *Advances in the sociology of language 2*, The Hague: Mouton, 1972, 126-149.

Delius, J. D. Irrelevant behaviour, information processing and arousal homeostasis. *Psychol. Forsch.:* 1970, 33, 165–168.

Hutt, C. Temporal effects on response decrement and stimulus satiation in exploration. *Brit. J. Psychol.*, 1967, 58, 3-4.

Hutt, C. Specific and diversive exploration. In H. Reese & L. P. Lipsitt (Eds.) *Advances in Child Development and Behavior*, Vol. 5. New York: Academic Press, 1970a.

Hutt, C. Curiosity in young children. *Science Journal*, 1970b, 6, 68-72.

Hutt, C., Forrest, S. J., Richer, J. Cardiac arrythmia and behavior in autistic children. *Acta psychiat. Scand.*, 1975, 51, 361–372.

Hutt, C., & Hutt, S. J. Heart rate variability: the adaptive consequences of individual differences and state changes. In N. Blurton-Jones & V. Reynolds (Eds.) *Human Behaviour and Adaptation*. London: Taylor and Francis, (in press).

Hutt, S.J., & Hutt, C. Stereotypy, arousal and autism. *Human Development*, 1968, 11, 277–286.

Oswald, I. Human brain protein, drugs and dreams. *Nature*, 1969, 223, 893.

CHAPTER 11

THE VALUES OF THE IMAGINATION

Jerome and Dorothy Singer

INTRODUCTION

Dr. Sutton-Smith: The Singers follow an emerging tradition of research, not otherwise well represented at this conference, in which investigators have sought to establish (a) relationships between creativity and play (Lieberman, 1978), and (b) the ways in which to influence play so that it will have an impact on children's creativity (Singer & Singer, 1977). Their own extensive work within this tradition has been to examine the characteristics of those who have higher imaginative capacity and, more recently, to attempt to increase that capacity in training studies.

Questions are again raised about the problem of verbally-oriented researchers using measures of children's language as measures also of playfulness or imagination. How can they deal adequately with children whose imagination may be expressed in spatial terms, like Gardner's patterners? There is discussion also of the inverse relationship between imaginativeness and aggressiveness as well as the impact of television watching on both. There is a practical demonstration of some of the techniques used in increasing imaginativeness, and finally a lengthy discussion on the values and socialization of the imagination. To what extent, it is asked, is play *training*, the training of the liberal imagination?

Dr. J. Singer: I wanted to show you some examples of ongoing make-believe play in the age group that Dorothy Singer and I have been working with most recently: three- and four-year-olds in nursery groups and on up through the five-year-olds. Five is perhaps the golden age of sociodramatic and make-believe play. As the film suggests, pretend play gets pretty complicated. Some fairly elaborate group games were started there, some rather more individualistic games, some relatively primitive, involving just a few sound effects such as a fire siren, and some fairly sophisticated, involving rather elaborate language and role playing. And that dimension, the *range* of pretending games, is what we've been studying.

In terms of the overall research program, I suppose one of the things we might address first of all is the question we were charged with discussing here: what is play? I will not try to define play in its general form. My wife, Dorothy, has really been the specialist in the broader Piagetian aspects of play, while I've been focusing more specifically on imaginative play, make-believe, symbolic play, or what Piaget (1962) calls *ludic symbolism*. That is play that we can define fairly well operationally in terms of the introduction of novel elements into an ongoing play situation, features that are not given in the immediate environment. Make-believe characters, make-believe identities, make-believe changes in time and space represent such transformations of the immediate environment. *An attitude toward the possible* is implicit in fantasy games, rather than what is literally present in the situation.

We can train raters who are not psychologists simply to watch carefully children's spontaneous behavior, record it, and then to rate it reliably on a 1 to 5 scale for degree of *imaginativeness* (Singer, 1973). Another approach, of course, would be to score the specific items or components of the play, the specific number of transformations or pretend elements introduced. We haven't found that practical in terms of our opportunities for study, although it could be teased out of the very extensive protocols we have of ongoing imaginative play.

The theoretical thrust of the research would *view make-believe as a form of information-processing or cognitive behavior*. It's something that children are going to be doing almost inevitably as part of the accommodation-assimilation cycle, trying to take the moderately familiar and further reduce the incongruity. We would more or less follow Tomkins's model (Tomkins, 1962) that moderately complex or incongruous material arouses a positive affect of interest and then, as material is eventually assimilated into well-established schema, there follows the experience of joy or the smiling response. Something like that would be the sequence. It is similar in some ways to an arousal sequence, but we prefer to use more the cognitive, information-incongruity orientation, although Tomkins uses a term more like arousal: *density of neural firing*. Since I can't figure out how to measure that, I prefer to try to limit myself to the cognitive level in discussing affects.

There's obviously a relationship between imaginative play and exploratory behavior in the sense that in many ways the child continues to be interested, and persists in exploring words and phrases and notions that are not clear. The inherent novelty and attraction of new and unfamiliar phrases or experiences from stories or TV become a part of an ongoing make-believe game. There's so much in the world that is strange and interesting to the child that this keeps feeding in more and more of the make-believe as part of the Piagetian assimilation process.

One of the things that we've been concerned with is that while most children show some make-believe by the age of two and a half or three, the continuation and expansion of pretend play seems to require a certain kind of social nurturance. I have to think over what Michael Lewis said yesterday and decide whether fantasy play inevitably would come out of parent-child interaction. I've been tending to take more of a Piagetian view that make-believe grows out of natural cognitive development (the accommodation-assimilation cycle), but it's possible that even earlier there's a great deal of parental input. Some of Greta Fein's research on the effects of mother-child interaction also support that to some extent. At any rate, it's clear that once a kid gets to about age three or four there does seem to be much more necessity for parental involvement to sustain and develop a more elaborate quality of make-believe play (Singer & Singer, 1976a).

One of the questions concerns whether fantasy play is of any purpose. Well, I propose to you that since children spend so much time in all kinds of play, only one portion of which is make-believe, an argument can be made that the major early learning experiences of human beings take place around play activities. *Make-believe play has particular advantages for certain kinds of learning* that would be useful for the child as a child and then for the adult that's emerging from the child.

Dr. Lewis: You said that by age three or four it's clear that you need parental involvement to maintain and sustain. Elaborate on that.

Dr. J. Singer: We've found pretty striking differences among children who play imaginatively. We watch them playing spontaneously. We score them for imaginative play and then divide two groups of children at the median and go back and interview them or their parents. There have been several studies done by us and by others who have used some of the same procedures (Singer & Singer, 1976a; Singer, 1977; Shmukler, 1977); they all seem to suggest that the differences between the high and the low imaginative kids are attributable in part to parental tolerance, parental modeling, or specific opportunities for fantasy play. For example, Freyberg (1973) interviewed parents of urban ghetto children who differed in amounts of make-believe play. The degree of privacy and the number of people per room in the tenements they lived in differed. The ones with a little more privacy showed more make-believe play; there was more tolerance of such play on the part of their parents. So you get disinhibitory and facilitative modeling activies by parents; such factors seem to be at least a part of the process.

Dr. McCall: As I recall, these kinds of correlates are over and above differences in intellectual and educational accomplishment of the parents?

Dr. J. Singer: That's right. We have never done a comparative study of lower socioeconomic kids versus middle-class kids. Within a particular sample, we've studied lower-middle-class, middle-middle-class, and some upper-lower-class groups. Within subsamples like that there are no great differences in actual educational level of the parents anyway. The differences are modest, and they don't correlate with imaginativeness of play.

Dr. Schwartzman: Could you say something about what the differences are that you see in terms of the imaginativeness, and how you're scoring that?

Dr. J. Singer: We have a rating scale that describes the child as he relates to immediate properties of objects. It would be like the patterners who were described yesterday by Dr. Gardner. Such children would be the most clearcut examples of kids who'd likely get a low score on imaginativeness, a 1, because it's a 1 to 5 scale. A low scorer would literally be putting things together but treating them for their actual perceptual properties. The kid who gets a high score on imagination would be taking the same blocks but introducing a story line, maybe even treating them as airplanes instead of as blocks. You can train raters to quite a high degree of reliability after a while, once you've given them a common definition. So there are those differences between the high and low imaginative kids, and we seem to see them as related in part to the available stimulation. And that suggests the possibility that there are advantages to make-believe. There is now a series of studies that have begun to come out looking at the differences between high and low imaginative kids where IQ and other obvious variables are controlled. Briefly, the results are that there seemed to be at the very least a consistent correlation between imaginative play and happy children, at least as we measure happiness by smiling, laughing, and other mood states of that kind. If make-believe does nothing else than make children happier when they're playing spontaneously, it would seem to be worth doing something about it.

Question: They're happy while they're being imaginative. Are they happier in other contexts?

Dr. J. Singer: I can't answer that from our own work. There are, however, clinical studies that suggest that more imaginative kids are less likely to be in trouble, or if they *are* in trouble they respond better to psychotherapy—they can get into the psychotherapy more easily. There is that kind of evidence. I don't know if any of you have seen Rosaly Gould's book (Gould, 1972) on fantasy in children, but she goes into some detail attempting to document that kind of finding. It doesn't, perhaps, meet the highest standards of systematic research but it's more than just casual anecdote—it's a careful examination of verbatim reports of children's play by nursery school teachers.

Dr. Garvey: Isn't that more related to communication than to happiness?

Dr. J. Singer: What do you mean?

Dr. Garvey: Well, they seem more amenable to treatment if they're more capable of communicating with the therapist.

Dr. J. Singer: Well, I was taking "happy" in the most general sense at that point. The question is, are they happier outside? I was saying that even if they're troubled they are at least likely to have a better chance for happiness in the sense that they respond better to therapy. I was sort of dovetailing several concepts very quickly. They show better waiting behavior, self-control, capacity for self-entertainment, reality discrimination, and resistance to temptation (Singer & Singer, 1976a). We find, for example, a correlation between children who play imaginatively and children who expect internal reinforcement on the SPIES Test, the Stanford Preschool Internal-External Inventory that Michel, Zeiss, and Zeiss developed (Singer & Singer, 1976a). And actual observations of waiting behavior in children also support this. When I say *reality discrimination*, that's a tough one, but at least we can put it this way: the more imaginative kids who are told either stories or supposedly true accounts of incidents will actually remember the details more veridically; even though they're more imaginative, they can recall and report the details more accurately. This is when intelligence is controlled, so it's not a function of simple verbal capacity (Tucker, 1975). There are lots of reasons to think that the child, in the course of the make-believe play, is talking out all kinds of things; he or she is in a sense feeding back this same verbalization, creating elaborate alternative environments. The environment that the child attempts to create in a make-believe game is never quite the same and never quite what he or she expected it to be, and so in a sense there is a whole new dimension being developed. There is also related to this the opportunity to try novel words and phrases; over and above that there actually are some studies, such as the one by Dansky and Silverman (1975), which suggest that children in the course of make-believe play actually learn more about an environment and later on can identify objects there better.

Dr. Gardner: This is the same question that's been raised before, but I'm still not sure exactly what your view on it is. You say it's not language ability per se. You also said you didn't feel it was the same as ability to communicate, but to what extent are there differences in the way high imaginers use language? You say there's no evidence at all?

Dr. J. Singer: It's hard to get it independently of the ongoing play. That's the problem. We have a study in which we scored various language variables—modifiers, possessive nouns, verbs, and all that—and correlated them with scores of imaginativeness during play. We found pretty good correlations; the more imaginative kids showed more use of modifiers and other vocabulary indicators that one would expect. Even when you control total verbal output as a ratio of length of utterance you get differences (e.g., mean length of utterance). It's not as if they actually say more things than the unimaginative kids. They produce about the same amount of verbalization. It's just that their verbalization turns out to be richer in metaphoric or analogic kinds of statements, descriptive statements or predicate nominatives.

Dr. Fein: Helen Marshall (1961) presented some awfully interesting data which suggested there's a very strong setting factor—that when kids are in the act of dramatic playing there is a very different quality to their language, so that you get more language in dramatic play than you do in reality contexts. It's more complex. There's more friendliness and also more hostility in it. But the kids who do more dramatic play get higher sociometric ratings from the other kids, taken independently. So it is a kind of a *setting by person interaction,* and you have to have both parts of it in order to see the skill spread of the kids. In other words, they can operate in both modes, but when they operate in one mode they're using what they have in a very different way. The other nice little thing is that even though there's more hostility language in dramatic play there is not more hostility—aggressive quarreling on the part of the kids—in reality situations.

Dr. Lewis: It's still not clear to me, in a nonpretend situation, what is the difference, if any, in the language ability of children who are rated high versus low?

Dr. J. Singer: In the standard vocabulary test they don't seem to differ. I think there probably is a difference, but it doesn't come out in the formal kind of test.

Dr. D. Singer: Just the use of modifiers alone was strikingly different between the kids who were high in imagination and those low in imagination. They simply used more adjectives.

Dr. Lewis: But that would covary with your scale.

Dr. McCall: Not necessarily. There's a difference between confidence and production.

Dr. Lewis: Imaginative kids may be using all that they know in very ingenious ways.

Dr. J. Singer: But it's being measured during the same time that they're being rated for being imaginative.

Dr. McCall: That's right, and I've been concerned about that in the past. Nevertheless, even if, for example, you split up a session and rated imaginativeness for one five-minute period and language for the next five minutes, you might still have enough consistency to produce the relationship. It may or may not be generalizable to other contexts.

Dr. D. Singer: We have nine ratings on the children over a period of time, and some when they were not just in imaginative play but during the actual television viewing over a full period of time.

Dr. J. Singer: We also have a much larger study going on now in which we're recording the language much more systematically and have a much more elaborate manual for scoring the language.

Dr. Hutt: How about looking at it the other way around? What of an emphasis on nonlinguistic abilities? We're finding that children who are high on spatial and numerical abilities tend to show less imaginative play. So that there does seem to be a correlation between linguistic aptitude and amount of imaginative play. Do you find this?

Dr. J. Singer: To be honest, we have not looked at it from that standpoint. It's worth following up. I would like to see what you have and then see if we can check that out.

Dr. Gardner: I'd like to comment on what you just said because it leads to something I was thinking about. Do we have some way of getting at the question of whether children who don't engage in imaginative play but who are, let's say, good in spatial areas, would do a lot of stuff which was imaginative but of a very visual, spatial type? That is, they might see lots of images and flip them around and build things in their mind, but that would not be the sort of thing that you talk about. In fact, one might be considered bizarre if one said, "I'm seeing all these forms and I'm arranging them." Does anyone know of any way that anybody has ever tried to tap this?

Dr. Hutt: We're trying to do this at the moment, but it's very difficult to use an objective test because by definition there's so little verbalization. What are you measuring? It's very difficult to get reliable ratings of any kind.

Dr. Ellis: There are some data that come from a quite different group—professional football players. The stereotypical view of these guys is that they don't show well on conventional linguistic or numeric aptitude tests, but if you study their descriptions of meaningful events in their lives—for instance, a certain play in the game—they're using words in a different way and showing their ability to deal with inordinately fine details and the spatial relationships for the actors in the setting. The language that comes out when they're describing what was happening three-dimensionally, with many, many parts moving and all of these being processes, was as amazing to me as when I was reading Kate's [Garvey's] transcripts. I have a feeling that again we have a measurement problem here. Our conventional methods are biased towards particular aptitudes that are symbolic and concrete. To transcend the distance between the experimenter and the thinking subject requires a special mode.

Dr. Fein: I think it's something like the data that suggest that the dramatist can shift from one mode to the other. The patterner perhaps can't.

Now, if you are testing in just one mode you have no way of spreading the range and mode of tests that will produce these different kinds of competencies.

Dr. D. Singer: One of the students, a clinical psych. student who was an Olympic gymnast before he moved into clinical psychology, said he used to rehearse his gymnastic movements through his mind before he would ever go to a meet. He would actually play through and visualize where he was going to jump and fall. And he said one night he had an uncanny experience. He rehearsed everything, but at the moment when he was about to do a particular jump someone interrupted him, and he simply stopped the rehearsal. The next day, during his jumping, that was the point when he fell. It was a bizarre kind of thing. He's sure it was because he didn't have his usual prerehearsal in his mind, where he works out all the images and jumps in a schematic way.

Dr. J. Singer: Our position is not that imagination is all, or that it's the only great and good thing. I think we've been more impressed with the fact that there is simply a lot more potential available to children in that realm, and indeed to adults; that this is a whole dimension that we have never fully developed as human beings. We're interested primarily in seeing whether kids that don't have it are all automatically lousy or don't have other things. But let's just take this one capacity and see if we can run with it for certain purposes. Other capacities will be developed in other ways, and we also use a whole set of cognitive skill procedures which I'll mention in a moment.

Dr. McCall: I'm very intrigued by your work, and I think you're at a point now where sometimes, as a discipline, we don't keep our wits about us. As soon as we find something that is interesting, and a bunch of correlates that society values, we immediately make the inference that we can train or improve that skill. Then we slip in a cutie, and that is that all of those socially positive attributes that we found correlated with that behavior in the ecological context will come along, and also be improved, as a by-product of the training of imaginative play. But it ain't necessarily so. Are you, in your training studies, planning to measure, or have you in fact measured, some of these socially valued attributes as concomitants of imaginative play, to inquire as to whether they also come along with training in imaginative play?

Dr. J. Singer: I think that's an excellent point. We have indeed tried. In one study we did several years ago (Singer & Singer, 1976a) we were interested in testing a live trainer engaging in a series of make-believe exercises with children versus the children being exposed to what was being touted as a constructive, prosocial TV program—the *Mister Rogers' Neighborhood* show, which has its own neighborhood of make-believe as one component. We had a control group, then we had a group of nursery kids watching Mister Rogers daily for a couple of weeks, another group who watched Mister Rogers but with an adult sitting in the middle as an intermediary, and a third intervention group where there was simply a live adult who came in for half an hour a day and went through a series of make-believe exercises with the children. We subsequently looked at whether there was an increase in imaginativeness and at positive affect and indications of cooperativeness and certain other benefits. (We didn't look extensively at the other variables in this study.) The result was that the make-believe with the live adult had the large effect. Mister Rogers had a small effect, especially if the adult intermediary was there. In a more recent study we have looked at things like cooperativeness with peers, interaction with peers. In a study we did in a mental hospital with very severely disturbed children who were older than this group but psychologically more at their level, we found not just the increase in imaginative play, but certain other socially valuable things like cooperation along with it (Nahme-Huang, Singer, Singer, & Wheaton, 1977). But I wouldn't be prepared to say we have a definitive answer to that question. We're a long way from that.

Now let me just quickly outline the study we're doing now on television (Singer & Singer, 1977b), and then I'll turn things over to Dorothy, who would like to give you some feel for the kinds of materials we use and demonstrate some of the actual exercises. Parents are keeping logs for two weeks steadily of children's viewing, and over a year there will be four time periods of maintenance of logs by parents. We're double-checking the parents by questioning the children and also by asking the parents on other occasions about their children's programming, and we're also looking at the Nielsen ratings for that particular area. We have 150 families cooperating in this study. We've tested the children for intelligence, using the Peabody. (Again, negotiating something like this is very tricky. The best we can get is in the Peabody.) Of course we have age and sex as independent variables, and then we have a little thing we call *imaginative play predisposition* which in some of the studies does correlate with actual observed imaginative play. That score is based on a combination of a little interview with the child and some responses to Rorschach ink blots.

The dependent variables are a whole series of ratings which vary across spontaneous behavior such as *imaginative play* itself, *positive affect, concentration, aggression,* various mood states, *interaction with peers or adults, cooperation with peers or adults.* Aggression we score here as direct physical aggression, not make-believe aggression. I think make-believe aggression muddies up the issue completely. We're talking about slugging other kids or knocking over other kids' blocks or destroying school property as aggression. These are the dependent variables of the study, and they are being sampled by observers who are unfamiliar with the hypotheses of the study and who are trained to reliable rating ability on the various dimensions.

In addition, we have a parent-training intervention that's nested into this longitudinal study. This involves one group that is receiving TV control training and TV sensitization. We've excerpted examples of violent TV and of constructive TV, which we show to the parents. We have a whole series of training exercises and devices that we demonstrate to the parents, and manuals which we send out to them. In effect, it's like forming a little TV control club with the parents.

A second group of parents is getting training purely in enhancing imaginative play, the notion being that it's possible that children who play more imaginatively will be less susceptible to the more noxious influences of television even if they do watch it and don't modify their viewing habits; or else that they will take the material from TV and work it into imaginative play, rather than acting it out directly. The third condition is a cognitive training condition in which we're giving the parents a series of cognitive exercises that we think would be very useful. These have been developed to some extent by others, but we've elaborated on them. They use some of the Piagetian notions of cognitive training. This group represents a kind of control for imagination or for the control of the TV conditions. Then we have a group of kids who are just being observed in the nursery school. Parents are keeping logs, but there are no parent groups.

We will follow these three- and four-year-olds for a year, which is a big chunk of their lives, and if we get more money we'll follow them longer. At least we will have four separate time samples of extensive material. We're also looking at language along a whole range of dimensions.

Dr. Gardner: I didn't follow the prediction for the imaginative group. Are you saying that by virtue of the fact that the parents are trained to play imaginatively with the kids, it will be cathartic for the kids to fantasy-play things like aggression and therefore they'll be less troublesome? Is that the prediction?

Dr. J. Singer: Cathartic? No; I think that if you have imaginative play as part of your repertory and you see people fighting on television, you will work that into little games and you'll have a stick fighting like this— "bang, bang." You'll have a whole game that you'll do. I would take my chances with that any day against a kid who comes at you with a club. I don't consider that catharsis at all.

Dr. J. Gardner: Do you envision a situation where training might not lead to nonclubbing behavior but might actually encourage the reverse?

Dr. J. Singer: No, but there is evidence that there's an inverse relationship between imaginativeness and overt aggressive behavior. There's quite a series of studies that I think have already indicated such an inverse relationship (Singer & Singer, 1976a).

Dr. Gardner: So it really presupposes that the preschool child can make the discrimination between an act committed in fantasy and an act committed outside of fantasy. It goes very much against a strict social learning kind of model, where if you learn to do this sort of thing you'll do it and generalize it, etc.

Dr. J. Singer: I think that's a simple-minded version of a social learning view. I think that what you learn is a set of ways and settings in which you can play the things you see and imitate them without having to hit other kids. The fairly conclusive evidence that has emerged from the TV research is that if children who are already predisposed to aggression— that is, who go around bopping other kids—see violent television, they will increase the level of their violence. Now even if that's only ten percent or five percent of all children, that's a huge number of children when four or five or six million children are watching every day and there's so much violence projected on the screen.

Dr. Gardner: You're saying then you think there might be an interaction between the child's baseline amount of aggressiveness and his mode of using aggressiveness.

Dr. Collard: I've taught nursery school for seven and a half years. This was mostly four-year-olds at Yale, University of California, and University of Chicago. I have seen television progressively influence the fantasy and dramatic play year by year in the four-year-olds. I have only had one child out of over 200 children who took what happened literally, and this was a child from Taiwan. The first time he ever saw *The Three Stooges* he hit somebody over the head, because on the show it looked as if it didn't hurt. Out of 200 I get one child who acts out. So it's exceedingly rare.

Dr. D. Singer: A letter went out asking the parents in a private nursery school in New York City if they would start limiting the television. The incidences of aggression went down dramatically in the nursery school. It may be that children vary in the amount of television they're watching, and I don't know whether you had the actual data on how much TV they watched. I think that's a variable that has to be looked at. But they definitely found a significant drop. That happened in Milford, too. It was reported in a journal and there was a popularization of it in *Redbook* just last month. Fifteen families started to monitor and limit the television viewing of their children, and the incidences of aggression went down. As a matter of fact, some of the children began to do better in school. These were five- and six-year-olds. So I think it isn't a one-to-one situation. I think it varies so much with the children and the amount of TV they're watching, what's going on in the family, how the families interpret television to the children, the interaction of parents and TV. It's much more complicated than "take away the TV and it'll all be good." It's a very complex thing.

Dr. Collard: You're right. I have very few aggressive kids in my groups.

Dr. Gimblett: I wonder what these kids are doing when they're not watching TV. It may be not so much that they're not watching TV but that the time that they're not watching now has to be filled in some other way, and how it's filled may in fact be the critical factor.

Dr. D. Singer: This is exactly what happened in Milford. The mothers began to complain after the first week because the kids asked the mothers to do more things with them and "play with me."

PRACTICAL TECHNIQUES FOR ILLUSTRATING IMAGINATIVENESS

Dr. D. Singer: What I'd like you to do is just take a pencil and write down as many things as you can think of that you can do with a bed sheet. Things that a three- and four-year-old can do with a bed sheet. How can you use a sheet with a three- and four-year-old in an imaginative way? Now switch your set, and I'd like you to think of all the things you can do with a balloon. Okay, now the last one. I'd like you to think of all the things you can do to play *small* and *big*. All the things you can play to be little or big, small, tall—for children; this is still for three- and four-year-olds.

Let's stop now. Just before I use your brainstorming ideas, I will describe what we would do in the parent sessions. I'm just going to describe the imagination session, because I think that's the one we're most interested in. In training parents, we started out by giving them a lot of the literature on imagination (Singer & Singer, 1976; Singer & Singer, 1977; Singer & Singer, 1977a; Singer & Singer, 1977b): why should children play, all the purposes of play; we went through the benefits of play, through the Piaget theories, etc. The people were interested in this, but it wasn't until we got to the actual playing that the sessions began to come alive, and one of the techniques was to brainstorm. We threw out many ideas, and I'm just giving you a couple of examples. We had to train the parents in the evening, which meant that we couldn't bring the children in at night to Yale, so what we did during the day was to go to a studio with some children whom we had never played with before and have a young woman simply follow some of the ideas in the manual and try these games out on the children. We found, too, that since we were dealing with a wide variety of parents—some of them played all the time with their kids, some really didn't play at all, as we discovered—we had to find a common medium for reaching their level, which was not so easy, but we did a lot of brainstorming. What I'd like to do now is have Jerry [Dr.

Singer] write down some of the things you said about the bed sheet. Then I'm going to use Michael [Dr. Ellis], since yesterday he said he was a dramatist, to play some games with me to show you what we're going to do.

Just call out one or two of your best sheet things and Jerry will put them down and we'll see where we are.

Roll it up and play crack the whip. The kids hold onto it and whip it around.

Hide and seek. Some kids go underneath. You wrap a kid up and it's a casserole and the other kids have to guess who's the meat.

Trampoline. Use it as a hammock and swing kids.

Sail for a boat.

Creating a private space that was for tents, hideouts, and other things like that.

Costumes—trains for brides.

Cutting it into pieces, which would be the bandaid.

Creating a new object, such as a mummy.

Chain gang. Snail. Eskimo throw—you put in four people, put a little kid in the middle, and go up. (A little Canadian content. Actually it could be Alaskan.)

Tug of war. Peek-a-boo. We had some violent people. One was going to smother. And after doing that it was going to be used as a sling.

Dr. D. Singer: We're going to ask you to go under our sheet and it is going to be the sky. Sit down on the floor. Now what we would do is have some children underneath and say, "This is the sky and the reason it's white is because it's snowing. Can you tell us some of the things you would do in the snow?"

Dr. Lewis: I would eat the snow. I would build a snow person.

Dr. D. Singer: Let's do that. Why don't you start building the snowperson and show me how you would do that?

Dr. Lewis: Well, you take a snowball and roll it down a hill, and that makes a big snowball. Then you do another one and put it on top.

Dr. D. Singer: He's not playing like a three-year-old, because generally when we have two-, three- and four-year-olds under there they will already be sleighing. They'll be on their bellies. And they'll be catching snowballs. What we were trying to do in this imaginative game is let you all brainstorm and then go one step beyond, which is to take something like this sheet and make it the sky. And as it becomes the sky it leads to imaginative games. We played this game with blue crepe paper as the sky, and suddenly one little girl put on her bathing suit and dove into an imaginary swimming pool, and everyone was happy. This is what we were trying to do, to get your imagination to work.

Here's one other thing that we did. You get under the sheet (and you'd be smaller, of course, if you were three years old). We'd say simply "move" and watch the child move. And underneath the sheet we found some very interesting things happening. They'd make believe they were all kinds of people. Their inhibitions would go away.

Now let's take the balloon idea and see what we did with that. We have just one more minute, and I'll show you what happens with the balloon. What did you do with the balloon?

Dr. Ellis: We looked through it to change the color, we could make it talk by squinching it. We felt that you could make animals by twisting it. We were going to put pieces of paper in it. We were going to put some water in it before blowing it up and we were going to use it as a pillow. We were going to let it fly, and squeeze it, chew it, make little teeny bubbles out of it that you could bash people on the head with and scare them.

Dr. D. Singer: Did anybody have the children become balloons? And blow each other up? Okay, this is where we would stretch the imagination. This is what we mean by imagination. We're trying to get them not to use the materials for props. Everyone sits on the floor, and we say, "We're going to play balloons and blow each other up." And you see the children get bigger and bigger and become balloons, and then we blow them, and they begin to drift along the room. And then the teacher says, "Now I think I'm going to let the air out of you," and she opens the "balloon" and the little child (if you can see him) falls down. And she says, "There's another way of letting the air out of you," and she pricks it. What we're trying to do in the imagination and fantasy games is to eliminate materials as much as we can. In some of the sociodramatic games we use a few props. There's a whole realm of imagination and fantasy that we think isn't being utilized by some parents and teachers, which is really to use *yourself* to play; and the sheet suggesting the sky really lets you fill out the game, or the balloon being the person we think is much more fun than making something out of the balloon, painting it or using it in that way.

I think what I'll do now is describe two of the research techniques instead of showing them to you. In the cognitive group to show small and tall, instead of an imaginative game we used concrete cognitive materials. We had some blocks that were graduated sizes, some seriation materials: little lids getting larger, so they could do some ordering, and candles of different sizes for ordering. For sorting we used buttons. We had them sort the buttons into colors and different sizes and shapes. So in the cognitive games, and in the training of the parents in the cognitive group, it was very school-like learning—dull, I think, but the children sat there nevertheless. In a sense, while the children were playing and doing all of these games I think they were learning about small and big and they also were increasing their vocabulary somewhat. By contrast, in the pirate sequence, a part of the imaginative training, a whole flood of words comes out just getting ready for the game—tying on the scarves, learning what a mustache is, digging for pirate gold, making a treasure map. A great deal of vocabulary is involved in the sociodramatic game. The training that we attempted to do was to go from something like producing facial expressions to singing a song, making up a poem, acting out a familiar story, and then finally making up their own game. And although this may seem very rudimentary to you, some of the parents never did this with their children. They really didn't understand the value of it or why one would do it. Once we began to train them they could understand, and they began trying these things out with their children and found it was a lot of fun. So in a sense we were hoping that the more imaginative games we could introduce to families, the more they would try to do these things with their kids and, hopefully, stop watching as much television; but we won't know about that until the logs come in. Then we'll be able to monitor the effect of the imagination training as compared to how much TV viewing the children were engaged in. It may be that some of the TV viewing won't stop at all, and the kids who are getting the imaginative training will still keep on watching television, but we'll still be able to measure their imagination in the playschool situation, through our observations. We'll be looking at the logs to see if the TV viewing has decreased, and we'll be looking at the imaginative play. The television group has some TV tapes, too, as Jerry [Dr. Singer] said, of both the prosocial behavior and the violent kinds of commercials on television. We also had the parents interact with us trying to brainstorm ways in which they could use the television more effectively with their children. And some of them did come out with some of the Piagetian notions that they could deal with, such as temporal concepts and ordering and number concepts, as in *Sesame Street*; so they themselves were beginning to see that there are some effective uses of television, and that it's not all bad. We're saying you can use TV with your children. It can become another enrichment source in the child's life.

In addition to the tapings and classroom demonstrations that the teachers are doing, we do give the parents a written manual. Everything that went on in the classroom is in the manual, so they can have something to refer to. Then there are mailings that go out periodically to reinforce the learning, so that the parents will eventually have a "book," in effect, on imaginative play, on cognitive exercises, and on television viewing techniques. We promised the parents that at the end of the project they would get all the materials so they would see what the people in other groups had been doing.

Question: To what extent do the parents in the imaginative play group understand that you would like to see television viewing be reduced? I mean, that's one of your predictions.

Dr. D. Singer: We don't say that to them at all.

Question: You said the people who are training them don't know about your hypotheses, but you do talk with them a lot about how to use TV. Are they getting tacit messages? What do you think they think is going on?

Dr. D. Singer: I think it's interesting that the cognitive group thought they were the group that we were trying to influence in regard to TV viewing. They're our control group, but they don't think so. They think they're the experimental group.

Question: But they know about the other groups.

Dr. D. Singer: They know that other groups are going on. We've asked them not to compare the results of the training sessions or talk about them. We hope they don't. They come from eight nursery schools in the New Haven area. I don't think they really know each other that well. They've been randomly assigned. I think that they will be as confidential as any large group can possibly be, but I believe they're speculating about what we're doing.

Question: It would be ironic if the cognitive group, thinking it was the chosen one, would lower the amount of TV viewing.

Dr. D. Singer: The television group last week thought they were the chosen one. Each one has been tossing this about: "What are you trying to do?" "Are we the group?" And we just don't answer.

Dr. J. Singer: As luck would have it, we had one parent in the group who had been a subject in Zimbardo's prisoners' studies, and another one who had been a subject in one of Milgram's studies. You can't win.

Dr. D. Singer: They're wondering when we're going to start to torture them in some way.

THE VALUES OF IMAGINATIVE PLAY

Dr. J. Singer: I would like to summarize now some of the *values* of play that I see emerging from such studies of make-believe. One would be self-entertainment, waiting capacity, delaying; there seems to be some evidence for that. Empathic affect discrimination seems to have been demonstrated in a few studies, and a greater accuracy in recall of material, and then a whole series of what we would call prosocial behaviors, such as cooperativeness and less overt aggression. Less overt aggression pretty clearly comes up again and again. The more imaginative play kids seem to be less likely to be overtly aggressive. And then there's some divergent production I think we have to mention. That's been demonstrated very clearly in a number of studies.

Dr. Garvey: These are good things that we think may be consequences of play, but we could, perhaps, ask the question from a more ethological point of view. As Blurton-Jones says, the child's got to survive as a child, so what function or functions does play have in the child's business of surviving as a child, not just as a species, or to grow up into an adult? There was a very interesting hint here in a paper by Marshall that Greta [Dr. Fein] mentioned, that children themselves seem to value highly the ability to create make-believe. What sociometric looks have been taken at this? It seems the children themselves may recognize the ability to make-believe fluently as a highly valued capability; so it may make a difference from their point of view, too.

Dr. J. Singer: I'll limit myself for the moment to the symbolic or make-believe kinds of games. I think that those do lend themselves to the development of imagery skills of a mental kind, of role-taking capacities, of mental kinds of general playfulness, humor. I could imagine the ability to stand situations on their heads and get perspective on them as originating in early childhood experiences with imaginative, make-believe play. I can't prove that. You would have to track people over longer times to demonstrate it, but I believe that that is a likely possibility.

Dr. Hutt: You must have some basis for that belief.

Dr. J. Singer: There are some retrospective studies. People who have been chosen as especially creative in arts or in sciences are asked what some of their early childhood experiences were like, and the things that seem to discriminate them are reports of greater daydreaming in childhood and of having had imaginary companions (Singer & Singer, 1976a). Evidence of that kind has come up. There are other indications, perhaps more from anecdotal reports of early childhood experiences involving imagination and fantasy in which, in various subtle ways, these become a part of the adult life, sometimes leading directly to a literary or artistic career, many times leading to a kind of an interest in and lively style of relating to people. A competent mother can think up interesting ways of entertaining the children on a rainy afternoon because she has not lost contact with her own early experiences of play, so to speak, and she can use those skills as an adult, for effective behavior; yet she may never become famous as an artist or creative person. If you allow the following jump, people who look at Rorschach ink blots or at similar kinds of materials and give a make-believe response are showing these imaginative skills. It is a black and white ink blot, but they say, "These are two clowns playing patty cake." They give what are called *Human Movement responses* (M) to the ink blots. There probably are thirty or forty studies with reasonable degrees of control on them that indicate that people who show a lot of Human Movement on the Rorschach are more capable of self-entertainment in a variety of situations, can sit longer in waiting rooms without getting frustrated, are less troubled; or if they happen to be mentally ill, they're even less trouble on the ward, less likely to be violent. If they're prisoners in jail they are less likely to be continuously violent. They might have killed a person by shooting him six times, but otherwise they've never been violent the rest of their lives; or they are embezzlers, the white collar criminals. Prisoners who have very few of these Human Movement responses tend to get into lots of fights and disruptions. There is a tremendous amount of literature suggesting that people who give that kind of response are more imaginative and more playful, self-entertaining, planful in their behavior, in general showing this capacity to take an attitude toward the possible or the symbolic realm (Singer & Brown, 1977). And that kind of data also holds for children, but nobody has taken a group of children and followed them into adult life, measuring their Rorschach M responses.

Dr. Gardner: Actually, there would be some data in the Berkeley study. Erikson did play configurations with the children in that study thirty to forty years ago, and he's gone back to see them.

Dr. J. Singer: I think he tended to look at the play more in terms of content-conflictual areas, and not enough in terms of the structural properties or the imaginativeness of the play.

Dr. Gardner: I'm sure he had some subjects who were reluctant to imagine, and that information might be retrievable.

Dr. Hutt: In relation to that, can you be absolutely certain that this is the evidence we have up until now, that there is a causal relationship, as opposed to a correlational relationship, between play and late success? Insofar as there is a divergent cognitive style in play, is it manifesting itself later in imagery, imagination, complexity, etc.? And is it the same cognitive style that later on is going to be manifested in creativity, divergent thinking, etc.? Are you able to say whether it's one form of relationship as opposed to another?

Dr. J. Singer: I would have to say no; I can't say that. What we do have are a large number of correlations, but I would have to back off from saying I know of any clear-cut causal studies.

Dr. Sutton-Smith: You mean long-term causal studies.

Dr. J. Singer: Yes.

Dr. Sutton-Smith: Because there are the immediate causal studies, the training ones.

Dr. J. Singer: You can find evidence, for example, that people who improve in psychotherapy show an increase in Rorschach Human Movement responses. There are studies like that.

SOCIALIZATION OF PLAY

Dr. Chase: There is one general question I'd like to pose for those of you who have schemes for looking at individual differences; that is, between children who imagine easily and those who have difficulty, or the dramatist and the patterner distinction. In terms of development which is relatively unencumbered by conflict and perplexity, do we think about matching? That is, first to help people understand what they are—their own particular profile of strengths and weaknesses— and then to define a way for them to intervene to expand the repertoire. I'm purposely caricaturing the options. Is the social responsibility, as in the case of the precocious children, to intervene and say, "You might be having trouble finding your way, and we'll help you to see earlier the map of possible social context in which expectations are made and supports are given"?

Dr. Fein: What I keep hearing people saying is that it will be very hard for us to proceed unless we know more exactly when and how playing becomes socialized. Where do children hear, "Now's the time to eat. Don't play." "Here's the time to go to the toilet; it's not the time to play." "Here's the time to sleep; it's not time to play"? This kind of thing starts very, very early. And there must begin, with our marvelously compliant organism, a growth of some terribly important separation of life functions, such that each one permits some kind of flow process to occur with minimal confusion across them. And what is striking is that we really don't know how parents want kids to define those times to do this and to do that. If we could somehow have that understanding, we would begin, perhaps, to find out how the kids come to match or reach these social definitions and then, having achieved that, what they do with it. How do they handle the frames that they come to negotiate with their caregivers? Then I think one can begin to better understand transitional schemes and maintenance schemes and exit schemes. But it seems to me that all this has to be thought through in terms of the fact that kids are really complying with a lot of divisions in terms of how labor is to be allocated and what that labor is to be called.

Dr. Sutton-Smith: There's an anthropological example in the Aymara Indians, where the parents try to prevent the kids playing all the time, but the children play furtively anyway (Miracle, 1976). They're supposed to be looking after the goats, and sometimes the goats destroy the vegetables while the kids are playing around and the kids get into trouble. This culture defines these kids as adults only when they don't have to play any longer, when they feel no compulsion to be furtive and do these behavioral things. What the children were really being socialized towards here, interestingly enough, was a sort of furtiveness. These Aymara have persisted for thousands of years in the face of Incas and Spaniards and others, and they have a very strong internal life and a very clear capacity for maintaining an external face which is static and obedient, without giving up any internal resources. The play socializes this habit.

Dr. Fein: I wonder if we negotiate that here within our children. We say, "Now it's time for sleep and it's not time to play," but when you listen in to the nursery you know that playing is going on, but it's at a level that's acceptable, a level which, in terms of our inferences about arousal, will allow sleep to take over. When it gets too high, we step in and say, "Now's not the time to play; settle down." So in a sense we negotiate the furtiveness, but the kid eventually learns how he can evade even further. One of my students said the other day that she had it all over her parents. She had two flashlights for reading after the lights were out, and her parents never discovered that. After the first one would go, then there was the other one.

Dr. J. Singer: I think there are very striking individual differences in families in relation to how much leeway they will give the child to play, and especially to play imaginative kinds of games. The more formal, structured games are more generally acceptable to a wider range of families, but the make-believe, the fantasy, the talking to oneself games—that's where there are subcultures and idiosyncratic family groups that come down very hard on children. My hunch is that the urge just gets suppressed and is not even internalized, as in the Aymara. I think it just withers away for lack of practice and for lack of effective development. And again, there is some evidence that kids who get into difficulties in school, or middle-class kids who have gotten into trouble because of delinquency and antisocial difficulties turn out, by various interview and testing techniques, to show much less of an internal imaginative life; they don't have a private set of games and fantasies that they have internalized in one way or another. Instead they move directly to some kind of action (Spivack & Levine, 1964). If they want something they don't play it out mentally before they try to get it. They immediately try to get it, in which case they often get caught or get into difficulties.

Again, there's literature taken from the Thematic Apperception Test which shows that kids who are prone to be overtly violent will tell a story like: "This boy sees this other kid; they don't like each other; he hits him on the head." That's the end of the story. Another child might show the same amount of hostility in the story—"This boy sees this other kid; he doesn't like him; he feels like hitting him on the head, but then he thinks, 'Boy, they're gonna catch me!'" so he thinks of a clever trick in which he can get this kid's schoolbook and color it all up so he won't be able to use it for his homework. He does that, the kid gets into trouble in school, but then afterwards he apologizes. Now that's the kind of story you get with the built-in inhibition from the kids who do not act out overtly. If you rate the actual amount of aggression or hostility it comes out the same, but the difference is in the amount of inhibition that's put in, which would seem to correspond with an internalized playing out of the situation (Klinger, 1971), and playing out all of the consequences of it also.

Dr. Csikszentmihayli: If I understood, Dr. Chase, you were asking whether society's responsibility should lie in training and encouraging a one-dimensional skill, or in trying to provide alternative skills. This is something I've been thinking about a lot. On the one hand you would like the person to develop that metier, a skill that will allow him to function perfectly within one medium and increase the challenges there. The problem with that is that, life being as changeable as it is, it's very easy to run into a metier or a skill that is crowded, so that you can't use your skills in that particular area, or where you run into a ceiling, at which point, if you have no other skills, you are stymied. This happens—for instance, to chess masters; once they reach a certain point they practically go bananas. They have no other alternatives. They put all their skills into that one medium and they can't recycle into another set of skills. So in terms of the fact that challenges can be exhausted, or skills cannot be used, it's very important for people to have alternative possibilities. Here I wanted to make another point, in terms of skills. A group of people I studied were concentration camp survivors who came out of situations where all of the objective supports for their skills were removed. They had to work in a completely barren environment, where everything was forced on them— forced labor, incredibly structured, no possibility of play. The survival of those people seems to me to have been predicated on their ability to have a symbolic form that they carried with them—a kind of portable skill such as reciting poetry, or remembering symbolic forms. Mathematicians and poets were the two groups that seemed to survive in these camps because they had a set of clearly ruled and structured symbolic forms to play around with. It's amazing how these people could actually transform this kind of labor camp experience into make-believe. There were people who remembered the concentration camp as being the high point of their life, although they are now successful professionals, because there they were able to transform the situation in terms of their own rules. They made competitive little games out of chopping trees or mining coal. They had periods of storytelling, riddling, poetry reciting; remembering a poem was one of the greatest resources that any person could have in that situation, and poems would be passed on and memorized and repeated. In our school system, the fact that we practically frown on memorizing, on rote learning of this kind of symbolic material is, I think, one of our greatest losses. Not that we anticipate living in concentration camps, but even in everyday life the ability to retrieve these kinds of symbolic structures and to play around with them is something that we are lacking.

Dr. J. Singer: I'd like to amplify that with some other examples. There's an architect named Herman Field who was taken prisoner by either Czechoslovakia or Poland back in the 1950s as a presumed American spy. He was on a mission from the United States to one of these countries, and he was arrested and kept incommunicado for several years. He told me that during this time he was in a sensory deprivation situation; they were trying to force him to confess to being a spy, but he was adamant about this because he wasn't a spy, merely a representative of a refugee agency. He developed a whole elaborate novel about his experience, and began writing it in his mind, chapter by chapter. Out of that he got certain ideas which he could actually use to manipulate his captors to get certain things he wanted, but he says mainly it sustained his sanity and kept him able to deal with the situation. More recently, not a very nice man, Albert Speer, the Nazi leader, has described in his book how he dealt with twenty-five years of imprisonment in Spandau prison by taking an imaginary walk around the world. He started at a certain point—I forget the details—but he would literally be walking around the world and imagining how far he could get on a given day before he would get tired, and what sights he saw. He did this every day and again managed to sustain himself and emerge reasonably sane from the situation. So I think that dimension could be a very broadly useful one. In picking up on what Mihaly (Dr. Csikszentmihayli) was saying, I think one might look at play experiences in childhood—and I would include the games with rules and more structured play as well as the fantasy play—as comparable in a way to a liberal arts education in college. We say that someone who has a liberal arts education can go out and handle a lot of different kinds of jobs and situations and settings, whereas the person who is trained in one highly specific skill doesn't have that degree of flexibility. I think we ought to look at play as having that sort of potential in the childhood experience. We may be minimizing the values of this form of early childhood experience and also underestimating the extent to which there are real prejudices against play on the part of whole segments of our society.

Dr. Sutton-Smith: I have a feeling that we are ethnocentric with respect to imagination in this group. I am totally sympathetic to everything you're saying. That's what makes me distrust it. I think we may be doing all the physical game players of the world—the sporty characters, all those violent sportsmen—a disservice. There are a lot of other play routes, I suspect. It's the scholarly crowd that's gotten it in the neck in organized sports through the last hundred years. The scholarly internalizers and fantasizers were not given great scope, except furtively and in literature, etc. But increasingly there is obviously scope for a lot more fantasy and innovation in the world. I suspect that there is a wall between types of training systems, types of play systems. There's indeed a relevance to us putting emphasis on internalizing now as an adaptive function for subsequent years, but there's real danger in us putting emphasis only on that. There are probably all sorts of other competencies, like dancers, who I understand have low Human Movement responses to the Rorschach. They move outside. They don't have much inside mental movement, but a lot of behavioral movement. So that's another whole way of flowing which presumably doesn't have much to do with internalizing imaginative activity, and that may be true of other physical-skill-type kinetic aesthetic forms. So I'm saying let's not forget who we are and bias the situation in a unidimensional sort of way by our own flow proclivities.

Dr. J. Singer: I would say that there is increasing evidence that people who are good athletes do a great deal of mental practice. They have come on this to some extent just be themselves, but in addition, actual training programs are now being instituted. Alan Richardson did work with gymnasts quite a number of years ago which demonstrated that they could be more effective through mental practice. So the addition of symbolic skills to game-playing skills enhances the likelihood that you're going to get into the flow condition in the actual athletic activity.

Dr. Gardner: The Sutton-Smith assumption is that the imagination occurs in the medium in which the real-life activity occurs. I imagine if you had given Mozart a Rorschach with pictures he would have given you terrible responses. But if you had given him ten little sequences of three notes and said, "Go to work . . ."

References

Dansky, J. L., & Silverman, I. W. Play: A general facilitator of associative fluency. *Developmental Psychology*, 1975, *11*, 104.

Fein, G. G. A transformational analysis of pretending. *Developmental Psychology*, 1975, *11*, 291–296.

Freyberg, J. Increasing the imaginative play of urban disadvantaged kindergarten children through systematic training. In J. L. Singer (Ed.) *The Child's World of Make-Believe*. New York: Academic Press, 1973.

Gould, R. *Child studies through fantasy*. New York: Quadrangle Books, 1972.

Klinger, E. *Structure and functions of fantasy.* New York: Wiley-Interscience, 1971.

Lieberman, N. *Playfulness.* New York: Academic Press, 1978.

Marshall, H. R. Relations between home experiences and children's use of language in play interactions with peers. *Psychological Monographs,* 1965, 75, #5.

Miracle, A. W. Functional analysis of Aymara Games and Play. Paper delivered at T.A.A.S.P. Atlanta, 1976.

Nahme-Huang, L., Singer, D. G., Singer, J. L., & Wheaton, A. Imaginative play and perceptual motor intervention methods with emotionally-disturbed hospitalized children: An evaluation study. *American Journal of Orthopsychiatry,* 1977, 47, 238–249.

Piaget, J. *Play, dreams and imitation in childhood.* New York: Norton, 1962.

Shmukler, D. An investigation into some of the familial and home background correlates of imaginative play in children. Doctoral dissertation, University of Witwatersrand, Johannesburg, South Africa, 1977.

Singer, D. G., & Singer, J. L. Family television viewing habits and the spontaneous play of preschool children. *American Journal of Orthopsychiatry,* 1976, 46, 496–502.

Singer, D. G., & Singer, J. L. *Partners in Play.* New York: Harper and Row, 1977.

Singer, J. L. (Ed.) *The child's world of make-believe: Experimental studies of imaginative play.* New York: Academic Press, 1973.

Singer, J. L. Imagination and make-believe play in early childhood: Some educational implications. *Journal of Mental Imagery,* 1977, 1, 127–144.

Singer, J. L., & Brown, S. The experience-type: Some behavioral correlates and theoretical implications. In M. C. Rickers-Ovsiankina (Ed.) *Rorschach Psychology.* New York: Kreiger, 1977.

Singer, J. L., & Singer, D. G. Fostering imagination play in preschool children: Television and live model effects. *Journal of Communications,* 1976a, 26, 74–80.

Singer, J. L., & Singer, D. G. Imaginative play and pretending in early childhood. In A. Davids (Ed.) *Child personaltiy and psychopathology* (Vol. 3). New York: Wiley, 1976b.

Singer, J. L., & Singer, D. G. Television viewing and imaginative play in preschoolers. NSF Grant Progress Report, 1977a.

Singer, J. L., & Singer, D. G. *Creativity and imaginative play in the preschool child.* Film strip series. New York: Parents Magazine Films, 1977b.

Spivak, G., & Levine, M. Self-regulation and acting-out in normal adolescence. Progress report for National Institute of Mental Health Grant M-4531. Devon, Pennsylvania: Devereaux Foundation, 1964.

Tomkins, S. S. *Affect, Imagery, Consciousness* (Vol. 1). New York: Springer, 1962.

Tucker, J. The role of fantasy in cognitive-affective functioning: Does reality make a difference in remembering? Doctoral dissertation, Teacher's College, Columbia University, 1975.

CHAPTER 12

SPEECH PLAY
AND VERBAL ART

Barbara Kirschenblatt-Gimblett

INTRODUCTION

Dr. Sutton-Smith: Dr. Kirschenblatt-Gimblett introduces several quite new approaches to this conference. The first is a critique of the relatively culture-bound nature of the discourse to this point. She shows that there are both similar and different ways in which cultures use speech play. For some groups the main emphasis in play is on make believe, for others it is upon nonsense, and for others on the manipulation of the play frame itself. Although she does not emphasize the matter, these explorations of the varying roles of play in culture are amongst the most exciting in modern research. They suggest that the relationships between play and creativity established in psychological research extend to the use of the phenomenon in culture, also.

Her second contribution to the understanding of speech play uses riddles as her vehicle. She demonstrates the extent to which speech play is a form of *foregrounding*, a concern with process rather than product, with non-instrumental rather than goal-oriented behaviors. Speech play deals with the absolute surface. It pushes language to its limits, but it does this in different ways within the genre, proceeding from preriddle to true riddle to riddle parodies, the latter being a play on the riddle frame itself. She emphasizes the contribution of these competences to the child's development in the verbal arts.

Dr. Kirschenblatt-Gimblett: I'd like to frame my remarks with some comments about the emphases so far and the areas that will emerge now that we're moving into the anthropological approaches.

Diagnostics. First of all, a major interest, in play so far has been from the point of view of what play behavior can tell us about children; that is, how children manifest cognitive or other kinds of behavior in play. In the case of young children, play is a particularly plentiful source of data for examining a variety of problems in the cognitive and psychological development of the child. Sometimes we even see children performing at a higher level in a play situation than outside of it. For example, Dan Slobin (1967), in his manual on communicative competence, provides evidence of children replicating adult discourse in a play setting but not in other settings. I think that Dr. Garvey demonstrates this point beautifully, too; her data demonstrate the complexity of what's going on among young children in a play setting.

Prerequisites. Second, we have been concerned with what kids have to know or be able to do in order to play, that is, the prerequisites for certain kinds of play. Roberta Collard's material was very interesting and relevant when seen in that light.

Play/Nonplay. Third, we weren't particularly worried about the problem of distinguishing play from nonplay, because in large measure we haven't really been talking about play proper except in connection with the arousal discussion. Most of the work has been done with the very, very young, where it is especially difficult to distinguish play from nonplay. Roberta's [Dr. Collard's] material on exploration versus play and Brian's [Dr. Sutton-Smith's] attempts to distinguish the antecedents of play contribute to this distinction.

Ethnocentrism. Fourth, one thing we haven't been very interested in is cultural definitions of play that are ethnographically derived. We have not asked what constitutes play in a given community. In fact, we've been somewhat ethnocentric—either academic-centric or American-centric. For the most part we have been studying play in our own culture and therefore have not been forced to question our own cultural notions of play. In contrast the definition of play becomes very problematic in the anthropological literature when nonwestern societies are compared with western ones and when generalizations are made about the absence or presence of play behavior. For example, in American society lacrosse is a game; among the Cherokee the very same activity could be defined as sacred work. Therefore our discussion of biological and other factors associated with play proper must also be considered in connection with ritual in North American Indian society, for example. Which activities count as play is culture specific. Cultural definitions of play must be considered.

Language Play. Finally, the interest in language has also been secondary in our discussions; language has been viewed as something that happens during play rather than as a play medium. We haven't really attended to how children play with language. As a result, I will emphasize the problems of defining play in general and speech play in particular.

Speech play is part of everyday interaction for adults and children, probably everywhere. Furthermore, each speech community has its own definition of speech play relative to other uses of speech. A basic problem then is to discover ethnographically what counts as play, or speech play, in a given community; that is, what may be used in what ways for purposes defined as play. What we need, therefore, are ethnographic, empirically-oriented studies of particular cases, to develop a cross-cultural perspective on how various speech communities play with language. How do they select and group certain features from their linguistic and social resources to produce speech behaviors that they define as playful? How do they use such speech patterns in social life? Interestingly, Huizinga (1938), the distinguished Dutch theorist, was sensitive to this matter and included a chapter called "The Play Concept as Expressed in Language" in his classic work *Homo Ludens*. Although I don't agree with some of his conclusions, I think the implications of his comments are worth pursuing.

Games and Routines

Speech play should be distinguished from language games. Games in general have been somewhat loosely defined, especially in the work done on infants. I would prefer to use the term *routine* for some of the things which were called games (by Dr. Hays) and to reserve the term *games* for the kind of definition we get from Roberts, Arth, and Bush (1959). According to this definition games are a special kind of play behavior. Games are competitive. They are organized in terms of sides and there are criteria for determining a winner. Whereas play is a cross-cultural universal, games by this definition may not be, but routines would be.

SPEECH PLAY

Let me now deal with the problem of defining speech play proper. Various groups speaking Mayan languages agree upon three characteristics in their definitions of speech play: it is *voluntary, rule governed, and intrinsic;* that is, it is carried on for its own sake. The various Mayan speech communities diverged with respect to other features of speech play. For example, in Zinacantecan and Chamula, two Mayan languages, it is the make-believe quality of speech play that is given priority; the translation of the term for speech play is "frivolous language," which indicates the hypothetical, nonserious, nonfactual status of what is said. The Blackfoot have a prefix, *kip,* which when added to a word means "for fun," "not serious." The Zuni have the term *nonsense talking,* which includes slang, punning, telling tall tales, and other things. Although all of these communities have a category and a term for speech play, the kinds of behavior included in the category are culture specific. We do have some taxonomies for ways of speaking in nonwestern societies and can locate speech play in the taxonomy. It has been done for the Chamula (Gossen, 1970) and it is being done for other societies.

In other speech communities, the nonserious or hypothetical nature of what's being said is not primary; rather, the way the code itself is being manipulated is critical. A good example is play languages—what we would know as pig latin, op talk, bop talk, etc. Play languages can be used to express erious messages; the focus is on the manipulation of the code rather than on the status of the message.

Dr. Gardner: You're telling us cultures give different names to something. Is what they're giving names to the voluntary, rule-governed, intrinsic thing you have been talking about?

Dr. Kirschenblatt-Gimblett: Right, with respect to language use.

Dr. Gardner: But that doesn't help me very much. All language is voluntary, rule governed and intrinsic unless somebody is putting a gun to my head.

Dr. Kirschenblatt-Gimblett: "Carried on for its own sake" stands in contrast to instrumental referential uses of language, the use to which we put language most of the time.

Dr. Garvey: What about poetry?

Dr. Kirschenblatt-Gimblett: It is a beautiful example of this kind of thing. Let us consider a *continuum* from speech play to verbal art, rather than discrete categories. In the work of the Prague School (Todorov, Mukarovsky, Jakobson, and others), speech play is terribly important because in it we explore the "poetry of grammar," a prerequisite for discovering the "grammar of poetry."

Dr. Gardner: Are you saying that it's a noninstrumental use of language?

Dr. Kirschenblatt-Gimblett: I don't want to make that a defining characteristic. That's why I selected voluntary, rule-governed, and intrinsic as being basic definitions. I want to make the other criteria problematic; that is, they may or may not be part of a particular society's own definition of what constitutes speech play. Noninstrumentality is certainly important. At the extreme end of the continuum, speech play takes the form of nonsense, and functions of language, which are the instrumental and referential so important in everyday talk, assume very low priority. But in poetry priorities are different, and the interests in language as form and language as reference are delicately balanced.

We have the basic criteria of being voluntary, rule-governed and carried on for its own sake. Criteria of nonseriousness, hypotheticalness and frivolousness are culture specific and may or no may not enter a definition of speech play. Let's look more carefully at the matter of intrinsicness. Stephen Miller's recent (1973) attempt to define play is useful here. Miller and many others have been inspired by Huizinga's (1938) notion that play has its aim in itself. For Miller the center of interest in play is *process* rather than *goal,* or outcome. As a result, the way of doing something assumes top priority. The way of doing becomes what gets done. Secondly, process is not streamlined, but rather is voluntarily elaborated and complicated in various patterned and culture-specific ways. These two aspects of process—the emphasis on the process rather than outcomes and the complicating of process—are terribly important. We see the usefulness of this notion of play very clearly in the speech play material. This concept of play is not new, and even Huizinga didn't invent it. We have it from Groos in 1901, who discussed play as "psychical damming up." We have it from Curti in 1930 as "overmotivation." We have it from Piaget in 1962 as deliberate complication in his book *Play, Dreams and Imitation.* I'm not suggesting that the notion of play is new, but rather that it might be useful to re-explore and consider the applications of this approach.

This approach to play is closely related to Jakobson's notion of the poetic function of language, which involves focusing attention on the shape of the message and exploiting language for its own sake. The notion of *foregrounding* is useful here too. When the "poetic function of language" assumes priority, there is a foregrounding of features of discourse that are normally not emphasized. Todorov (1971) states that in literature—and I would say this is equally true of speech play—*linguistic signs stop being transparent instruments of communication or understanding and acquire an importance in themselves.* Play becomes a central element in such notions of literature and literary meaning, and is integral to the nonreferential, noninstrumental nature of much literary discourse and of much play discourse. This leads us back to Huizinga's position that play is a prerequisite for literature and art.

I want to emphasize that the poetic function of language and speech play as well can involve *any component of speech and any relation among the components. There are no restrictions on what you can play with.* A primary determinant is the culture-specific basis for selecting what and how to play. For example, it would be worth doing comparative studies with Japanese children. Since rhyme is not a feature of Japanese poetry, what do children do when they play with sounds?

The question as formulated by Dell Hymes becomes "to what extent and in what ways and for what purposes is speech manipulated for its own sake or for kinds of effects recognized as play and art?" One of the things that we found in working with middle-class children in Texas was that children and adults set the priorities differently. We tried to account for child-adult differences in what was selected and how it was played in terms of the difference between child and adult language structures.

I have suggested that the epitome of speech play at the far end of the continuum would be nonsense. An especially interesting essay on nonsense is Michael Holquist's "What is a Boojum" (1969). His work on Lewis Carroll and other work on the great classic nonsense writers is particularly informative because these writers expand our whole notion of language, of how language works,and of what can be done with language.

Dr. Hutt: What do you mean by "nonsense?" Edward Lear's nonsense verse, for example, is referential. It just contradicts the conventions. What I understood you to mean by nonsense is something more like randomness.

Dr. Kirschenblatt-Gimblett: I would distinguish between jibberish—

Dr. Collard: It's a logical nonsense.

Dr. Kirschenblatt-Gimblett: Right. I indicated that you can play with anything, which means you can play with semantic relationships and with referentiality. But the kind of sense that is made is contained within a system that's defined by the playing rather than by a set of relationships that one works with in the everydy.

Dr. Hutt: Egocentric?

Dr. Kirschenblatt-Gimblett: In the sense that it's a private system.

Dr. Hutt: But not necessarily playful.

Dr. Kirschenblatt: Not necessarily playful.

Dr. Collard: Kids just verbalize their thoughts. A lot of egocentric speech is speech that hasn't become internalized. It just comes out.

Dr. Kirschenblatt-Gimblett: Okay. Let me say a little about nonsense, then I want to move on. The beautiful thing about nonsense is that, like play, it constitutes a system of its own and it's untranslatable; therefore, you have to deal with nonsense within its own frame of reference and you can't translate nonsense by referring to something outside of it. That's why it's of such special interest. In Holquist's term, it is *absolute surface.* Nonsense at its most extreme compromises the status of words as linguistic signs; nonsense pushes language to its limits. I think much speech play does that too. Speech play and nonsense are ways of pushing language to discover its limits in all kinds of ways.

There's a lovely statement by a twelve-year-old: "We like nonsense because all the squares think something has to mean something all the time" (Jablow & Withers, 1975). In nonsense and speech play the tyranny of a certain kind of meaning gets played with or abdicated in favor of other principles.

RIDDLING

What I'd like to do now is to take some riddling material and briefly suggest ways in which it illustrates the problems we've been considering. To summarize, we suggested that ethnographically derived concepts of play and speech play might lead us in productive directions, and we offered a working definition of speech play as voluntary, rule-governed, intrinsic, and in, some societies, nonserious discourse. Speech play is process- rather than outcome-oriented and involves a complication of means. Any component or set of relationships among components within language may be played with. Referentiality and instrumentality have low priority, presumably because we associate them so strongly with "serious" uses of language and because we so often associate speech play with the frivolous or nonserious. Speech play is essentially a metalinguistic activity— that is, speech play is largely language about language or, to make language a social act rather than a cultural artifact, speech about speech.

Dr. Gardner: Metalinguistic? Does that imply that there's some kind of consciousness about what's going on?

Dr. Kirschenblatt-Gimblett: Yes, especially in the "disciplined" speech play I have examined. Babbling and much spontaneous speech play are different from traditional or "disciplined" speech play. We are very interested in how speech play relates to other kinds of verbal art. For example, I'm specifically interested in the ways in which children's speech play can illuminate our understanding of how adult verbal art is put together. Children have this beautiful way of acquiring things in an order which suggests that adult forms are organized in ways we never even thought about. And the riddle material is exceptionally interesting for this reason. To anticipate a little, the riddle appears to be a primary form. For example, kids ask riddles before they use proverbs. This is true cross-culturally. We have evidence that in some societies proverbs are introduced as answers to riddles; children first learn these proverbs as riddle answers and only later learn to use the proverbs as proverbs. We know that riddling precedes narrative jokes and that riddles precede wellerisms ("What did the monkey say as he pee'd in the cash register drawer? This is going to run into money!" is a wellerism). Therefore we find the sequence of riddle to proverb, riddle to joke, riddle to narrative. Furthermore, riddling involves a manipulation of social interaction. Dr. Sutton-Smith deals with riddles as an exercise of arbitrary power. There is also Dr. Shultz's (1974) work on riddles as incongruity and resolution, and Brian's [Dr. Sutton-Smith's] work on riddles as problems of classification (1976). And I'm going to talk as well about MacDowell's work (1974) on riddles and classifications. These studies indicate that children work their way sequentially through the different problems addressed by the various types of riddles. They opt to do riddles first and they select which riddles to do first. In their own selecting process they move through a sequence of traditional forms in their cultural environment, which reveals a great deal about the nature of these forms and what needs to be mastered in order for a child to be able to handle the more complex ones.

Dr. Collard: Don't riddles get important when children first learn what is true logic, then enjoy the things that don't fit logic—aren't they perversions or variations on logic?

Dr. Kirschenblatt-Gimblett: There's interesting riddle work going on. The work that Brian [Dr. Sutton-Smith] has done (1976) has dealt mainly in terms of problems of classification and the kinds of classification problems that surface in riddle preferences across age. But there's other work that suggests that kids are first interested in descriptive questions; that is, questions that demonstrate that language is miraculous because it really can refer to things in the world. So you get questions like "What's red? An apple." "What's yellow? A banana." Children will do those over and over again and will revel in the capacity of language to refer, in the transparency of language. Later, children introduce a block element which demonstrates language's inability to refer, language's limits. Paradox, ambiguity and multiple meanings all pose challenges to the clarity of language. In addition there is the interest in language as a social art, and this is expressed in riddling behavior that McDowell calls "ludic routines of victimization." These routines shift from physical abuse—"Would you like some Hawaiian Punch?" "Punch!"—to verbal abuse where you insult people verbally to routines where you make them victimize themselves. For example: "Say after everything I say, 'key.'" "I am a house-key; I am a door-key; I am a car-key; I am a mon-key." These routines are developmentally arrayed in children's repertoires. The array shows that children are working on several things at the same time—logical problems, classification, social interaction, etc.

Dr. Gardner: I'm having a lot of trouble understanding what you're saying. You're making the argument that there are developmental patterns in these different realms. You're making the argument further that there is a kind of an agenda, if you will, whereby children highlight different aspects of language from adults in their language play, and you're making the argument that if we study what young children do this will give us insight into the organization of adult language which we may not have. What else are you saying? I'm not saying that I don't think that's important. I think it's crucial. You're saying a lot, but I'm not sure if you're just trying to reinforce the same arguments.

Dr. Kirschenblatt-Gimblett: I am saying different things. What the paper essentially does (Sanches and Kirschenblatt-Gimblett, 1976) is attempt to account for and characterize speech play productions of children in terms of the child's language model. Children's speech play productions and preferences are compared with adult ones, and the differences are accounted for in terms of the child's language model. Another interest that I have as a folklorist is in the extent to which children's ways of playing with language help us to understand the nature of language and the nature of adult productions. We know from the child-aquisition literature that people have been looking to the child's acquisition of language for insights into the nature of language. I don't think we've really explored that approach, although I'm personally interested in it.

Dr. Fein: Are you saying that there is a relationship between the developmental sequence for these forms and the timing of the original acquisitions of the language models in children?

Dr. Kirschenblatt-Gimblett: Yes. We found that even after children were presumably competent in certain features of the language they were interested in playing with that feature. Furthermore, even after they were presumably competent English speakers (at age four or five), phonological structure still had priority in their speech play and language model. Again, the relative priority was different for an eight-year-old child than for an adult, even though the child is presumably competent in his language.

Dr. Fein: Then there would be a general lag between the acquisition of language and the acquisition of the metalinguistic system which knows what you've acquired. The development of the metalinguistic system in a sense parallels the original acquisitional sequence, so that before you really become competent you have to begin to know something about your competence in a superior way, in a more reflective way, in a more deliberate kind of controlling way.

Dr. Kirschenblatt-Gimblett: I would argue that babbling and a lot of play behavior precede all kinds of regular language competencies, but that some basic language competence is a prerequisite for disciplined speech play, the kind that we're looking at here. This kind of disciplined speech play in turn is a prerequisite for verbal art, so that there's a kind of reciprocity involved.

Dr. Gardner: Even though there may be a décalage between the child's acquisition of competence as a nonreflective speaker and his ability to capture some forms of knowledge in different kinds of verbal play and verbal art, you're implying that the order may not be the same in each case. I think it could be empirically just as interesting if it were much more complicated, which I would guess to be the case.

Dr. Kirschenblatt-Gimblett: Right. I'm not suggesting that the order is parallel; that is to say, that the priority of certain features of the language system necessarily parallels the order in which they're acquired.

Dr. Schultz: You asserted a few minutes ago that riddling was somehow primary in comparison to other forms. Is there something profound about that that I'm not grasping, or is it merely a matter of riddles being much easier for the child to produce? All he needs to do is remember how to ask the question. He doesn't have to construct a whole story.

Dr. Kirschenblatt-Gimblett: I'll tell you some of the things that are involved. Wolfenstein (1954) argues that one of the reasons why riddling precedes joking, for example, is that riddles are short and ready made, and jokes are longer and improvised. Riddles are therefore easier to control. But there's so much happening in riddling when you watch kids in a session. If you simply ask children to write down or tell you all the riddles they know you miss a lot of what's going on. We have to observe a naturally occurring riddling session—the sequence of the riddles and the ways in which the session is constructed. For example, one riddling session that was transcribed showed very clearly that the riddling activity involved downward classification. The children were dealing with the class of things that move and distinctions among things that move. They asked questions such as "What is it that has two legs and walks?" "What has four legs and walks?" "What has no legs and rides?" "What has two legs and flies?" McDowell took the whole series and displayed the classification generated by the riddles. First we have animate and inanimate. Then we have animal and human. Then we have four-legged animals and two-legged animals. The inanimate are divided into land and air categories. The land category was subdivided into cycles and cars. The result was a beautiful exercise in downward classification. Furthermore, the riddles were improvised, rather than being a recital of stereotypical fixed-phrase formulae. So much of this early riddling is improvised, spontaneous and very conceptual. When you relate the operations involved in riddling to the operations involved in using proverbs and telling jokes, you begin to see some of the reasons why kids ask riddles first. For example, proverbs are exercises in upward classification. With proverbs you look at a situation and classify it up. That is, you have to include the specific situation in a more general principle rather than work down from the general principle to the specific cases. Riddling occurs early; it relates to other genres (proverbs, jokes, etc.) in complex ways and also entails developmental sequence within riddles themselves.

Dr. D. Singer: What about the kinds of kids who riddle and the kinds of play they do? I would be curious about some of the other variables that are involved in riddling. Does a child have to be highly imaginative to riddle? Or do all children riddle? Do you find variations among riddles?

Dr. Kirschenblatt-Gimblett: I don't believe that the predisposition to riddling or the interest in riddling proper has really been examined. It's just been assumed that kids riddle, and then *how* they riddle has been looked at.

Dr. D. Singer: To make up a riddle you do have to have a lot of image-ry. It isn't just playing with words, it's imagery not only for what the thing really looks like, but the thing in juxtaposition to what it is not.

Dr. Kirschenblatt-Gimblett: Well, you do and you don't. It depends on the kinds of riddles.

Dr. D. Singer: Unless you memorize them all.

Dr. Kirschenblatt-Gimblett: Riddles can be metaphorical or literal; a traditional riddle is "What swims in the sea? Fish." It's literal. There's nothing metaphorical about it. Or riddles can be oppositional or nonop-positional. That is, they can involve some kind of logical contradiction or not involve a logical contradiction. You can also have metaphorical rid-dles: "Twenty-four white horses on a red hill, they chomp and they stomp and then they stand still." That one is metaphorical but not oppositional. The answer is "Teeth in the mouth." It's an Anglo-Saxon riddle. Riddles can therefore be metaphorical-nonmetaphorical; they can be opposition-al-nonoppositional; and they can work with other strategies for confu-sion. Here is a false gestalt: "What is it that a dog does on three legs, a man does standing up, and a woman does sitting down?" "Shake hands." Or you can work with too little information. There are a variety of strate-gies that can be used to confuse, and what I'm trying to suggest is that kids work with different strategies at different points. We can show that there is developmental input there in terms of preference for strategy. So that, for example, the descriptive riddles work by incomplete information but they do not utilize contradiction or metaphors. Let me give you some examples and you'll see exactly what I mean.

Here are descriptive routines that you get from your five- and six-year-olds regularly. "What's red?" "A rose." "What's yellow?" "A banana." "What's orange?" "An orange." "What's in the dirt?" "There's a hole." "What's inside the hole?" "An ant." "What has long legs and is hard to walk?" "A seagull." "What has three wheels and pedals?" "A tricycle." "What has four wheels, no pedals, and a steering wheel?" "A car." "What's round and has a lot of jelly?" "A jelly donut." Well these are exer-cises in description, and they may work by relatively little information but there is no contradiction, there's no metaphor, there's no false gestalt, no confusing with superfluous, irrelevant information. All of those other tac-tics become block elements and challenge the function of language to re-fer clearly. An interest in these "block elements" comes later.

Dr. Collard: When does the logic for it being denied enter? I remem-ber the first riddle I ever thought of, when I was six—"What can go all the way around the yard and leave only one track?" (You've got to remember this is a six-year-old riddle.) You know what? "A wheelbarrow." You've got to have lived back when I did.

Dr. McCall: Where do these nonsense jokes come in? I can deal with it when my kid comes home and says, "Why did the elephant stand on the marshmallow?" and the answer is "Because he doesn't want to fall into the cocoa." I can deal with that. But not when he comes home and says, "Why did the kangaroo slam the door? Because the mouse was purple." They get a big charge out of this, not only because I sit there and go, "Pffff, it's absurd," but you can see them in the corner telling each other this and they're rolling in the aisles. What's the pleasure in this? I missed it someplace.

Dr. Kirschenblatt-Gimblett: It depends on whether he's five or whether he's twelve. It'll mean something different. For a five-year-old it's what Brian [Dr. Sutton-Smith] calls preriddles. His work really demonstrates this beautifully (1976). If you examine the riddle productions of children at various ages, you'll understand what concept of riddle underlies their productions. Now the absurd riddle you presented is based on a conception of a riddle such as "A riddle is a question with an arbitrary answer." For a four- or five-year old, the deciphering of that incongruity is impossible, so all the child understands is that a riddle is a question of some kind and that the answer is arbitrary in its relationship to the question.

Question: So it's an incomplete imitation of a riddle?

Dr. Kirschenblatt-Gimblett: Fair enough. Yet the preriddle is not simply an incomplete riddle or a poor imitation of an adult riddle. It's based on a model of riddle that says a riddle is a question that has an arbitrary answer, or an answer that doesn't have a connection to the question the way answers usually do, and people laugh. One of the things that's interesting about riddles is that they are a special kind of question, and the interesting thing about mock riddles and parodies of riddles is that they play with riddling, they play with the genre. Therefore, *riddles play with questions, and mock riddles play with riddles.* People have expectations about what a riddle is, and at a certain juncture they start to play with those expectations. They start to play with riddles as a genre, and therefore giving you a totally arbitrary answer is to defeat your expectations that, no matter how bizarre and tenuous, the answer will have some connection to the question. That's why we need to know the context in which an absurd riddle was asked in order to determine if it was a preriddle or a mock riddle.

Dr. Lewis: What you're suggesting is that if the five-year-old does it then it reflects the lack of competence to the genre of riddle. Yet when the twelve-year-old does it he's already captured the genre and now is playing with it.

Dr. Ellis: So the nine-year-old will riddle in the acceptable structure of riddle, where there is a logical but tenuous connection between the answer and the original question.

Dr. Kirschenblatt-Gimblett: Yes. But that expectation can be played with too. People can be quite cruel, as in the "no soap radio" joke. You know that everybody feels obliged to laugh at a joke and you look stupid if you don't understand the joke. There's a traditional conspiracy in which all but one person is informed that they are to laugh at a meaningless joke—"No soap radio." Only one person doesn't know what's going on. Everyone else laughs uproariously and waits for this other person to laugh; everyone knows that they are laughing at a meaningless "joke." Finally the one person who's not in on the conspiracy is embarrassed into pretending he understands the joke and laughs. That's conspiratorial. But the conspiracy is based upon a knowledge of what the expectations are.

Dr. D. Singer: I'm curious about "the dozens," which is an adult kind of play with words. How would you classify that?

Dr. Kirschenblatt-Gimblett: That's speech play and it's not really adult, it's adolescent behavior, certainly among Afro-Americans. Verbal dueling is extremely interesting because verbal dueling from what we know cross-culturally (Zinacantecan, Tzeltal, Chamula, Afro-American, Turkish) is by and large played among adolescent male peers. It's extremely interesting because adolescent males use this playful discourse to establish a temporary hierarchy where there isn't one; the hierarchy only lasts for the duration of the duel. Dueling is invariably done in public; that is, it isn't done privately between two people, it's almost invariably done in front of other people. And I think it's part of a whole constellation of adolescent ways of playing with language that are very special. I'd like to emphasize what we could call *continuing acquisition*, something we should examine as much as initial acquisition, which we have emphasized here. We have had the expectation that there is not much new learning later on. In fact, a lot of the adolescent material that we have for language and for speech play suggests that much learning goes on later that should be viewed as continuing acquisition.

Dr. J. Singer: I wonder if you could say something more about the cultural differences in patterns of speech play. Is riddling universal? Is punning anything like universal? Are there different developmental series of that? And then I wonder also whether in the history of language, or in the history of culture, there are changes?

Dr. Kirschenblatt-Gimblett: Absolutely. For example, we've got good material from the Elizabethan period, the French Renaissance, nineteenth-century America, and others to indicate that there are vogues or fads where a certain kind of play with language is very much in fashion. Today we ostensibly see punning as the "lowest form of humor." First we excuse ourselves—"pardon the pun"—and then we indulge. Presumably we are ambivalent. But there is material to suggest that historically, preferences for certain kinds of speech play do change. Also there are cross-cultural differences in the ways speech play is organized. As to which aspects of speech play are cross-cultural universals, we don't have enough data to say that everybody puns, or that everybody asks riddles. We know that not everybody engages in verbal duels and that not everybody organizes things in terms of metaphorical couplets, a strong Mayan pattern in many speech-play forms.

Dr. Schultz: I wanted to speak to that question. We recently completed a cross-cultural survey of the structure of humor and indeed we found, as Barbara [Dr. Kirschenblatt-Gimblett] said, cultural variations in the particular forms that were used. Some cultures told riddles, some didn't, etc. Some cultures, such as the Japanese, had very complicated forms of riddling. Some had very simple forms, as we do. But what did seem to be culturally universal were the structural characteristics of these things. And in every culture we sampled, whether it was literate or traditional, the structure of humor appeared to be characterized by incongruity and resolution. Something which acted to increase arousal, if you want, and something else which acted to decrease arousal.

Dr. Ellis: Asimov has a book, *Treasury of Jokes,* of which the most important part is not the jokes, but his anlysis of jokes; and the central feature of that analysis is the building up of an expectation and then its destruction. If the expectation is realized, then the punch line is redundant, so there's a requirement that there be incongruity of a nonsalient kind. If the stimulus is too salient, and produces a critical effect on your existence, then it's not perceived as funny.

Dr. Kirschenblatt-Gimblett: Another reason why the speech-play material is so important is that it lets us investigate novelty in directions we would not normally take if we used language only in the conventional way. So whether you take riddling as an exercise in novel classification, or play languages as an exercise in reorganizing the phonology of your language, you find that exploration and novelty are maximized in speech-play activity.

Dr. Fein: It might be worth making a distinction between a play form that is present in a culture (meaning if you look hard enough you find some evidence for it)—a play form that the average person in the culture can understand—and a play form which the average person in the culture can invent. My guess is that most of them are imitated. I'm skeptical about how many original riddles there are.

Dr. Kirschenblatt-Gimblett: Children invent them. They generate them. They really do. You know the problem, and I think that it's a point that Helen [Dr. Schwartzman] brings up; namely, that scholars who have collected riddles have been interested in their traditional character. They haven't attended to unique riddles. They've been concerned with riddles as cultural products and have gone after ones that are recognizable as traditional rather than as individual creations. As a result there's been a bias against riddles created by individuals, whether child or adult. Collections don't reflect the unique creations of individuals.

Dr. Fein: I don't deny they exist. We have the best subjects, our own children. My daughter never riddled and she never riddled originally. I'm not saying never was she caught saying a riddle, but it's not something that she did often. Her younger brother does it frequently and does original ones. My intuition, having been a school teacher and watched kids, is that you will find kids who will engage in lots of instances of one kind of riddle play or in lots of instances of lots of kinds of riddle play. But I think that most kids can understand them and appreciate them.

Dr. Kirschenblatt-Gimblett: I should also refer to the Forman and Roberts (1971) cross-cultural study of riddles based on the Human Relations Area Files materials. Their study deals with hypotheses about enculturation and preferences for certain kinds of play forms in cultures where oral interrogation is a form of socialization. I'm interested in looking at naturally-occurring riddle sessions and in treating them as a totality. I want to see how they're organized and structured. I'm interested in the relationships that are established among the riddles and also in the wrong answers that are offered. For example, the wrong answers are very interesting because they indicate a set of possibilities. We know that riddlers, in that they exercise arbitrary power, have the power to refuse possible but not traditional answers. So "What's black and white and red all over?" is a great one because you can just stand there till a person goes blue in the face saying "A nun rolling down the stairs, a newspaper, a blushing zebra." The guessers spin out all the answers they can think of and you say no because as the exerciser of arbitrary power you have the power to determine which of the logically possible answers you will accept. All the rejected answers are very useful in understanding the riddling process. Therefore naturally-occurring riddling sessions with wrong answers offer possibilities for a study not available in the kind of corpus that you get in a collection of riddles from oral tradition as, for example, "1100 riddles from the English language" collections.

Dr. Sutton-Smith: The value of Barbara's [Dr. Kirschenblatt-Gimblett's] data is that it's across several age levels and therefore we begin to get a sense of a play sequence: you begin with questions and answers, then a parody of the reference within questions and answers, then a parody of expectations of parodied reference within questions and answers. You get a successive reversal of frames. We have asked here about the unit in play, "What's the unit?" Here the frame or unit is provided us. Of course there are many sorts of frames in riddles, interactional ones as well as verbal ones, but just looking at the riddle as play we have here a successive series of frames. That is not a bad model for thinking about most of the play material we've been looking at and then asking if what we're calling play is a reversal of some frames. We've established that play begins with some kind of competence. We've usually used the words *competence* or *exploration*. We could use the word *frame* for a prior set towards establishing an adequate response to some stimulus or other. If you look at it that way, then the play becomes some way of manipulating a prior frame so that it is inverted or reversed.

Dr. Ellis: It seemed to me your frame is a notion of a reversal or a cyclical appearance of a particular way of dealing with a phenomenon, and, from my field, competition is a kind of a frame. First of all you try something out, and very soon you require sufficient skill so that the only way to generate a further level of development is to introduce the uncertainties inherent by competing with somebody else; so that looks like a frame. And then very soon people come out of the competitive mode again. They go beyond competition. I'm just wondering if that's a frame. I was thinking that there are a few people who go on and develop those activities at a different level which again becomes competitive. I can deal with it in terms of sailing. First you study sailing and how to do it. When you've acquired control of the thing, the only thing left is to see if you can do it better than someone else, so you have sailboat races. And very soon they're boring as hell because why do you want to charge around three buoys under very constrained circumstances? Even the uncertainties inherent in beating other people or, as in my case, regularly being beaten, lose interest. Then what happens is a few guys go on to see if they can get around the world. In a lot of sailboat races you can see the starting point out there, then they go to there, and you come back to here, and you do that a couple of times. Everything is visible to you. Then you say to hell with that, and you go cruising around, which is beyond competition, but after a little while you begin to see if you can cruise better than somebody else. Then you have a very different kind of racing. I can't think of what you would do next.

Dr. D. Singer: Then you sail across the ocean single-handed.

Dr. Ellis: Then you do it the wrong way 'round.

Dr. D. Singer: Don't you ever just get on a boat and say, "Gosh, this is great; it feels so good."

Dr. Ellis: At intermediate stages you do that. I'm sort of one and a half frames in, so I'm a leisurely sailor, but I begin to feel that if I got very good at navigating I might want to try that out. Is that a frame? Bring me back to riddling.

Dr. Sutton-Smith: There's a better example in Bernie DeKoven's work (1978). There is a group of people who are into metagames and gaming. That is, they start a game, they get it going, then they sit down and say, "What the hell's wrong with this game?" There are basic rules, such as: if anybody doesn't like it, everybody has to stop and sit and listen to that person and change the rules. So there's this constant free play, as it were, with the frame of the game itself. I think that's the next step up from the competitive game or the old-fashioned organized game. It's a sort of self-conscious manipulation of game frames.

Dr. Ellis: In Asimov's analysis of jokes, the first step was sort of a pre-riddle—you don't understand it but it has the surface appearance of a riddle—then the actual use of the riddle, then the inversion. You kept seeing this kind of thing happening.

Dr. Kirschenblatt-Gimblett: There are also transformations. Riddles may be embedded in jokes. In fact, if you look at the construction of jokes, a lot of jokes are convertible into riddles and a lot of riddles are convertible into jokes. You begin to see not only the kinds of inversions that Brian [Dr. Sutton-Smith] talks about, but also embedding operations where you embed these smaller forms and begin to expand them. We also have transformations by inversion. I consider the proverb to be an inversion of the riddle.

Dr. J. Singer: I think we'd all agree on the incongruity and breakdown of expectation element. I wonder if there isn't also the private stretching, the additional stretching at the level of imagery. For example, I still can't get that nun rolling down the staircase out of my mind. I mean, that's a great image. To do some of those riddles or to grasp certain jokes, you do have to generate some type of visual image. It's not just the play on the words themselves. Although it can be done without that.

Dr. Kirschenblatt-Gimblett: It depends on the kind of riddle, too. For example, "A plane crashes on the border of the United States and Canada. Where do they bury the survivors? Since when do you bury survivors?" In this case I don't focus on an image of an airplane with people in it. It is a parody of a riddle, because instead of making you attend to the answer it asks you to find out what's wrong with the question. Riddle parodies tell you so much about how riddles are constructed. The parody calls attention to what makes a riddle a riddle.

Dr. D. Singer: I would still think there are children who will drop riddles and then move on to something else—who are more imaginative. I just think there are so many variations in the kinds of kids who keep riddles, and maybe the next step would be to examine the kinds of play these kids indulge in. Maybe this is a major part of the play for some of these kids, just this verbal play, and they may be patterners for all I know. But I think it would be interesting to see if there is any correlation between their play and the type of riddles they prefer.

Dr. Kirschenblatt-Gimblett: I don't believe individual differences have been examined in connection with riddling.

Basically, I wanted to address myself to the definition of play, and specifically of speech play, and to argue for a culture-specific approach. I suggested that disciplined or traditional speech play as opposed to spontaneous and improvised speech play was of special value in understanding various developmental questions. One question I consider particularly important is that of what leads us to competence in verbal art or various other aesthetic uses of language, rather than just to basic competencies. Most of what we've been talking about are basic, and initial, competencies. I was interested in the relationships of speech play and verbal art as well.

Dr. J. Singer: Do you have any information at all as to where the riddles really get started? How much of it comes from parents or adults directly, and how much is generated within peer culture?

Dr. Kirschenblatt-Gimblett: That's a good question. Because of the lack of an ethnographic interest, context has often gotten lost in the wash. I'd like to distinguish between immediate context and broader context, because there are multiple contexts and we've tended to talk about them as if they're all one. The immediate situation is one context, and a broader cultural frame of reference is the other. Very often they've been ignored, so that we don't know as much as we need to know about the occurrence of riddling in a child's life. I know that for the Chicano children studied by McDowell a lot of riddling was generated by children in child-child interaction. I know in my own experience I used to open the centerfold of *Children's Digest* each month, stand at the kitchen sink, and ask my mother riddles; and there was no greater pleasure than in stumping her repeatedly. That was my own personal pattern, but for these Chicano children it is a peer activity. It is an ethnographic problem that we should look at cross-culturally: who riddles to whom under what circumstances?

Dr. Schultz: Certainly the work of the Opies would suggest that in our culture this is really a part of the culture of childhood and is passed from one generation of children to the next, rather bypassing the adult culture altogether.

Dr. Kirschenblatt-Gimblett: The Opies are biased. They acknowledge that there's children's lore and nursery lore, lore transmitted from child to child and lore transmitted from adult to child. But they only deal with nursery lore in its most conventional form, namely, nursery rhymes. They don't really examine the content of dangling rhymes and lullabies and all that traditional lore that adults transmit to infants and young children. It's not that there is no adult-child lore; the Opies just don't talk about it much.

Dr. Sutton-Smith: We know informally that adults are constantly putting bits of information into the child play culture. In my own earlier work in schools (1959), kids would actually tell you, "Well, we got this game from Mr. So-and-so." Although it wouldn't be regular, there was enough of it to indicate some incalculable amount of input going on, usually from playful adults who were out on the playground or read riddles in a classroom.

Dr. Gardner: My own experience, though, is that my kids don't like my knock-knock jokes. They like their peers' knock-knock jokes, and I think the reason is that it's hard for parents, at least for this one, to come up with a joke which is at a child's level of assimilation, whereas peers usually have the jokes which are at the right level.

Dr. Sutton-Smith: I think even those arbitrary preriddles of theirs are not quite as arbitrary as they may seem. When we try to give an idiosyncratically arbitrary response ourselves, it never quite works. Then again there's the social interactional context. The kid doesn't expect it from you. The whole thing's mainly a mockery of you, the parent, anyway. That's the import of the Roberts & Forman research (1971). It showed that in cultures where they socialized by interrogation, they had riddles. You have to see the riddle as in part a reversal of the adult interrogative situation, so that when children tell riddles, and you try to get into the game, you're really defeating the whole inversive social purpose of the thing.

Dr. Kirschenblatt-Gimblett: Right. It's their turn to exercise the arbitrary power.

Dr. Schultz: Why would you want to define speech play arbitrarily as being noninstrumental? Isn't it possible that it might indeed have very instrumental functions for play itself, or for modulating arousal, or for governing and controlling social interactions and that kind of thing?

Dr. Kirschenblatt-Gimblett: That's a very good point. I also think, in support of your argument, that we've underestimated the nature of ordinary language and made too strong a dichotomy between instrumental and referential language on the one hand, and play language on the other. I really wanted to set up a continuum and to array various types of speech along it; at one end of the continuum you have the guy in the control tower in the airport giving instructions for how to land a plane. You really don't care how he speaks as long as he communicates clearly. At the other end of the continuum you have the idea it's not *what* you say but *how* you say it. You're right; a continuum is more useful than a dichotomy.

Dr. Sutton-Smith: The instrumental functions of the particular riddles are probably long term in outcome. They're a consolidation of flexible management of various routines. They probably do have an instrumental outcome later, but we haven't dealt with that.

References

DeKoven, B. *The well played game.* New York: Anchor Press, 1979.

Gossen, G. H. Time and space in Cahmula Oral Tradition. Ph.D. Dissertation, Harvard University, 1970.

Huizinga, J. *Homo Ludens.* Boston: Beacon, 1955.

Holquist, M. What is a Boojum? Nonsense and Modernism. In P. Brooks (Ed.) *The Child's Part.* Boston: Beacon, 1969.

Jablow, A., and Withers, C. Social sense and verbal nonsense in urban children's folklore. *New York Folklore Quarterly,* 1965, *21,* 243-257.

Jakobson, R. Poetry of grammar and grammar of poetry. *Lingua* 1968, *21*,579–609.

Kirschenblatt-Gimblett, B. *Speech Play.* Philadelphia: University of Pennsylvania Press, 1976.

McDowell, J.H. Interrogative routines in Mexican-American children's folklore. *Working Papers in Sociolinguistics* #20, Austin, Texas, 1974.

Miller, S. End and means and galumphing: Some leitmotifs of play. *American Anthropologist,* 1973, *75,* 87–98.

Mukarovsky, J. Standard language and poetic language. In P. L. Garvin (Ed.) *A Prague School Reader on Esthetics, Literature and Style.* Georgetown: Georgetown University Press, 1970.

Opie, P. & I. The Language and Lore of Schoolchildren. Oxford: Oxford University Press, 1959.

Roberts, J. M., Forman M. L. Riddles: expressive models of interrogation. *Ethnology* 1 1971, *10,* 509–533.

Roberts, J. M., Arth, M. J., & Bush, B. R. Games in culture. *American Anthropologist,* 1959, *61,* 597–605.

Sanches, M., & Kirschenblatt-Gimblett, B. Children's traditional speech play and child language. In B. Kirschenblatt-Gimblett (Ed.) *Speech Play.* Philadelphia: University of Pennsylvania, 1976.

Slobin, D. A field manual for the cross cultural study of the acquisition of communicative competence. Berkeley: University of California Language-Behavior Development Lab, 1967.

Shultz, T. R. Development of the appreciation of riddles. *Child Development,* 1974, *45,* 100–105.

Sutton-Smith, B. *The Games of New Zealand Children.* Berkeley: University of California Press, 1959.

Sutton-Smith, B. A developmental Structural Account of Riddles. In B. Kirschenblatt-Gimblett (Ed.) *Speech Play.* Philadelphia: University of Pennsylvania Press, 1976.

Todorov, T. Meaning in literature. *International Review for the Theory of Literature,* 1971, *1,* 8–15.

Wolfenstein, M. *Children's Humor: A Psychological Analysis,* Glencoe, Ill.: Free Press, 1954.

CHAPTER 13

THE SOCIOCULTURAL CONTEXT OF PLAY

Helen Schwartzman

INTRODUCTION

Dr. Sutton-Smith: Dr. Schwartzman, like Dr. Kirschenblatt-Gim-blett, begins by emphasizing the relativity of most psychological concepts of play. While the psychologists struggle for some overall insight as to what anthropology has to say about play, Dr. Schwartzman emphasizes the great limitations of the anthropological evidence in this area.

But along with Lewis, Ross, Garvey and Kirschenblatt-Gimblett, she once again takes up the importance of the interactional context of the play. She proposes that children borrow their play relationships from the interactional systems they know (mother-child, child-child, etc.) and then use these both to work out their own relationships and to engineer new relationships for themselves. There is argument as to how open these relationships are for the discovery of novel relations. Schwartzman also gives special emphasis to the time phasing of play, pointing out the various steps children go through in defining, maintaining or breaking down establishing frames for play. Perhaps her most important contribution is in making it clear that one cannot think of the drama of the play without thinking of its management. As in Garvey's example, she emphasizes that play is both negotiation (context) and drama (text). They are inseparable from any definition of play.

ANTHROPOLOGICAL PERSPECTIVES

Dr. Schwartzman: Let me first make a qualification about anthropological data, and that is that since unfortunately most of us anthropologists are Western, and often American or European, therefore we have obviously incorporated our own categories of what play is and what work is in that particular dichotomy, which may not necessarily be unique to this culture, but is certainly not found in all societies. But at any rate we've incorporated that distinction into our studies of other cultures, and this has manifested itself in a variety of ways. One way, the most obvious way, is that we haven't studied play to any great extent, although there are a variety of ways it's been looked at. Another way is that when we have examined it, we've thought it as organized games and not as children's unstructured play. Another way that we've looked at it—and this was particularly true for the culture and personality studies, and still true for many of them, particularly the six cultures series—is as a kind of projective test. And then we've *used* play to study other things, but we haven't really found out very much about play itself. And the last thing done is to consider it as simple imitation. When you look at the anthropological literature, it's amazing to me that you find people who are studying vastly different societies saying exactly the same thing. You find almost word for word the same kind of description, such as *all play is imitative. Kids all over the world imitate, and this of course prepares them for growing up and taking on tasks in the adult world.* Period. That's the end of the description. Because of our tendency not to look at play it's easy to look at it as imitation, because then we can study the adult world and since we know that play is imitative, why bother to look at it? If we study the adults we'll know what the kids are doing because they're just imitating adults.

One other thing is that verbal play until recently has been, I think, more neglected than any of these other forms because to study verbal play you have to be fluent in the language. You must be able to understand its nuances and the subtleties, and even when anthropologists have worked in a culture for a couple of years, depending on the language, it's very hard to acquire that kind of proficiency. So verbal play has not been looked at in any extensive way. There are a few examples; I think I mentioned some, and in her book, Barbara [Dr. Kirschenblatt-Gimblett] (1976) discusses a great many more. That is my two-minute summary of the anthropological literature on children's play. This isn't to say that there aren't interesting studies or interesting things to read. I've summarized some of the research in my article (Schwartzman, 1976).

Dr. Lewis: Is there a word in other languages for play? Barbara [Dr. Kirschenblatt-Gimblett] mentioned *frivolous* or *nonfrivolous.* Can you give us some idea what other words there might be—either or both of you?

Dr. Schwartzman: It's very hard because there are so many different cultures. There are some that Barbara talked about in which there's a term for work—in some ways it's similar to what we think of as work—and then there's a term for play. In other instances there are no terms that would differentiate between work and play.

Dr. Kirschenblatt-Gimblett: Huizinga (1938) claims that a special type of play is so seldom found in Indo-European languages that he infers from this that maybe they don't have a concept of it. He makes the argument that in very few Indo-European languages do you actually find a term that specifically means "play." On the other hand, we do have the example I gave you of a prefix. If we add that prefix to anything it means "in a playful way, in a non-serious way." *Kip* could be kip eating, kip sleeping, kip drinking, whatever. It's kind of like a marker that will transform anything.

Dr. Schwartzman: I think that probably the best example would be the Marshall study of the Bushmen. Marshall has just come out with a book (1976) that includes some information—in fact a whole chapter—on play. One of the things that's been very interesting about the Bushmen material is that we tend to think that this is a very harsh environment where people must be spending all their time working. In fact when researchers (e.g., Lee, 1968) have done studies of their daily activities they've found that the Bushmen are a very "leisured," in our sense of the term, society; so that there's a good deal of time for people to spend doing things that we might talk about as play. This is particularly true for the males.

Dr. J. Singer: You mentioned pretend play. In Beatrice Whiting's book (1963) she mentions different degrees of pretend play and in part relates this to the demands of the society; so in some societies children have no real demands placed on them and they generate much more imaginative pretending. There's another society where the children are put right to work.

Dr. Schwartzman: I think that some of the material in Whiting really needs to be reinterpreted. I happen to have written a book (Schwartzman, 1979) in which I've tried to do that. First of all, in the Whiting text play is arbitrarily defined as a projective system; so in the authors' sense it has no real formative or generative part to play in cultures. Right away, therefore, they were biased towards really not looking at play very carefully. But it's true there are some interesting differences in the six societies that were studied, and the most obvious one is the Levine material with the Gusii of Kenya (Levine & Levine, 1963), where they were living in the community of Nyansongo and reported that there were only two instances of fantasy play, or pretend play as we might look at it, in the two years they were in that culture. I know Brian has made some interpretations of that [Sutton-Smith, 1977], arguing that if kids are put to work early in a society then you generally see less play. However, in many of the other societies in the six cultures study, kids are also put to work, as caretakers or working in the fields or whatever, at a much earlier age than we would ever conceive of doing, and they play as well. There's a wonderful example in the village of Taira in Okinawa, studied by Thomas and Hatsumi Maretzski (1963), where the kids will be caretakers by the time they're five or six and have an infant strapped on their back while they're playing. That sort of work doesn't necessarily stop them from playing and engaging in games. And the interesting thing about the Kenya study is that while it's true that the kids are put to work earlier, be-cause the women are the major providers in this society—they work in the fields, cultivating and harvesting the crops—the men, who in the past were cattle-herders, have fewer responsibilities in this area (e.g., they may build fences or plow). Today the men spend most of their time poli-ticking and being involved in very complex legal negotiations, so that in one sense you could say they're playing. Because the women have a very large work load, they bring in their kids to take care of the younger chil-dren and to help in the fields. So while this culture seems to not allow for children's playing, the men have a great deal of time to engage in some-thing that we can talk about as play in one form.

Dr. Gardner: I thought you were about to say something that I would like to hear you say, and that is that it's a mistake to go to different cul-tures and try to define an area called *play*. What you really need to do is see what the people do, and play will necessarily be found surrounding that, because there isn't such a thing as an activity which people spend a lot of time at that doesn't have its playful aspects. In a way, an academic conference is sort of a funny thing, because any intuitions you have, have to be coded in a language with a certain degree of jargon. Never having spent any time in any other culture but reading, and being a reasonably introspective human being, I sort of assume that has to be the case. Is that what you think, as an anthropologist who does know something about cultures—that whatever people do there's play surrounding it? Whether there's something artifically called *play* is going to vary a lot. That the people could spend all their time around political negotiations or in working in the fields and not have play activities intermeshed with that seems to be really antihuman. Even antiprimate. I'm proposing a culture-free definition of play: that every culture obviously does certain things, and whatever things it does will have play surrounding them, and the children will follow suit.

Dr. Hutt: In Bali there's a lot of ritualized dancing. How would you classify that? Because I think the Balinese themselves presumably take that as something outside their serious work.

Dr. Kirschenblatt-Gamblett: That could be sacred work. There's a lot of expressive behavior that comes under the category of sacred work in a tradition-oriented society. I think Dr. Gardner's point is an interesting one. We've been trying to look for an activity to demarcate play as being discrete rather than exploring a play component in a whole variety of activities, which is what I was going to say about language not being so ordinary that one cannot be playful with it. There can be a playful component running through just about everything. Well, not everything, perhaps, but certainly it is never possible to say that this is play and only play and nothing but play.

Dr. Ellis: Then you run the risk of the decision being solely in the head of the person who's doing the activity. It would be very difficult then to discover anything about play, whatever that might be.

Dr. Fein: You'll also find out that we operate as people in trained worlds where entries are fairly discrete, without a lot of overlap, so that having made an entry one can push it to the boundaries of various world components. For example, in giving a very serious lecture you can make it very funny, if you're that kind of lecturer, and play with the contrast between the serious and profound. But again it's all somehow situationally appropriate.

Dr. Sutton-Smith: Howard's probably right, that every culture plays with certain of its ingredients. But we haven't yet worked out theoretically which ingredients are played with. I think that's the right way to go, but at the same time, if you look at the six culture study and again use Western frames, the more complex the culture, the more you see of the sort of thing you're looking for. That could be a totally subjective thing. Still, it looks as if the more complex the culture, the greater the variety of children's plays and games that the anthropologists have listed. The other thing that seems to be happening, if you look amongst the more complex societies, is that the ones that seem to play more seem to have more leeway. In the societies with the longest play lists, the kids seem to have more free time and are less confined in who they can play with. In the Rajput society (Minturn & Hitchcock, 1963) for example, children are confined in their back yards with their siblings. In Taira, by contrast, the kids could roam all over their world, a little bit like our concept of the rural American Tom Sawyer village. And those kids had a wider variety of play objects than the Indians did. But there's nothing very definitive or final about this. It was, however, the same for the games and culture data from the Human Relations Area Files (Roberts & Sutton-Smith, 1962). For the basic types of games of skill, strategy and chance, the variety of games increased as the complexity level of the culture increased. This does fit information-arousal notions. As you have to deal with more elements it takes more systems to deal with them. In cultures where you're subjected to more stimulus input there have to be more systems to handle it. The other thing is that as you come up the culture-complexity series you get more stress, and one of the things we did find in the game and culture study was a tremendous amount of socialization conflict in relation to the presence of games. I see those as two kinds of norms in the situation—complexity-stress and leeway for playful response. That's a beginning, and then I think you have to look at it Howard's [Dr. Gardner's] way and ask what are the elements in this culture that are really forms of competence. What are the frames they really care about, where they also can go into states of playful reversal? Although another point I have is that it seems that in some cultures, where things are very routinized, there may not be the flexibility subsequent to the imitative play. There can be a culture where you have ritualistic riddling, but you don't have playful inversions of it. I have a feeling that certain sorts of work orientations aren't predisposed to being flexible. Responsible cultures need chores done and the play is relatively sober. They don't need dilettantishness about chores; they don't need flexible ways of thinking about them. That's another possible variable.

Dr. Schwartzman: I think there's a problem, though, in terms of the complexity issue. It's relative to your definition. I think that the six cultures, as I interpret them, do not really fall out that way (i.e., more "complexity" equals more play), and that to me is a great problem. I think that the issue Howard [Dr. Gardner] raised is another very great problem. I think the fact remains, as I started out saying, that anthropologists are American or Western, so that it's not likely that we go into the field without preconceptions. I'm sure the psychologists like to pretend they don't have any preconceptions about what they're looking at, but the fact is that they do. In a way we're inventing a culture (or a concept or motivation or belief) in terms such that we can understand it, just as an anthropologist does. We teach the people that we're dealing with how to invent in our terms, so that the whole interaction becomes very confused and very much mixed with a kind of pretend play (see Wagner, 1975). I don't really know how to resolve that problem.

Dr. Gardner: You could do simple concept-formation tasks or game tasks or sorting tasks in a culture, where you set up what we would consider to be a play-work dichotomy and see whether you can get people to categorize on that basis. It's called ethnoscience.

Dr. Kirschenblatt-Gimblett: These people try to get at native categories, and they can do it. One can actually make the category of *play* a kind of ethnoscience problem and then proceed to elicit it. What bothers me is that a lot of the activities that we would consider play activities may not be defined as play by those who are doing it.

Dr. Gardner: You could have photographs of different things and say, basically, "make two piles."

Dr. Kirschenblatt-Gamblett: What kind of activity is this? Thus you find out whether it's work, ritual, play—nonserious, serious, or whatever?

Dr. Fein: I'm intrigued by the way you use a lovely combination like "sacred work." I want to say, okay, economic work, political work. For each form of work there is nonwork, and for each unit there is both excitement and danger, so that if your cancellation of sacred work is *nonwork* you're into the profane; that can be dangerous, or it can be an undercurrent which somehow makes the sacredness more salient. And for each one of those components of survival, serious survival, there can be the opposite and its dialectic and its cancellation, which the human mind can engage in and somehow use as a part of the construction of meaning or of social purpose. I don't think you can really understand a purpose unless you can cancel it out.

Dr. Schwartzman: Or that you can play at your work or work at your games. I think Mihaly [Csikszentmihayli] has some interesting material on that.

Dr. Ellis: The real question is, when do you do that? When do you work at the work and when do you play at the work?

Dr. Schwartzman: But Kate's [Dr. Garvey's] question is: what is the logic of ought, will, can, should, would? When do you, when can you, when should you, when ought you, when mustn't you dare?

Dr. Lewis: We've avoided the whole issue of emotion and affect. Does play turn out to be a positive affect? Can you ever have unhappy play? Or is play more often associated with joy and work with sobriety?

Dr. D. Singer: I'm thinking of the case that Erikson talks about in *Childhood and Society*, where the child keeps playing over the death and coffin business. The dominoes with his grandmother, and his play configurations always take the form of the domino which was the coffin.

Dr. Schwartzman: Is that play? Would most of us even say that was play?

Dr. D. Singer: He calls it play therapy.

Dr. Lewis: We work at our play and play at our work, and it seems that this is not going to help us. I'm wondering if we need to bring in another dimension having to do with a feeling state, with the feelings about the activity.

Dr. Hutt: The fact that we can distinguish when something is done playfully means that the affect is acting as a marker. The child enjoys it; the activity is pursued for its own sake. This implies an enjoyment.

Dr. Lewis: From that point of view, the reason why play is good is that it's enjoyable, or at least that's one of the reasons. I'm thinking of it as light. What was that expression, Brian [Sutton-Smith], that you mentioned as the most consensual definition in Huizinga? It was "light, quick movement" which has a flavor of emotional tone as opposed to information. I think the arousal dimension has been the only emotional tone that we've been giving to the concept. If we look at ourselves, we seem to be very nonemotional about play.

Dr. J. Singer: I thought I mentioned positive affect today, and yesterday gave a list of the correlations between positive emotionality and pretend play—linkages that seem to come up in our data consistently. It's hard to tease out which is the cause and which the effect, but we see it pretty consistently. Rating of the children smiling, laughing, and showing liveliness goes along pretty consistently with clearly defined make-believe situations.

A SIDEWAYS VIEW

Dr. Schwartzman: I may be able to help define that. I think that we might be able to tease out some of these issues if I just quickly describe what I view as play. I'm going to read you one play event and then give you my interpretation of it. I try to be flexible and playful about how I look at things, so I believe that there could be many interpretations of this. The dimension I want to illustrate is something that I call a *sideways view*, and it has to do with using the social context of the play. This is difficult to do if you haven't had experience with children over a long period of time, getting to know the history of their relationships with each other both in and out of play situations. In this particular project I was studying a group of kids in a day-care center in Chicago, most from low-income families, whom I worked and played with for a year and a half (Schwartzmann, 1973). I got to know them and their situations quite well. I had various ways of collecting information, such as taking field notes on what was happening and keeping a diary of kids' behavior. I made some films and I did a sociometry study and interviews, I collected drawings and so forth.

This way of looking at play I take from Gregory Bateson (1955, 1956), from Clifford Geertz (1972), and from Jacques Ehrmann (1968). I want to look at play as communication; that is, as characterized by the production of *paradoxical statements* about objects, about persons, about activities— the transformation of objects or persons by saying "This both is and is not what it seems to be." I think both those things are important. I don't think it's just a "not-or" statement. It's a dialectic between those two things, and that's something that needs to be stressed. I also want to look at play as a text, in the sense that in play, kids are telling themselves stories about themselves, and you can only see that dimension if you know something about the history of their relationships with one another. And finally I want to argue after Bateson (1956) that play is not something whereby kids learn particular styles or particular roles or particular cognitive skills, but instead, in his term, *they learn how to learn,* and specifically they learn that *behavior is influenced by context*—that it is "contexted"—and *play itself is a context, so it's both a text and a context,* and that's what I want to stress. In this regard I think in play you *learn how to comment on things.* In the examples I'm going to be giving, the play event can be interpreted as a comment, the kids commenting about their relationships with each other. And once you have learned to do this, then you get into the kinds of comments and critiques and challenges and satire illustrated by Dr. Kirschenblatt-Gimblett.

After collecting a large number of play events at the day-care center, I came up with a series of different kinds of statements that the children used in those play events. In this sense I talk about formation statements, definition statements, disconnection statements, maintenance statements, counter-definition statements—this kind of thing. I'm going to use these to analyze a particular event. I want to say that in some instances with these kids—and I think it would be true with any kids—it can get very confusing. There was one child in the day-care center who turns out to have been the most dominant kid in the center on the basis of sociometry—my observations, kids' reports, what not—and was very adept at creating situations where she would play and then say that she was not playing. She would end up being out of the so-called defined play space and say that she wasn't playing, or she would define herself in a subservient role and abstract herself from the situation, but everyone knew that she was in fact leading the group. When they would want to play with that particular group they wouldn't go to the two little girls, or whoever was in the defined play space; they would go to Linda (which is what I call her) and ask if they could play, and she would say, "I'm not playing; why are you asking me? Go ask so-and-so. She's the one that's the mother," or something like that. But of course she was defining that person in that role, so that everyone knew she was the leader and the one you had to check out. You had to make your *formation statement* to her, and not to those other little girls who seemed to be playing in the play space. It can get very complicated.

This was not a daughter of Mayor Daley! Just bear with me as I read this and I'll try to do it fast. This is just one part of a very long incident that went on for thirty or forty minutes, which was not unusual with this particular group, particularly when Linda was playing.

Thomas, Paul and Karen are playing in the block corner. Sonia enters the area and asks if she can play with Thomas and Paul. They emphatically say "no." Karen says, "Yes, she can. I know; you marry me" (and she points to Thomas) "and Sonia can marry Paul." Thomas and Paul respond again, "no." Karen replies, "Okay; I'll marry her and you can marry each other." Again they say no to this proposal, but then they respond reluctantly, "Okay, she can play." Karen says to Sonia, "We'll be nurses and you sleep in the tent." Karen explains to Sonia where the boat, tent, water, etc., are. (This is a very elaborate construction, with the blocks outlining the boat, then more blocks beyond that, that defined the quicksand area, and then there were "alligators" mixed in, and I attempted to write all these things down. But anyway, you can imagine what this involved in terms of communication. Kids understand what all these things are.)

Linda comes in from playing in the outside yard. She observes the play group briefly and then immediately comes over to the block corner and falls in the designated "water" area and screams, "Help! something is biting my legs." The group responds to Linda's action and then Karen announces that "Captain Paul is dead." At this point Thomas acts very upset and says very forcefully, directing his statement to Paul, Karen and Linda, "You guys never know what to do." Karen leaves the group here and says, "I'm not playing any more." During this period Sonia is busying herself in the "water" area, saying, "Oh, I found a small snail, look, a baby alligator, a baby raccoon . . ." she goes on and on. She becomes absorbed in this activity and the rest of the group ignores her. Thomas, Paul and Karen shift their discussion now to a discussion of angels in heaven—wings and what not—and at this point Thomas, with very agitated body movements, falls to the ground saying, "I'm dead." Linda responds to this by declaring that "Thomas is an angel." Paul now begins to fidget and act restless and states his desire to return to the original boat play theme. Linda responds by saying, "Well, I guess it was just a dream," and then the boat play theme is resumed. Obviously, this is an interpretation of what happened.

I want to give you my sideways interpretation of what was happening here, and I think there are many other things happening also, so I don't want to appear authoritarian about this and not believe that there are other ways you can look at it.

First of all, you have to know that Thomas and Paul almost always played together as a dyad, and Thomas almost always dominated Paul, which in my term is to say that he made *definition statements*—and Paul generally accepted them. He didn't challenge them. In other words, he didn't say, "No, this isn't rice; this is meat," or something like that.

However, as I've already said, Linda was the most dominant child in the classroom—she never really needed to make a formation statement, which is to say, "Can I play here?" or "Can I be this person?" She would just come into a group and define an activity for herself, and the kids would have to respond to it. That is another measure of her dominance. The other thing is that Linda, Thomas and Paul very often played together, and Linda generally dominated that group. Karen, however, who was also a participant in this group, and who often played with this group, often had difficulty accepting Linda's leadership role; so, to try to assert herself in the situation she would often bring in kids who were notoriously submissive, which is to say that she would make definition statements and they would always accept them. Sonia happened to be one of those kids.

I'll start with my particular analysis where Sonia comes in and asks "Can I play here?" and is rejected by Thomas and Paul. Then Karen, who wants to bring Sonia into the group, defines a possible activity for them— marriage—so that she can bring her into the group. This is rejected by Thomas and Paul. Then Karen does something that she was very adept at doing in play groups, and this is what I call a trick, which is a type of for- mation statement. She reformulates the original marriage proposition; she says, "I'll marry her and you marry each other." I suspect she knew this was not going to be a tolerable solution, but hoped that by her persist- ence she might be able to get Sonia into the group this way, which in fact is what happened. So they say, "Okay, she can play." So Karen assumes control and starts making definition statements: this is, this will be this, this will be that, this is where the alligators are, and the water and what not; but when Linda comes into the classroom she looks at the group briefly and then goes right over to the group and falls down into the water area and immediately makes a definition statement. She doesn't ask if she can play. She just falls down and says, "Help; something's biting my legs," and the group immediately responds to that. And then Karen responds to that definition statement on Linda's part by saying, "Captain Paul is dead." At this point, as you have probably noticed, a number of kids have been making definition statements; so it's not really clear who's in com- mand. I think Thomas responds appropriately to this by saying, "You guys never know what to do," which is to say that if someone here isn't making clear statements this play is not going to be able to continue. So Karen then *disconnects out* and says, "Well, I'm not going to play any- more." In the meantime Sonia has gone into her own sort of solitary play, which is very common for her, and the group is not paying any attention to her; even though she's in the same space, she's really not involved in the same event.

Then the group shifts to a discussion of angels in heaven and wings and what not, and Thomas falls down and says, "I'm dead." I would sug- gest that in fact Thomas is dead as a potential play leader at this point, and in response to this Linda defines the whole sequence, in which she becomes very clearly the leader, as a dream. She says, "Well, this was just a dream," and then Paul starts acting restless and Linda goes back and they start doing the boat-play business again.

That is my perspective on this particular event. I think that one of the things that's obviously going on here is that these kids are very concerned with issues of control, issues of manipulation, issues of dominance, and that their play was in fact a reflection of these concerns and a commentary on their own ability to control their own interactional styles. Because these styles exist in a context where there are various types of relationships experienced—symmetrical relations, asymmetrical relations— they're commenting on the nature of these kinds of relationships which they have experienced. So one of the things I did with all of these various play events that I collected was to try to come up with a discrimination among these texts in terms of the kind of authority structure that seemed to be being commented on, and I talked about these as different kinds of genres (see Table 13-1). This had to do with the various kinds of relationships that seemed to be getting commented on and that also were related to a particular relationship model that the kids have probably experienced, or are experiencing, in that context. I listed five different kinds of genres, which I won't describe in great detail. There were some events that seemed to deal with asymmetrical dyads or triads, which I think relates to a familial sort of model: parents-children, older sib-younger sib, this kind of thing; playing house seemed to be associated with that particular kind of relationship genre. On the other hand, there are asymmetrical *group* relationships; for example, teachers with children, younger children versus older children. In this center there were two classrooms, younger children and older children, so this was clearly a discrimination that was important to them. Playing school often seemed to be related to this kind of relationship model. Another kind is something that I call group confrontations, or "bad guys versus good guys," which are modeled, of course, after TV and stories. For this particular group, examples were "cowboys versus Indians," or "Batman and Robin versus the bad guys." But what I want to stress is that these relationship models were *not simply imitated* by the children but in fact were being used by them as *formats* for commentaries on their own relationships to each other, and so certain groups of kids might be associated with certain sorts of genres. For example, there was a particular group in the class that was defined by the teachers, as well as by some children, as "disruptive." These kids often played "bad guys versus good guys." Of course when they played this it often involved chasing and using guns, both of which were defined by the teacher as something you were not supposed to do in the classroom. So frequently this particular play brought them into confrontation with the teachers, and the teachers would have to stop the game. Or they might disrupt another group of children. This kind of confrontation was really an effective comment on their status in the classroom, what their definition was in this particular classroom; so it's not surprising that this was the kind of play that they most frequently engaged in.

Dr. Gardner: I'd like to get clear about how your analysis proceeds. At times you seem to be talking very much in a language that one would be comfortable using for animals: dominance hierarchy and control and

TABLE 13–1
Play Genres

Genre	Relationship Model	Play Theme
1. Asymmetrical Dyads	Parent(s)–Child Older sib–Younger sib	"playing house"
2. Asymmetrical Group Relationships	Teachers–Children Older children–Younger children	"playing school" "witch" "trains"
3. Symmetrical Dyads or Groups	Friend–Friend	"name game"
4. Meta-complementary Relationships	Relationship confusion, where relationship is defined as symmetrical but in fact is asymmetrical	— — —
5. Group Confrontations	Bad guys vs. Good guys	"Cowboys vs. Indians" "Batman"

stuff like that. But I gather from your introduction to your remarks that you are really thinking of it in much more symbolic terms—texts, and comments, and so forth. I don't think those things are necessarily at odds, but in reaching the conclusions I think it's important to know whether you really draw them primarily from what the kids say—from a human symbolic kind of model, as opposed to a more social interpersonal interaction kind of model in which you wouldn't need to have any kind of symbolic communication in the usual sense. You said you were analyzing this in terms of texts, which is obviously a linguistic-symbolic approach, and you talked about the children using language in order to interpret situations. That's fine, except at the same time you were also talking about dominance hierarchies and interpersonal rivalries and things like that for which you don't need to have any kind of language or symbol system in order to draw interpretations. I want to know whether the analysis you do is based primarily on the linguistic information you get, or whether it draws on both sources and whether you can do the same analysis without language. In other words, how human-specific is the way you're thinking about what's going on?

Dr. Schwartzman: The way I talked about dominance was derived not just from my observing the kids and saying, "This kid seems dominant;

this kid seems submissive." It was derived in a number of ways, but the one that I would cite as the most indicative was the kids' response to a question that I asked them in a sort of mini-interview that I did with all of them. The question was: Who are your favorite friends in the classroom? That was something they reported to me. I had observed and I had some ideas and hunches about who seemed to be dominant and who wasn't, but I tried to check this out with the kids and with the teachers, who had a longer experience with some of the kids. So I'm not sure I see the distinction.

Anyway, I think that one of the things the kids are learning here is that *behavior is "contexted" and that contexts influence the authority structure of relationships,* so that there are differences between symmetrical and asymmetrical relations and so forth. These relations can in fact be commented on, and because children most generally experience hierarchical relationship in their lives—in the day-care center and in the family—it's not surprising to find that they then use these models to interpret their own relationships to each other. And at another level (and here I'm using Geertz's [1972] analysis of the Balinese cock fight) it's possible to suggest that these play events are in some way a commentary on the whole idea of organizing relationships on the basis of this kind of hierarchical model; that they provide children with an opportunity for making commentaries on the relationships, or interpreting them. I think that play also suggests that there are possibilities for reinterpretation, for challenges, and possibly even for changes in relationships, so that in this case what seems to be reality can be presented as if it's unreality. So there's a possibility for change and, as I've already said, we can see here relationships to humor, to what we talk about as art, to the whole idea of social satire, challenges and reversals.

Dr. Gardner: I can't quite visualize what shape your evidence is in. You've classified these different kinds of statements; are you counting them? Are you counting them in certain time frames?

Dr. Schwartzman: No, I haven't counted them, but I have collected a number of these play events. When I constructed the genres I decided that I wasn't going to designate something as a genre unless I had ten events that seemed to be recurring, but that was obviously an arbitrary decision on my part. I don't have counts. When I make such statements as: "So-and-so frequently played together with this person," I didn't in fact count how many times they played so that I could present that kind of information to you. I'm giving you my intuition on that.

I'd like to look at this in a middle-class/upper-middle-class nursery school. I'd like to look at this in another culture, in a non-Western culture, but then of course you have the whole problem of language, which is why I ended up doing my study in Chicago, and not in Africa, where I wanted to go originally.

Dr. J. Singer: There's a cognitive level that I don't think you made explicit enough. These kids have established a game. The game is not just what they're actually doing; it's also a kind of private image that each of them has, or a set of private plans about what they're going to do in the game, which don't, as it happens, mesh too well—which is why they have some difficulties. One of the girls, Sonia, goes off—she's playing the game with the ocean, and she doesn't give it up. She just goes off by herself and she's picking fish or mussels or crabs, or whatever she can find in there, and she continues the game. Having developed her mental plan, she sticks with it for a while. Tommy, I think, is disappointed that the others aren't sharing the game, but he doesn't succeed in maintaining his plan and he wants to be a part of the group. He can't, for whatever reason, go off the way Sonia does. And so he sort of suffers and it becomes less of a game for him. He's disappointed.

Dr. Schwartzman: I think that all of these things are going on. I think all of them would be compatible with one another. The main thing that I want to cite is that here is a relationship feature of play that I hadn't seen being revealed by most of the studies of this kind of play. And it seemed to me that the reason was simply that the other studies were being done in other kinds of contexts, or with a methodology that did not allow the researcher to find out this kind of information, or they did not see it as important; so they could not use it in their interpretations of their particular data.

Dr. Fein: At one time I thought, based upon what we'd seen eighteen-month-olds do when they were playing by themselves, that if you saw them in a group situation, with the very early beginnings of the sociodramatic forms, you would find eighteen- and twenty-four-month-olds playing with a doll as a baby, but not playing with themselves as a baby. In other words, if you had two kids you wouldn't have a child that young able to adopt a baby role, because that would be too close to where he actually was. After watching kids playing in a group, I found that's obviously just not true. Even at eighteen months, children do play "babies," with other children being "mothers." But what I don't see at all is a role shifting. There seem to be fairly standarized roles that kids agree upon, and the kids who are going to be the mothers and fathers are usually that, and the kids who are going to be the babies are usually that.

Dr. Schwartzman: There's another role that I found was even lower on the hierarchy scale—the "pet." In the material I had, the kids that were the least popular very frequently played the pets. This was even below "babies."

Dr. Fein: With our older kids there seems to be some beginnings of the possibility of challenging or commenting on reversing these authority or asymmetrical relations. But what you're saying is that by and large that's not true, that they become standardized, that those roles are not reinterpreted within the play situation. In order for a kid to reinterpret his place he has to find another kid who's lower down or is willing to fit into his attempt to explore another status position. It's not reversible with the play group; at least, in the material I had it was not frequent.

Dr. J. Singer: In the film I showed, if we had played the whole thing through you would have seen that the little boy who plays the nurse at the beginning and is very officious and clearly a dominant person in that setting, later on comes over to these two little girls who have got a very elaborate kiddie house game going. He asks into that game, and he has to become a pet within that game, which he does. He takes his shoes off. He doesn't lose some of that forceful quality, but he does change roles from the top boss role in the beginning to a much more menial position.

Dr. Fein: Then does he keep that role, or is he using it instrumentally in order to get into a dominant role?

Dr. J. Singer: That I don't know.

References

Bateson, G. A Theory of Play and Fantasy. *Psychiatric Research Reports,* 1955, 2, pp. 39–51.

Bateson, G. The Message "This is Play." In *Group Processes: Transactions of the Second Conference.* New York: Josiah Macy Foundation, 1956, pp. 145–246.

Csikszentmihalyi, M. *Beyond Boredom and Anxiety.* San Francisco: Jossey-Bass, 1975.

Ehrmann, J. Homo Ludens Revisited. *Yale French Studies,* 1968, 41, 31–57.

Geertz, C. Deep Play: Notes on the Balinese Cockfight. *Daedalus,* 1972, 101, 1–37.

Huizinga, J. *Homo Ludens.* Boston: Beacon, 1955.

Kirschenblatt-Gimblett, B. (Ed.) *Speech Play.* Philadelphia: University of Pennsylvania Press, 1976.

Lee, R.B., & DeVore, I. What Hunters Do for a Living, or, How to Make Out on Scarce Resources. In R. B. Lee and I. DeVore (Eds.) *Man the Hunter.* Chicago: Aldine, 1968, pp. 30–48.

Levine, R., & Levine, B. Nyansongo: A Gusii Community in Kenya. In B. Whiting (Ed.) *Six Cultures: Studies of Child Rearing.* New York: Wiley, 1963, pp. 19–202.

Maretzki, T., & Maretzki, H. Taira: An Okinawan Village. In B. Whiting (Ed.) *Six Cultures: Studies of Child Rearing.* New York: Wiley, 1963, pp. 363–539.

Marshall, L. The *!Kung Nyâe-nyae.* Cambridge: Harvard University Press, 1976.

Minturn, L. & Hitchcock, J. The Rājpūts of Khalapur, India. In B. Whiting (Ed.) *Six Cultures: Studies of Child Rearing.* New York: Wiley, 1963, pp. 203–361.

Roberts, J. M., & Sutton-Smith, B. Child training and game involvement. *Ethnology* 1962, *1*, 166–185.

Schwartzman, H. *"Real Pretending": An Ethnography of Symbolic Play Communication.* Ph.D. Dissertation, Northwestern University, Evanston, Illinois, 1973.

Schwartzman, H. The Anthropological Study of Children's Play. In B. Siegel et al. (Eds.) *Annual Review of Anthropology.* Palo Alto, California: Annual Reviews, Inc., 1976.

Schwartzman, H. *Transformations: The Anthropology of Children's Play.* New York: Plenum, 1979.

Sutton-Smith, B. Towards an anthropology of play. In P. Stevens (Ed.) *Studies in The Anthropology of Play.* New York, Leisure Press, 1977, pp. 222–231.

Wagner, R. *The Invention of Culture.* Englewood Cliffs, New Jersey: Prentice-Hall, 1975.

Whiting, B. B. (Ed.) *Six Cultures: Studies of Child Rearing.* New York: Wiley, 1963.

CHAPTER 14

THE CONCEPT OF FLOW

Mihaly Csikszentmihayli

INTRODUCTION

Dr. Sutton-Smith: Dr. Csikszentmihayli will shift our attention to adult play, which he suggests has too often been construed in terms of children's play. Heart rates are constant here, not variable as in children's play (Hutt). A phenomenology of adult *flow* is outlined as a particular quality of behavior that can occur anywhere. It is totally involving, under self-control, has a clear sense of goals, immediate feedback, and a lack of self-consciousness. Operationally it is most likely to exist where challenges match skills.

The group discussion centers on the relationships between play and flow. It is suggested that flow is more like Piaget's concept of equilibration, and play more truly the one-sided imbalance of assimilation over accommodation. In play, skills exceed challenge, but in flow (and in games) they are matched. Mihaly cautions against taking for granted the usual play-work dichotomy and looking at play or flow only in those culturally prescribed settings where it has been culturally established.

Dr. Csikszentmihayli: I would like to make my presentation in four parts. The first will be a brief introduction that lays out my approach to the problem of play. I will follow this up with a brief theoretical model, some applications of the theory, and then at the end will try to formulate my answer to the three questions that were proposed at the beginning of the conference.

ADULT VERSUS CHILD STUDIES

The first thing I want to talk about is the way in which my approach is different from the ones that have been presented so far at this meeting.

There are essentially two main differences in the way I come at the problem of play. The first one is simply that since the subjects I have studied are adults, I'm raising some issues that are different from yours. I have never looked formally at play in subjects under fifteen years old. Most of them are either adults or young adults, and this raises several issues. The first general one, I suppose, is what happens to play in adulthood. One thing that ethologists have remarked on over and over again is that adult organisms decrease their play or stop their play, that play essentially disappears with age. But since there are no good longitudinal studies of the phenomenon, we don't know what disguise play takes on in adulthood or if it does so. The only study I know of was done with some baboons in captivity; it was found that those that played more ended up as more aggressive adults. There are a lot of problems with that study, which I don't want to go into, but it's certainly a legitimate question: what happens to ludic behavior or play behavior in adults. One of our students at Chicago, Jeannie Altman, just came back from a year and a half in Kenya where she has been studying infant-mother interaction among baboons from birth to one and a half years of age. She plans to go back and gather further data when the babies are adults. Provided there is no great attrition in the sample (out of twelve pairs one baby was eaten by a leopard and another by a hyena), she will begin to find out what kind of adults playful baby baboons grow into. And, of course, we need studies of this kind with humans.

There is also a methodological problem when you look at adults. Do the same behaviors get counted as play in adults as in children? For instance, I went to another play symposium where, in order to demonstrate that scholars can still play, we were expected in the evening to chase around with painted faces and wallow inside a bin filled with plastic pellets and do all kinds of childish ludic things, with the assumption that this is how adults play. This might be a very limited and distorted understanding of what play is to adults. In a study we are doing now with assembly-line and clerical workers, we have been following two groups: those who love their work and those who hate their work, the two extremes on the distribution of job satisfaction. We found that the people who enjoy their work describe their job exactly in terms of what you would expect ludic answers to be. For instance, they say the reason they like to work is because work is not real. The problems at home are real and they don't know how to handle them, but at work problems have no personal consequences. Whether they work well or badly doesn't bother them, whereas what happens to their children, their husband, etc., are problems they can't face. At work, reality seems suspended, which is one of the classic criteria for play; so this is another example of the difficulty of knowing what happens to the need for play or the actual experience of play as you grow up.

A third problem refers to a point in Corinne's [Dr. Hutt's] presentation. It's interesting that in the most ludic types of adult behaviors, instead of variation in attention there is an enormous concentration of attention. We haven't measured heart rate or other physiological measures, except for chess players playing against each other, and there we find an incredible physiological concentration. I'm sure you will find this kind of reduction of variability in attention during other forms of play as well.

Dr. Hutt: Why are you calling that ludic behavior?

Dr. Csikszentmihayli: That's the question. For most adults, chess is a way of withdrawing themselves from the kinds of problems they have in life; so it corresponds to a certain extent to your idling behavior, except that it's not idling. I think we have to redefine what *ludic* is for adults, and that presents some interesting problems. All of those activities that for adults correspond to play show increased concentrations. I'm just stating this as a problem.

A PHENOMENOLOGY OF PLAY

So these are the first differences. They have to do with the fact that we are looking at a different developmental stage; namely, adulthood. The second difference is the kind of theoretical framework that I have been using and that I feel comfortable with. This is what I would call a *phenomenological approach,* for lack of a better term. When I started getting interested in play six or seven years ago, I looked over the available theoretical frameworks and was attracted to the arousal and information-processing theories, but I found that for my personal taste they dealt with the phenomenon I was interested n at a reductionistic level. That doesn't mean that they were wrong or inappropriate. The kind of model I worked out is in fact complementary to theories based on arousal, but I'm interested in the performance of the whole organism which has goals, has intentions, has whatever we want to call self-consciousness or self-reflective abilities. I prefer to look at the phenomenon from that point of view, as a kind of holistic, systemic view which takes into account the level of complexity of the organism. That doesn't mean that most, or all, of behavior can't also be explained by a different slicing, by a different level of analysis which focusses on physiological processes. In fact, I'm interested in those processes also and I try to use as many physiological indicators as possible. But essentially I would like to start by looking at the organism as a self-reflective agent.

This is a kind of dialectic like the one Brian [Dr. Sutton-Smith] is talking about. You have to proceed by differentiating yourself from a schema that has been established. As Thomas Kuhn says, when you change a theoretical paradigm you're almost forced to differentiate yourself by negating another paradigm. But this doesn't mean that the two approaches cannot account for the same data, only that they account for them in different terms. Basically it's a question of choice or preference in terms of which of these approaches you choose to take. So that, briefly, is the kind of introductory setting I want to establish.

Now I would like to talk about the model, or theory, that I worked out as the basis of my research. Very simply, I wanted to study the *experience of playfulness,* rather than play itself. To do this, we interviewed groups of people who spent much time and energy on activities that provided few or no extrinsic rewards: that is, people who seemed to be motivated to act by intrinsic concerns, by rewards provided by the activity itself. These were chess masters, rock climbers, dancers, basketball players, etc. We finally interviewed 175 people with a finished interview protocol which lasted anywhere from two to four hours, and each transcript was about thirty single-space typed pages. So it wasn't just a man-in-the-street kind of thing, but a very detailed interview about how these people felt when the activity they were engaged in went well.

Out of this initial study we collected a number of extremely similar descriptions of how the experience felt when it was going well. Later on we replicated the same kinds of dimensions that emerged with a variety of other people: thirty surgeons, teachers, mathematicians, secretaries, and workers, all the way from assembly line to management. In each case the descriptions coincided amazingly in describing the subjective dimensions of the experience.

I'm going to rattle off these dimensions, just to establish a baseline. The first thing people mention is the issue of *concentration,* or involvement, which is described as a merging of action and awareness. You are not thinking about doing something, you are doing it, and while you're doing it you are not aware of alternatives, nor are you aware of certain other problems. There's a filtering out of irrelevant stimuli which happens almost automatically. As some people describe it, your memory becomes very short term. You remember only a few seconds before and you are thinking only a few minutes ahead of what's happening, and it's a kind of concentrated involvement in an activity, which is the first sign of an enjoyable, intrinsically rewarding activity.

Now usually, in all these situations, there is a clear *noncontradictory goal* that the person perceives in the activity, and rather clear means-end relationships. There is usually *immediate feedback.* It is clear when you are doing right or wrong. In tennis you know whether the ball went in or out of the court. In climbing you know whether you are still on rock or you're falling. You're always getting feedback related to the goals of the activity. *Time sense becomes warped.* Time either disappears completely, or it seems very short, or some part of the experience seems to occur in a terrifically compressed time dimension; or the time dimension may expand very dramatically.

There is in general a feeling of *control of affectance or influence,* as Bob [Dr. McCall] mentioned before. You feel you are influencing whatever is happening, and of course the feedback tells you that, and yet paradoxically this feeling of control goes hand in hand with a kind of a *loss of ego,* or loss of a personal kind of caring about the results. Later on when you reflect on it you feel, "Gee, I did it, I accomplished it," but as you're doing it, because of the focusing of attention—this merging of action and awareness—you are not concerned about your performance. There is no splitting of the observer or the ego reflecting on the performance. In fact some people describe it as a transcendence, as a merging with the environment, as a union with the activity or with the process.

Now these are all the subjective characteristics of the state of involvement or experience which we call the *flow state* because it's a native term that many people, such as composers of music, climbers, etc., spontaneously produce in talking about this. It's like flowing, it's like being carried away and yet being in control of the direction of the flow.

It's also clear that in these activities there are some objective characteristics which parallel dimensions of experience. For instance, any activity that produces flow reliably helps people to *focus attention,* to *give goals,* to *give feedback,* and to establish a *feeling of control.* Games are sit-

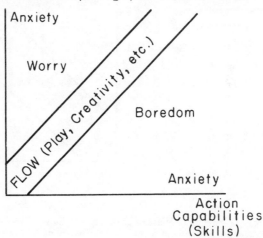

FIGURE 14-1. Model of the Flow State. When action opportunities are perceived by the actor to overwhelm his capabilities, the resulting stress is experienced as anxiety. When the ratio of capabilities is higher, the experience is worry. The state of flow is felt when opportunities for action are in balance with the actor's skills. The experience is then autotelic. When skills are greater than opportunities for using them, the state of boredom results, which again fades into anxiety when the ratio becomes too large.

(Adapted from Csikszentmihayli, 1975 a)

uations where through rituals, through equipment, the rules of the activity allow this concentration and screening out of everything that's irrelevant.

There are other characteristics of flow activities that I'm not sure how to describe—whether to call them *preconditions for entering the state* or *structural characteristics.* But the best way to show how this works is that in every one of these activities the person perceives what we could call action opportunities or *challenges* and action capabilities or *skills* that can vary anywhere from low to high on these two dimensions.

In spontaneous reports people place themselves somewhere along this diagonal when they are reporting enjoyable experiences. So this area along the diagonal is where the flow experience seems to occur. Obviously this theory has a lot in common with the arousal, information-processing theories we have been talking about before, but here we look at the same phenomenon from the subjective view of how the person records his perception of what his challenges and skills are.

This simple diagram has interesting properties. It can be used in all kinds of ways. For instance, a person who learns how to play chess and

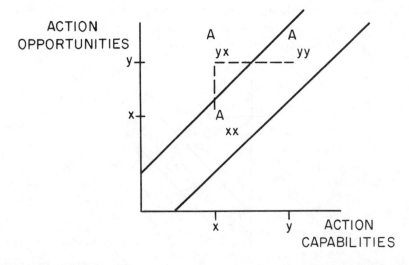

FIGURE 14-2. Two Ways of Experiencing Flow. Chess Player A, with x level of skills, playing against someone at level y, will be worried. A person in such a situation can choose a number of ways to re-enter the state of flow (e.g., by playing only against opponents of skill level x, or by increasing skills to level y). The opponent can also handicap himself until challenges match Player A's skill level at x. (It is to be noted that flow state Ayy is more complex than flow state Axx, since the former involves the use of greater skills in overcoming greater challenges.)

(Adapted from Csikszentmihayli, 1975a)

has low skills can get involved in this activity in a variety of positions. If he starts playing against a very good opponent, for example, his skills are low, and the challenges are high.

Let us call this chess player "A." Chess player "B" has high skills and is facing an opponent with few skills, so he's going to be bored in this situation, while A should be worried if he knows what's happening.

Now, one of these two people is going to enjoy the situation. If you are bored or worried you lose intrinsic motivation in the situation right away, but there are several possibilities for regaining it. For instance, if B sacrifices his queen at the beginning of the game, to equalize the skills, the challenges for him are increased artificially because he is at a disadvantage. Or person A could choose to play against another person of his own skills, and move down to the flow state in this way. Of course the other possibility is for A to increase his skills so he will move up and be able to enjoy interacting against someone of equal competence.

The vertical dimension along the diagonal represents increased complexity; this is, how many new action opportunities one can integrate into one's action. Here on the vertical you are flowing also—the activity is involved and concentrated, but you are dealing with many fewer challenges than higher on the vertical.

Let me illustrate further how this model works. Take a group of surgeons. First of all, they say that performing operations is habit forming. It's like taking drugs, like taking heroin. Once you have got used to the activity, it's very difficult to do without it. If they go on a vacation to Acapulco, within two days some of them are volunteering to work in a hospital for free just to get back to surgery, and it drives their wives crazy to be left alone on the beach. Surgeons describe an operation as having three phases. There is the opening, which has relatively few challenges. Then there is the middle part of the operation, which is usually much more complex, and finally there is the closing, which is the simplest part. There's a range of these, of course, depending upon the type of operation. When you talk to surgeons who are just beginning to work, who are relatively unskilled, you find they enjoy closing. When they are closing they forget everything; they are really involved. But in the beginning and the middle of the operation they are worried. They are aware of things happening around them, they're very self-conscious, and they don't enjoy it and would rather be sailing or something. An experienced surgeon is bored all through the easy parts of the operation. The ideal for such a surgeon is to intervene only at the crucial point. We had surgeons who would do four or five operations during the same morning, and just do one little cut, especially in open heart surgery. They move from one operating theater to the other and do these little performances and everyone applauds them and they love it. But if they are stuck with the routine parts they are bored out of their skulls, and they resort to other kinds of strategies.

Dr. J. Singer: A lot of them engage in daydreaming.

Dr. Csikszentmihayli: Daydreaming. They engage in joking behavior. It's interesting that the type of joke is very different when an operation goes very wrong for some reason. It is a kind of de-arousing joking, whereas when they are bored, the jokes or the little routines become arousing.

Dr. J. Singer: Did you see the program *M.A.S.H.?* That typifies what you are describing. There's a good deal of that sort of humor.

Dr. Csikszentmihayli: Horsing around.

Question: Are there any data on complications? A surgeon once told me that the easy stuff is where he makes his mistakes. The operations he's never performed before, he thinks he does a good job on. He was telling me this while he was cutting me. He said, "It's the simple stuff we really screw up."

Dr. Csikszentmihayli: Yes, you find some surgeons, like ophthalmic surgeons, for whom the whole operation, the cutting and the sewing, is all terribly important. Corneal transplants, things like that. Those people are in flow during the whole period. Other surgeons become careless. Their concentration starts wavering and they get bored unless they have a challenging set-up like a research hospital where they can be doing new things all the time.

Question: There's a similar situation in intensive care nurseries. Some of these have a constant situation of life and death. Some doctors can't take it and in maybe five or six years they have to get out, because the minute they walk in it's one crisis situation after another.

Dr. Csikszentmihayli: That probably is highly stressful. There are studies of control tower people in airports, who are faced with challenges over which they have little control. Surgeons love operations where they can prepare in advance. The ones that come up all of a sudden, where you have to start whether you're ready or not, are quite different. If they can plan it out, things are under their control.

Well, let me present just one of the applications of this model to a study which shows how it works in research. We have been studying all kinds of groups, from workers to mathematicians, but this is a group of high school students where we tried to show at least internal consistency of the model in action. In a long interview we asked students to identify their favorite activity, what they liked to do best in their life. Then we asked them to put that activity—let's say basketball—on a ten-point scale on ten different dimensions which we got from the model of the experiential state of flow. Such dimensions as the clarity of goals, or whether you

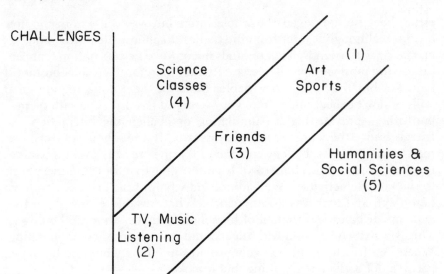

FIGURE 14-3. How high school students rate their favorite activities (Nos. 1, 2, 3) and school classes (Nos. 4 & 5) in terms of challenges and skills

(Adapted from Mayers, 1977)

get consistent information about whether you're doing well or badly, etc. After they positioned basketball, or whatever the favorite activity was, then we asked them also to put whatever courses they were taking in high school on the same dimension, and adding up for each activity over the ten scales we got a flow rating for that activity. As you would expect, all the scales were very highly related. The favorite activity was always at the appropriate extreme of the flow activity. Subsequently we gave them this coordinate that we talked about before—challenge and skill—and we had it marked off with little squares. We gave them a penny, and after instructing them what *challenge and skills* meant, we asked them first to put the penny in the position where their favorite activity would fall and then to position their school activities, their classes—French, trigonometry, etc.— on the same dimension. Well, we found that first of all, 80 percent of the favorite activities fell along the diagonal, as one would expect. There were three interesting groupings. Up here you had a bunch of activities which tended to be either sports or artistic activities—music, ballet, theater, basketball, hockey (#1).

Question: Participant rather than spectator?

Dr. Csikszentmihayli: Yes, things that people can do. Now here you had a bunch of spectator activities, and most of them were watching TV and listening to music (#2). Then you had a third cluster which was interesting because it bridged the whole range but was still within the flow channel, although it went from the highest to almost the lowest, and this was being with friends. That reminds me of Mike Lewis's notion that people are the most variable. These are friends; therefore they are constant, I suppose, but they are also variable. Some of them don't require great skills or don't expect much from you—you just pass the time with them—and others provide highly stimulating or challenging interactions; so friends bridge the whole scale of complexity. In the school subjects, you tend to have physics, biology and chemistry up here (#4), and humanities types of subjects down here (#5). It's interesting that there are exceptions to the favorite activities. We had one kid who put his first activity down here (#5), and that was playing cards. What was interesting about him and similar cases was that all of his school activities were up here (#4). This is a sixteen-year-old with ulcers, and he's obviously compensating. When he's free to do it, he's going to do something which he has down pat. It's not a challenging thing, but it makes him feel skillful. Of course there were also school activities within the flow channel, but a much larger proportion were placed at these two extremes.

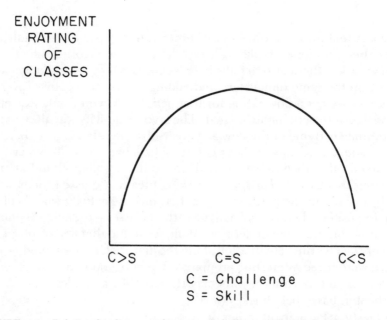

FIGURE 14-4. Relationship between the ratio of challenge/skill ratings and enjoyment of classes in school

(Adapted from Mayers, 1977)

To test the internal validity of these dimensions for each of these activities, we transformed the scores given in terms of whether the challenges were equal to the skills, the skills were greater than the challenges, or the challenges greater than the skills—each one was scored as a deviation from the balance. Then for the same activities we used the total flow rating on the ten dimensions, as I explained before. What you get is an almost perfect quadratic curve, a very significant curve. In fact, the experiential states that we predicted are covariant with the balance between perceived challenges and skills in the activity. So this was a nice way of confirming that there is a coherent pattern between the state of the experience and the perception challenges and skills. They go together.

We did another check on this model, using a technique that we call the *experiential sampling method,* which we started using about a year ago in Chicago. We give a person a little electronic pager to wear for a week, and we randomly beep the person about seven times a day over that week. Every time the pager beeps, the person takes out a little booklet and writes down what he is doing, where he is, what he is thinking about, and then rates his moods on semantic differential scales and in general gives a little snapshot of his experience and his activity at that point. So we were beeping the students fifty times a week in their classes. (Actually we didn't use a beeper but a vibrating unit, so as not to disturb the classes.) It's amazing how this technique is motivating to all subjects, but especially to kids. They love to be the center of attention when this thing goes off, and there are all kinds of methodological caveats here. Yet we find it's a fairly unobtrusive and reliable way of getting information. What we found was that classes rated higher on flow two or three weeks before are the ones where the moods of the person are much higher when they are beeped in those classes. The best single item that correlates is one where we ask a person to rate himself on a ten-point scale on the variable: "I wish I was doing something else," from "I wish very much" to "I wish very little." The correlation between the flow rating of the classes two weeks before and during actually being in the class was .59 ($p<.\phi\phi1$) with about 1,400 observations in 354 different classes (Mayers, 1977). This shows that there is a consistency there. The students who had rated the class as being most like the flow state of their favorite activity would not wish to be doing something else when they were actually beeped in that class. Incidentally, semester grades correlated .50 with the enjoyment of classes (with scholastic aptitude controlled for).

QUESTIONS

At this point I am ready to try to answer those three questions we started out with.

The first question put to us was, *what is play?* I would say that play is the experience of flow in a setting or frame of action in which the activity is perceived to be voluntary or autotelic; that is, the goal is in the activity itself, and unrelated to "real-life" consequences. You notice this is a standard definition of play except for the inclusion of the experience of flow. In other words, I am definitely trying to focus on the experiential state of the subject. At the same time, I don't think play is the most interesting subject here. I'm really interested in flow as being the critical category. First of all, flow need not be voluntary, as play is. You can get into flow in almost any situation; it doesn't need to be autotelic. The surgeon is saving lives or earning his living, and yet he can be in flow. And again it need not be unrelated to real-life consequences, because the rock climber can fall off and kill himself and the surgeon can kill a patient. So play seems to be a culturally structured form, or an individually structured form, for experiencing flow. It's a frame, a setting, where you can have this experience which is voluntary, autotelic, and unrelated to real life. But I'm interested in how this same experience can be gotten out of real life situations and involuntary situations, and out of extrinsicly rewarded situations too.

The second question was, *what is the role of play?*

Dr. J. Singer: You'd have to define flow as you have, in effect, operationally, as an optimal balance of challenge and skill.

Dr. Lewis: Isn't flow the feeling of having it, not the balance of challenge?

Dr. Csikszentmihayli: I understood Jerome [Dr. Singer] to mean it's a subjectively perceived balance, which of course very often corresponds to the objective parameters of a situation; but play tries to maximize the possibility of arriving at that subjectively through objective means. What is the role of play in child development? If you asked what the role of flow was, it would be an easy question to answer, because its role seems to be the same as that of life itself. You can also have some functional explanations—evolutionary or whatever—but essentially, to get that experience is the same as *living at your optimal capacity.* I don't feel you would have to justify that. But the question, what is the role of play? is a different proposition. Perhaps you can explain the role of play as a compensation for the lack of flow in everyday life, or as a preparation for flow in everyday life in terms of producing more competent people. I'm not sure. Since I'm not focusing on play per se, I never really thought about this problem. Probably there are people here who are more competent to define that.

The third question was, *how can the quality of play experience in children be improved?* Here again I'm not sure exactly how I stand. I'm worried about the separation of play and "real life," play and work, play and study. I'm afraid that if we focus too much on play rather than the experience of the optimal interaction of flow that we may unwittingly, with the best intentions, sidetrack the whole enterprise into separating out what should be the focus—the flow experience—and relegating it to a dimension of play which is only autotelic and voluntary. I think we need to know more about play to understand how best to produce the experience. Then we have to be very careful that we don't end up isolating it from the rest of life.

Dr. J. Singer: I wonder if we don't produce transformations in our work that allow us to bring challenge and skill into better balance. If we were to be really serious in all of our work we couldn't get into a state of flow, because presumably none of us is that good in our job. None of us has mastered the literature that has to be known in our field, and we're well aware of how much more needs to be known. So if we don't suspend judgment a little bit, we can't get into that kind of flow, and at a certain point we have to say, "Well, the hell with it, I'm going to go ahead and do this research even though I haven't mastered all the variables." Once you make that slight transformation of the situation, you can then get into the enjoyment of doing the work.

Dr. Csikszentmihayli: You're phrasing all of this within the context of work, and that I agree with perfectly. What bothers me is when we separate play and ask how we can play better rather than thinking how we can produce better, or do the thing that we are best at doing. If we separate play out, it is more difficult to make exactly the kind of transition you're making, which is how to work better rather than how to play better.

Question: Let me push your position to an extreme. Would you be suggesting that the reason there is no single set of behaviors that we define as play, the reason why we're having such a difficult time defining or delimiting play, and all of these other problems that we've voiced ad nauseum here, derive from the proposition that there are innumerable routes to this state of flow, that it may be arrived at in many different ways, across the classifications of play, work, etc., such that anything can be done ludicly?

Dr. Singer: There are parts of traditional definitions of play as a positive affective component which are not defined in any more detail than that.

Dr. Fein: In sociodramatic play, if the child has mastered some of the physical properties of the objects that may be involved in play, then the child establishes a controlled world that has some challenges, in the sense that he can predict orderly outcomes of the game once he starts off the make-believe play structure; so he has created a miniature world that has some degree of novelty as the game starts to unfold. He can't predict what's going to happen to all of the characters right from the start, so there is that amount of exploration involved, but at a relatively controlled level, so that challenge and skill do come into a fairly good balance, and the child is enjoying that happy feeling as he goes through the play.

Question: But the fantasy play is only an imagined way of getting out on the diagonal (as in the diagram) without cost.

Dr. Hay: To me the word *flow* is a dynamic, not a static word. Might we really be talking, not about the point at which your perceptions of your skills and challenges are, but rather about the process by which you test your skills against your challenges? Are we talking about flowing as a verb rather than a state? If we are talking about that, I'd like to ask people who know more about Piaget than I do if we're talking about assimilation and accommodation.

Dr. McCall: It's occurred to me that information intake and influencing are also very similar to those things.

Dr. Hay: I guess I'm talking about growth in the process. Is this troublesome to anyone except me? This state of flow—it seems to me it's in flux, as it were.

Dr. Csikszentmihayli: Okay. It is certainly a dynamic state, and you find people always moving in and out of it and going above it and below it, and when you freeze that process you can talk about it as being *in the state,* but essentially it is a dynamic concept. That's why I talk about activities, and by activities I also mean fantasy or any process which unfolds. That's where all of these things happen, when you are interacting with the environment.

Dr. Hay: You can talk about it as a process. You might be able to fit it into some of the things Corinne [Dr. Hutt] talked about, as a shift from epistemic to ludic behavior. In any behavior you have to spend some time figuring out how good you are at it and understanding the properties of the situation, and this might indeed be epistemic. And then once you gain that information that's both internal and external you can flow with it, and that might be ludic.

Dr. Csikszentmihayli: I think so.

Dr. Kirschenblatt-Gimblett: A very important consideration here is that first of all, not all ludic behaviors necessarily generate an experience of flow. I've played many a game that I've been absolutely bored to tears with. So that's bothered me, this insistence of affect and ludicness. Too, even in the course of a play activity there may be moments of flow, or more sustained periods of flow. This experience of flow which comes closest to what we've been trying to talk about as a characteristic of play experiences can also occur in a nonplay context, learning context, problem-solving context, all kinds of contexts. And I think what's critically important here is being able to separate out this full experience from any particular example—what Turner calls *flow mechanisms,* borrowing from your work. He argues that with the Industrial Revolution there has been a major transformation in the kinds of mechanisms through which flow experiences are had, so that whereas today spectator sports and football and institutionalized play activities may assume a much greater role in providing a setting for flow experiences, before the Industrial Revolution religious and sacred activities may have been the major cultural flow mechanisms. So what we must do is try to separate out this kind of qualitative experience from any particular type of institutional activity proper.

Question: Also it wouldn't be necessary for every "play behavior" to achieve flow in a highly symbolic organism. For example, I play squash. I feel pretty lousy about some games, but there's always the hope, the seeking after the reward that I can imagine might derive from this game, the flow that I know is a possible consequence, and that's what I mean by reward, or maintaining a behavior.

Dr. Kirschenblatt-Gimblett: There's a good reason for that, because there are some givens in many particular game situations that would tend to maximize the possibility for a flow experience: the clarity, the immediate feedback, the lack of ambiguity. If you like, certain kinds of play activities certainly maximize the conditions that are required for flow experiences to happen, but it doesn't necessarily mean they will happen.

Dr. Csikszentmihayli: Vietnam veterans I have talked with characterize their experiences very similarly to flow. When they were fighting in the front lines, they experienced the war as a situation that demanded concentration, provided clear goals and clear feedback. And to their surprise, it was enjoyable. I'm not using *flow* in any evaluative sense at this point. I'm just saying there's a tremendously important motivating factor which can occur everywhere, even in war. It can occur in fighting, in aggressive behavior; it's important to realize that some forms of flow are very socially undesirable. But we have to understand the experience before we can talk about whether it's positive or negative, and under what conditions.

Dr. Gardner: The question I want to raise takes off from what Barbara [Dr. Kirschenblatt-Gimblett] said. I find your analysis very impressive. For me, it opens up not only a new way of looking at things, but a whole new set of questions. What I'm wondering about is the extent to which you're dealing with a vocabulary and a way of thinking about things which is distinctly Western, which comes out of the Western intellectual tradition—the kinds of issues that Nietzsche and many others wrestled with. If one could somehow translate this set of concerns in your measures, and your vocabulary, etc., into a very different cultural setting, would one find something that's isomorphic to flow, or might this be something which would have to be grafted onto another social setting?

Dr. Csikszentmihayli: The only evidence I have is that the first, and so far the only, translation of my book on boredom and anxiety is in Japanese, and of course that's an exception that may prove the rule because Japan is in tune with Western thought. I have been impressionistically comparing these descriptions with what people in the highly developed Eastern traditions have been doing, and I don't find terribly much difference in the experience itself. There is a tremendous difference in the *ways of arriving at the experience.* But the flow experience itself is similar to what you find in Zen yoga or many other non-Western practices.

Dr. Garvey: Lest play become a bit ephemeral here and we lose track of it, if flow is a process or an experience to be desired, and one that we can work at, is it possible, in our make-believe kind of play, that the child is both imagining the challenge and imagining the skill level, and that one measure of success in coming up with a good, satisfying play episode is the extent to which you can maximize both of those areas? The player is imagining that these dimensions exist in the play activity.

Dr. Lewis: But you could even increase challenge so that the intensity would increase, or you could match them at a very low level, as in the TV watching.

Dr. Csikszentmihayli: That's a connection with what Barbara [Dr. Kirschenblatt-Gimblett] was saying about word games and literature and art. You can push the imagination and fantasy and play to higher levels of complexity, and then you reach a ceiling. Or the fantasy becomes redundant after a while and there's no way for it to develop.

Dr. Lewis: Even within the fantasy, you might want to track this out: if in the fantasy the child produces a challenge that he's not capable of matching with a skill, then the child should drop out of it. That is, within a fantasy as it builds you might have the same modulating process, which would be driving the fantasy itself to a higher level.

Dr. J. Singer: In the dual games presented by Dr. Garvey, one of the children is always a little bit ahead of the other, is trying to get the other one to move into higher levels of complexity, and gets impatient when the younger or less verbal one lags behind and can't get into the flow.

Dr. Schultz: I've been thinking of a possible answer to Dale's [Dr. Hay's] question about how your model might relate to Piaget's theory of assimilation and accommodation. It seems to me that the area where a challenge is beyond the skill of the player is roughly equivalent to what Piaget talks about in terms of accommodation, or predominance of accommodation over assimilation, in that he has to work and worry about trying to match internal structures to external requirements. The area where he's way ahead of the game is just the opposite. His internal structures are quite capable of easily assimilating or mastering any environmental input. The flow area is what Piaget might call a state of equilibrium, where there is a relative balance or match between external requirements and internal structures.

Dr. D. Singer: He says equilibrium is when you're in the realm of cognitive behavior; when assimilation prevails, you're in the realm of imagery or ludic play.

Dr. Schultz: I think this model leads to somewhat different predictions about play than Piaget's model would, because Piaget talks about play as a predominance of assimilation over accommodation. This model suggests that flow experiences are more likely to occur near the state of equilibration than when you have a predominance of assimilation over accommodation, but maybe that again is the difference between young kids and adults.

Dr. Ellis: Gambling and risk taking support this idea, in the sense that it is most attractive to highly skilled players to operate in systems where the challenges balance their abilities; in other words, where there's a .5 probability of the outcome being A or B.

Dr. Fein: What I thought Dr. Schultz was getting to and didn't finish was to see how Piagetian tension between assimilation and accommodation, with equilibrium as a developmental state, was like flow. Now if you want to make Piagetian equilibrium similar to what Mihaly's [Dr. Csikszentmihayli's] saying about flow, then you'd have to say childhood is characterized by nonflow and nonequilibrium, that children are expressing that their tensions aren't at the middle yet. They're bouncing up, they're bouncing down, they've got a skill here, an opportunity there. And so much of this is a shifting back and forth—a kind of nonflow, play, divergent, bounce a bit, roll a bit kind of thing, which makes play a very special kind of opportunity for children such as it cannot be for us, because presumably we've moved on from there.

Dr. Hay: I think that child's play is part of the natural world, a phenomenon within the natural world. It may have some connections with flow experiences that adults have, but there are other translations that don't work. What Greta [Dr. Fein] is describing is a phenomenon to be studied in its own right, partly with implications for adult experiences, and partly as a natural phenomenon of interest to us.

Dr. Sutton-Smith: I follow the Schultz paradigm as having the equilibrium and flow down the middle, with assimilation down in the lower corner. Both assimilation and flow are pleasurable, but the assimilation is a much more passive, internalized sort of thing. I have it plenty of times as an adult, but it doesn't flow in the sense of being gripping or urgent. It's a much more receptive, withdrawn, private envisagement of things. Does that fit? In other words, I can see play for adults as well as for children, with flow and play as quite distinct for both children and adults.

Dr. Hutt: I would still like to reserve play for the sort of idling behavior with no compunction, with no structured format, that Greta [Dr. Fein] is talking about: arbitrariness, free movement—that kind of nuance.

Dr. Kirschenblatt-Gimblett: What happens to games and tennis and chess and all that stuff?

Dr. Sutton-Smith: They're not play. They're models of flow. I think play and games are distinct.

References

Csikszentmihayli, M. Play and intrinsic rewards. *Journal of Humanistic Psychology*, 1975a, *15*, (3), 41–63.

Csikszentmihayli, M. *Beyond boredom and anxiety.* San Francisco: Jossey-Bass, 1975b.

Csikszentmihayli, M. Intrinsic rewards and emergent motivation. In M. R. Lepper and D. Greene (Eds.) *The hidden costs of reward.* New York: Erlbaum, 1978.

Csikszentmihayli, M. Attention and the wholistic approach to behavior. In K. S. Pope and J. L. Singer (Eds.) *The stream of consciousness.* New York: Plenum, 1978.

Csikszentmihayli, M., Larson, R., & Prescott, S. The ecology of adolescent activity and experience. *Journal of Youth and Adolescence,* 1977, *5,* (3), 281–294.

DeCharms, R., & Muir, M. S. Motivation: Social approaches. *Annual Review of Psychology,* 1978, *28.*

Mayers, P. L. Flow in Adolescence and its relation to school experience. Doctoral dissertation, University of Chicago, 1977.

CHAPTER 15

OVERVIEW: PLAY OR FLOW

INTRODUCTION

Dr. Sutton-Smith: Although this conference began with the three questions, (a) how to define play? (b) how does it change developmentally? and (c) how to enhance it? one has to conclude that not even the first was answered to anyone's satisfaction. And in the final discussion the interrelationships of play and flow so intrigued all the speakers that they overwhelmed most other considerations.

The discussion begins with the recommendation that definitional problems might be solved by closer empirical textual analysis. There did seem some general agreement that all play was either subject to rules, had rules as its subject matter, or had special procedural rules for its own progress. Play was felt to be similar to flow by some discussants and quite different by others. It was argued on the one hand that the feeling tone of both may be similar even when the structure is different; also that in both cases there is an attempt to match challenge and skills. On the other hand, it was argued that play is merely a childish simulation of flow, a simulation of a challenge-skill match, which prepares the child for the flow experiences of adult life which have a more objective quality to them. Attempts were made to distinguish between play and games in terms of their relative degrees of openness and closedness, their uncertainties and their control. The relativity of the play concept to Western cultural usage led some to advocate dispensing with the notion altogether and substituting *flow,* a notion which they found to be more culturally free, less embedded in the customary dichotomies of work and play.

While there was less time given to the issue of the enhancement of play, it seemed relevant to some to think of play as a training ground for the more adequate adult life of flow in any kind of experience (work of play). The question of whether that training should be in play itself or in skills to allow the matching of challenges was not resolved by this panel. As this was the last session of the Conference we decided to serve champagne. The focus on flow was perhaps an inevitable outcome.

HOW IS PLAY TO BE DEFINED?

Dr. Garvey: There is one aspect of play that I don't believe we've touched upon, or at least taken as seriously as I would like. We haven't thought about using fantasy and make-believe play as a way of observing the social construction of reality in process, so that the obvious in play is often played out before us. By looking at play only for what it might do, for what it might be good for, for its contextual correlates, we may miss a great deal that we could find by looking at it more closely.

Dr. Chase: That is what you have been doing, is it not?

Dr. Garvey: Not in very great depth.

Dr. Chase: To me, the striking thing about your presentation was that it was a modest piece of text which we found amazing for its complexity. And yet in terms of a sample of behavior, you gave us a modest portion of what you considered to be a modest effort. Obviously imaginative and ambitious, it was still a modest text, and we were all amazed; and people started counting up the number of roles and saying, "Oh my, look at how much is going on here!" It was an example of the examination of the fine structure.

We've had trouble in our search for definition, in our search for the understanding of the role of play in human development. We had no trouble feeling discouraged about finding a resolution of these objectives in the morphology of behavior. Play isn't a certain kind of behavior which can't at other times be nonplay, so that doesn't help. It seems to me that lurking in the background has been the hope that a successful generalization would be about some kind of positive affect occurring in association with play in some unique relationship that gives play its special character and its special quality. We haven't quite reached an agreement that positive affect of the unique kind is not going to be the way of identifying play, but it seems to me there have been a pitter-patter of comments that suggest that we are not generating a collective optimism about that either. If our answer isn't to come from a particular morphology of behavior, and if it isn't to come from a particular affective accompaniment of behavior, there seems to be an agreement that it is at least something multidimensional that has importance in the life of the individual, in the life of the group. And Kate [Dr. Garvey] has suggested that it might be more productive to look at some of the fine structure of those experiences and episodes that we all agree are productive to examine, to ask what they are telling us about ourselves, and to look for the more obvious elements.

PLAY MAY BE DEFINED IN TERMS OF RULES

Dr. Chase: It seems to me that there have been ever so many more comments about play as a dimension of the experience of the individual learning how to survive as a social organism, and far fewer from the perspective of the group maintaining the social organisms of which we're all a part. It's a perspective that we might want to give more attention to in the discussion this afternoon. For example, there's a kind of diplomatic immunity that seems to me to obtain when we are at play. For one thing, we have to negotiate the permission to be at play from a society that basically attends most seriously to the business of its moment-to-moment, day-to-day survival. So it's commonplace to help children play, protect them in play, etc. When we say to a child, "Stop playing with your food," we're saying that at least under these conditions we want the food to have to do with nutrition and eating or conforming to the rules of the dinner table, and we're not going to be tolerant of an exception. But in so many instances it seems to me that what we do do when we allow play to occur, or when we get permission to play, is to relax certain kinds of expectancies that have to do with the literal business of group life, and we don't have to be productive in the sense that a group has to be in order to keep itself together. We don't have to conform as strictly, which is a way of minimizing conflict and any kind of eccentricity that can otherwise be very threatening to the life of the group. That's all tolerated much more abundantly, in the hope, I would guess, that part of this immunity allows us to share very private experience in a public way. Play therapy would then be a way of saying to somebody who is troubled and in terrible conflict: "Make it all obvious and overt, because under these conditions it's safe to do that." It seems to me that this is true for people who are well, and for adults, as well as for children. For example, walking around Bourbon Street last night, you could see that this is a big playground, this district of New Orleans. And all of these discriminative stimuli seem to me to be saying, "We're not going to bring the expectations of all of you into this context in the way that we do in the literal business of maintaining group life."

Dr. Kirschenblatt-Gimblett: I think what we do is just substitute one set of constraints for another. I find that a chess game is very constraining, and a basketball game, incredibly so, and punitive too, in the sense that in everyday life the punishment may be a lot more subtle than in a game where you lose points or you're excluded or you're out.

Dr. Chase: I don't know all of the things that are going on in a chess game, but if it is a highly ritualized, highly intellectualized form of combat, such a game of contest which has winners and losers can, in terms of an internal psychological autonomy, represent a very adaptive and happy resolution of what otherwise might be a life with the Special Army Forces or this or that gang.

Dr. Ellis: Our society has some ambivalence about this with relation to sports, where we're mainly observers and only a small number of people are participants. We accord those participants some of the privileges that we accord players, but that has led to some difficulties. For example, last year a hockey player was finally arrested for rather brutally beating up somebody else. Up until that time no one ever thought that one ought to be arrested for having a fight in the middle of a professional sporting contest. Maybe we're beginning to take that sort of thing a little more seriously; but up until now a player has been protected by the rules of the game, whereas that wouldn't have been true if those same men had gotten into a fight on the street or at work. One of them would have gotten arrested. It's related to the notion of creativity. It's very difficult for me to imagine anybody being creative without a problem. It would strike me as being very difficult to have a challenge without a boundary or a constraint. A limiting condition has to be dealt with, as in your chess game, and that's how I see the relation of the problem to the creative outcome: take away all constraints and any response becomes possible—there's no challenge.

Dr. Kirschenblatt-Gimblett: What's the challenge of fantasy?

Dr. D. Singer: I think it's not so easy to maintain a story line. A kid has a bunch of blocks but still has the challenge of putting them into some order, developing a narration, and that's where the very youngest kids can't hold out very long. It really does get beyond them, and the story does break down. It's easier for one child, as we heard in that recording yesterday—Sonia wandered off by herself picking sea shells. She could maintain the story, whereas for the other kids who were trying to keep more of a group structure the thing fell apart. So some individual kids can carry on a longer sequence than others. There is some challenge to that.

Dr. Hutt: I'm with Barbara [Dr. Kirschenblatt-Gimblett] here. Children make this distinction—and therefore I think it's important—between what they find to be constraining activities with an explicit objective and those situations which are unconstrained, or where the constraints come from within. And imaginative play, fantasy play, is just such an area where there is no explicit objective to be realized. There are no sanctions, and the contraints that apply are those that they impose themselves. Children do articulate this sort of distinction.

Dr. Gardner: When you say there are no sanctions, I'm not sure I know what you mean because my observations suggest that there are many households in which you're told very strongly not to engage in fantasy. The message is given fairly directly: "That's pretend; you shouldn't do that."

Dr. Hutt: But that's a social sanction. It doesn't emerge from the play itself.

Dr. Gardner: You mean it isn't a physical constraint like a rock or something that's blocking the way.

Dr. Hutt: But in games with rules they're constrained by the objective. Chess, for example, is such a game where there are constraints. There is an objective to be realized and there are sanctions whether you win or lose.

Dr. Ellis: But I think the fantasies have a structure, and the structure is often a sort of antistructure in the sense that in our society this is what would happen next. What can I do about it to have that not happen in my fantasy? So there is the challenge to continue to fantasize: can I come up with something that's not conventional or stereotyped?

Dr. Lewis: I could want to fantasize because I'm bored, or because I am anxious over what's happening now and I want to be somewhere else. It seems to me that the motives for fantasy or symbolic play can be multiply determined; I don't think we need to generate a single rule.

Dr. Ellis: Just because I used one example doesn't mean there is only one rule. Barbara [Dr. Kirschenblatt-Gimblett] gave a whole host of strategies for dealing with riddles, and they got more and more complicated. You can extract from those and say, "Here is the strategy for producing another riddle like that." In other words, it involves structures of jokes. You establish an expectation and you break it; that is actually a strategy, a rule.

Dr. Hutt: That comes from the child?

Dr. Ellis: Yes, and I'm happy with that. Without these strategies I don't think you could sustain fantasy.

Dr. Garvey: Play with rules is an ambiguous phrase. We have play with rules that are the subject matter of what we're playing with, and then there's play that's constrained by rules in Piaget's sense. I think I'm agreeing with you 100 percent if you're saying that when you fantasize you are playing with rule systems; that is, regularities in systems. You're either keeping them consonant or you're varying them in some way, but if that rule-governed system didn't exist, then you couldn't play, *because you are playing within a system, a system of relevances and coherences.*

Dr. J. Singer: If a little girl says, "I'm going to be Mommy and you be the baby," and then the baby gets into a make-believe car and drives away, the one that's playing mommy will say, "Babies can't drive," or something like that. There *are* some structures, and the child will become dissatisfied with the game if it stretches them too far.

Dr. Hutt: But there are also situations where that would be permitted . . . "You're a funny baby" . . . one's heard that. Children will take the conventional model and deliberately contradict the convention, and this is equally permissible. It's what the child decides to do with the rules and the conventions.

Dr. Schwartzman: I don't know how we got into this, but it seems to me that you could make the argument that it's more challenging to play with the ambiguity that's inherent in the symbolic or the sociodramatic play, an ambiguity that is really ruled out in games, as far as I can see.

Dr. Kirschenblatt-Gimblett: It may depend on how old you are.

Dr. Schwartzman: Yes.

Dr. Fein: It's hard for me to continue to convince myself that play is really antiflow, and I think that's why the concept is dangerous. I think that generally the involved experiences, however they may be defined, are usually safe culturally, and that it's the antiflow that is upsetting and disturbing, and possibly rule violating and inside-out turning. I have a feeling that when kids turn up imaginary companions capable of doing all sorts of bizarre things, there is an element of a real violation of stability, of equilibrium, of an optimum. Somehow it seems to be too disordering, too separating out from one thing to another. I don't know where to go with that, but at this point it makes me more comfortable to feel that there is a kind of play experience which is not a flow experience as Mihayli has described it.

Dr. Sutton-Smith: One of the rules for the manipulation of rules in play is to do the opposite of some rule that you already know, and there may be other rules for the manipulation of rules. That manipulation itself would perhaps be a play-intrinsic rule system, not found only in play but apparently generated quite often there, because kids do reverse things a great deal more in play than elsewhere. What sense do you have of the portion of time that children are reversing things? We have rites of reversal, and Barbara's [Dr. Kirschenblatt-Gimblett's] speech-play material was also a beautiful example of reversal. We have a sense, too, that children spend a lot of time modeling, much of which seems to be fairly straight or nonreversive, although I suppose it's a reversal insofar as they're in power.

PLAY AND FLOW: SAME OR DIFFERENT?

Dr. McCall: I have come to some integrating thoughts which are undoubtedly too simplistic, but they do bring some order to my experience. I have come to accept in the beginning, and lasting through life, an idling concept: that there is a disposition of the organism to maintain some motor activity and some mental activity, even in sleep. However, that alone doesn't get me to the intensity of physical and/or mental involvement that can occur in play, although I can understand there are arousal limits. When you're too aroused you don't do certain things. When you're not aroused enough you don't do certain things. There are other dispositions of the organism that get it into situations that provide challenges in one way or another. In the very young baby, at the most primitive level, you have the intake of information about physical objects. I see my discrepancy curve as essentially a blend of new but processable information; that, in its most primitive sense, is the channel of challenge and skill. The new information is the challenge in this case, because the organism is disposed to take in information as an adaptive mechanism. Now there are hints not yet empirically well established that there is a positive affective component to that resolution, to the accomplishment of the processing of information. We are currently involved in a study directly attempting to assess that component. There is another disposition: that of influencing, or having contingent commerce with, the environment. There is partly anecdotal, partly empirical evidence of incredible affective blossoming, as John Watson says, by very young infants—two months old, perhaps younger—when dependable contingencies in their behavior are established. They are cute stories, but we've told enough such stories. There are possible affective consequences to these dispositions. Those can in turn reinforce such behaviors if necessary, though I'm not captivated by this necessity, but it does form a primitive state of flow in an extraordinarily young infant. Now as the infant develops, his cognitive skills permit new challenges to be taken up as, according to my steps or Piaget's steps or anybody else's, new challenges are posed. As his symbolic capabilities improve, the child can anticipate and plan to achieve flow states, if that is the desired goal. Importantly, he is then able to imagine situations which balance challenge and skill. A global definition of play would suggest that *play is meeting challenges with skills for the sake of making that match,* the primary goal being to match skill with challenge. Imaginative play is going after that not quite veritable goal with skills that are not quite veritable, but which are filled in imaginatively. Children become capable of that at around two years of age. I think there is a disposition of the organism to exercise newfound capabilities in the process of exploring their ramifications. Between two and six years of age there is a veritable plethora of imaginative activities which permit that child to experience flow all along that dimension because, by virtue of his imagination, he is no longer restricted to challenges or skills that are real in his real domain. As his mental capabilities increase, as that child reaches the point where he can now meet challenges with a greater range of society's valued skills, there is less need for imaginative filling in along this diagonal. Since there are many routes to achieving challenges, since there are many challenges, their very format changes with development. There are no particular sets of behaviors that are play. It makes it incredibly complicated and difficult for people who are trained in the way we are trained to deal with this kind of problem. When you get sufficiently skilled, the imaginative component becomes less, except, interestingly enough, in those situations which are morphologically the same as for the child; that is, where you cannot accomplish the challenge, or the challenge is not available in society for moral reasons. The consequences of such imagination may be undesirable, as in the case of divorce. You fantasize meeting certain challenges that for other reasons are undesirable to you. You don't want to carry them out in actuality. Games, complicated rules, thrill seeking as in mountain climbing, also fall into the matching of challenge and skill in this way.

Helping children then would amount to helping them to achieve flow, however that is defined; and this help would change with the age of the child. It would be to match tasks to a child's skill level at that moment, which is what a good teacher does, and to develop in him skills which will meet the challenges you know society will present to that child as a normal course.

Dr. Sutton-Smith: What I hear from that is that play prepares for flow and becomes the opiate of those who don't make it!

Play and Flow As Different

Dr. Fein: I don't play tennis to play. To me tennis is a deeply involving, totally preoccupying activity—I want to get that ball across and fast so badly. They used to say as I went to serve, "Greta, you're fantasizing." They were right. I was fantasizing how to get that ball just right and come down on it just right.

Dr. D. Singer: We had a very different experience when we were playing with you.

Dr. Sutton-Smith: One man's play is another man's flow?

Dr. D. Singer: We thought, "Gee, what great games. Greta got the shot; great!"

Dr. Fein: I think play, on the other hand, is like what happens when my family and I are sitting around the dining room table, horsing around and fooling, and people are knocking about ideas or whatever, and it's totally free. It's not a preoccupied, intensely ordered, organized thing like the tennis. It's up for grabs. When I play with a baby, I'm just riding and rolling. There's no beginning and there's no end.

Dr. Chase: Aren't you making a new point that we really have not focused on? I'd like you to give some names to what you're describing. For example, I have associations such as "it's unpredictable; I don't know how it will end."

Dr. Fein: To me playing tennis is a time-bridging, enclosed kind of operation, and when I'm playing with a child, or involved in a play exchange, it's totally open-ended. I don't know and I couldn't care less what's going to happen there. When I play tennis, I care what's going to happen next. I really do. I try to control what's happening next. But the thing I'm enchanted with when I watch kids play and when I play with kids and when my family are playing together, is that we're just sort of tuning in moment to moment. Nobody knows exactly where it's going to go and we're up for grabs. It's a different spirit.

Dr. Gardner: I'm a little bit upset by what Greta [Dr. Fein] said. It may be just my misunderstanding, but I think there's an attempt here to map incommensurate uses of the term *play*. You can talk about play in terms of definition—what the dictionary says or what somebody smart says. You can talk about play as a psychological process, which would either be an operationalization by a psychologist or just some kind of a measure that you make; or you can do what I think people are now doing, giving a phenomenal definition of play, which is what Mihayli began by asking people. He wasn't talking about play, but by asking people to describe their feelings. I think that's what both Barbara [Dr. Kirschenblatt-Gimblett] and Greta [Dr. Fein] are doing. Don't demand of the thing that you happen to find affects you a certain way that it to map on the language developed or the way the discipline developed. Those are separate levels of analysis.

Dr. Fein: I guess I want to make a distinction, Howard [Dr. Gardner], between sociodramatic play—as Kate [Dr. Garvey] talked about it and as Helen [Dr. Schwartzman] talked about it, it has an inconclusive tone—and making up a performance, creating a production to present to an audience. I think if we lose that distinction, we've lost something important. It's the *kind* of organization we're working on when we or children participate in these different activities.

Dr. Hay: I think for a while it seemed as if we were going to make the leap that play is flow, and it seems to me that that is not what at least some of us have been talking about. I would hate to have us make that leap because I think it creates a problem.

Dr. Sutton-Smith: I'm hearing different play textures. I play tennis and I can flow in tennis too, but conversational horsing around the dinner table is the best fun of all when everybody's up. They are different textures, but very clear flow. I'm just as gripped by one as the other. I'll tell you, I feel better about myself in horsing around the table or when I'm writing stories. I feel better about that flow because I feel it's where I am now in my development. In tennis, and when I play soccer and go around killing balls, I feel, on subsequent reflection, a little bit embarrassed, but there is there a primitive quality of flow that's unlike anything else. It's like total blindness or tunnel vision as you go after that ball and kick and mangle. And that reflects the sort of childhood I had. It exists in me now, but it's still flow, and quite a different texture.

Dr. Hay: If you're going to use the term that way, it seems as though we're redefining flow. In Mihayli's description it seemed that you had to be aware of the end; you had to be aware of the goal. This ambiguity that I find in Greta's [Dr. Fein's] table play, or children's sociodrama, was not a part of that description. I don't think that is present in these other kinds of games we're talking about.

Dr. Csikszentmihayli: Most of what I've been trying to do so far has been to understand play and playfulness, play and flow, and to point out that when they coincide it's lucky, but they don't *have* to go together. At the same time I don't want to throw away completely the notion that play has a special function in the flow experience. The way I tried to get around it was to define play as the experience of flow in a particular situation where it's voluntary, autotelic, and has no implications for real life. There is a particular frame within which flow is play. As to that business about texture—I'm not sure but whether that depends on the challenges that you're confronting at a given time. When you're fooling around with people, especially people you know, who happen to be predictable because of the conditions of the situation, the setting—there is a possibility of abandoning yourself and interacting with the totality of your feelings at that point. As Greta [Dr. Fein] pointed out, there is no concern with the outcome in any given sense, but still I assume there is sense of skills—of responding appropriately, of producing the appropriate response in the other person, etc.—which is what makes this kind of interaction interesting and involving. There too you get the same kind of variables involved, except it is a different medium and it may be more satisfying. The problem is that in a game like tennis or soccer there is the constant intrusion of the self into the activity because the goal, or the point in tennis, becomes something that affects your life outside the activity. I mean, your self-esteem is riding on the activity, and you can't completely block out that consideration; so you keep alternating between flow and being very self-involved—but in a wrong sense; I mean sense in the sense of ego.

Dr. Sutton-Smith: You come in and out all of the time in all these things.

Dr. Csikszentmihayli: That's right, but when you are in a situation like that with your family around the dinner table there is less self-intrusion.

Dr. J. Singer: When we started playing tennis with Greta [Dr. Fein], she couldn't serve. She was really down pretty low on that skill part, and so it wasn't a flow experience for a couple of times, but it was wonderful to see how much better she got so soon—then it really did become a flow experience. I think Dorothy and I experienced it in that way.

Dr. McCall: I'd like to get some resolution of these points of view that I've heard. I have some sympathy with all of them. Let's suppose we define play as the attempt to achieve flow purely for the sake of attaining that state. Since behaviors typically have multiple causes and motives, a given act is directed more or less purely for the sake of achieving flow. Some attempts to achieve flow may be more or less likely to be successful, and happiness requires some degree of reality testing. So that if you are hopeless at tennis, but you learn and work at it, although it may be painful for years you are still attempting to achieve flow—that is, to the extent that there are no other criteria or goals to be served by this activity. Do we have a pure instance of that? No.

Dr. Hutt: That's teleology.

Dr. McCall: I believe human organisms have intentionality, and I don't find that teleological.

Dr. Ellis: You only have to say it the other way around and put in an extrinsic consequence that you would normally talk about as the product of work. Then you say the same thing. It's multiply motivated, and each one of those motives changes from time to time. And yet there are also possibilities of achieving flow in work.

Dr. Gardner: Might it not be the case that if we look for morphological behavioral parallels between what little kids do that we call play and what adults do which since this morning we call flow, we will find no particular relationship between them, but that the phenomenal experience we call flow is in fact what the child feels during play but cannot reflect upon because that's what being a young child is like. I'm suggesting that maybe the experience that we call flow gives a lot of insight into how the child feels doing what we say he's doing when he's playing.

Dr. Kirschenblatt-Gimblett: Greta [Dr. Fein] and I were talking about this, and saying that in the adult view, almost all of what children do is defined as play. In talking about children's activities, keeping it nice and neutral would make me more comfortable. But what happens is that when you're not feeding them or diapering them or putting them to sleep, and when they're not crying in distress, all else is presumably play, except for those few attempts to try and sort out what we call exploratory behavior. So that in a way it's an adultcentric view of kids' activity, and it may be a view of it as being essentially nonserious, noninstrumental, and voluntary, and, therefore, play.

Dr. Chase: It seems to me Greta was making some very specific points, such as being comfortable with uncertainty, a lack of structure, a lack of clear predictability of when and how the activity will end. Corinne used the word *idling*. The word *nonproductive* has been used. Since we haven't worked on this very much, what I'd like to invite you to do is sift and sort through this list, add things, see what kinds of labels seem to move us towards some consensus about a subset of behavior that would be worth looking at.

Dr. Lewis: I'm just reminded of Greta's question, which seems to be more than reasonable, as to whether or not there really is uncertainty. And I go back to our early comments that in fact that analysis would suggest that although it's uncertain, it really isn't uncertain; or it's a range of uncertainty that's narrowed in such a way that any one of those uncertain outcomes isn't too bad. I would suspect that there is a structure there, rather than this free expression. There is in fact a constraint, a very nice constraint, which allows for the free activity. That would also fit into arousal levels or into fear situations.

Dr. Fein: I think you're also talking about structures.

Dr. Lewis: I think that kind of modification is necessary to what you were saying. I believe that's a good way of doing it.

Dr. Sutton-Smith: It could well be that the whole point about play, as distinct from the games and flow, and the like, is that, as for example in the idling, repetitive behavior, the boost comes from your control, not from your uncertainty. The arousal is that you're in charge. The contrast comes when you're not in charge. So the boost comes now—"You're in charge"—and that's a boost of excitement, if you like, but it's not uncertainty. You're excited because you're now doing what you can competently control, and maybe that's a pleasure and makes play quite different from flow—where we have this whole matching notion of uncertainty and of challenge and skill. The flow is much more of an interactive concept. It's not just you by yourself with your skills and challenges. If you get the right match then you have this great excitement because your skills have appropriately and objectively matched the challenges. But fantasy is subjective play. I'm always fantasizing, and there's no great uncertainty about which way I'm going. I've been the same way millions of times. It seems to me that the arousal there is that I'm doing it. This is a very primitive analysis, but there seems to be a potential subjective/objective distinction between play and flow.

Dr. Kirschenblatt-Gimblett: What's the difference between control and skill? Would the control be as interesting if that which was being controlled was too easy?

Dr. Garvey: Aldis in his play/fighting book (1975) makes a great deal of this point, especially in the latter part, which is not so much about rough-and-tumble play as about thrill seeking. He uses a number of interesting analogies from videotaped behavior in amusement parks, about seeking fear up to a certain level, but always having to be in control. You see certain points where the child seems to feel that maybe he has lost control of the fear that he has invited, and then suddenly something happens.

Dr. Hutt: I'm glad you brought that up. There are the Russian workers whom Berlyne quotes. He terms this sort of activity *arousal jags*: you go out seeking a certain amount of uncertainty—challenge, if you like—but you are in control. You know that you can opt out of the situation if things get too much for you. Again, I'd like to link this up with animal work, simply because the mechanisms are easier to elucidate. In the diversive exploration situation—that is, where external cues are not governing behavior (it's intrinsically motivated)—we have animals bar pressing for life-contingency changes. Those bar presses aren't the most rewarding, because if you allow animals to choose between an externally imposed schedule or their own temporal schedule or a rhythmic schedule, what they prefer is their own spontaneous schedule. So that this again seems to suggest that in the intrinsically motivated situation, what is most rewarding is for the animal to be able to control the output and contingencies, and to opt out of the situation if things are going awry.

Dr. J. Singer: Childhood is not all fun. It's really not a very pleasant time. There's a lot of confusion in the child, difficulty in organizing experience and in regulation. Play becomes one medium by which the child can have some sense of control and can acquire new information at a rate that it can control, then influence. So I think they set up a variety of situations where there is an optimal balance between challenge and skill, where information processing capacities can function at a moderate rate so as to provoke positive affecting interest.

Cultural Differences in Play and Flow

Dr. J. Singer: I think there are a lot of specific cultural group differences in play. For instance, why do the Aymara mentioned by Brian [Dr.

Sutton-Smith] have this prejudice against play? I don't know. I think there are subcultures that have clear-cut prejudices against play. I think in this country some of it comes out of Protestantism, in which there was a clear dichotomy between work and play. Play was sinful. What was that place where they used to dance around the maypole near the Puritan campsites in Massachusetts? Merrymount. The cavaliers were there and they were happy and playful, and the Puritans looked on them as sinners. That whole Puritan tradition was part of our ethic in this country. Then I think there are very specific subcultural group patterns.

Dr. Csikszentmihayli: On the other hand, it's really fascinating to see, for instance in Weber's book on the Protestant ethic, how he attributes all the characteristics of flow to work, and how he dichotomizes play as being something that distracts him from the serious business of enjoying himself by working hard and *not* enjoying himself.

Dr. Lewis: It's a deprivation of the feeling state, and not the activity—that you shouldn't feel good.

Dr. Kirschenblatt-Gimblett: Feeling good and feeling joyful should be sacred.

Dr. Chase: They should be approved activities. This is one thing I was after. We haven't yet tried to enlarge our understanding of play by asking who's against it, who has a very rigid definition of what is is and what it isn't. We have such a hard time deciding. Are there people who know the conditions under which it's allowable, the conditions under which it's not? I think there are in some contexts.

Dr. Singer: You were asking before who are the *enemies of play*. I'll tell you about one enemy. We were working in the valley town of Shelton, which was about a fifteen-minute ride from New Haven, with people who were mainly blue collar workers, workers in factories; they really were very much against play. In the nursery school where we did the experiment the teacher gave the children a lot of cognitive skills each day. The parents paid their fee for that nursery school and wanted their children to have reading and writing and to do better in life than they had. And the parents asked for a group, so they could begin to work with us and understand what we were talking about—what was all this imagination and fantasy and play. They really wanted to understand that. Now, we had a little girl who for two weeks during the experiment sat near me as I was doing some clay modeling and always looked at me in a very dour way, and I kept thinking, "I can't seem to win this child over." She never would play. She had been rated very low on imagination before the experiment began because she sat in corners and did nothing with any of the toys. But during the modeling period, which went on for two weeks, a half hour every day, she would sit quite close and just stare at me with an angry look on her face. At the end of modeling period, I was there one day when the students were observing, and there was this tremendous excitement going on; so I peeked around the corner to see what was happening. This girl was sitting in the garden at the table with four children around her. Before this she had always been isolate, with no peer contact. She had been really low on all of our variables, and yet here she had a game going. She said to one, "Here's your food" (there was no food), "set the table" (there were no dishes)—did the whole thing. Then after she fed everyone she reached under the table and fed this imaginary dog, and it was fantastic. The students were just jumping. The vibes were going all over the place. And then when she was through serving the dinner she said, "Okay, everybody, let's go into the living room," and she moved them from this table to a grassy knoll which was now the living room, turned on the fake television set, got everybody organized, called the dog over. I've never seen such play. At the same time the mother began to report to us that this kid, who would not allow her hair to be washed, who was frightened, who never related to the mother, was now beginning to talk to the mother, and the mother to talk to the child. And in the parent group this mother then told why, out of her own experience, she felt it was important to begin to play. So little by little we were winning over the people—good, sincere, honest parents who felt that play was going to interfere with the real business of work and success, which meant: you're going to go to college because we didn't; and, if you're playing you're not learning. But it took a long time. So there are some true enemies of play.

Dr. J. Singer: It sounds like the group Corinne [Dr. Hutt] mentioned before.

Dr. Kirschenblatt-Gimblett: It seems to me that our emphasis on play has been both ethnocentric and childcentric and I think one of the great benefits of Mihayli's discussion this morning was to point out that a flow experience is very much what we have had in mind as we've been talking about play. And it might be very liberating to ask ourselves, what are the broad range of activities and areas in which people can have flow experiences, and to what extent is that culture-bound? Ritual festivals, social life, humor, literature, art, theatre, music, crafts—what is the range that wouldn't be defined by us or by them as play? I think we've invested too much in play as being kind of ultimate vehicle for this experience that we're now calling flow, and I really don't believe it is. I believe there are lots of other flow mechanisms or activities. To separate the two, and look to the others as well, might be very helpful in our thinking. Even "enemies of play" might be great promoters of religious ritual, masses with fantastic music and costume and color and stained glass windows, and you may have regular flow experiences on Sundays. Does it matter? You have to be able to conceive of play without flow. Just speaking for myself, the things I get most fun, or most enjoyment from, or most exhilaration, euphoria, whatever, aren't conventionally defined as play. They would come under some other category—aesthetic experiences or puttering. So there's a possibility of play that either fails or that has low flow realization. In other words, we've somehow or other seen play as some kind of salvation for mankind in terms of positive affect, optimal arousal. But it may or not be—for the individual, for the particular instance. Further, my feeling has been that much of what Mihayli described as flow has been implicit in many of our characterizations of play, and that if you acknowledge that that kind of positive experience can be had from a whole variety of other kinds of activity not defined as play, what then is left? If a significant amount of play activity need not necessarily generate that kind of experience, then what's our vested interest in play?

Dr. Collard: It's a living!

Dr. Kirschenblatt-Gimblett: If you can get the goodies from something else, and if you don't always get them from play, then what's with play? If we agree, as a way of getting a common frame of reference, that much of what we've been characterizing so positively about play is very much like what Mihayli was talking about when he talked about flow; and if we agree that that kind of experience can be had from many other things than play—music, art, literature, good humor, religious experiences, festival, whatever; and if we also acknowledge that a substantial amount of play activity doesn't necessarily yield the kind of experience that he described (there's many a boring game of Hearts, and many a boring Monopoly game. I've sat through and been thoroughly bored by many football and baseball games—all those traditional things we call play), then what is our investment in play? It seems to me also that it's something of an illusion when we assume so easily that play in its classical sense is without consequences in real life. It's very idealistic. Wouldn't it be wonderful if there were some area of activity that was essentially immune from consequences in real life? The fact of the matter is that there's more business settled on the squash courts and handball courts and the men's locker rooms at the university than in the board rooms or the committee meetings. That's what I'm told. What I'm saying is that the assertion that the proficiencies displayed at play have no spillover in terms of one's esteem afterwards, or that relationships that are negotiated during play have no repercussions on one's relationships outside of play—that play is in fact immune from life, or life is immune from play—is an illusion and a fiction that we've been maintaining. And that this self-consciousness, in and out of flow, is a much more fundamental aspect of the nature of play than we might like to admit.

THE IMPROVEMENT OF PLAY

Dr. Gardner: I'd like to reflect a bit on the questions that Dick [Dr. Chase] posed at the beginning. The reason, quite frankly, is that I have a lot of difficulty with them and I haven't at all been able to sort them out in my mind. Maybe my difficulty will be helpful, and I'll try to state it in kind of a strong form. As for (1) the *definitional question,* I think play is very difficult to define. Basically, definitional exercises haven't been terribly successful in psychology, although we all feel the need to indulge in them from time to time. (2) With the *development question* I ran into a real impasse in my own thinking which was to some extent alleviated by Mihalyi's presentation today. I don't think you can indulge in developmental psychology unless you have an end state in view, some sense of what it means to be developed in the particular area you're looking at. It's easy to study language development because we all agree on what competence, grammar, etc., should look like. Until this morning I don't think anybody put out any kind of elaborate notion of what *developed play* might be like. I think flow is a good candidate, but only to the extent that I'm willing to accept flow as what I would like my developed player to exhibit. This causes real problems to the third question, which is, how do you *get somebody to be more developed,* or how do you improve the extent to which they exemplify the trait which you're studying? This is where I see what I think may be a real dysfunction between the kinds of activities which most of us have been describing with the adjective ludic, and the sorts of states which, following Mihayli, we might value in the adult. To put it very starkly, I think that the person who is a developed player is the individual who has acquired a lot of skill in a given area, is good at it, has got a competence, often in the symbolic medium though not necessarily; it could be in a sport or something else. And what usually goes along with this is that they feel pretty good about this kind of competence. Yet in talking about play in children we seem to have shied away from talking about the development of competence, because when we talk about kids' play it is defined as those times when the heart variability is great, and the organism doesn't seem to be very goal directed. And so the kind of contrast I've been playing in my mind is between a character in John Updike's novel *Rabbit Run* and, say, a very gifted musician or scientist. The man in *Rabbit Run* is a person who was a very good player as a child, and would have scored well in our different measures, and yet is pretty dysfunctional as an adult. His golden day was in the past. I think the people whose lives are characterized by flow as adults may in many cases have been the people who wouldn't have impressed us an being particularly good players, but rather people who were isolated and working very hard at developing skill at something. They would be getting feedback from that, and living now in an adult culture where it isn't very important how much ludism you can entail, but rather that you have a metier in which you can gain satisfaction and make sense vis-a-vis the rest of the community, they would have achieved the kind of thing which is the adult payoff for play. I'm curious as to whether people feel that they can tie the kinds of behaviors we've been talking about in young kids more closely to some kind of an end state of development than I can. Or, alternatively, maybe you think that's not a good way to look at it—to think about an end state in relation to what we're looking at in the course of early development.

Dr. Sutton-Smith: It's not only that sort of contrast between play and flow. The other potentiality is that there are various kinds of play states that become different kinds of adult end states which may be play *or* flow. The fantasizer, the imaginer, may go into drama or not. He or she may go into novel writing or not. The physical gamester may go into sports. The tic-tac-toe gamester may go into chess. And all of them may also apply these play shifts in business, war, politics, and so forth, and flow in those areas.

Dr. Chase: The gifted are not a very ludic group, and this is one of their difficulties. They also have a great many other ways in which they don't fit with their peers; it's one of the things that people find difficult about them. Adults find them too much like other adults. In Stanley's study, the researchers go out and find these children, so that they identify them rather earlier than is customary. Then they are brought to Johns Hopkins and they take their mathematics course with the undergraduate and graduate students. That's considered to be sensible in terms of matching skill with challenge and I think it is, because they're terribly bored and frustrated and perplexed in a conventional school setting. But what about the rest of their lives and the dilemma of being precocious? No, they're not very ludic. I'm sorry I don't know more about it, but at least that's one population we could look into.

Dr. Gardner: I've made an argument in favor of developing a lot of skill in something because I think in the end that's where flow comes from. I think Jerry Singer has made an equally good if not stronger argument in favor of a kind of generalized capital as opposed to investment in one stock. Possibly these notions can be combined in an educational way by trying to figure out what one or two or three domains a child has real strengths in and building the play, imagination-expanding exercises around them. These exercises don't have to be formal, but they should create a kind of atmosphere around those areas. This approach doesn't have a disembodied playfulness which, in the absence of having knowledge about how to go around the world or about poetry or whatever else, doesn't really do you much good except at cocktail parties.

Dr. Kirschenblatt-Gimblett: I wonder if maybe play is so important a part of childhood because it becomes the method for enculturating people into flow experiences. This is the idea that since play is so prevalent a mode it's one in which the possibility for flow experience is maximized, particularly in structured play where there's a lot of control of the circumstances. And the end result isn't that you would play more and better later, but that you would be capable of more flow experiences in general in whatever spheres, whether play or nonplay. And perhaps it's those people who've never been able to make the transfer of the flow experience from a play to a nonplay setting for whom play continues to occupy such an important role as adults, the most exhilarating moments of their lives still being at soccer games, football games, wrestling matches, or whatever. I think Mihayli's data shows that there is that kind of separation; that those who get the most exhilaration from work aren't getting it from home, and those who are getting it from home aren't getting it from work. It's rare that somebody is getting it right across the board. There is a tendency to get it from one place or another, and so I wonder then if play in the early years can be seen as a prime mechanism for learning how to flow, with the hope that one can extend one's possibilities for that kind of experience across a greater range of activity and not confine it simply to play.

FINAL COMMENT

Dr. Fein: Let's take this business of *now it's time to eat and it's not time to play, don't play with your food.* I think maybe that's a first partition. Subsequent to that partition a new way of looking at eating is possible, which is eating as a gourmet experience, as an aesthetic experience. I feel that maybe what's happening is that these human functions become separated out into ways in which new human experiences, dimensions of human experiences, can become organized. My eldest son came home after he went climbing up in the mountains and said that one of the greatest things about being in the Wing Rivers with nothing but a pack on your back was in the morning when you went to the bathroom. It was a great experience, going to the toilet and looking at these gorgeous mountains and the sun coming up; it was a total alteration of a human function.

Dr. Hay: Someone told me last summer that studying nuclear physics is child's play compared to studying child's play. What's the source?

Dr. Sutton-Smith: That's Bergson.

References

Aldis, O. *Play Fighting*. New York: Academic Press, 1975
Berlyne, D. E. *Conflict, Arousal and Curiosity*. New York: McGraw-Hill, 1960.

CHAPTER 16

EPILOGUE: PLAY AS PERFORMANCE*

Brian Sutton-Smith

There is no proper conclusion to a conference of this kind. All the researchers have had an opportunity to present their own way of looking at play, both in a formal presentation and during the manifold discussions that occurred. We reached as near a conclusion as was possible in the long and excited discussion over the interrelationships of play and flow which, in the final session of the three days, was itself a "flowing" experience of some value to the participants.

This is an epilogue by the editor which has no greater or lesser status as a statement on play than those already made by the other participants. Its value lies in the attempt to bring together what I have had additional time to perceive as some of the trends of this conference. This is obviously a personal statement, and the colleagues of the conference have no responsibility for this attempt. The problem continues to be how the two major groups can be reconciled—how one can unite primary paradigm energy concepts and cognitive processing concepts and secondary paradigm interactional concepts. Only one member of the conference made an explicit attempt to do so. This was Dr. Hutt, who presented her material on play in terms of various levels of analysis: physiological, linguistic, interactional, and so on. So unusual was this attempt for such large-scale coherence that she felt obliged to defend the "promiscuity" of her effort by reference to the potential fertility of the analysis.

In an earlier work entitled *The Dialectics of Play* (1979) I have attempted to reconcile some of the approaches in terms of what was dominantly a cognitive processing approach to the field. The organization of

*As in Ben-Amos, D., & Goldstein, K. S. *Folklore, performance and communication.* The Hague: Mouton, 1975.

the research issues in the introduction to this conference, in terms of antecedents, transitions, structure, development, and consequences was derived from the organization of that particular work. It is apparent to me now, however, that that very primary paradigm "psychologistic" approach does not do sufficient service to many of the matters raised in this conference, and particularly, to the interactional concepts that were presented here. It is possible to argue, for example, that from the idealistic play theorizing of Schiller to the phenomenological play theorizing of Csikszentmihayli nearly all play theory has proceeded on the basis of individualistic philosophical premises. One might define this implicit theory of play as follows. Play in the bulk of play scholarship (Herron & Sutton-Smith, 1971) is *defined as a voluntary and solitary activity of the individual as a result of which he increases his mastery or his creativity.* Clearly this is the kind of play that has been available to the children of upper status parents. It is the kind of definition that springs naturally to the minds of those who spend their life in solitary scholarship, or have sufficient wealth to make their recreation an avocational pursuit. There is much in common between this kind of play theorizing and the class based "amateur" doctrine of sports of the nineteenth century.

One can gauge the social class relativity of this way of viewing play, by contrasting it with the play theory developed by some play theorists to handle the special case of the poor. At the turn of the century the streets of the urban world were flooded with the children of immigrants from other countries and rural parts. These "urchins," "larrikins," "pests," "snipes," "waifs," as they were variously called, were accused of idleness, gambling and depravity. The play theorists of the Playground Movement sought to prescribe a theory of play which was suitable for their case. We have in mind, in particular, Henry Curtis (1915), Stanley Hall (1907), and Joseph Lee (1922). They prescribed playgrounds, organized sports, gymnastic apparatus, military drill, boy scouts and Indian troops. Their common assumption about play seems to have been that *it should be organized, and that it is a collective phenomenon of character training value which brings happiness to the participants.* Now this may well have been a play theory made up by the rich for the poor as we have described it elsewhere (Sutton-Smith, 1979). But whatever it was, it contrasts markedly with the kind of play theory of the former sort, and the kind primarily discussed throughout this conference. The existence of this socially determined and important play theory, and its avoidance in most play theorizing, strongly supports the argument of Kirschenblatt-Gimblett, that much of the conference doings were themselves of an ethnocentric character. One might argue that just as the play theorists of the early twentieth century sought to bring the supposed virtues of upper status games and outdoor camping to the *depraved,* similarly we are now attempting to bring the virtue of make-believe and "flow" to the *deprived*. But in both cases we are arguing as if discussing certain universal psychological functions, rather than seeing our endeavor as itself an arm of social policy, and, therefore, involving definitions of play relative to our social situation.

At this point, however, rather than taking a further sideways step into the sociology of play theory, I would like to reconsider the kinds of issues discussed in this book, but from a theoretical stance which attempts to ground play theory in social events from the very beginning.

THE PLAY QUADRALOGUE

The difference between primary paradigm thinkers with individualistic premises and secondary paradigm thinkers with collective premises is not unlike that within linguistic theory between those who analyze language from the point of view of its grammar (Chomsky, 1965) and those who analyze language from the point of view of speech (Hymes, 1964). The first are concerned with language as a text with an underlying structure, and the second are concerned with language in context, as an act of communication. Each tries to make predictions as to how language will proceed on the basis of its own set of researched variables. The same problem has arisen in the present conference. On the one hand we have the groups concerned with those individual and object-related variables that trigger the drama of play; and on the other hand the smaller group concerned with those collective kinds of communication that make the play frame what it is. To transcend this difference, it seems, we require a theory of play which deals with it both as an act of communication and as a dramatic occurrence.

If one adopts the very traditional developmental psychologists' ploy of asking what the final form of the play phenomena is to be, then we end up with such things as sporting contests, Miss America Pageants, the Olympics, theatre, and ballet. And in all of these there are not only the players or the contestants (the performers), there are also the directors and the audiences (as well as gamblers, critics, columnists). It follows then that if language is always a *dialogue*, a situated act, and not merely a text, that all expressive forms, of which play is only one, are a *quadralogue*. They always involve at least four prototypical parties: the group or individual that stages (or creates) the event, as actors and co-actors; the group that receives this communication (the audience); and the group that directs the race or conducts the symphony (directors).

The "staging" will vary by culture, as Dr. Kirschenblatt-Gimblett so well illustrated. In modern society what is on stage is thought to be optional behavior, and what is not staged is thought to be obligatory. But Dr. Csikszentmihayli's new approach begins to suggest that even that well-established dichotomy may no longer serve us so well. We may take our "theatric" stages with us wherever we are. But in other societies what is staged has been regarded as the sacred as against the profane (Turner, 1974), the disequilibrial versus the equilibrial (Lévi-Strauss, 1966), the equilibrial versus the disequilibrial (Adams, 1978), the animal versus the human (Geertz, 1971), and so forth. The varieties of possible dichotomies increase with our knowledge of the human array. The argument to be presented here, however, is that the "expressive" sphere is always mediated by the formal quadralogic of communication. In what follows we will not be concerned so much with these broader cultural questions as with illustrations of the way in which this kind of model might usefully integrate the types of disparate data presented in the conference. The theory of *play as performance* is a theory which says that play is not ever simply solitary action, but always a performance before real or imagined others. The player may be both director and player on his own stage, as he is in solitary play. He may be audience for some other. The mother may be player, director and audience for her baby who is the counter player. But in all cases, thinking in quadralogic terms helps us to highlight the actual or implicit characteristics of the play phenomenon.

In what follows we will be concerned in particular with the genesis of play in the mother-infant communication. Once again the matter is approached through a consideration of research issues relevant to play antecedents, play transitions, play structure, play development, and play consequences.

ANTECEDENTS

The first question in the introduction concerned the issue of how play arises and what leads to it. By and large the literature on animals was ignored in this conference apart from passing mention by Drs. Shultz, Collard and Hutt. But any approach to play presumably would need to take into account what evidence there is to hand on the biological parallels to human play. Those data seem to show that play is

1. More likely when there is a long period of delayed maturation;
2. More likely when the organism is protected and secure in its surroundings;

3. More likely under moderate, not intense, degrees of arousal.

4. They show too that moderate arousal is more likely to lead to complex learning than intense arousal.

In this conference, and with respect to humans, Dr. Lewis in particular, but also Drs. Garvey and Schwartzman emphasized, consistent with these points, the importance of social determinants in establishing the playful interactions. It is known for example that infants supplied with more stimulation are more likely themselves to be stimulus seeking in subsequent years. We know also that the infants themselves play a role in evoking stimulation from their own parents. There was no resolution of the extent to which solitary play with objects is itself affected by, or independent of, the earlier interactions with the parents, though it seemed probable that each epistemic system (social and solitary) has some relative autonomy, but with the social determinants having the predominant effect. The evidence, both psychological and anthropological, would seem to show that the most important single prerequisite for play is that it is modeled by other persons. Child-rearing behaviors have been empirically related to play behavior in various ways. The most general finding is that the amount of demand and stress is associated with more complex games (Roberts & Sutton-Smith, 1962). Complex cultures have more play and more games of all kinds, as well as more severe socialization. Perhaps these conditions of parent-child interaction approximate the definition of moderate degrees of arousal.

While it seems probable that both social play and symbolic play are very much affected by the conditions of mother stimulation (the amount, the elaborativeness, and the like), there is also well-documented indication that solitary play can be preceded and perhaps instigated by solitary exploratory behavior alone (Collard, Hutt). What was suggested in the conference but never clearly resolved was that the transition from exploration to play may find sufficient explanation in the state of the organism alone (boredom, shift to functional conceptualizing, disposition to exercise influence). Drs. Collard and Hutt, along with Dr. Ellis, have shown, for example, that as objects become uninteresting, play responses increase in number, apparently because the subject seeks now to increase stimulation which the objects can no longer provide by themselves. Both kinds of play, however, social and solitary, are subject to the kind of ecological variables mentioned—privacy, a playroom, accepting adults, and supporting playgroups, all of which help to define the communicational context as one suitable for this activity to occur.

In the rest of this section, however, I would like to bring together the biological and the human data to give special weight to the mother-infant relationships as providing the prototypical antecedent play situation. In effect, I will take a lead from Michael Lewis and add some details of my own which I see as steps towards the formulation of a theory of play as performance.

The Mother-Infant Paradigm

Analysis of the comparative animal data and the cross-cultural data on play suggests that the essential and universal precondition for play is the protection and stimulation of the young by the nurturing older member of the species. The mother typically provides the safe expressive frame within which her stimulation and the infant's responsiveness can assume those characteristics commonly known as play. As Lewis says, she is both a constant and a variable. The communicational frame she provides includes at the least the following expressive attributes:

a proxemic bubble:	closeness of faces
a play face:	raised eyebrows, open mouth, wide-open eyes, mock surprise
a play gaze:	infatuated gazing while talking
play vocalization:	higher pitch, elongated vowels, slower speech
face presentations:	zooming in and out
play time:	usually after meals and before the infant's sleep
a play place:	usually in the crib, on her knee, or in her vicinity

Within this communicational context, which we derive chiefly from the work of Stern (1977), she and the baby engage in a series of dramatic episodes, the nucleus of which is an alternation of contrasting actions. These action contrastives are themselves supplied by the contrasting roles of the participants to the actions. The play can be limited to one such episode or more. As the child grows older, the normal tendency is for these episodes to be joined together in a cumulative way rising to an emotional climax after which there is a release of euphoric energy. Each episode itself is a microcosm of such excitement arousal and reduction. In sum, *we postulate as the aboriginal paradigm for play, mother and infant conjoined in an expressive communicational frame within which they contrastively participate in the modulation of excitement.* We call this a *paradigm* for all ludic action, because we suggest that other play itself is a metaphoric statement of this literal state of affairs. Ludic action, wherever it is, always involves the analogous establishment of the secure communicational frame and the manipulation of excitement arousal through contrastive actions within that frame. The amount of playfulness in subsequent years is a direct function of the mother-infant involvement, variability (Lewis), and elaborativeness (Fein) in the establishment of these norms (Collard; Clarke-Stewart, 1973).

Kinds of Communicative Ludic Competence

We deal here with some of the first modes of interaction of mother and infant as they play together. It is our view that quite fundamental implicit rule behaviors are established here which provide a model for play behaviors in later years. In rough order of appearance, beginning by the second month of life, the play routines are as follows:

The Exchange Routine. The mother imitates the baby, establishing a contingency between her own response and the baby's earlier act (for example, vocalization), which causes the baby first to examine the mother carefully, then later itself to intentionally repeat its own earlier sound (Lewis). After a time mother and infant become engaged in a turn-taking "round," within which each does the same thing, usually with increasing enjoyment, smiling and laughter. Turn-taking communicational routines of this sort can be adopted as early as one year of age by little children playing with each other. One places a toy in the other's hands, the second one returns it; it is given, it is returned (Hay). By three years of age, these "rounds" often become vocal, with children repeating after each other the same words (Garvey). Here the contrast is supplied for each party by the similar (but really different) action of the other. The excitement is in maintaining the linked steps in the performance. These exchange routines are not limited to *similar* performances, although that is how they begin. Players increasingly take turns at novel behaviors within a general category of repeated actions.

Central Person Routines. Here the mother is the performer and the infant the counter-actor. (In exchanges they are both performers and co-performers for each other.) The mother manipulates either the situation or the child itself to provide increasing excitement, as when she plays hand games, tickling games or peeping games with the infant. (These games are fully described in other works—Sutton-Smith & Sutton-Smith, 1974; Singer & Singer, 1977.) By one year of age, the same infants can play the same games with the parents, thus becoming themselves the performers rather than the responsive counter-actors. Most games of children between the ages of four and ten years involve a similar situation, in which one child is the central actor and the others are mainly responsive to that actor's initiatives. Games of chase are of this character (Sutton-Smith, 1959).

By this age level, of course, we have central person *games* rather than

routines, because the other players do have the chance to enter into and
alter the course and outcome of the game, not just be responsive as is the
young baby. Furthermore there is in games an uncertainty as to the final
outcome, which along with the fact that it must be a different outcome
for the different parties is what helps to distinguish a game from a routine
where the outcome is always roughly the same and neither party tri-
umphs (Avedon & Sutton-Smith, 1971).

Unison Routines. If much of society rests on turn taking and on performing for each other, even more rests on our ability to act in concert
with each other. The ways in which the mother burbles or sings along
with her infant, or dances with her infant or walks with her infant, where
they both share the same sounds and the same movements and the same
rhythms, are innumerable. They are the bases of social order rather than
social exchanges and may well be more fundamental than the other kinds
of routines being discussed here.

Contest Routines. The mother-infant interaction which is most like a
game is the one-sided manipulation by the parent of an episode in which
either she or the baby get a different result depending on a contest between them. Thus, the baby holds and pulls the mother's hair or the
mother escapes; or the baby twists her mother's nose or the mother escapes; or bites her finger or she escapes. These have the character of
games because there are "tacit" sides, rules and outcomes that determine
who is the winner. However, because both sets of players are not equal
before the rules, and the whole is staged by the benevolent parent for the
entertainment or excitement of the child, it is better to call them contest
routines.

I should note at this point that because the mother *stages* the exchange, the central person performance, the choral action, and the contest, her roles are more complex than just to be the player with the child.
She really has three roles to the baby's one. First she *directs* the whole
event. Then she is a *performer,* and finally she is a *spectator.* The baby is
at first counter-actor, and perhaps a spectator, although that is at first less
certain. Furthermore we can make a logical distinction within these four
roles (actor, counter-actor, director and spectator). The director and
spectator roles must come first. Without them the play cannot occur.
They establish the initial communicational frame, whatever it is to be. It
seems that expressive signals are most relevant to this initial communicational frame because they signal its character. Then within this communicational frame the interaction between actor and counter-actor
takes place which is the dramatic structure of the play event. So at this
early age level we have a *communicational structure* of director and spectator (the mother) and a *dramatic structure* of actor and counter-actor
(mother and infant). For further clarification of this distinction see
Abrahams (1976).

TRANSITIONS TO PLAY

We have been presented with certain general conditions (dependency, stimulation) as necessary antecedents for play to occur across species, as well as with some more specific suggestions about the way the mother-infant interactions provide the infant with a model of kinds of interactive playing (exchange, central person, unison, contest) and some suggestions about the state of the organism (moderate arousal) and the state of the environment (moderate complexity) that is likely to lead to solitary play. While we must concede that these may well all be independent as sources of play, it is worth considering how the mother-infant play quadralogue may also affect the solitary play.

Solitary Play Forms

Even before the age of six months, for example, the baby will exchange faces with the mirror just as the mother has exchanged faces with him (Lewis). The routine here is particularly successful because of the instantaneous contingency of the baby's own facial movement to the mirror's reaction. The bulk of Piaget's and McCall's examples of solitary play in the first year can be seen from this point of view as a recapitulation of the actor/counter-actor role of mother and infant. But now instead of the infant being only counter-actor to the parent, as central person performer he or she is now both performer and audience. He kicks the side of the crib and then watches and laughs as the toys that are tied there rattle furiously. "Making interesting things happen" is just what the mother has already done to the baby. It is not invented by the baby! In solitary play, then, the child is both participant and spectator. We have a new intrasubjective kind of bipolar communicational competence, abstracted from the objective bipolar social relationship with the mother. Thus solitary play, while being at a lower level of complexity than can be maintained by an actual interaction with the parent, nevertheless has a structure that the play with parent cannot have; namely, that the child is both performer and spectator in the same episode. That is, we have control of a communicational competence but within a monologistic form. Ruth Weir's account of *Language in the Crib* has many examples of such communicational complexities *within* the play monologues in which baby plays spectator to its own language. Adult reverie provides further examples.

The symbolic play of the second year of life leads to an even more complex, even if subjective, rendering of communicational competence. Now the child begins to use the doll or the truck as the central performer. This central performer interacts with other things and settings. The doll is put to bed, is fed, is clothed (Fein). This interaction between doll and event is itself a form of interaction staged by the child in its own play. So the doll and the event are like the original situation of mother and child. Only now in addition to this parallel, the child itself is (as deus ex machina) manipulating the whole situation and also viewing the results. The doll provides the central person routine (as did the infant itself in its own physical play in the first year); but the child is now director and spectator, not merely actor and counter-actor. So we have a fourfold statement of the communicational relationship: there are actor and counter-actor (doll and bottle), and there are director and spectator (the child player). These are the same two- and three-year-old children who are said to be "egocentric" in relationship to other people. It is said that they cannot take the point of view of the other. Yet here we see them framing in their own subjective world a complex relationship of communication which borrows from the polarities of their earlier relationships to the mother and even gives us a paradigm for the theatre. It is a subjective expression in which their own lives (if egocentrism is correct) are objectified as a way of uniting objects outside of themselves (dolls and bottle) on a stage of events.

The communicational frame is provided by the child as director and spectator, and the drama is provided by the contrastive relationships of doll and bottle or truck and garage. This is to say that the child has now taken the part of the mother who, as mother, controlled the infant and watched what happened but also as *central person* created interactions with the infant as respondent. Now the child makes the doll into the central person interacting with things as the respondents. The mother who was frame manager becomes the child as frame manager.

It follows that it is not accidental that in their acquisition of ludic actions children usually first acquire the communicational frames and only later gain as much control of the principles for manipulating the contrastive dramatic actions within those frames. Thus children can manage the setting of telling riddles before they can actually follow the logic of riddles (Kirschenblatt-Gimblett). They will make up questions and give answers which have the correct intonation, but do not make any of the absurd sense that riddles require. They are absurd but not in the way that is meant. Still this shows that these children have first acquired the communicational competence of the expressive frame, even if they have not yet learned fully the inner secrets which make the drama work out. All of which means that the fourfold roles of performer and actor, director and spectator, do not always arrive developmentally at the same time. The director and spectator establish the communicational network within which the actors and counter-actors do their work.

The point of these illustrations is that it is most probable that in varying degrees children carry around with them from their prior experience a disposition to set up the kinds of subjective community of which we have been speaking. Much of their solitary play may be really a transmutation of their prior interactional play with parents. When they are provided with the appropriate setting for play (their bedroom, the playroom, the nursery playroom, playmates, toys), which is also learned, then it is probable that these dispositions are triggered into action. To what extent the state of the organism and the complexity of the toys operate within this framework or as separate principles, it is difficult to say. But most probably, given the social disposition as well as the appropriately complex setting and toys and a low state of arousal, play is more likely to occur. We would tend to locate the transition into play in the confluence of these antecedents, rather than in any one of them alone.

However, in addition to the *social frame* that the child brings as a disposition from earlier interaction (director, audience, actor, counteractor), young children cannot usually get play going with peers without learning how to negotiate the frames they wish to establish. Framing is not only a necessity for play performances; it must also be negotiated. We will speak of the two separately as *play frames* (like game rules) and *frame negotiation.*

Frame Negotiations

From as early as one year onwards the child becomes engaged in a protracted series of negotiations with other children and parents in order to sustain his own play frames. Communications within this world of power management involve learning how to set up play frames with other children, for which there are various signals systems about pretending or not pretending (Garvey, 1977). Over the years these negotiations can become routinized in terms of counting-out rhymes, methods for choosing players, etc., and in adulthood by the use of referees, umpires, and the like. At the earliest stage the children must negotiate before they can play, or alternatively negotiate during the course of play at its various junctures. With age, the negotiation goes on largely prior to the play, at least until it breaks down. By adulthood negotiations become a part of the larger vicarious sports organizations, coaches and associations. Although I will not go into it here, one can clearly speak of a negotiational framework within which communicational and dramatic structures get to be established.

While it is possible to think of the negotiational frame as something that must be at first established (the context) before the playframing can occur (the text), what this conference shows so well in the work of Drs. Garvey and Schwartzman is that this is a falsely dualistic way of looking at the matter. Play is as much the activity of oscillating in and out of negotiations as it is the dramatic content that those negotiations allow. Further, in Batesonian theory (1956) the making of choices about playframes is as much a part of the conceptual work of play as what it is that goes into the frames, dramatically speaking. To "play with something" means conceptually to frame it in another way. While you and I might do such things in our heads, children must run the frame through behaviorally as an index of their own thinking.

In sum then, I have argued that it is artificial to separate the prior negotiations and the framing from the play itself. While such a duality is clearer in adult play, even there the referee is active throughout. I have suggested there is real value in thinking of even solitary play as a *performance* first modeled for the child by the mother in social play. A performance, I have stressed, involves the existence of actor, counter-actor, director, and audience. I implied that the child imports this into his solitary play or his social play with other children as a frame which he is seeking to establish. However, he cannot do this without some negotiations with them about how the frame will be defined or maintained (Schwartzman), which is, to put it in Bateson's terms, *the metalanguage of play*. Negotiations are the language about play, which because they are inseparable from its initiations and its continuations must therefore be seen as intrinsic to the play. This I have sought to summarize here by talking of *play as performance*.

Even if we look back to solitary play in terms of the notion of exploration preceding play, it is clear from the data (Collard's figures) that while there is a gradual shift from exploration to play, this is not a suddenly qualitative leap. There is constant oscillation between the two. And that suggests, in turn, that throughout solitary play the child re-examines the objects for novel facets and then reframes his play activity in accord with new findings. Reframing of director and actor roles is probably ever-occurring, though in solitary play negotiations with others are not necessary.

But what of the children's native reaction to objects regardless of people? What of the "patterners" of whom Gardner speaks who seem to find most of their symbolic enjoyment in direct concourse with the nature of things? It is most probable that children enter into relationships with objects partly mediated in the social ways which we have discussed, but undoubtedly mediated also by the very texture, shape and sensory qualities of the objects themselves. All we wish to stress here is that we psychologists have tended to take our own individualistic philosophical premises for granted when examining children. We have tended to see them as like ourselves as individual experimenters and explorers. And in doing so we have neglected the incredible dependence (but not sole dependence) of their explorations on preceding social events. Of Piaget, for example, we might say that in studying his own children's explorations, he seems to have neglected both his own role as experimenter, but even more important the role of Mrs. Piaget as mother. How can we expect to understand those infant interactions with objects without knowing how relations to others, and relations through others to objects, have already been mediated?

THE STRUCTURES OF PLAY

We come next to the play text or the drama that takes place within the frame. In making up stories, for example, children have to negotiate the telling ("My turn to tell a story"), establish the play frame with markers ("Once upon a time," the use of the past tense, repetitions, fictional characters, and terminal markers, "they lived happily ever after"). Having done all that they still have to get on with the story, which is where narrative and plot enter. So also in play there is some entity within those frames.

Our own model of play structure, borrowed from the mother-infant paradigm, is that it is at least minimally a modulation of excitements, or (the same) a modulation of uncertainty. It may not be necessary to base that excitement modulation on underlying neurology as Dr. Shultz implies, although it is reasonable that it should have such a relationship. In the mother-infant play, the tension of increasing excitement and the laughter at the denouement seem to be essential to that dramatic structure. What we do not know is whether in social play with others or solitary play by themselves children also seek to develop crescendoes of excitement. The description of children playing in terms of arousal (Shultz), subjective uncertainty (McCall), and activity level as a response to functional complexity (Ellis) or as flow (Csikszentmihayli) could be interpreted in this way. But the description of play as idling behavior (McCall, Hutt) with much peripheral attention and heart rate variability does not seem to fit this model. Perhaps excitement modulation is a model for only one kind of play, or for only one intensity of play.

In what follows, however, I will take the view that in solitary play the child does attempt to produce the kinds of modulation that the mother has shared with him. As much of his voluntary activity is exploratory or framing behavior, rather than dramatic, it may not look particularly exciting to the outsider. But when it is underway I would maintain that it does have its peaks of excitement, as when the child is feeding the doll or flying the airplane in its hand.

Following Bateson, I believe play requires as a cognitive base a logical act of *negation* (1971). The usual way of framing classes and relations must be temporarily suspended. At the sensory-motor period this negation is only such a logical act by implication, though as infants children already show the ability to shut their eyes, turn their heads away, and actively suspend the ongoing series of events in order to initiate a new series in their own way—to have an influence, as McCall puts it. I prefer to think of this act of negation as a reversal of the usual contingencies of power and see in it the embryonic form of what will later become rites of reversal as described in anthropology. Given this innate *conative* competence present from the beginning, what can then occur *cognitively*, I believe, is that the infant can select freely from amongst its own prior instrumental behaviors and manipulate these in new ways. Freed from their prior contingencies, behaviors can be explored in new ways. During the conference this kind of process orientation was referred to a number of times as foregrounding (Kirschenblatt-Gimblett) and as ends-means manipulations (Lewis). Apparently a characteristic of this foregrounding process is the exaggeration or caricature of the abstracted instrumental behaviors. But in larger play schemas the abstraction refers to a whole rule system which is being created by the child out of prior life. Consistent with Bateson's notion that the player plays in order to create novel frames and therefore create novel thought for himself, Vygotsky saw play as the very process whereby meaning was created. He said, "Imagine two girls who are sisters playing a game called two girls who are sisters." Clearly they intend a selection and formulation which is novel and has not occurred in that way in nature.

In fairly authoritarian cultures it seems that the children's negation is little more than putting themselves in power (instead of the adults), then staging the adult world in their own slavish microcosmic imitation. But the freer the cultural conditions, the more likely they seem to move on to increasing flights of reversibility, to cultural parody and amusement. Perhaps Schwartzman's analysis of anthropology's concern with imitative play refers to a real, if historical, reality which is changing.

In this conference there was considerable agreement that the *affective* quality of play structure is positive. Classically, play is associated with feelings of fun (Huizinga, 1934). It is my position, however, that it depends on the phases of play being studied. Play can be biphasic. There is a phase of increasing excitement and then, after the climax is reached, one of general tension release and euphoria. I feel that the first mounting arousal phase is characterized by a most vivid involvement, which we have termed the *vivification phase* (pure flow for Csikszentmihayli), with the *euphoric phase* being the down slope after the peak. While excitement can be much higher in social play because the different roles of the players can provide the contrastives and the tension, solitary play can also be characterized by doing increasingly novel (and risky) things with one's toys, reaching for ever higher levels of excitement.

It seems that in talking about antecedents and transitions we talked only of this biphasic structure being modeled by the parents. But children in their own play clearly select from their own experience, not just that experience modeled for them by their mother. While there are no clear guidelines, the general view is that they prefer to play with those areas of competence which are not fully mastered and yet not completely unknown. This is certainly the implication of cognitive humor research (Schultz). We may thus speculate that they deal in their modulations with the moderately unmastered, with matters which they cannot fully control. Babies, for example, are constantly subject to both arousals and reductions of tensions, by their own organism or by other persons, over which they have no control. Yet in play they can both increase tension (kicking the side of the crib) or reduce it (not kicking) at will. We like to use a dialectical metaphor for this situation and say that play permits the subject a controllable and dialectical simulation of the moderately unmastered arousals and reductions of everyday life.

Our definition of the "drama" or structural part of play, then, is that it is a subset of voluntary behaviors (so does not include exploration which is also intrinsically motivated), involving a selective mechanism which reverses the usual contingencies of power so as to permit the subject (or subjects) to frame a controllable and dialectical simulation of the moderately unmastered arousals and reductions of everyday life in a way which is alternatively vivifying and euphoric.

Games are an even more obvious example of the way in which incompatibles outside of play are brought into new forms of synthesis. Winning and losing, which are relatively unmanageable outside of play, in games become operating principles for a continuing series of cooperative engagements. Both play and games are, in these terms, examples of what we term the *ludic dialectic.*

In sum, I have presented briefly a structuralist theory of the drama of play, in which play and games provide a peculiar synthesis for oppositions arising outside of play. It is a dialectical theory in the sense that play is a unique synthesis. For me, one virtue of the theory is that it allows scope for the formulations of Drs. Shultz, Ellis, Collard or McCall within its own terms. Whether the biphasic modulations be couched in neurological or informational terms, there is agreement here that the intrinsic drama of play has much to do with some kind of arousal control. It also makes clear that these investigators are not talking about the same thing as are Drs. Lewis, Garvey, Schwartzman and Kirschenblatt-Gimblett, who talk to the larger matters of framing the performance. The drama is only a part of the performance. The performance also involves being on stage, at least mentally, and taking into account audience, director, actor, and counter-actor. It means setting up the frame as to how these shall be arranged. It may even mean negotiating the establishment of that frame. Obviously the inherent drama is dependent on all these other facets of performance for its existence. Still the internal dramatic text can at least abstractly be distinguished from these other contextual arrangements. So also we can distinguish the rise and fall of excitement in the game from the arrangement of teams and rules without which it cannot proceed.

Yet to define play to include both kinds of orientation we must proceed as follows: *play is that subset of voluntary behavior within which the participant(s) negotiates or subsumes an agreed arrangement of actors/counter-actors, directors and audience in order to frame a performance in which the usual contingencies of power are reversed, so as to permit the actor(s) a controllable and dialectical dramatization of the moderately unmastered arousals and reductions of everyday life in ways which are alternately vivifying and euphoric to both performers and their audience.*

DEVELOPMENT

The conference contains several whispers of emerging *synchronic* notions, whether referred to as biphasic, biorhythms, idling or otherwise. It begins to look as if there may be some special tempos to play or at least tempos that vary with the kind of play. These tempos may have a basis in the organism (Shultz, Ellis), they may have a basis in the structure of excitement (see the previous discussion), or they may have more to do with the kind of context in which the play takes place. According to Dr. Hutt, play is much more susceptible to interference of these tempos than is exploration. It may also be that the kind of idling behavior discussed by Drs. Hutt and McCall alternates with periods of excitement or arousal, so that we get the kind of heart rate variability of which Dr. Hutt was speaking. It would be interesting to know if the kind of peripheral attention associated with play (Dansky & Silverman, 1975) is what permits the subject to bring the elements together into new and exciting combinations when all other factors are supportive. In sum, we look for some pattern of periodicity whereby idling and unfocused periods of peripheral attention alternate with periods of focused excitement. The earlier periods would be more flexible in the sense that the subject does not make a commitment, but ruminates subjectively; whereas the focused periods would be the bringing of all this together into some attempt at a match with environmental circumstances, some matching of skill and challenge in a flow pattern.

Diachronic changes, those occurring across age levels, are mirrored by the arrangement of the chapters in this book. We begin with the infant studies of Drs. Shultz, Lewis and Collard. From Dr. McCall we have an overview of some ways in which solitary play is organized between zero and two years. Dr. Hay introduces the social organization of which one-year-olds are capable, Dr. Garvey picks up the possibilities at the ages of three and four, and these are carried on by both Dr. Schwartzman and Dr. Kirschenblatt-Gimblett for four- to seven-year-olds. Meantime Dr. Fein has looked at object play in one- to two-year-olds, and Dr. Gardner has discussed different kinds of symbolic play in the same age period. Drs. Ellis and Hutt take up both object play and social play between the ages of four and seven years. The Singers provide illustrations of the role of the imagination between those years. Dr. Kirschenblatt-Gimblett shows some of the complexities of speech play and ritual play in the same age period. From there we have a large age hiatus, until Dr. Csikszentmihayli picks up the flow behavior of the adults he has studied. So this is a book largely about the under-ten-year-olds.

Clearly there is no attempt here to relate all these different phenomena in a neat developmental scheme, but one has the feeling that the data may well be here for such an organization. At least there are enough data for the developmentalist to consider more carefully what the problems are. How are the object-related plays, the social plays, the symbolic plays and types of symbolic play, the speech play and the fantasy play all to be knitted into one developmental system?

It seems most probable that in the first place there is considerable autonomy of development within each system (object play, social play, speech play, fantasy play). Each may well tend to have its own spatial and temporal contexts, its framing and performance sequences with development. At the same time we expect that there are parallels across forms and that they affect each other. There was the notable suggestion in Dr. Fein's work that after a period of prototypic examinations and nonprototypic variability, object relations might be reduced to a conventional level of reference in order to provide a common frame for children who on a social level were now looking into novel routines for behavior (shopping, chasing, doctors, and the like), rather than just examining and playing with objects as such. One could imagine in turn that in due course behavioral routines would become conventionalized in order to permit role diversification, and in due course roles be conventionalized to allow group diversification. There are some patterns of developmental interweaving here that are clearly worthy of much future interest. In addition there is the more general developmental issue of the way in which the codes for some forms of behavior can be conventionalized to provide a basis for exploration of novel behaviors on some higher level.

On yet another level there was the suggestion in Dr. Kirschenblatt-Gimblett's work that (1) the first forms of play might actually consist in a rather stereotyped adoption of the external expressive frame of the model (a hollow gestalt) in which the phonic, rhythmic and salient movements were copied without much sense of the inner form. (2) Next the child would proceed to a competent control of the internal logic (rule system). (3) Subsequently, however, he would be contented only with (a) subordination of this system within some larger pattern (as chase is subordinated to football) or (b) inversion of the expectancies of the system itself (as in parody riddles). This third phase could be called the metaludic phase, as it involves a more self-conscious capacity to manipulate the frames of the event that is central to the performance. There might then be (4) a re-entry, nonludic phase in which the competences now so flexibly mastered are reintegrated into novel adaptive acts, as when Dr. Kirschenblatt-Gimblett suggests that the riddler transfers his foregrounded skill into poetry (and, we might add, transfers his nonsensical interrogations into pedagogy). The system proposed by Dr. Fein overlaps the present one, and is relevant particularly to phases 2 and 3. Perhaps we can summarize our earlier statements about negotiations by pointing to at least a six-phase play process as follows:

1. Negotiations for control of the frame
2. Frame negotiations
3. Stereotyped expressive modeling
4. Rule competence
5. Metaludic competence (inversions and subordinations)
6. Extraludic applications.

In *The Moral Judgment of the Child* (1948), Piaget essentially outlines phases 3 to 5 in his discussion of the child's transformation from moral heteronomy to moral autonomy as illustrated through games.

But the largest developmental frame provided by this conference was that play may lead ultimately to the capacity for flow in adulthood; that those who have learned to engage in autotelic play behaviors when young will show more capacity for finding "flow" possibilities in their adult lives. It certainly makes sense that with fewer skills at their command children might well more often choose the subjective performance, where skills and challenges are only simulated. But one notices in play many things. There is the kind of play in which skills are simulated (as in flying toy airplanes), and there are the kinds of play in which threats are simulated (as in playing monsters in the dark). And there are the kinds of play in which we seem to have a match between skill and challenge (as in building ever higher towers of blocks). Dr. McCall suggested that perhaps all the time the child in his play is moving towards those moments when he can match challenge with appropriate skill in some appropriately objective terms, even though for some time this may happen only on a subjective and fantasy level as the preparations are laid down. There is room here for some future research monitoring of child play in challenge and skill terms. Perhaps in the meantime, however, we can say that play is not only frame and performance; on the performance level it varies in degrees of subjectivity-objectivity. Sometimes it veers to the subjective pole with little but a fantasy match; and at other times it veers to the more objective pole with a clear match with objects, events or other persons. It is the latter kind of objective match with which Dr. Csikszentmihayli was concerned.

This kind of view says there are both play and flow in childhood, or, in Piaget's terms (as presented here by Dr. Shultz), we find in children's play both examples of assimilative and equilibrating activity.

But now having given a special emphasis to the importance of framing in play in contrast to the drama which takes place on the stage, we must now enter a caveat. When play is looked at developmentally, there is an ever changing relationship between framing and drama, or between context and text. The infant, for example, was incapable of the game unless his mother maintained the situation. And so it is throughout much of childhood. It is only by adopting a fairly rigid frame that children can get their act onto the stage. As players or storytellers, they are not particularly sensitive to the roles of others (though not insensitive), but often seek to rigidify the frames, so they can attend to the difficulties of the textual performance itself. Not surprisingly the younger the children the more ritualistic are the games they play (Farmer in the Dell). Again, a great deal of solitary play could be said to be like a rehearsal of the monologues that they may later produce as dialogues. The monologues reflect the earlier communicative events, but at the same time they are a form of textual practice. Just as the player recites her lines in isolation, so must the child prepare his lines in isolation. And when he arrives at the stage, so often he will need special props and special distance from the audience to hold his act together. As the child grows older, however, and the skilled performer, the great artist, the true sports champion takes his place, then we get a more fluid relationship between the performance and the audience, the text and the context. Unfortunately a great deal of the discussion of framing in communicational theory is derived from this final adult state, and pays little attention to the vagaries of this relationship during child development. Much if not all of childhood expressive performance is only a rehearsal, and, therefore, as such, a limited kind of performance (Goffman, 1974). Again communicational theorizing is only partially a good model for thinking of play which is not, after all, a conversation. In play as in many forms of expressive behavior there is a larger distance between the performer and the audience than is normal in speech

(Abrahams, 1976). This means again that the frame is drawn tighter and is less permeable (consider the stadium in a football game, or the house corner in a nursery school), than is usual in ordinary conversation.

CONSEQUENCES (PLAY AND LEARNING)

What are the outcomes of play? What are its consequences? Or, to put it more simply, what do children learn through playing?

The classic theories of play's function were virtually that the player did not learn anything. Play was surplus energy, relaxation, recreation or catharsis. We could argue that these theories were themselves a by-product of the work ethic. They reflected the same duality of work and play which characterized the economic life of industrial societies, an ethic in which work is valued and play is not. In these theories, therefore, play is given only a derivative or a projective status. This kind of thinking is still widely prevalent in ordinary notions of play, and in ordinary disbelief in its value. In this conference some of the contemporary character of this belief is nicely described by Dr. J. Singer from his current research with adults. We have called this the "Scroogian" ethic of play, which can be summarized in the present terms by saying that those who must be cogs in an industrial machine cannot afford the luxury of reframing their possibilities. That luxury is reserved for the monied amateurs, or it once was.

In this century, however, there has been a gradual shift from "triviality" notions of play, at least in the upper and middle classes. Nearly all the theories of our time, beginning with Groos in the 1890s, stress that play makes some contribution to child development and growth. An effort is made to show that play is not trivial to the child: it is his work, and in it he prepares for his adult life. So important has been the job of conveying this new message that children learn through play, that its proponents have generally presented the message in the most sober of fashions. We have been told that play, games and sports socialize their participants into familial roles, sex roles, work roles and so on. And in the present conference we are shown very clear examples of learning in most of the presentations. We are not sure that children could not have learned those things elsewhere, but there seems little doubt that information is at least being consolidated in the play and possibly is actually being first acquired there, given the appearance of greater complexity in play than elsewhere in several of the papers. The object play described by Drs. McCall, Fein and Ellis, the social play of Drs. Hay, Garvey, Schwartzman and Kirschenblatt-Gimblett, seem to indicate we are dealing with novel behaviors in the play scene itself. The play as they presented it seems to be a frontier of behavior acquisition. But the point we are making here is that as a part of the rehabilitation of play in this century its protagonists have perhaps overemphasized its conventional import. They have overstressed its contribution to society as it is.

What we begin to see in more recent research stressing relationships between play and creativity (represented in this conference by the Singers' work), is relationships between play and possible novel object or social behavior. Play may socialize not simply by imparting behaviors that integrate the players into their cultural systems, but by providing them with innovative alternatives that they may be able to use to change that cultural system. Socialization may occur as well by innovation as by integration. It is our assumption that the ratio of these two, integration-innovation, changes with the kind of cultural system. In a more authoritarian system the children's play is more strictly imitative; in a relatively open society like our own, the play is much more reversive and transformational, as children feel free to attempt varying permutations of the possibilities before them.

We can look back to the structural analysis already presented, however, and frame these possibilities in terms of the kinds of cognitive, conative, and affective learnings that might result specifically from play.

Cognitive Learning

The message from my earlier statements, and from Drs. Schwartzman and Garvey in this conference, is that play is in the first place a reframing of activity. To play with something is to open it up for consideration and for choice. Play opens up thought. As it proceeds it constitutes new thought or new combinations of thought. These thoughts may at first be rudimentary, but they are alternatives to prior involvements. At the integrative levels, playing a new game introduces the child into conventional sex-role or social behaviors for his age level. The new frame for the child may be an old frame for the culture, but it is always a venture into new rule systems and new rule subject-matters that have not been a part of the child's accomplishments beforehand. As far as we can tell, this novelty for the child can occur because of the ends-means and foregrounding distinctions, the process rather than product orientations, as discussed earlier. It is the separation from the usual consequences that allows the kinds of abstraction that permit a flexible dallying and rearrangement of behaviors. The Singers in their work showed at considerable length all the many indices of cognitive flexibility that their highly imaginative children and adults possessed: their capacity for delay, for redirection, for alternative routes. While there is much work yet to be done to prove beyond doubt the causal connection between the play and the flexibility, most of the research certainly points in that direction.

What is learned in these terms, then, is a new repertoire of negotiations, of frames, of behaviors, of ideas; but more important, the greater the encouragement and experience of play over and above this repertoire, the greater the chance that the child may become more flexible, in general more able to consider alternatives. As we have mentioned, we believe this to be more true of modern and complex societies than of more authoritarian and simple ones, where adult alternatives are limited in any case. It is remarkable that most of the socialization and preparatory theories of play in our time have almost always omitted the fact that a great deal of children's play is reversive; it is nonsense or absurd or hilarious or a nuisance to adults. That there is a logic to much of this was so well explained by Dr. Kirschenblatt-Gimblett in this conference. The number and kind of reversive plays probably indicate to us the extent to which the play training is a conventional one into prototypic (integrative) behaviors or the extent to which it is a play training into variable (innovative) behaviors, and the balance between these two in the group being studied. There is a difference between play that introduces children to necessary alternatives and play that allows children to consider the play of alternatives. It is our own information culture with its innumerable kinds of specialization and choice, which is providing the economic basis for the more radical theories of play as innovation training that we see beginning to emerge in this conference.

Elsewhere we have spoken of this kind of radical play theory as a theory which says play is the envisagement of possibility. Play is adaptive potentiation. It makes many alternatives possible, even though none are necessary. Play increases the repertoire, but whether the repertoire gets to be used depends on further cultural encouragement.

In sum, the major cognitive consequence of play is an increase in cognitive alternatives available to the player, as well as the flexible management of these. How many such alternatives and how much flexibility clearly vary with the cultural system.

Conative Consequences

As an act of reversal, play is also an exercise of autonomy. There are long-standing associations between play and the increase of autonomy (from the play therapy literature). People who can wait, who get more internal reinforcement, who can resist more temptation (to quote some of the Singers' data) are of different character and motive from those who cannot. Still, the conference yielded surprisingly little new information on these issues. Its focus was primarily cognitive.

Affective

Everyone agrees that there is more positive affect associated with play. Consistently we should expect the player to become the more confident, optimistic kind of person. But again there is little data on this, except from Dr. Csikszentmihayli's readings on flow, where his subjects who flowed most, certainly found more work satisfaction and were enjoying their lives to a greater than usual extent.

Social

An important issue which lay behind the thinking of Garvey, Schwartzman and Kirschenblatt-Gimblett, however, eluded this conference. Play is, after all, only one kind of social frame flexibility. There are other similar states of social being in which ordinary reality is suspended and in which there are special meta-messages about being in a new social frame. Religious life, rituals and ceremonials are of this order. What then is the relationship between play and ritual which in some respects are alike in not being taken as ordinary reality? Handelman, who has dealt with this issue extensively, argues that in ritual we *make belief,* while in play we *make believe* (1977).

In both cases we depart from the reality we ordinarily follow, but in the one case we do not take seriously our departure, and in the other we take it even more seriously than the so-called ordinary reality. Both play and ritual share this creating of frames which are not grounded in the usual material of natural and social life. However, what is called play includes several things. It includes (a) playfulness or nonsense in which we break frames in an unusual way or with quixotic rapidity. (b) It includes the childlike repetition of adult conventional frames but with the children themselves in charge so there is the joy in autonomy and role reversal, while the content is a facsimile of ordinary life. Here even the adults say the children are making believe, and the children say they are "pretending." There are good socialization grounds for arguing that they are *making belief,* not just making believe. They are gaining belief in the ordinary frames (social and object) by their voluntary control of their own buffered versions of those frames. It may not be, therefore, that most of children's play is much different from ritual in its intrinsic function, except that they are creating frames which will enable them to assimilate the ordinary frames, while the ritual adult is creating frames which transcend and give cosmological grounding to the ordinary frames. It is only with respect to adults who are not true believers that much of children's play must be disguised as make-believe. After all, many adults look at the religious activities of others as so many "fairy tales." Calling something a fantasy, or a

fairy tale or make-believe, is both a form of disparagement by nonbeliev-
ers, and a defense by those whose autonomous existence requires them to
reconsider the ordinary frames in their own particular way. (c) Then
there are those frames of play which do not seek to imitate everyday
frames, but to reveal the many other aspects of feelings and relationships
that the ordinary frames must deny. These are what Geertz (1971) has
called "deep play" and the psychoanalysts called forms of compensation
and Turner has called anti-structure (1974). There are many varieties,
which range all the way from obscenity to professional sports. Here the
new frames make belief about the whole earthly reality which experience
encompasses, even though much of it is left out of ordinary frames. (d)
Finally there is ritual, religion, etc. in which the groundings of ordinary
reality are encompassed in larger frames of the cosmological order.

Now I would argue that all of these, even including the first, are *making belief*. They all share the departure from the ordinary world. They do
differ in the range of that world that they encompass from the microcosmic play forms to the macrocosmic ritual forms. They differ also in social
status, and the lower their social status, the more often they must use the
defense of make-believe. Make-believe is in these terms a social defense
for the outrageous behavior of making new belief instead of merely following ordinary belief; for making *realms*, not accepting the *world* as it is,
which is how Goffman, to whom this discussion owes so much, might
make the distinction (1974).

When one takes this kind of view, however, and reduces play and ritual to novel frame construction, the creation of new realms, there are
problems. It does for sure accord well with everything we have said previously about flexibility and play. But how can it explain nonsense and playfulness? Here frame breaking becomes a thing in its own right. It becomes
functionally autonomous. The means become the ends, as we have had
emphasized throughout this work. Perhaps we must conclude that playfulness is the only really distinct kind of play activity which we should
consider. The rest is good earnest frame construction of various age levels
and various kinds. If we took this limited focus, of course, we would be
dealing with a much smaller portion of novel frame-constructing activity.
Playfulness, as Nina Lieberman has shown, is quite rare (1978). On the
other hand, when people are engaged in novel frame construction, playfulness often bubbles momentarily to the surface as if the voluntary engagement allows such greater looseness of spirit and thought.

Or looked at another way, perhaps playfulness, while a distinct affective state (positive, joyous), is just a highly charged way of making belief.
What seems to be inconsequential, what seems to be a dabbling with
frames, may be, in fact, once more a making of belief. To give an example, I am quite a playful father with my own children (Sutton-Smith &

Sutton-Smith, 1974), but when I look at some of my practices more carefully they seem to be examples of attempts to make frames for an ambiguous relationship. Thus I sometimes pretend to be Frankenstein or the
Werewolf and, baring my teeth, and lifting my arms stiffly, move in their
direction. When I galumph in this manner, they laugh and run and I
laugh. It is playfulness at its peak. Then on other occasions when they
scold me or protest, I do the opposite. I exaggerate my abasement. I pretend to cry. I sob and sob, head bowed. Again we all laugh. But taking a
cue from Bateson (1958) and Handelman's reinterpretation of same
(1978), what I am also doing besides playing, is saying that:

(a) I am your dangerous father.

(b) But my exaggeration shows that it is under my control and so not
unpredictably dangerous to you.

And again:

(a) I am your softhearted booby father.

(b) But it is under my control and I am not a complete pushover.

So once again I am making beliefs even while I am playing. I am saying to my children, all these contradictory feelings can continue to exist
and this is how it can be done. The joy of playfulness may thus be the
marvel and brilliance of our frame-making reconciliation of real-world
ambiguities, rather than any apparent dabbling with frames for their own
sake. Even when we appear to do the latter we may be, it seems, con-
structing transcending realms. Even if they are not to be taken seriously,
as in the nonsense of children, they are quite seriously suggesting that
ridiculing the world of letters, numbers, dates and alphabets is what they
deserve, given the way the world pressures us into accepting them. Making nonsense is making belief that we count for as much as the sense from
which it temporarily delivers us.

We conclude then that play, games, sports and ritual are all part of
novel frame-making behavior; that there can be either a zest to these novelties (called playfulness) or a sobriety (called religious fervour). We conclude that they are more similar in their fundamentally creative response
to life than they are dissimilar. And that their differential range and status
evokes the charge of make-believe or revelation, but that this has more to
do with how they function in the groups in which they are found for the
members of the different subclasses, than reveals their fundamentally
creative similarity. This makes sense too of the great variety of ways in
which play, games, sports and ritual are defined in different societies. The
variety is baffling if we take each of these categories as itself the activity
which we discuss, rather than a culturally relative exemplar of the life and
times of frame making in that situation.

Goffman entitled his work *Frame Analysis, An Essay on the Organization of Experience*. We should perhaps have entitled this epilogue, *Frame*

Creation, An Essay on the Role of Expressive Activity in Human Experience.

In sum, play is a form of frame creation, and that is the flexibility that it brings to its creator. As we have said earlier, however, it is more than that. First there are negotiations, then the frame is created or agreed upon, after or during that process the drama begins to take place, and the child as player keeping in mind his quadraloguic alternatives, puts his performance on stage. So the social consequence of all this social creativity, is presumably a greater competence at social improvisation.

CONCLUSION

As this is a book dominated by psychological modes of thinking, we will finish with the implications that the above analysis has on an individual level. If the individual is a rampant frame maker, this work tells you, then he is going to be more flexible, more autonomous and more optimistic. But we would also emphasize that play only *potentiates* all of these things in the individual. Whether they become adaptive depends upon many other elements in the larger culture. Playful persons are often found to be facetious and not serious, and to be discriminated against by others; so the conveying of these values leads to no simple transference to the larger cultural system.

The view of play as adaptive potentiation is not too different from that of Groos that play is a preparation for life, except that we put the matter on a probabilistic basis. One recalls the ancient custom of making the fool a king for three days, then killing him. On one occasion, however, the king died during the regime of the fool and the fool became king. That is the nature of adaptive potentiation. Play is the fool that might become King (Sutton-Smith, 1976).

References

Abrahams, R. D. The complex relations of simple forms. In D. Ben-Amos (Ed.) *Folklore Genres.* Austin: University of Texas Press, 1976.

Adams, C. R. Distinctive features in play and games: a folk model from Southern Africa. Paper present at The Association for the Anthropological Study of Play, Annual Meeting, Notre Dame, 1978.

Avedon, E., & Sutton-Smith, B. *The Study of Games.* New York: Wiley, 1971.

Bateson, G. The message "This is Play." In B. Schaffner (Ed.) *Group Processes.* New York: Josiah Macy, 1956, pp. 145–246.

Bateson, G. *Naven.* New York: Cambridge University Press, 1936.

Ben-Amos, D., & Goldstein, K. S. *Folklore, Performance and Communication.* The Hague: Mouton, 1975.

Chomsky, N. *Aspects of the Theory of Syntax.* Cambridge, Mass: M. I.T. Press, 1965.

Clarke-Stewart, K. A. Interactions between mothers and their young children: characteristics and consequences. *Monographs of the Society for Research in Child Development,* 1973, 38, 1–109.

Curtis, H. *Education through play.* New York: Macmillan, 1915.

Garvey, C. *Play.* Cambridge, Mass.: Harvard University Press, 1977.

Geertz, C. *The interpretation of cultures.* New York: Basic Books, 1973.

Goffman, I. *Frame Analysis: An essay on the organization of experience.* Cambridge, Mass: Harvard U.P. Norton, 1974.

Groos, K. *The Play of Man.* New York: Arno, 1976,

Hall, G. S. *Youth: Its Education, Regimen and Hygiene.* New York: Appleton, 1917.

Handelman, D. Play and ritual, complementary frames of meta communication. In Chapman & Foot (Eds.) *It's a Funny Thing.* London: Pergamon, 1977.

Handelman, D. Rethinking Naven: Play and Identity. Paper delivered at the Annual Meeting of the Anthropological Society for the Study of Play. Notre Dame, April, 1978.

Herron, R. E. & Sutton-Smith, B. *Child's Play.* New York: John Wiley, 1971.

Hymes, D. (Ed.) *Language in Culture and Society.* New York: Harper & Row, 1964.

Lee, J. *Play in Education.* New York: Macmillan, 1922.

Lévi-Strauss, C. *The Savage Mind.* Chicago: University of Chicago Press, 1966.

Lieberman, N. *Playfulness.* New York: Academic Press, 1978.

Piaget, J. *The Moral Judgment of the Child.* Glencoe: Free Press, 1948.

Roberts, J. M., & Sutton-Smith, B. Child training and game involvement. *Ethnology,* 1962, 1, 166–185.

Singer D., & Singer, J. *Partners in Play.* New York: Harper & Row, 1977.

Stern, D. *The First Relationship.* Cambridge: Harvard University Press, 1977.

Sutton-Smith, B. *The Games of New Zealand Children.* Berkeley : University of California Press, 1959.

Sutton-Smith, B. Current research in play, games and sports. In T. T. Craig (Ed.) *The Humanistic and Mental Health Aspects of Sports, Exercise and Recreation.* Chicago: American Medical Association, 1976, pp. 1–4.

Sutton-Smith, B. *Dialektik des Spiels (The Dialectics of Play).* Schorndorf: Karl Hoffman, 1979.

Sutton-Smith, B. & S. *How to Play with Your Children.* New York: Hawthorn, 1974.

Sutton-Smith, B. Play Theory of the Rich and for the Poor. In P. Gilmore & A. Glathorn (Eds.) *Ethnography and Education.* Philadelphia: University of Pennsylvania in press.

Turner, V. Liminal to liminoid in play, flow and ritual: an essay in comparative symbology. *Rice University Studies*, 1974, 60, 53–92.

Vygotsky, L. S. Play and its role in the mental development of the child. *Soviet Psychology*, 1967, 5, 6-18.

Weir, R. *Language in the Crib*. The Hague: Mouton, 1962.

AUTHOR INDEX

SUBJECT INDEX